Technology and the Future of Health Care

The Milbank Readers
John B. McKinlay, general editor

T & H

Technology and the Future of Health Care

Milbank Reader 8

edited by John B. McKinlay

The MIT Press
Cambridge, Massachusetts
London, England

362.1
T22

e.

© 1982 by
The Massachusetts Institute of Technology

Printed and bound in the United States of America

Library of Congress Cataloging in Publication Data

Main entry under title:
Technology and the future of health care.

(The Milbank reader series ; 8)
  Selections from Milbank Memorial Fund quarterly.
  Includes bibliographies and index.
  1. Medical innovations—Social aspects—Addresses, essays, lectures.
2. Medical innovations—Economic aspects—Addresses, essays, lectures.
3. Medical innovations—Economic aspects—United States—Addresses,
essays, lectures. I. McKinlay, John B. II. Milbank Memorial Fund
quarterly. III. Series. [DNLM: 1. Economics, Hospital—Collected works.
2. Technology, Medical—Collected works. QY 4 T256]
RA418.5.M4T4   362.1   81–13718
ISBN 0–262–63084–2 (pbk.) AACR2
        0–262–13183–8 (hard)

Contents

Foreword

During 1973–74, the Milbank Memorial Fund, in conjunction with Prodist (New York), produced four edited volumes that drew together and organized published papers from the well-known and respected *Milbank Memorial Fund Quarterly*. In producing these four initial resource books (*Research Methods in Health Care, Politics and Law in Health Care Policy, Economic Aspects of Health Care*, and *Organizational Issues in the Delivery of Health Services*), the Fund had attempted to respond to heavy and continuing requests for accessibility and economy of the Milbank papers. The success of the four books exceeded even the most optimistic expectations, and all are now, unfortunately, out of print. They were adopted as course texts by many different health-related disciplines, were used widely throughout North America and abroad, were acquired by many university and professional libraries and were favorably reviewed in internationally respected professional journals.

The foreword to the earlier series noted that we always "planned to keep this series active and responsive to changing needs. Suggestions for future volumes will be welcome." Since their release, there have been numerous inquiries, requests, and suggestions for further volumes dealing with new and emerging issues concerning health care and social policy. The titles included in this second wave of edited volumes attempt to respond again to this widespread enthusiasm and need.

A venture of this nature has several obvious limitations. First of all, the universe from which the contributions were selected was limited to the *Milbank Memorial Fund Quarterly/Health and Society* and to several books produced by the Fund as a result of roundtable meetings on particular health-care issues. However, more than enough rich material by eminent scholars was available for at least the present volumes. For the editor, a major problem was to decide which of several excellent papers had to be omitted (for reasons of economy, coverage, datedness, etc.) rather than what was available for inclusion in each volume. It should be emphasized that all of the authors represented here have progressed in their thinking and have advanced their work in other journals and books since original publication of the papers. Some have altered their theoretical orientation and some even their substantive interests. Wherever possible the editor has selected contributions published since the early 1970s. Indeed, most of the articles were first published within the last three or four years. Articles that were widely recognized as classic statements were selected from earlier years. Finally, several contributions dealt with a breadth of issues and were of sufficient quality to warrant their inclusion in more than one volume. Since each volume is likely to appeal to somewhat different readerships, this duplication was not considered problematic but rather enhanced the treatment of some health-care issues and the value of each volume.

It is hoped that this new series will help teachers, researchers, policymakers, public administrators, and especially students to overcome an ever-increasing problem: namely, how to gain easy and economical access to the rich resources contained in recent Milbank Memorial Fund publications.

Introduction

The ever-increasing proliferation of new medical technology continues to profoundly alter just about every facet of health/medical care around the world. For example: It affects the epidemiology of mortality, morbidity and disability; it changes patient/consumer expectations as to what is possible and influences utilization behavior; it profoundly affects the organization and financing of hospital services; it changes the scope and content of medical work and alters the status balance among various medical workers; it continues to influence the scope and content of the medical curriculum; it contributes to the worrisome problem of health care cost inflation; and it dramatically increases state expenditures thereby raising the most profound issues concerning the proper role of government, regulatory intervention and so forth. Many other important ramifications could be added to this list.

This volume touches on these and many related questions. The first section contains three papers which orient the reader by dealing with more general issues concerning technology and health care. David Mechanic considers some of the ways in which national policies regarding the financing and organization of health care increasingly seek to control "technological imperatives." Obviously, no country is able to fulfill all of the public's demands upon valuable medical resources and the physician seems to be centrally involved in the inevitable system of rationing. Rationing can be expected to shift the locus of influence from consumers/clients and even providers/professionals, to officialdom. With the rise of bureaucratization in medical care, one can reasonably expect challenges and changes in the expectations and obligations inherent in the traditional roles of patient and physician. The matter of rationing is discussed further in section V.

Prior to the mid-1930s, the major infectious diseases killed those people who were already debilitated by other causes. Since then, technology appears to have changed that situation dramatically, adding years to sick rather than healthy lives. Ernest Gruenberg argues that the resulting increase in the prevalence of chronic disease and disability represents the "failure of our success." He believes that we are beginning to recognize that our lifesaving technology of the past four decades has outstripped our health preserving technology and that the net effect has been to perhaps worsen the public's health. For a period at least, health saving must take precedence over lifesaving. It seems that we will be unable to move forward in enhancing overall health status until the prevention of nonfatal chronic illness becomes a top research and policy priority. In the third paper, Kenneth Warner critically examines the early optimistic search for more effective, safer and less expensive health care triggered by the medical technological revolution. The remarkable increase in health care costs over the last several decades and associated imperfect expectations have resulted in a range of programs and proposals for hospital cost containment that may eventually impede the development and use of new technology. Warner believes that concern for the most important issues of care and economic cost will best be served by selective shifts in the types of technology employed and appropriate incentives for its use.

In the second section, medical care technology is considered in relation to the worrisome health cost spiral. The proliferation of high cost medical technologies is viewed by John Iglehart as one of the key elements in the medical care cost spiral. At their lifesaving extreme, they may be society's most valued services; at their cost-generating extreme, increased governmental involvement and regulation appears unavoidable. Indeed, legislation already enacted and some proposed for the future will directly regulate the development and diffusion of technology. Other informal policy processes will present further mechanisms by which the state will evaluate medical treatment practices, procedures and technologies. The results of such evaluations are likely to be used in deciding which services will be reimbursed under Medicare, Medicaid and eventually, perhaps, through National Health Insurance. In the second paper, Judith Wagner and Michael Zubkoff discuss what the proliferation of medical technologies portend for hospital cost inflation. They are alarmed at the way new equipment, procedures or systems are introduced by hospital decision-makers without knowledge of, or concern for, their relative effectiveness or efficiency. Technology, particularly hospital technology, is attracting increasing attention because of the convergence of at least three lines of criticism of our health care system. First, there is now evidence that technology is linked to increased hospital costs. Second, there is mounting evidence that many medical services (perhaps even a majority) have made little difference to any health outcome measure. (Nonmedical factors, particularly improvements in nutrition and water supply among other public health measures, appear to have been more important in reducing mortality and morbidity rates over the last fifty years.) Third, programs designed to control hospital capital expenditures have generally been disappointing failures. One example which these authors consider is Salkever and Bice's study of the effect of certificate-of-need (CON) legislation on hospital investment, which is reprinted in the fourth section of this volume. Wagner and Zubkoff provide a useful discussion of some aspects of the diffusion process and conclude that there remain major gaps in our knowledge of both the process by which technologies become established and their real impact on social costs and benefits. Policymakers in the future will face difficult choices as they seek to determine where we should be on the trade-off curve between health care costs and benefits and how to ration the availability of those technologies that offer clear benefits.

The five papers in the third section consider aspects of the diffusion process as it involves hospitals. Arnold Kaluzny and his colleagues investigate the differential contribution of various organizational variables that affect the innovation of high-risk versus low-risk health service programs in two types of health care organizations: hospitals and health departments. They find that variables are differentially related to both the type of program and the type of organization. Organizational size appeared to be a critical factor in program innovation as it relates to high-risk services in hospitals and low-risk services in health departments. Excluding size, such staff characteristics as cosmopolitan orientation and training were prime predictors for both high- and low-risk programs in health departments and low-risk programs in hospitals. The degree of formalization was the primary predictor of innovation of high-risk programs in hospitals. Cosmopolitan orientation of the administrator was a critical factor in the innovation of high-risk programs in both hospitals and health departments.

Edward Morse and his colleagues employ survey data from 388 government, nonfederal and voluntary general service hospitals to examine the impact of several dimensions of organizational structure on indicators of hospital efficiency and level of adoption of new medical technology. They focus particularly on the degree to which resource allocation decision-making is centralized and levels of visibility of medical and economic consequences. It appears that, in terms of efficiency, organizational structure is an important factor in determining whether gains in effectiveness outweigh expenses associated with the adoption of new medical technology. The third paper by Gerald Gordon and his colleagues presents a contingency model for research administration that suggests ways in which the effectiveness of problem solving in diffusion research can be improved. The authors employ the concepts of urgency (the social need for rapid applicable research results) and predictability (the extent to which researchers can predetermine the steps needed to reach their objectives) to develop administrative guidelines as well as predict the probability of tangential research, the emergence of anomalies, the probable sources of conflict and the personality attributes required by researchers in different research settings. Building upon the background provided by the work of Wagner and Zubkoff, John McKinlay traces the way in which medical innovations (diagnostic techniques, surgical procedures and medical interventions) typically become part of established medical procedure. He identifies seven stages in the career of an innovation: promising report, professional and organizational adoption, public acceptance and third-party endorsement, standard procedure and observational reports, randomized controlled trials, professional denunciation, and erosion and discreditation. He then discusses the different types of information associated with each stage. An alternative approach to the allocation of public funds to health care based upon evidence from randomized controlled trials is advocated. Finally, Ann Lennarson Greer identifies some areas where, seemingly, we need more information on the diffusion of innovations in health care organizations. She suggests that federal government programs of the 1960s, which were designed to assist the rapid diffusion of technologies, have been displaced in the 1970s by various efforts to constrain costly technological growth. It is suggested that, as a guide to action, the understanding of the reasons for the adoption of an innovation is essential. Unfortunately, the utility of available diffusion theory is limited by its focus on the speed of diffusion rather than on the reasons for its adoption by formal organizations. She believes more is known about the administrator as decision-maker than about those increasing situations in which physicians play a central role. It is suggested that until coherent, empirically grounded theories of organizational innovation become available, many of the large-scale tests currently underway are somewhat premature and wasteful.

The fourth section contains two papers that describe the failure of two policies affecting the utilization of technology as applied to medical care. The first by David Salkever and Thomas Bice reveals how CON controls over hospital investment enacted since 1974 appear to have actually backfired. They review some questions that have been raised about the effectiveness of CON controls and then develop quantitative estimates of the impact of CON on hospital investment. They show that CON did not in fact reduce the total dollar volume of investment, but altered its composition, retarding the expansion in bed supplies but actually increasing investment in new services and equipment. The second paper by Anne-Marie Foltz and Jennifer Kelsey discusses the fact that the annual Pap test became a recommended standard for women without ever having been subjected to properly designed and conducted controlled trials to estimate its efficacy and effectiveness. Unfortunately, after more than thirty years of routine use, the Pap test fails to meet most of the generally accepted criteria for a mass screening program. The procedure and its associated policy persists, however, because the nation's ideology supports the maximum utilization of new technologies. Furthermore, special-interest groups have promoted the test as a major weapon in the declared "war on cancer." The authors raise important and legitimate questions concerning the wisdom of this allocation of both public and private health resources.

The fifth section contains two papers that discuss the fiscal crisis and the possibility of rationing medical technology by science. The first paper, by the Office of Health Economics of London, suggests that the assumption that a centrally planned national health care system could match resources to needs has proved to be a chimera. It is suggested that shortages are inherent in any system that is more or less "free at the point of access," while it still permits unlimited scientific innovation for its patients. Rationing by science is considered as unsatisfactory as political or economic rationing. It is concluded that equality in health care cannot be in balance with uncontrolled technological innovation. The final paper by John McKinlay is essentially a case study that illustrates a number of the issues raised in the earlier sections of the volume. He argues that macroeconomic factors have everything to do with informed social policies concerning public health—they determine the very nature and range of policy options available. He considers aspects of social policy concerning medical technology in New Zealand and reviews several problems besetting that country's economy. The overall medical care system is described, highlighting some issues that are affected by, and themselves compound, problems associated with high technology as applied to medicine. Finally, he considers some specific medical technologies and offers suggestions for a future social policy in this area.

John B. McKinlay

I General Issues

The Growth of Medical Technology and Bureaucracy: Implications for Medical Care

DAVID MECHANIC

Center for Medical Sociology and Health Services Research,
University of Wisconsin-Madison

Despite significant differences in ideology, values, and social organization, most Western developed countries—and probably most countries in the world—face common problems of financing, organizing, and providing health care services. As populations increasingly demand medical care, there is growing concern among the governments of most nations to provide a minimal level of service to all and to decrease obvious inequalities in care. To use available technology and knowledge efficiently and effectively, certain organizational options are most desirable. Thus, there is a general tendency throughout the world to link existing services to defined population groups, to develop new and more economic ways to provide primary services to the population without too great an emphasis on technological efforts, to integrate services increasingly fragmented by specialization or a more elaborate division of labor, and to seek ways to improve the output of the delivery system with fixed inputs. Although all of these concerns to some extent characterize national planning in underdeveloped countries, they particularly describe tendencies among developed countries as they attempt to control the enormous costs of available technologies. Throughout the world there is increasing movement away from medicine as a solitary entrepreneurial activity and more emphasis on the effective development of health delivery systems.

Having discussed these trends elsewhere in detail (Mechanic, 1974, 1976), what I will do here is examine how changing technology and organization affect not only the provision of medical care, but also the underlying assumptions of practitioners and patients. My thesis is that medical care constitutes a complex

M M F Q / Health and Society / *Winter 1977*
© Milbank Memorial Fund 1977

psychological system of assumptions and meanings that is significantly affected by the bureaucratization of medical tasks and the growing specification of the technical aspects. Public policies everywhere in the world increasingly play a role in the financing and organization of care, but when such public policies violate the psychological assumptions and social expectations of health practitioners and patients, they may have consequences very different from those intended.

Modes of Rationing Health Services

Medicine has in recent decades undergone an enormous development in specialized knowledge and in technology. While these advances have brought considerable progress in treating some diseases, most of the major diseases affecting mortality and morbidity—from heart disease and the cancers to the psychoses and substance abuse—are only poorly understood, and existing efforts, while they ameliorate suffering and sometimes extend life, are not able to cure or prevent the incidence of most of these conditions. The technologies that do exist are often extraordinarily expensive, require intensive professional manpower, and must be applied repeatedly to a patient during the long course of a chronic condition. Take an example where success has been quite impressive, such as in hemodialysis and transplantation in end-stage kidney disease: intensive and expensive efforts must be made over a long period to sustain life and functioning, which on a per capita basis consume a very high level of expenditure (Fox and Swazey, 1974). As these halfway technologies have developed—intensive care units, radiation therapy for cancers, coronary bypass surgery—the aggregate costs of medical care have continued to move upward, with medical services consuming a larger proportion of national income. In the United States, for example, where in 1940 the cost of health care was $4 billion and 4 percent of the gross national product, 1976 costs were almost $140 billion and 8.6 percent of the gross national product. While the proportional increase is not as large in nations having a centralized prospective budgeting process, as in England, the trend, nevertheless, is the same and a source of concern among all thoughtful people.

Since the prevalence of illness and "dis-ease" is extremely high in community populations, as has been repeatedly demonstrated by morbidity surveys (White et al., 1961), there is almost unlimited possibility for the continued escalation of medical demand and increased medical expenditures. As people have learned to have higher and more unrealistic expectations of medicine, demands for care for a wide variety of conditions, both major and minor, have accelerated. No nation that follows a sane public policy would facilitate the fulfillment of all perceptions of need that a demanding public might be willing to make. As in every other area of life, resources must be rationed. The uncontrolled escalation of costs in developed countries results in part because techniques of rationing are in a process of transition, and most countries have yet to reach a reasonable end point in this transitional process. The process is one of movement from *rationing by fee* through a stage of *implicit rationing* through resource allocation to a final stage of *explicit rationing*. In this process the role of physician shifts from entrepreneur to bureaucratic official, and medical practice from a market-oriented system to a rationalized bureaucracy. These shifts, in turn, have an important bearing on the psychological meaning of the doctor-patient relationship, on the uses of medical excuses for various social purposes, and on the flexibility of medicine as an institution to meet patient expectations and to relieve tensions in the community at large. The remainder of this paper will explicate each of these points.

Types of Rationing

In the traditional practice of medicine, and in much of the world still today, the availability of medical care has been dependent on the ability to purchase it. Those with means could obtain whatever level of medical care was available, while those without means were dependent on whatever services were made available by government, philanthropists, the church, or by physicians themselves. Since affluence was limited, and medical technology and knowledge in any case offered only modest gains, the marketplace was a natural device for rationing services. Indeed, it worked so well that physicians were often supporters of government intervention and direct payments for care since such support increased their opportunities for remuneration.

Fee-for-service as an effective system of rationing broke down due to a variety of factors. First, medical technology and knowledge expanded rapidly, greatly increasing the costs of a serious

3

medical episode, and imposed on the ill a financial burden that was large and unpredictable. Associated with this was a growing demand on the part of the public for means of sharing such risks through benevolent societies and insurance plans and, as costs mounted, for government to assume a growing proportion of these expenditures. Because of the traditions of medical practice, however, and the political monopoly that physicians had gained over the market-place, the rise of third-party payment was not associated with care-ful controls over the work of the physician and how he generated costs. While third-party payment increased access to services, the orientations of increasingly scientific and technologically inclined physicians resulted in a large acceleration in the use of diagnostic and treatment techniques. The consequence has been the escalation of costs which we now almost view as inevitable. Physicians have been trained to pursue the "technological imperative—that is, the tendency to use any intervention possible regardless of cost if there is any possibility of gain (Fuchs, 1968). This contrasts with a cost-benefit calculation in which there is consideration of the relative costs and benefits of pursuing a particular course of action. The "technological imperative," when carried to its extreme, incurs fan-tastic expense for relatively small and, at times, counterproductive outcomes.

In a provocative analysis, Victor Fuchs (1976) asks why almost all the developed countries in the world pursue national health in-surance when such a policy is "irrational" from an economic point of view in that it encourages the overconsumption of services relative to other needs. Moreover, he argues, it often results in the purchase of the wrong and, perhaps, less useful types of care. He comes up with the intriguing suggestion that the thrust toward national health insurance may have relatively little to do with health.

> Externalities, egalitarianism, the decline of the family and traditional religion, the need for national symbols—these all play a part. In democratic countries with homogeneous populations, people seem to want to take care of one another through programs such as national health insurance, as members of the same family do, although not to the same degree. In autocratic countries with heterogeneous popula-tions, national health insurance is often imposed from above, partly as a device for strengthening national unity. The relative importance of different factors undoubtedly varies from country to country and time to time, but the fact that national health insurance can be viewed as

serving so many diverse interests and needs is probably the best answer to why Bismarck and Woodcock are not such strange bed-fellows after all.

Many developed nations shifted quite early away from fee-for-service rationing to what I have referred to as *implicit rationing.* Under health insurance plans in various European countries, ration-ing was imposed either by the centralized prospective budgeting procedures of the government, as in England, or through the limited resources available to "sickness societies" that contracted with physicians and hospitals for services for their members. For exam-ple, in England under the National Health Insurance Act of 1911, and later through the enactment of the National Health Service in 1946, the central government budgeted fixed amounts for providing community medical services on a capitation basis, and hospital ser-vices as of 1948 on a global budget. Similarly, sickness societies in other countries had to make contractual agreements with physicians within the means available, thus limiting the extent of services that could be rendered.

In European countries that adopted national health insurance through an indirect method, such as mandated employer-employee contributions, governments increasingly assumed a larger propor-tion of the costs of physician services and institutional care. Since government had little control over how costs were generated by physicians and hospitals, there was continuing pressure for in-creased expenditures by both patients and physicians. Governments took on the obligation in making up deficits between costs generated by health professionals and the funds available from employer-employee contributions. They did so either by raising the social security tax rates or by making larger contributions each year from general revenues. In England, where the government had direct budgetary control, costs were more successfully contained, but there were constant pressures from health professionals for increased ex-penditure, nevertheless. Despite direct control, the proportion of national income allocated to health care escalated, but at a lesser rate than in many other countries that had more open-ended budgeting systems.

Implicit rationing depends on the queue. Limited resources, facilities, and manpower are made available, and the health care system adapts to demand by establishing noneconomic barriers (Mechanic, 1976: 87−97). Health professionals, having their own styles of work and professional norms, accommodate as many patients as they can, making judgments as to priorities and need. Access to services may be limited by long appointment or referral waiting periods, by limited sites of care (and therefore greater barriers of distance and inconvenience), longer waiting times, bureaucratic barriers, and the like. Rationing also may occur through the control exercised over the extent of elaboration of services: the laboratory tests ordered, the diagnostic techniques used, the rate of hospitalization, the number of surgical interventions, and the time devoted to each patient. Capitation or salary as a form of professional payment tends to limit the extent of these modalities; fee-for-service increases the rate of discrete technical services for which a fee is paid (Glaser, 1970; Roemer, 1962).

Implicit rationing has the effect of limiting expenditures, but not necessarily in a rational way. Such rationing is based on the assumption that the professional is sufficiently programmed by his socialization as a health practitioner to make scientifically valid judgments as to what constitutes need, what treatment modalities are most likely to be effective, and which cases deserve priority. It is supposed that the exercise of clinical judgment will result in rational decision making. But as Eliot Freidson (1976:136–137) has noted, evaluation of medical judgment by professional peers is so permissive that only "blatant acts of ignorance or inattention" are clearly recognized as mistakes. Moreover, it is the more knowledgeable, more aggressive, and more demanding individuals who get more service; and these patients are usually more educated, more sophisticated, but less needy (Hetherington et al., 1975). In short, under implicit rationing the assumption is that physicians exercise agreed-upon standards for care and that services are equitably provided in light of these standards. The fact is that these standards are very murky, if they exist at all, and even the most obvious ones have little relationship to any existing knowledge on the implications of varying patterns of care for patient outcome. Under these conditions, the most effective and vocal consumers may get more than their share of whatever care is available. Moreover, given the ambiguities of practice, physicians and other health professionals may play out their own personal agendas, cultural preferences, and professional biases. Being remunerated on salary, they may work at a comfortable and leisurely pace; and they may choose to emphasize work they find most interesting, neglecting important needs of patients, such as needs for empathy and support, which may be perceived as professionally less fulfilling functions.

There is considerable evidence that systems of implicit rationing provide care at lower cost because of the limited budget available and the containment in provision of resources and manpower, but there is little evidence to support the contention that the result is a fairer allocation of social resources. Under implicit rationing, large disparities continue in the availability of facilities, in allocation of manpower and resources per capita (and in relation to known rates of morbidity in the population), and in access to services (Cooper, 1975; Logan, 1971; Hetherington et al., 1975). Affluent areas tend to retain more facilities, manpower, and other resources, and relatively little redistribution takes place. There are very large variations from area to area and institution to institution in the procedures performed, work load, ancillary assistance available, and the level of technology.

Increasingly, governments are seeking means to move from implicit to explicit forms of rationing. The idea of explicit rationing is not only to set limits on total expenditures for care, but also to develop mechanisms to arrive at more rational decisions as to relative investments in different areas of care, varying types of facilities and manpower, new technological initiatives, and the establishment of certain minimal uniform standards. The difficulty with establishing such priorities and standards is the overall lack of definitive evidence as to which health care practices really make a difference in illness outcomes. While standards for processes of care are readily formulated, it is difficult to demonstrate for most facets of care that such process norms have any clear relationship to outcomes that really matter. Indeed, health services random trials tend to show that such expensive innovations as coronary intensive care or longer hospitalizations for a variety of diseases seem to make little difference in measurable outcomes for populations where they are routinely used (Cochrane, 1972).

The difficulty of imposing explicit rationing, however, is more political than scientific. While there is always danger in establishing general guidelines that the overall formulation will not fit a specific case, there are many instances in medical practice where intelligent restrictions on practices of physicians are likely to lead to both improved and more economical practice. The fact is, however, that physicians resist such guidelines as intrusions on their professional judgment and autonomy, and tend to do whatever they can to subvert them. Even with a certain amount of slack, intelligent guidelines—sensitive to the realities of medical practice and human behavior—can be an important contribution toward more effective rationing than usually exists under the implicit system.

There are a variety of techniques that are used under many insurance systems to restrict the options of health practitioners (Glaser, 1970), and these are becoming more commonly adopted. The most straightforward is the simple exclusion or restriction of certain types of services that may involve large costs but dubious benefits—for example, psychoanalysis, orthodontia, rest cures, plastic surgery for cosmetic purposes, etc. In the case of essential components of treatment, the program may set maximal numbers of procedures that will be paid for or establish required time intervals between procedures that can be repeated and remain eligible for coverage. These limitations have the function of restricting the physician's discretion although to a modest degree. In theory, however, they can be very much extended. Another technique is to limit the cost of a treatment by requiring the physician to provide justification if he wishes to exercise a more expensive option. Since physicians tend to dislike additional required paperwork, if the guidelines are reasonable they are likely to be effective.

In the United States emphasis is now being given to mandatory peer review, a process whereby utilization practices and, in the future, the quality of care as well will be evaluated. Moreover, justification under federal programs must be provided if certain established norms are to be exceeded. While these requirements are still very weak, and frequently insufficiently responsive to contingencies at the service level, and involve a great deal of unnecessary administrative effort, in theory they can be quite valuable if the review process is an intelligent one and if control over the review mechanism is not captured by physicians who wish to maintain ongoing practices. The necessity of any guideline or standard should be evaluated in terms of its costs and benefits. When the costs exceed the benefits, the rule is obviously pointless.

Some countries require pre-review for specified expensive procedures. If pre-review is used too extensively it becomes a costly and inefficient technique but, if used sparingly to control expensive work of dubious effectiveness and possibly dangerous as well, it can have effects both as a deterrent and as a means of controlling irresponsible practitioners. Particularly in the area of surgical intervention and perhaps also in the use of dangerous classes of drugs, pre-review functions both to reduce costs and to encourage a higher quality of care. In short, both government itself and nongovernmental insurance programs are becoming more bold in intruding on areas that physicians regard as within their discretion. We have every reason to anticipate that this trend will continue.

Rationing and Primary Medical Care

The most salient aspect of medical organization in modern countries is the enormous growth of specialization and subspecialization that has occurred. While much of this development is due to the growth of biomedical science and technology, specialization is also a political process bringing economic advantages and greater control over one's work and responsibilities (Stevens, 1971). Specialization, moreover, allows physicians to dominate a specified domain and to restrict competition. While the traditional concept of the specialist was as a consultant physician who assisted the generalist with puzzling problems or those of greater complexity, existing specialties are organized around varying population groups such as pediatrics or geriatrics, types of technology such as radiology, organ systems such as nephrology, etiologies such as infectious disease, and disease categories such as pulmonary disease. The most recent distortion of the concept of the consulting physician was the development of a specialty in family practice, which in effect defines the generalist as another type of specialist.

While there are many issues relevant to the manner in which specialization has emerged, the distinction with the greatest importance for rationing is the one between physicians who engage in primary care and those who provide specialty care or more complex hospital services. Everywhere in the world, nations are seeking to define the appropriate functions and responsibilities for each of the levels of care and their most efficient balance. Most discussions of primary care, particularly in countries that retain the provision of services at least in part within the private marketplace, suffer from confusions among the organizational, service, and manpower dimensions of the situation.

The most typical view of primary care is that it is the care given by certain types of practitioners who work as generalists: general practitioners, family practitioners, nurse practitioners, and so on. It is assumed that the training received by such practitioners prepares them adequately to provide first-contact care and to take continuing responsibilities for overall needs of the patient. While convenient, this definition includes as primary care highly complex medical and surgical procedures that are more adequately performed by physicians who are highly conversant with the field and who perform these procedures sufficiently frequently to do them expertly. While a considerable amount of major surgery is performed by general practitioners in the United States and elsewhere, major surgery is not appropriately included as primary care. Similarly, many specialists insist that they devote significant amounts of their time to primary care, and thus the shortage of primary care physicians is exaggerated. It should be clear then that this approach to understanding the appropriate role of primary care is not particularly helpful.

It is frequently suggested that one way of resolving the issue of primary care is to divide arbitrarily medical functions into primary, secondary, and tertiary. Such an approach, however, misses the major point which is that the practice of medicine is a conceptual and intellectual endeavor in which physicians with diverse training perceive, evaluate, classify, and manage comparable patients differently. The evaluation of a patient in good medical practice comes from listening to the patient, getting to know the person, and developing a clinical context in which the patient is willing to reveal himself or herself. How physicians will come to view a patient's problem depends on their orientations and how accessible the patient is to them psychologically as well as physically. The key point is that differences between primary and specialist practitioners are not simply a matter of what they do, but also a matter of how they do it. An essential aspect of primary care is the physician's attitude, assumptions and storage of information about the particular patient, and the way the practitioner goes about evaluating the patient's complaint. Many patients first contacting a physician are in a stage in which their symptoms are unorganized and fluid (Balint, 1957). What the physician defines as important, what he inquires about, and how he evaluates the patient's symptoms and illness behavior are molded by his knowledge of the patient as well as his training and orientations. In understanding how varying types of general and subspecialty training affect medical practice, it is necessary to have a good appreciation of how patients with comparable presenting complaints are evaluated and managed differently.

Still another way of viewing primary care is as part of an organizational system. Here the emphasis is less on a particular type of practitioner and how he is trained, and more on how different levels of care are organized and how they relate to one another. For example, in most organized medical care systems there are designated primary care physicians who have responsibility for first-contact care, for assuming continued responsibility for an enrolled population, and for dealing with the more common and less complicated problems of their patients. These systems are often established so that patients are required to seek more specialized services through the referral of their primary doctor. Similarly, secondary and tertiary care facilities are organized in relation to the system as a whole, and attempts are made to specify the conditions for coordination among varying levels of care. Although the particular type of practitioner used at varying levels of care is not an unimportant issue, the major focus shifts to defining responsibilities for care functions at each level of care. Primary care services, however they are defined by the system, may be organized in a variety of ways with alternative types of personnel as long as the necessary functions are performed. In this context, primary care is a level of service, not a particular type of practitioner.

The formulation of a planned system of primary, secondary, and tertiary functions has important implications for rationing. When the primary practitioner is the source of entry into the care system and a gatekeeper to access to more specialized practitioners and technologies, the rate of use of specialized technologies can be very much diminished. Systems of care that use primarily a sole source of entry through a primary physician make do with many fewer specialists and specialized facilities, and without any major loss in effective care. As Paul Beeson (1974:48), who has held responsible positions in both England and the United States, has noted:

> There are 22,000 in family practice in the United Kingdom and 70,000 in family practice in the United States. There are 8,000 in specialist practice in the United Kingdom and 280,000 in specialist practice in the United States. . . . The striking difference is economy in the use of specialists. To me this is the most obvious reason why America has a badly distributed, excessively costly system.

An effective system of care, moreover, allows an opportunity to organize manpower rationally relative to population groups, thus limiting the extent to which doctors generate marginal efforts due to their excessive concentration in any area. Also, by emphasizing functions and patterns of care, rather than types of medical specialties, it is much less difficult to develop functional substitutes to physicians in performing many primary care services. Because the emphasis is on a service, it is more possible to develop participation of health practitioners who are trained and willing to perform functions that physicians are unwilling to do, that they do poorly, or that they provide inefficiently—for example, health education, patient monitoring, medically related social services, and the like.

When primary care is defined as part of a system, problems still remain in coordination and motivation. The point at which referrals should take place from one level to another, for example, is left to the individual practitioner and is often affected by the implicit incentives built into the organization of health services or in how health personnel are remunerated. A common complaint in organized systems of care based on a capitation arrangement is that unnecessary referral is made to secondary services because of the lack of incentive for continued care at the primary level (Forsyth and Logan, 1968). These problems can be alleviated, if not avoided, by a good understanding of the epidemiology of help-seeking, with specification of standards for referral and with incentives promoting good care.

The Structure of Doctor-Patient Interaction under Varying Rationing Arrangements

Each of the types of rationing described tends to be associated with a particular mode of physician-patient interaction, although there is great variation within each type, dependent on the personalities of the actors involved, the work load and work flow, and the incentives operative in any particular situation. Eliot Freidson (1961, 1970, 1976) has written extensively on these types of relationships, and in this section I draw heavily on his work. Very simply, it is my contention that, as rationing varies from fee-for-service to implicit to explicit rationing, the types of influence shift from client control to colleague control to bureaucratic control. Similarly, the nuances in the physician's role shift from "entrepreneur" to "expert" to "official."

Freidson has convincingly illustrated how the shift from fee-for-service practice to prepaid group practice is accompanied by lesser flexibility and responsiveness of the physician. When the retention of the patient is no longer an economic issue for the physician, there is no need to "humor the patient" nor bend to the patient's wishes when they are contrary to the physician's best judgment. Freidson argues that in the prepaid situation colleagues are a more important reference group, and while the physician may be more inflexible he may practice a higher standard of medical care. The extent to which differences between fee-for-service and prepaid practice will exist depends greatly on the competition for patients existing in any practice area. As competition increases, physicians may be more willing to provide greater amenities to patients and to be flexible to their requests in order to retain their patronage. When the physician has more patients than he requires, there may be little client control even in the fee-for-service situation. As the physician becomes less dependent on the patient—either because he is only one of a large number of physicians servicing an enrolled population or because he is in a favorable competitive situation—he can more easily play the role of the neutral expert, one whose decisions are quite isolated from any personal financial stake he may have in his work.

In theory, implicit rationing encourages the physician to play the role of the expert, but in actuality the difficulty lies in the ambiguity of his expertise. Since the physician by the very nature of his work is required to come to many social decisions quite irrelevant to his technical expertise, and since physicians differ radically on these social judgments, there is no clear basis for these decisions. For example, consider the frequently occurring issue of whether a hospitalized mother should be sent home or retained for a few more days because the physician anticipates that her family will expect her to resume usual duties, or because she may be inclined to quickly reassume responsibilities. In theory, when the patient must incur part of the fee, such potential cost will influence the decision. However, when third parties assume the cost, neither the physician nor the patient has any incentive to choose the more parsimonious decision. If the physician acts as an expert, his bias is to use resources if he sees any potential benefit. Incentives to do otherwise come only when he is personally faced with a limitation of resources. A global budget without further guidelines, although it may restrict the physician's actions to some extent, does not insure rational decision making and may encourage highly preferential behavior depending on the physician's perceptions of and attitudes toward the patient.

Although the evidence is not fully clear, most existing prepaid group practices seem to conserve resources more by controlling inputs—numbers of primary care physicians, beds, and specialists—than by directly affecting the manner in which physicians make decisions in allocating resources. While it has been alleged that the incentives for physicians to avoid unnecessary work may be an important factor, there is no impressive evidence that such incentives substantially affect decision making itself (Mechanic, 1976). Most of the rationing that takes place seems to be at the administrative planning level, and then physicians seem to adjust to whatever resources are available. Thus, in most prepaid group practices or in health centers or polyclinics, physicians still very much retain the role of "expert."

As health care plan administrators or government officials attempt to tighten expenditures by moving toward a system of explicit rationing, physicians are pushed to a larger degree into the role of bureaucratic official. The case of the Soviet physicians, described by Field (1957), who were limited in the number of sickness certifications they could issue, provides an extreme example of how bureaucratic regulation can substantially limit the options available for physician decision making. While no explicit rationing system in the world has gone this far in any systematic way, there is a discernible tendency toward greater administrative control. In such circumstances the physician must explicitly determine which patients are more needy of a particular service, and he must develop ways to discourage or influence other patients who insist on such service. Increasingly, for example, the physician will require pre-review of certain decisions or have other decisions reviewed after the fact. The intrusion of such requirements or review, if seriously performed, can have a significant effect on decision making, particularly on the "technological imperative."

Everywhere in the world physicians have retained considerable autonomy; even in such highly bureaucratized contexts as military medicine, industrial medicine, and the health services of communist countries, physicians have persisted in their roles more as experts than as bureaucratic functionaries. The shift is more nuance than drama, and while such tendencies will grow throughout the world, rationing is more likely to be imposed on the total framework of services and less on the decisions of the individual physician treating a particular patient. In any case, the growing bureaucratization of medicine poses some serious dangers, and I conclude this paper with a brief consideration of these.

The Effects of Bureaucratization on Medicine as a Social Institution

Medicine as a social institution has extremely broad functions. Not only does medicine deal with the prevention and treatment of pain, disease, disability, and impairment, but it also provides an acceptable excuse for relief from ordinary obligations and responsibilities, and may be used to justify behaviors and interventions not ordinarily tolerated by the social system without significant sanctions. The definition of illness may also be used as a mechanism of social control to contain deviance, to remove misfits from particular social roles, or to encourage continued social functioning and productive activity. Thus, the locus of control for medical decision making is a key variable in examining the implications of medical care for social life more generally.

In the case of fee-for-service medicine, the physician acts as the agent of the patient. Although his own personal economic interests may intrude in the relationship, his role is to defend the interests of the patient against any other competing interest. The increasing employment of physicians by health programs or complex organizations involves changes in the auspices of medical care that depart in significant ways from traditional concepts (Mechanic, 1976). As I have noted throughout this paper, and specifically in my discussion of rationing, bureaucratic medical settings involve multiple interests, thus putting the physician under pressure to sacrifice certain potential interests of an individual patient to satisfy organizational needs. In the case of such institutions as health maintenance organizations, for example, increased administrative directions for rationing, as well as financial incentives, are developed to encourage physicians to avoid providing unnecessary services. But since the concept of "necessary" is itself vague, the determination may reflect the balance of pressures on the physician.

The bureaucratization of medicine also has the effect of diluting the personal responsibility of the provider, making it more likely that interests other than those of the patient will prevail. By segmenting responsibility for patient care, the medical bureaucracy

15

relieves the physician of direct continuing responsibility. If the patient cannot reach a physician at night or on weekends, obtain responsive care, have inquiries answered, or whatever, the problem is no longer focused on the failure of an individual physician, but on the failures of the organization. It is far easier for patients to locate and deal with individual failures where responsibility is clear than to confront a diffuse organizational structure where responsibility is often hazy and the buck is easily passed. To the extent the physician knows that a patient is his or her charge, the physician feels a certain responsibility to protect the patient's interests against organizational roadblocks and requests that may not be fully appropriate. But when responsibility is less clear it is easier to make decisions in the name of other interests such as research, teaching, demonstration, or the "public welfare," whatever that might be.

The growth of bureaucratic medicine is in many ways an effective response to the development and complexity of medical knowledge. But it also involves some significant threats to the concept of physician responsibility for the best interests of the individual patient and for the empathic and supportive relationships that are so vital to effective care of the whole person. It also involves a shifting in the balance of power in dealing with the broader problems for which patients use the medical system such as in alleviating anxieties and excusing failure. The physician's role as advocate of the patient derives from a close and continuing relationship and knowledge of the patient and a certain relational alignment to him. Bureaucratic structures tend to promote more segmented and detached relationships and ambiguities and conflicts in relational alignments. While in theory bureaucratic structures could be developed to promote empathy, continuity, and humane care, the tendency is for bureaucratic and technical functions to be given higher priority. Physicians are rewarded more for being good managers and researchers or for coping with a large work load than for providing interested and humane care. While physician care in bureaucracies is often humane, such behavior seems to occur despite bureaucratic structure rather than because of it.

Bureaucratization in medicine is inevitable. The challenge thus is to promote organizational arrangements that ration wisely and fairly, and that provide incentives for listening to the patient and caring for him. Humane medicine is an effective component of good patient care. Medical outcomes often depend on the understanding and cooperation of patients and their willingness to engage their problems in a serious and committed way. Medicine without caring, no matter how effective the technique, has a limited capacity to fulfill the broad potential of medicine as a sustaining institution for those who come to depend upon it. The development of bureaucratic incentives, thus, must be designed to enhance humane values while capitalizing on advances in knowledge and technology (Howard and Strauss, 1975). In my estimation this can be most effectively accomplished by upgrading the role and performance of the primary care sector and by regulating carefully through the planning process the availability and provision of the more expensive, complex, and dangerous technologies. Within broad guidelines, physician and patient must remain as free as possible to negotiate satisfactory solutions to the personal and social dilemmas that bring them together.

References

Balint, Michael. 1957. *The Doctor, His Patient, and the Illness.* New York: International Universities Press.

Beeson, Paul. 1974. "Some good features of the British National Health Service." *Journal of Medical Education* 49 (January):43–49.

Cochrane, A.L. 1972. *Effectiveness and Efficiency: Random Reflections on Health Services.* London: Nuffield Provincial Hospitals Trust.

Cooper, Michael. 1975. *Rationing Health Care.* New York: John Wiley (Halsted Press).

Field, Mark. 1957. *Doctor and Patient in Soviet Russia.* Cambridge: Harvard University Press.

Forsyth, G., and Logan, R. 1968. *Gateway or Dividing Line: A Study of Hospital Out-Patients in the 1960's.* New York: Oxford University Press.

Fox, Renee, and Swazey, Judith. 1974. *The Courage to Fail: A Social View of Organ Transplants and Dialysis.* Chicago: University of Chicago Press.

Freidson, Eliot. 1961. *Patients' Views of Medical Practice.* New York: Russell Sage Foundation.

———. 1970. *Profession of Medicine: A Study of the Sociology of Applied Knowledge.* New York: Dodd-Mead.

———. 1976. *Doctoring Together: A Study of Professional Social Control.* New York: Elsevier.

Fuchs, Victor. 1968. "The growing demand for medical care." *New England Journal of Medicine* 279:190—195.

———. 1976. "From Bismarck to Woodcock: The 'irrational' pursuit of national health insurance." Center for Economic Analysis of Human Behavior and Social Institutions, Working Paper No. 120. National Bureau of Economic Research.

Glaser, William A. 1970. *Paying the Doctor: Systems of Remuneration and Their Effects.* Baltimore: Johns Hopkins Press.

Hetherington, Robert, et al. 1975. *Health Insurance Plans: Promise and Performance.* New York: Wiley-Interscience.

Howard, Jan, and Strauss, Anselm, eds. 1975. *Humanizing Health Care.* New York: Wiley-Interscience.

Logan, R.F.L. 1971. "National health planning—An appraisal of the state of the art." *International Journal of Health Services* 1 (February):6—17.

Mechanic, David. 1974. *Politics, Medicine, and Social Science.* New York: Wiley-Interscience.

———. 1976. *The Growth of Bureaucratic Medicine: An Inquiry into the Dynamics of Patient Behavior and the Organization of Medical Care.* New York: Wiley-Interscience.

Roemer, Milton. 1962. "On paying the doctor and the implications of different methods." *Journal of Health and Social Behavior* 3 (Spring):4—14.

Stevens, Rosemary. 1971. *American Medicine and the Public Interest.* New Haven: Yale University Press.

White, K.L., et al. 1961. "The ecology of medical care." *New England Journal of Medicine* 265:885—892.

Prepared for the Colloque International de Sociologie Medicale, Paris, July 1976. Supported in part by a grant from the Robert Wood Johnson Foundation. Full rights reserved by the author.

Address reprint requests to: David Mechanic, Professor of Sociology, Center for Medical Sociology and Health Services Research, University of Wisconsin, Social Science Building, Madison, Wisconsin 53706

The Failures of Success

ERNEST M. GRUENBERG

Johns Hopkins University School of Hygiene and Public Health

I would like to begin by taking you back to the years preceding the
Second World War, because the problem I wish to discuss must be
seen as a historical process if it is to be understood. I am going to
talk about a particular chapter in the history of disease, a chapter
characterized by the surprising fact that the net effect of successful
technical innovations used in disease control has been to raise the
prevalence of certain diseases and disabilities by prolonging their
average duration. The beginning of this historical period coincided
with the introduction of the systematic clinical trial and of the
sulfonamides in 1937 and 1938.

The health situation regarding modern man's chronic diseases
and disabilities immediately before that period was well described
by Osler in 1904 in his famous textbook, *The Principles and Practice of Medicine*, and the same description was still present in the
1935 edition revised by McCrae (Osler, 1935):

> There is truth in the paradoxical statement that persons rarely die of
> the disease with which they suffer. Secondary *terminal* infections car-
> ry off many patients with incurable disease.

Osler could not have anticipated the coming successes in curing the
terminal infections associated with these incurable, or chronic, diseases that were to be introduced by a new era of medical research—
the era of the clinical trial. What happened was that at the beginning
of the era, in 1936, on a very small grant from the Rockefeller Foundation, a group of investigators searching for a cure for puerperal
fever revealed to the world the antibacterial powers of sulfanilamide. The impact that sulfa drugs were to have on pneumonia, the
most frequent of the terminal infectious diseases at that time, was as
dramatic as it was serendipitous. Figure 1 shows the steep decline in
death from pneumonia after 1936, following the introduction of sulfa drugs.

M M F Q / Health and Society / *Winter 1977*
© Milbank Memorial Fund 1977

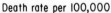

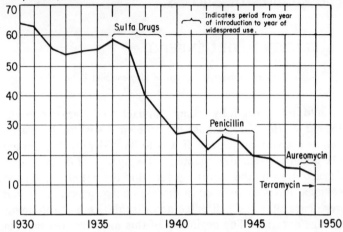

FIG. 1. Curve of the mortality rate per 100,000 from pneumonia between 1930 and 1950 as prepared by the Metropolitan Life Insurance Company.

From Reimann, Hobart A., *Pneumonia*, 1954. Courtesy of Charles C. Thomas, Publisher, Springfield, Illinois.

Coincidental to the discovery of the sulfonamides was the invention of the clinical trial, the seeds of which had been developing for many years. In 1937 Professor A. Bradford Hill gave researchers a means for comparing a new treatment with an old one on a carefully selected population, and getting a definitive answer, usually within a few months. Quite by accident, the first new treatment that was tested adequately by the clinical trial was sulfanilamide. The clinical trial was then used to examine the efficacy of treatments whose effects, while not so apparent as those of the sulfa drugs, represented major clinical successes.

The rate at which new, effective remedies were discovered accelerated suddenly. The most important of these turned away impending death by simple techniques. The once fatal disease or injury might be in an otherwise healthy or vigorous person. As it turned out, these successful life-saving measures were disproportionately needed in people suffering from an incurable disease or disability. But these new techniques did not cure the chronic diseases, nor did they prevent them in the next patient.

If we assume no change in the age-specific annual incidence of the diseases formerly terminated early by now curable infections, and that, in fact, the anti-infectious drugs have been postponing death, then the average duration of these conditions has presumably been increasing. Therefore at the same time that persons suffering from chronic diseases are getting an extension of life, they are also getting an extension of disease and disability.

It is obvious that, with increasing duration, we would expect the proportion of the population in any given age group suffering from these conditions to rise. And, in fact, as the result of advances in medical care, we are seeing a rising prevalence of certain chronic conditions which previously led to early terminal infections, but whose victims now suffer from them for a longer period. The goal of medical research work is to "diminish disease and enrich life" (Gregg, 1941), but it produced tools which prolong diseased, diminished lives and so increase the proportion of people who have a disabling or chronic disease.

That is a major but unintended effect of many technical improvements stemming from health research. These increasingly common chronic conditions represent the failures of success. Their growing prevalence and longer duration are a product of progress in health technology.

Mongolism

How much does the elimination of fatal complications increase the proportion of the population with a specific chronic condition? That depends on how much the duration is increasing.[1] The increased duration has been measured best for mongolism (Down's syndrome).

Mongolism has long been known to be associated with a high susceptibility to respiratory infections (Record and Smith, 1955; Penrose, 1932). Children born with Down's syndrome rarely reached maturity until the 1940 birth cohort started to age. Persons in that cohort are now passing their thirty-sixth birthdays. However, their predecessors who managed to survive the first few years of life have also experienced an increased life expectancy—a much larger increase than that of the general population. For the first time in human history we are seeing 70-year-old mongoloids. Spain's ex-

[1]The duration of each person's illness extends from the time he becomes ill until he no longer is ill. A person with an incurable chronic illness will remain ill until he dies.

21

cellent pathology text (1963) on diseases resulting from medical advances does not describe the consequences of this new type of extended disease process in adults which the pathologist sees at the autopsy table. According to the director of the new Institute on Aging, Robert Butler, the geriatrics program will have to include plans for mongoloids, a situation that would have been unimaginable 40 years ago!

Several sets of life tables for mongolism have been prepared, but none allows us to measure with precision how the life expectancy has changed and how much the prevalence rates have been rising since 1939. However, Carter (1958) makes what I think is a reasonable set of estimates of the prevalence rate of mongolism at age ten years. The rate doubled between 1929 and 1949, and doubled again in the following decade, reaching a level of more than one per thousand by 1958.

If we look at prevalence data from Victoria, Australia, in 1961 (Collmann and Stoller, 1963) and Salford, England, in 1974 (Fryers, 1975), we see that this trend is continuing. The overall prevalence rate increased by about 150 percent between 1961 and 1974. For children aged five to fourteen years, the prevalence rate per 1,000 was 1.3 in 1974, or almost twice the 1961 rate of .70.

Prevalence rates for mongolism would have risen dramatically even if nothing had been added to medical technology beyond antimicrobial drugs. Cardiac complications, which today are the most common cause of mortality among mongoloids (Deaton, 1973), usually do not occur until the teens or twenties, whereas previously most mongoloid children died of pneumonia before the age of six years. The most dangerous period of life for mongoloids is still the first year, but gains in survivorship have also been the most dramatic in this early period.

Of the mongoloid children who survive to age five years today, 50 percent live on into their fifties (Øster et al., 1975). Even this situation is changing. As more and more cardiac and gastrointestinal lesions are being surgically corrected, and patients with leukemia and other cancers are receiving life-prolonging treatments, we can expect to see an even greater rise in the prevalence of Down's syndrome.

Yet, no large scale searches for preventable causes of mongolism are underway. Such inquiry seems to represent no one's priority. Even the door to new studies, which opened dramatically in

1959 when mongolism was shown to be due to trisomy, has given us no new insight into how to keep this condition from beginning. Fetal diagnosis of the trisomic condition followed by elective abortion does indeed represent an attempt to reduce the incidence of live-born mongoloid infants. At best it is a method for recognition of the condition early enough in fetal development so that women willing to do so can arrange for an early termination of the pregnancy. But this is merely a method of precipitating death, not an attempt to find preventable causes of the condition itself.

If this phenomenon of rising prevalence had occurred only in mongolism, the situation would be disturbing, for mongoloids now represent one-fourth of the severely retarded population (Kushlick, 1966). But because the prevalence rate of the severely retarded has been growing in general, it becomes alarming. The lives of youngsters with other causes of severe mental retardation are also being extended more rapidly than those of the general population due to the falling neonatal, infant, and childhood mortality rates associated with these conditions. The best data on the subject of rising prevalence rates come from Salford, the industrial suburb of Manchester, England (Fryers, 1975). There the school-age prevalence rates of the severely mentally retarded more than doubled between 1961 and 1974. We do not have much information on the diagnostic groups represented, but if I interpret correctly the criteria for severe retardation, many young people are going to live handicapped lives of unpredictable duration.

Senile Brain Disease (SBD)

Another example of the failures of our successes occurs at the other end of life. We have long known that the age-specific prevalence of serious mental disorders rises rapidly in the last decades of life (Fig. 2). We also know that the general population is aging.

With the exponentially rising age-specific prevalence rates of mental illness with age, and with an increasing number of aged in the population, it is clear that we are headed for a great increase in serious mental disorder associated with aging. I can see no reason to think that the incidence of senile brain disease might be falling, nor do I think there is evidence that it is rising. I suspect that psychosis with cerebral arteriosclerosis may be getting more common,

23

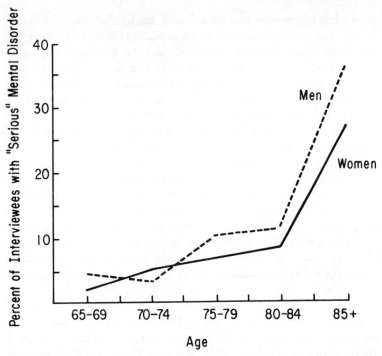

Fɪɢ. 2. "Serious" mental disorder. "Serious" in this study meant with enough evidence of danger to self or others, or, more commonly, inability to care for self that an involuntary mental hospital certificate could have been properly signed by a physician *if* those in the individual's home situation stopped being able and willing to provide care.

SOURCE: Staff of the Mental Research Unit, New York State Dept. of Mental Hygiene. 1960. A mental health survey of older people. *Psychiatric Quarterly* (supplement) 34(1):34−75. (Constructed from data in Table 3.21, p. 56.)

because coronary artery disease is getting more common, but I know of no assembled facts on this issue.

However, since senile brain disease was probably the condition which led Osler to think of pneumonia as the old man's friend, we may properly ask whether the large-scale conquest of pneumonia has reduced the usefulness of this friend, stretching out the course of senile brain disease, which produces the mental manifestations of "senile dementia."

We have some facts from a small (approximately 2,500), south Swedish population which was carefully screened for psychiatric illness in 1947 by Essen-Möller (1956), and rescreened in 1957 by Hagnell. Hagnell and I selected two diagnoses believed to be dominated by cases of senile brain disease, although the classification might be slightly contaminated by cerebral arteriosclerosis and depressive states. (The silent cases of senile brain disease which occur will, of course, be missed by the type of clinical screen used.) (Gruenberg and Hagnell, in press.)

There were twenty-four people over the age of sixty with senile dementia in 1947, and there were forty-eight over the age of sixty in 1957. All twenty-four of the people found to have senile dementia in 1947 died by 1953, but of the forty-eight cases prevailing in 1957, five were still alive in 1967. The average duration of the episodes had at least doubled in a decade. The data suggest no concentration of this doubling in either sex or in any age group, but the number of cases is too small to examine this issue with confidence.

From 1947 to 1957, the prevalence rate of senile dementia in women over sixty years old rose from 3.2 percent to 5.7 percent, and in men from 2.3 percent to 4.9 percent.

Survivorship of the cases prevailing in 1957 closely resembled that of the general population, whereas cases prevailing in 1947 died off faster than the general population. The evidence suggests that this process did not end in 1957, but probably still continues today.

Who Else Was Killed By Pneumonia?

The chronic disabilities I have discussed so far—Down's syndrome and senile brain disease—are only two examples of the failures of success. What other conditions have been extended because of the elimination of fatal complications? First let us ask what other conditions have risen in prevalence due to the advent of antimicrobial drugs. Collins and Lehmann (1953) examined the excess death rates caused by conditions other than pneumonia during local influenza and pneumonia epidemics in the 1920s and '30s. From this material, they were able to provide us with evidence regarding those diseases which were frequently terminated by these respiratory infections in the days when the treatment resources against them were limited. From their data, we can infer what those conditions were (Table 1).

If no other causes of death had been conquered by modern medicine except those which respond to the sulfa drugs and antibiotics, we would be justified in suspecting that the durations of

TABLE 1
Conditions Showing Excess Death Rates
During Epidemics of Influenza and Pneumonia

Heart Disease
Tuberculosis (especially before 1921)
Intracranial vascular lesions
Nephritis (especially before 1929)
Diabetes
Puerperal diseases
Cancer
Chronic bronchitis

After Collins and Lehmann, 1953.

these conditions were being prolonged. They are conditions which
do not recover spontaneously. They are also diseases for which no
cures have been developed, and for which no preventions have been
found.

But there have been other major advances against the killing
complications of chronic diseases, some of which I will mention to
illustrate the fact that the rising prevalence of chronic diseases and
disability is not merely the result of a decreased case fatality rate in
pneumonia.

Some Other Conditions

In Table 2 are listed some of the conditions which should be looked
at from the same point of view—diseases made more prevalent by
medical progress. I have listed them approximately in their rank
order in terms of prevalence rates, regardless of which age group experiences the highest prevalence rate. In doing this I have taken the
unusual step of eliminating discrimination by age.

Arteriosclerosis

Most cases of arteriosclerosis cannot be recognized by clinical examination. We have no good estimate of the prevalence of subclinical cases, but we do know that arteriosclerosis represents the
most important single cause of chronic brain disease interfering with
mental functioning, as well as the largest cause of chronic heart disease in this country. Chronic kidney disease and hypertension are
also closely related to this condition. Previously, cases of arterio-

sclerosis were terminated by a number of complications: pneumonia, coronary occlusion, and ruptured arteries in the brain (stroke) and aorta. In the last forty years, medical research workers have developed a variety of means for outmaneuvering each of these fatal complications.

Hypertension

The prevention of fatal complications by moderating the level of hypertension with diuretics seems to be working. Most hypertensive patients lead almost normal lives and experience only a low level of disability. We have discovered an ideal way to control this disease, but we have yet to learn how to prevent it from occurring.

Schizophrenia

This is a common enough condition to worry about and a damaging one. While the highest point prevalence rates run only a little over 1 percent (Kramer, 1976), the proportion of the population who will at some time in life get clinical treatment for a schizophrenic episode is close to 5 percent. Its prevalence may be rising because in the recent past schizophrenic patients in mental hospitals had much higher mortality rates from many conditions than the general population (Malzberg, 1934). Yolles and Kramer (1969) have shown that since then this high mortality rate has declined. The pattern of community care has reduced the implications of these institutional death rates radically. But the frequency of schizophrenic diagnoses has also risen with the expansion of outpatient treatment and the broadening of diagnostic criteria. Balancing these two forces which affect the available data, I estimate that the life expectancy of schizophrenics has been increasing faster than that of the general population.

Diabetes

The discovery of insulin in 1922 dramatically changed the life expectancy of diabetics. While formerly the majority died of fatal complications (in conformity with Osler's paradox) over 40 percent died in diabetic coma. This figure rapidly dropped to a tiny fraction. Pneumonia continued to account for over 10 percent of the deaths until approximately 1944. By the 1960s over three-fourths of the diabetic deaths were due to vascular complications (Marble, 1972) which must be occurring at older ages.

Spina Bifida

In 1963, a British surgeon developed a marvelous operation to save newborn babies with extreme spina bifida, a congenital anomaly of the spine. Over half those who survived this surgery were severely or very severely disabled (Laurence, 1974; Hunt, 1973). They were doubly incontinent, immobile, and often retarded and incoherent. Ford (1970) estimated that this surgery would add 358 children with severe mental and physical handicaps to the British population each year. Routine use of this surgery in the United States would result in about 1,700 families each year being "blessed" with totally crippled children (Eisenberg, 1975). No one yet knows how many years these children will survive because this is a new "advance." Previously they would have died in the newborn nursery; now they will be saved to live crippled lives.

Other advances have had similar effects. The fatal complications of pernicious anemia have been thwarted, since this condition can now be suppressed with medication. Cases of Huntington's chorea have been prolonged by successfully treating terminal pneumonia. Hemophiliacs can now be treated so that they less often die of hemorrhages. The thoughtful reader will undoubtedly be able to list numerous other examples.

Discussion

Why are we preventing death in the presence of illness and disability? Why these successes which produce these failures? Is it because the scientific period of modern medicine and public health continues to gain its drama from the idea of a life and death struggle against the causes of death? Public health departments once routinely put falling death rate curves on the outside cover of their annual reports. This was their index of success. They only gave up using crude death rates as a selling point when their successes in lowering childhood deaths increased the proportion of old people in the population, which resulted in a rise in the crude death rate. In fact, many health officers no longer know what the death rates in their jurisdictions are or how they compare with those of the country as a whole.

I, among others, predicted that morbidity would become the priority of public health once the giant killers had been conquered and the average age of the population rose. Events have refuted my hopeful expectation. Yet our research programs continue to put primary emphasis on causes of death rather than on causes of non-killing chronic diseases. More and more of the health dollar is being used to provide services to the chronically ill and disabled. A recent estimate (R. Morris, 1976) of the health and medical care and transfer expenditures for the chronically disabled was around $83 billion—almost as much as the hotly debated defense budget.

The major advances in medical science have in fact been against killing diseases. It is noteworthy that the sulfonamides emerged out of the fight against maternal mortality in a search for a treatment of puerperal sepsis. The other effects of the sulfa drugs were all serendipitous to that goal.

Next Steps in Research

It seems obvious that the rising prevalence rates of serious conditions should lead to new priorities for research. We should focus on furthering our understanding of the forces which determine the patterns of occurrence of these conditions, and thus try to identify some modifiable causal factors. Intensive searches for preventive measures are at least as important for bettering the people's health today as were the searches to gain control over plague, smallpox, cholera, diphtheria, tuberculosis, pellagra, and lung cancer a generation or so ago. In principle there is no reason to think that different types of epidemiological forces are at work in the causation of these diseases. Infections, poisons, genes, physical agents, and nutritional deficiencies are the classes of agents we have come to worry about, and we should continue to worry about them. The epidemiologists of the future must seek out such modifiable agents in the causal chains which lead to these newly stretched out diseases of medical progress.

In order to indicate that this precept is not just empty rhetoric, I have undertaken to suggest a next step in epidemiological research for each of these conditions (Table 2). In selecting a next step I have

TABLE 2
Conditions Showing Increased Prevalence in the Last 30 Years

Condition	Highest Prevalence[a]	Next Steps in Research
Senile brain disease[b]	300/1,000 (80 years)	Case-control; autopsies; laboratory diagnosis
Arteriosclerotic[c]		
Heart disease	140/1,000 (65–74 years)	Case-control
Brain disease	100/1,000 (65–74 years)	Case-control
Hypertension[c]	150/1,000 (Over 65 years)	Case-control
Schizophrenia[c]	12/1,000 (35–44 years)	Penetrance factors
Diabetes[b]	9/1,000 (65–74 years)	Case-control on individuals with similar indices for metabolism of glucose
Severe mental retardation[b]	4.7/1,000 (5–15 years)	Nutritional preventive trials
Spina bifida[b]	2.5/1,000 (birth)	?
Down's syndrome[b]	1.3/1,000 (birth)	Is increased incidence in older women due to more trisomic mutations or decreased lethal effects of trisomy?

[a]Author's best estimate, based on available data
[b]Pretty certain
[c]Inferred

tried to keep in mind Sir Peter Medawar's excellent dictum: "If politics is the art of the possible, science is the art of the soluble" (Medawar, 1967). Selecting the next issue to investigate is not a science but an art—it is a matter of judging what problem is soluble today with today's understanding and research techniques. "Any fool can ask a question, the trick is to ask a question which can be answered" (Lemkau and Pasamanick, 1957).

Trisomy 21

We have known for some time that mongolism (Down's syndrome) is the most common of the human trisomic disorders. I will confine my suggestions to those cases caused by nondisjunction, the failure of the chromosomal material to divide properly when the ovum is being formed in the mother's ovary.[2] The obvious approach to this

[2]The normal human cell has twenty-three pairs of chromosomes, one of each pair coming from the father's sperm and one from the mother's ovum. The ovum and sperm each have only twenty-three chromosomes. Nondisjunction in oogenesis results in an egg having twenty-four chromosomes because one pair failed to split. When fertilized such an egg has three chromosomes where a pair normally exists, hence the name "trisomy."

problem is to look for the causes of nondisjunction and to look at its epidemiology. The nondisjunctions which occur in the various trisomic conditions (for example, mongolism, Turner's syndrome) may be caused by different agents or they may have a single underlying cause. If all nondisjunctions have similar causes and result only in different patterns of trisomy because they affect different chromosomes, we should then turn our attention to all the nondisjunctions including those which do not cause human disease. Most trisomic patterns are likely to be lethal to the embryo, so the obvious research step is to compare fetuses which spontaneously abort with those that do not. We would then be able to tell whether trisomy of chromosome 21 (which produces mongolism) is the most common human trisomy, or only the most common one which survives the fetal period and produces disease.

I suspect that trisomies are fairly common and that quality control occurs by weeding out the "misfits" during fetal development. One way to pursue that hypothesis is to determine whether the much higher rate of mongoloids born to older women is associated with a higher rate of trisomic conceptions or with a decreased ability for discriminating weeding through resorption, abortion, and miscarriage. There is abundant evidence that the mortality rate in mongoloid fetuses is enormous. How does it compare in women of different ages? That, I think is a soluble problem.

Senile Brain Disease

Clinical diagnosis of senile dementia is not terribly difficult but this does not identify the frequent asymptomatic silent cases of it. So we need autopsy surveys on clinically surveyed populations. Case control studies cannot yet be done because we know too little about the age of risk. There is some evidence in Hagnell's data that incidence rates, which soar between age 70 and age 80, begin to fall off after age 80. Perhaps everyone who is going to develop this condition does so by age 85 or 90. If so, we know that our case control studies should be done on people who have passed their ninetieth birthday. All of the important questions about the epidemiology of senile brain disease would become rapidly answerable if we had a reliable, valid means of knowing whether senile plaques were present during life. The new evidence about aluminum deposits in the senile plaques suggests the possibility that some clever biophysicist might develop a noninvasive device for ascertaining the presence of such deposits.

Arteriosclerosis

We need a means of identifying people in the early presymptomatic stages of this group of diseases. These early stages can be detected at autopsy, and autopsy surveys for this purpose can be done on young people who die of other conditions, particularly accidents. This would provide an opportunity to compare the characteristics of cases and non-cases—a simple case control study.

Schizophrenia

The next fruitful step in elucidating the pathogenesis of schizophrenic conditions may be reached by identifying populations with high levels of familial aggregation of the condition and comparing these families with the families of schizophrenics in which the concentration of secondary cases among first degree relatives is low. This is based on the general notion that there are two types of factors which must interact to produce clinical schizophrenic syndromes: factors associated with the family of origin (polygenic mechanisms, dominant gene with low penetrance?) and external environmental factors. Comparing the environments and living habits of these two sets of families would be an attempt, through a type of case control study, to identify risk factors other than the familial tendency to develop schizophrenia. That is a long shot, but it attracts me. I have used the single word "penetrance" in Table 2 to signify this line of reasoning.

Diabetes

The individual's inability to metabolize glucose, which was earlier thought to be the hallmark of the diabetic condition, is no longer an adequate criterion for case identification. Survey findings have revealed that the indices which measure the ability to metabolize glucose fall with age in the general population, whether diabetes is present or not. This has made the task of the epidemiologist more difficult, as has the fact that these falling indices are accompanied by greater variations in value for older age groups. A next worthwhile step for research would be to compare diabetic and nondiabetic individuals who have low index values with respect to factors associated with clinical diabetes (overweight, familial aggregation, and so on).

Severe Mental Retardation

Epidemiology cannot help us to find causes for this group of conditions when approached collectively. Some forms of retardation are associated with genes. Some are caused by the trisomic conditions discussed above. But there is a large group which are not familial and are probably associated with brain damage early in fetal development. The "continuum of fetal damage" concept introduced by Lilienfeld and Parkhurst (1951) and elaborated by Pasamanick and Knobloch (1961) has not been picked up and elaborated sufficiently in more concrete investigations. Causative agents often interact with suboptimal nutrition to produce disease, and many women who become pregnant are in a suboptimal nutritional state. Preventive trials in which nutritious food is supplied to pregnant women would seem to be the logical next step in research.

There have been so many examples in the last forty years of how our health technology too often advances by postponing death and thus increases the duration of chronic conditions, that one might conclude that this trend is inevitable. But there is one great victory during the same period which went just the other way. It may not be as impressive as the conquest of smallpox, but as a consequence of the discovery that a very large proportion of tooth decay was due to a correctable deficiency of the trace element fluorine, millions of persons who would have lost their teeth in early adulthood have been able to keep them. The final link in the chain of evidence came from the great preventive trial which compared the incidence of caries in Newburgh and Kingston (New York) after one of the towns had fluoridated its water supply. Our techniques for treating dental decay have improved only slightly, but we have made great strides in reducing the incidence of decay. The fact that more dentists are making more money than ever should relieve any anxiety that the medical fraternity might have about successful disease control programs.

Envoi

In assessing the effect of our technical advances in the past four decades, I have attempted to demonstrate that the net contribution of our successes has actually been to worsen the people's health. The prevalence of chronic diseases and disabilities depends on both the frequency with which they occur and their average duration. It is true that we have lowered the occurrence of certain chronic conditions through preventive measures; the prevalence of dental decay and lost teeth has diminished, and the prevalence rate of paralytic poliomyelitis has fallen. However, these few reductions in the occurrence of chronic conditions have been more than offset by the increased average duration of a wide range of conditions whose fatal complications we have learned how to postpone.

You will recall that Semmelweis was led to connect puerperal sepsis with contamination from the autopsy room after a close friend of his, a pathologist, had died with tissue changes similar to those seen in puerperal sepsis after he had been pricked with a knife during an autopsy on an infected person. I can give you no such dramatic episode which forced me to the conclusions outlined in this paper, but I do have enough recollection of transient ideas and insights to know that I was extremely resistant to the generalizations laid out here. I now recognize that we should have predicted by 1940 that some chronic diseases and disabilities would become more common because we had better techniques for thwarting killers which had been weeding out the chronically ill.

I tell you about this resistance within myself to let you know that if you find alien the whole idea that the techniques we have to improve life expectation perpetuate sick lives more than they do healthy lives, I was recently of your company. I know that part of my resistance and caution stemmed from a feeling that colleagues would also be resistant and that I would have to be able to defend myself against much methodological quarreling. But after looking at the issue from many angles, and examining multiple sources of information, I am convinced that this unpleasant proposition is true.

The paradoxical fact about death is that it is at once the great leveler and the great discriminator. It is the greatest of all equalizers because it is everyone's ultimate end, and the lowliest beggar can be no more dead than the most eminent monarch. But it is also a great discriminator because it comes later for those more privileged than for those less privileged. As Sir Thomas Browne (1642) said so elegantly in *Religio Medici*, "There is little difference between one man's death and another's except in the time and the manner of dying."

While the universal fear of the great plagues might leave us with the impression that they were no respecters of persons, in fact, all the great killers have discriminated, more readily taking those who were half dead or half grown than those who were healthy and in their prime. There are a few examples of killers which discriminate in the opposite direction. The generals have always wanted the flower of our youth for cannon fodder. Paralytic poliomyelitis selected people of strong athletic build who were more vigorous than the average person (Draper, 1917). In this instance, it was later discovered that higher social status was associated with a lower chance of having a subclinical immunizing attack of poliomyelitis in early childhood. But the few real exceptions only underline the general rule that the large-scale killers are cowardly and select those least able to defend themselves. That greatest of all iatrogenic killers, puerperal sepsis, was concentrated in women of childbearing age, but from all the records I can find, showed special favoritism for the weakest of them.

But now our technological successes defy death's claim on the sick and the weak. We are proud of these successes, and perhaps it is partly our pride which prevents us from seeing that the successes result in the prolongation of sick lives.

Surely another reason why it has been so difficult to see the effects of our medical successes is that we have been suffering from that terrible ailment of modern technological man, his fragmented specializations. I did not see, for example, the way that chronic brain syndromes are made more common in the population by the systematic application of new health technologies until I stopped thinking of mental disorder epidemiology as somehow isolated from general epidemiology. It seems obvious to me now that general epidemiology also needs to be capable of dealing with the mental conditions which are manifestations of brain disease or of cerebrovascular disease. But our thought processes have been suffering from excessive hardening of the categories.

It is easy to see, in such cases as Karen Ann Quinlan's, that maintaining the vital systems artificially is not maintaining an intact person. And it is easy to see that there are profound ethical, professional, and legal questions involved. But my concern is not these small gains in extending life at the last moment before death. Such cases, which Jerry Morris (1975) has aptly called "snatch victories," make up only a minute part of the paradoxical effect of medical progress which I am trying to make more visible to you. The vast bulk of the increases in prevalence rates consists of only slightly impaired lives: memory loss in elderly people who are continuing to get and give pleasure in their lives, generally well-controlled cases of diabetes, or early hypertension. I am myself a handicapped person who survives by courtesy of modern medical care at its best. The extensive antishock and reconstructive surgery procedures I had following an automobile accident saved my life. The same injury would have been fatal a few years earlier.

So the successes I have been referring to are real successes representing real advances. But the increase in disease and disability which ensues is also real and must be faced. What then are the proper lessons to learn from these failures? Not the silly notion that we should give up our efforts to overcome the killers. Not that we should go backward to a pre-enlightenment stage of society in which we throw away the umbrellas and say, "If God meant you to stay dry, he wouldn't have made it rain." Nor should we conclude that the cheapest solution to chronic disease is the best solution. Hitler knew that the cheapest "solution" to cases of chronic illness was death. If our technology has blunted the edge of the grim reaper's scythe, that's exactly what it was meant to do and we should rejoice. We cannot avoid the successes. We must learn to overcome the ensuing failures.

As a first step, we must come to recognize that the socially organized application of health technology is one of the greatest epidemiological forces in the world. We have seen how the provision of medical care, while it has served as an important means of postposing death, has done so, to a great extent, by defeating the fatal complications that used to terminate the diseases people were suffering from, thus making those diseases more common in the population.

Today's socially organized campaigns to prevent killing diseases can have a similar effect; that was the object of the swine flu vaccination program. The eradication of smallpox from the earth—perhaps public health's greatest single victory—may have a similar effect. Smallpox must have been weeding out some individuals with chronic conditions. Who had it been killing? I admit to feeling foolish in raising this question only after the campaign has been completed. If we had posed the question before the campaign got started, we would now be in a position to state what conditions will become more common as a result of the eradication of smallpox. If we are to be more sensible in our efforts to improve the people's health we must have the foresight to look for these failures as soon as we recognize the possibility for advance.

The increase in chronic illness and disability which results from our advances makes finding ways to prevent these chronic conditions a matter of top priority for research programs. We are now over thirty years late in recognizing the failures that are bound to follow such successes. We should not waste time crying because we are so tardy, but rather hasten to see how quickly we can catch up.

I have indicated in the last column of Table 2 a few ideas which I think are worth pursuing. To my eye, what is dramatic about these conditions is the paucity of existing epidemiological data. We don't even have good case control data for many of them. We haven't failed in our efforts to find preventable causes of these conditions— we have hardly made any effort at all! There are whole sequences of investigations which are obvious even when we have no clues. But even in cases where we do get a clue, I think that we are unduly passive in our approaches to preventing chronic diseases.

Preventive trials are interventions based upon an accumulated body of experience. Their great value lies in their ability to prove or disprove seemingly credible hypotheses. If preventive trials were done often enough, most would yield negative results, and we could rid ourselves of a number of erroneous "common sense" ideas. But preventive trials are not used to the extent that they should be. Most often, they are thought to be too expensive. Frequently they are viewed as "manipulations" which raise social and ethical problems, even though in most applications (like improved maternal nutrition) they are innocuous and involve interventions known to be desirable. Frequently, preventive trials are not done because they call for stable research teams which cannot be organized under the present project grant system.

Our weakness today in finding preventive measures for chronic illnesses in contrast to our strength in finding curative measures for fatal complications is due largely to the way health research money is organized. I think the time has come to examine afresh the administrative mechanisms by which research is supported. Can't we find new ways to encourage research which will emphasize chronic disease *prevention*? If we don't, research which produces means for thwarting fatal complications—research which, when applied, increases the frequency of postmature deaths—will continue to advance more rapidly.

I have always been mortified by public health's preoccupation with death. We have always known that there are fates worse than death. But epidemiology and biostatistics have never sufficiently weaned themselves from John Graunt's great bills of mortality studies and William Farr's brilliant use of birth and death records. I have long been sick and tired of this morbid preoccupation with the first and last months of life. But it doesn't matter that this back-wardness in public health made *me* sick. Now that we know that instead of enhancing the people's health this kind of deathly thinking has been increasing the people's sickness and disability, it is time to call for a change.

Now that we recognize that our life-saving technology of the past four decades has outstripped our health-preserving technology and that the net effect has been to worsen the people's health, we must begin the search for preventable causes of the chronic illnesses which we have been extending. Epidemiologists must play a key role in finding these causes, but without the application of social pressures in that direction, few will take up the opportunity. For a period, at least, health saving must take precedence over life saving. And we will not move forward in enhancing health until we make the prevention of nonfatal chronic illness our top research priority.

References

Brown, T. 1642. *Religio Medici*. Reprinted in *Religio Medici, A Letter to a Friend, Christian Morals, Urn-Burial and Other Papers*. 1889. Boston: Roberts Brothers.

Carter, C.O. 1958. A life-table for mongols with the causes of death. *Journal of Mental Deficiency Research* 2:64−74.

Collins, S.D., and Lehmann, J. 1953. Excess Deaths from Influenza and Pneumonia and from Important Chronic Diseases During Epidemic Periods, 1918−51. *Public Health Monograph* No. 10. Washington, D.C.: Government Printing Office.

Collmann, R.D., and Stoller, A. 1963. Data on mongolism in Victoria, Australia: prevalence and life expectation. *Journal of Mental Deficiency Research* 7:60−68.

Deaton, J.G. 1973. The mortality rate and causes of death among institutionalized mongols in Texas. *Journal of Mental Deficiency Research* 17:117−122.

Draper, G. 1917. *Acute Poliomyelitis*. Philadelphia: P. Blakiston's Son & Co.

Eisenberg, L. 1975. The ethics of intervention: acting amidst ambiguity. *Journal of Child Psychology and Psychiatry* 16:93−104.

Essen-Möller, E.; Larsson, H.; Uddenberg, C.E.; and White, G. 1956. Individual traits and morbidity in a Swedish population. *Acta Psychiatrica et Neurologica Scandinavica*. Supplementum 100.

Ford, A.B. 1970. Casualties of our time. *Science* 167:256−263.

Fryers, T. 1975. Life expectancy and causes of death in the mentally retarded. *British Journal of Preventive and Social Medicine* 29:61.

Gregg, A. 1941. *The Furtherance of Medical Research*. New Haven: Yale University Press.

Gruenberg, E.M., and Hagnell, O., with the assistance of L. Ojesso and M. Mittleman. The rising prevalence of chronic brain syndrome in the elderly. Symposium: Society, Stress and Disease: Aging and Old Age. Stockholm, June 14−19, 1976. In press.

Hunt, G.M. 1973. Implications of the treatment of myelomeningocele for the child and his family. *Lancet* I:1308−1310.

Kramer, M. 1976. Population changes and schizophrenia, 1970−1985. Paper presented at the Second Rochester International Conference on Schizophrenia. Rochester, N.Y., May.

Kushlick, A. 1966. A community service for the mentally subnormal. *Social Psychiatry* 1 (2):73−82.

Laurence, K.M. 1974. Effect of early surgery for spina bifida on survival and quality of life. *Lancet* I (7852):301−304.

Lemkau, P.V., and Pasamanick, B. 1957. Problems in evaluation of mental health programs. *American Journal of Orthopsychiatry* 27(1):55−58.

Lilienfeld, A.M., and Parkhurst, E. 1951. A study of the association of factors of pregnancy and parturition with the development of cerebral palsy: Preliminary report. *American Journal of Hygiene* 53:262−282.

Malzberg, B. 1934. *Mortality among Patients with Mental Disease*. Utica, New York: State Hospitals Press.

Marble, A. 1972. Insulin—Clinical aspects: the first fifty years. *Diabetes* 21 (Suppl.) 2:632−636.

Medawar, P. 1967. *The Art of the Soluble*. London: Methuen.

Morris, J.N. 1975. *Uses of Epidemiology*. 3rd ed. London: Churchill Livingstone.

Morris, R. 1976. Alternative forms of care for the disabled: developing community services. In *Developmental Disabilities: Psychologic and*

Ernest M. Gruenberg

Social Implications, edited by D. Bergsma and A.E. Pulver. New York: Alan Liss, Inc.

Osler, W.O. 1935. *The Principles and Practice of Medicine*. 12th ed., revised by T. McCrae. New York: D. Appleton-Century Company, Inc.

Øster, J.; Mikkelsen, M.; and Nielsen, A. 1975. Mortality and life-table in Down's syndrome. *Acta Paediatrica Scandinavica* 64:322–326.

Pasamanick, B., and Knobloch, H. 1961. Epidemiologic studies on the complications of pregnancy and the birth process. In *Prevention of Mental Disorders in Children*, edited by G. Caplan. New York: Basic Books. pp. 74–94.

Penrose, L.S. 1932. On the interaction of heredity and environment in the study of human genetics (with special reference to mongolian imbecility). *Journal of Genetics* 25:407–422.

Record, R.G., and Smith, A. 1955. Incidence, mortality and sex distribution of mongoloid defectives. *British Journal of Preventive and Social Medicine* 9:10–15.

Spain, D.M. 1963. *The Complications of Modern Medical Practice: A Treatise on Iatrogenic Diseases*. New York: Grune and Stratton.

Yolles, S.F., and Kramer, M. 1969. Vital Statistics. In *The Schizophrenic Syndrome*, edited by L. Bellak and L. Loeb. New York: Grune and Stratton. pp. 66–113.

This paper was presented as the Rema Lapouse lecture at the Annual Meeting of the American Public Health Association, Miami, Florida, October 19, 1976.

The preparation of this manuscript depended upon the excellent help of Linda LeResche, Sc.D., in assembling and organizing the relevant facts, and upon the writing skills of Janet Archer. Abraham Lilienfeld, M.D., gave very useful advise. David Willis kept us going with presistent encouragement and suggestions through numerous versions.

Address reprint requests to: Ernest M. Gruenberg, Dept. of Mental Hygiene, Johns Hopkins University School of Hygiene, 615 N. Wolfe Street, Baltimore, MD 21205.

Milbank Memorial Fund Quarterly/*Health and Society, Vol. 56, No. 2, 1978*

Effects of Hospital Cost Containment on the Development and Use of Medical Technology

KENNETH E. WARNER

*Department of Health Planning and Administration,
School of Public Health, University of Michigan*

O NE OF THE DOMINANT CHARACTERISTICS of modern American medicine is the development and widespread diffusion of sophisticated technology. Originally considered an unequivocal blessing, the technological revolution in medicine has of late acquired something of a bad name. This change reflects a shift in the nature of current technology and its presumed contributions to the costs and benefits of medical care. In the 1940s and 1950s, biomedical science contributed the antibiotics that dramatically reduced the morbidity and mortality associated with a variety of infectious diseases. This true "high technology" of medicine was effective, safe, and inexpensive to administer (Thomas, 1974). Today, however, the public and many professionals view the medical technological revolution as expensive and complex, characterized by resource-intensive capital equipment of unestablished efficacy, which frequently requires hospitalization and serves to inflate the cost of care while delivering little demonstrable health benefit.

Increased awareness of the opportunity costs of resources devoted to expensive "halfway technology" is poignantly illustrated by Gaus and Cooper (1976):

[W]e spent 4 billion dollars for new technology [for Medicare patients in 1976] and we do not know if it did any good, much less how much . . . .

. . . If we had continued providing hospital services to the aged, as they were in 1967, then we could have spent that 4 billion dollars last year [to] . . . have

• Brought *all* aged persons above the poverty line [with at least 3.3 million currently living below it]; or

• Provided the rent to raise 2 million elderly from substandard to standard housing units; or

• Brought all the elderly above the lowest accepted food budget and more; or

• Provided eyeglasses and hearing aids to all who needed them [estimated at 18 million needing or wearing glasses and over 3 million needing hearing aids], and more.

Which would have helped the most, [medical] technology or food?

The "technology problem" is simply a reflection of the fundamental dilemma of American health care: how to provide accessible, high quality care to all and at the same time restrain inflation in the cost of providing care. The profusion of expensive medical technology has been cited as a cause of rising costs and one of the effects of attempts to provide quality care. The question is how to search for, develop, produce, distribute, and utilize technology that will truly contribute to the higher quality and economic efficiency of health care, and how to simultaneously weed out technologies whose benefits are not commensurate with their costs.

The severity of the inflation problem is reflected in Congress' willingness to seriously entertain proposals for national hospital cost containment.[1] Concern has also been demonstrated recently by several government-sponsored inquiries into diverse technology

---

[1]The Carter Administration's Hospital Cost Containment Act, as amended in the Subcommittee on Health and the Environment of the House Committee on Interstate and Foreign Commerce, is HR 9717. The Senate version of the bill is S 1391. The competing alternative, S 1470, introduced by Senator Talmadge and others, is limited to Medicare and Medicaid reimbursement. The major provisions of these bills, prior to amendment, are described in Committee on Interstate and Foreign Commerce, 1977.

issues: the deterioration of technology's research base; the safety and efficacy of technology; the role of technology in inflation; and so on (the President's Biomedical Research Panel, 1976; Office of Technology Assessment, 1978; National Academy of Sciences, forthcoming). In this paper we merge these policy interests by asking: How might hospital cost containment affect the development and use of medical technology?

Perspectives on the Technology Problem

The concerns with which different observers voice this seemingly neutral question indicate the diversity of perspectives on "the technology problem." The major perspectives are not inherently incompatible, but they do reflect a tension that pervades the cost containment debate. Proponents of medical technological development ask the question with trepidation, fearful that the economic discipline in cost containment will retard the development of useful medical technologies. These individuals believe that regulatory meddling by government coupled with the inherent public-good problems of research have erected barriers to the pursuit of promising biomedical research and development (R&D). Cost containment might exacerbate the situation, further weakening American leadership in biomedical science and restricting productivity growth in the practice of medicine.

Proponents of cost containment generally believe that the current system fosters excessive adoption and use of medical technology. They ask the same question in the hope that cost containment will direct the allocation of medical resources more efficiently, producing more cost-effective technology and reducing the waste they perceive to be associated with much existing technology. The dimensions of that waste include the following:

The current system fosters the production of too much technology, *i.e.,* technology whose social benefit is not worth its social cost.

New and existing technology is too widely distributed; new technology often diffuses too rapidly and indiscriminately.

Technology is used excessively and in many instances improperly.

The R&D and medical practice systems have led to the production of the wrong mix of cost-saving and cost-increasing technology, with the system heavily biased toward the latter.

The "pro" and "anti" technology views are not necessarily incompatible, because they focus on different stages of the R&D-use spectrum. This difference suggests a subtle but important point that has eluded most discussion of the technology cost issue: while there is general agreement that technology contributes to the medical cost inflation problem (Warner, 1977), there is little consideration of the *mechanism* linking technology to inflation; yet for cost containment to be effective, policy must be tailored to the source of the problem. For example, if the problem results from an excessive stock of capital equipment, policy ought to focus on hospitals' acquisition of equipment, as do Certificate of Need (CON) and a ceiling on hospital capital expenditures. If the problem derives from excessive use of a reasonable stock of equipment, legislators should concentrate on reimbursement policies.

Alternatively, the inflation problem may result from the flow of new technology into the system, namely, the rate of increase in available new technology and the consequent pressures to adopt it. This might call for policy focusing on the medical technology R&D system, and not on hospital or physician behavior *per se*. Finally, it may be that "the tendency to overinvest in and overuse sophisticated services is just part of a larger tendency to overuse health services or to invest too many labor or nonlabor resources in the production of hospital services"(Wagner and Zubkoff, 1978). If this is the case, the contribution of technology to inflation should not be isolated as a "technology problem." Rather, cost containment policy should concentrate on general reimbursement and regulatory mechanisms, without an explicit technology focus. (See also Schroeder and Showstack, 1977.)

Medical technology comes in all sizes and shapes. Similarly, cost containment has many forms, varying from a dichotomous decision on whether to grant a hospital's request for a specific piece of equipment, to a general cap on hospital revenues. Each of the cost containment forms may have different effects on the development and use of medical technology; indeed, a single form may have very different effects on different types of technology. Thus for purposes of analysis it is necessary to define the meanings of both cost containment and medical technology. In this paper, cost containment will refer to a limit on hospitals' inpatient revenues, as proposed by the Carter Administration, with separate consideration of a ceiling on capital expenditures, a second significant component of many proposals. The operation of these limits and details on specific proposals are described elsewhere (see the bills referenced in footnote 1 and Committee on Interstate and Foreign Commerce, 1977). Medical technology will refer to non-labor inputs, with interest focused on sophisticated, high-priced capital equipment, *e.g.,* computerized axial tomography (CAT scanners), and other equipment and supplies having significant implications for hospital costs due to frequency of use, *e.g.,* automated electrocardiography. To an economist, technology means a defined configuration of all inputs, both human and nonhuman, used in a specific production process. The emphasis in this paper on "hardware" reflects the popular usage of the term, and concern about, "medical technology."

The remainder of this paper suggests some tentative answers to the issues raised by our question: How might hospital cost containment affect the development and use of medical technology? We begin by analyzing the environment in which medical technology develops, is adopted, and used. The purpose of this discussion is twofold: to provide a context within which one can understand how hospital cost containment might influence the development and use of technology; and to provide a perspective for assessing the desirability of alterations in the status quo. The following section suggests what some of those changes might be.

Factors Affecting the Development and Use of Medical Technology

Advancement of medical technology depends on a robust system of biomedical R&D and on demand for the products of R&D. In most industrial settings, these two factors are inextricably linked: the nature and amount of R&D depend principally, if not exclusively, on the productivity of firms' R&D departments (measured as contribution to profitability). In contrast, frequently in biomedicine much of R&D appears to function as an entity unto itself, dependent more on the mood of Congress and the public than on its innate productivity. In part, of course, this simply reflects the great difficulty in measuring the productivity of biomedical R&D, especially that of basic research. But it does raise an important point: some aspects of medical technology development and advancement are quite independent of the medical care delivery system and hence are unlikely to be affected by changes in the technology use patterns of hospitals that result from cost containment; other aspects do depend on changes in the delivery system and seem likely to be affected by cost containment. We will discuss these distinctions in the next section of this paper, after briefly examining herein the factors that influence both the development and use of medical technology.

Much of biomedical R&D, including almost all basic research, is the ward of the state. Through the National Institutes of Health and other agencies, the federal government dominates determination of how much and what type of research will be undertaken. Decisions about funding levels, categorical disease emphases, and the mix of fundamental and targeted research all reflect a combination of professional and political influences. Even many of the immediate beneficiaries of the government's largesse—medical schools and biomedical researchers—have little interest in the economic implications of the fruits of biomedical R&D. In short, market forces play only indirect roles in governmental R&D allocations, despite the fact that "Many . . . research funding decisions [which] appear to be million-dollar decisions at the time they are made . . . turn out to be billion-dollar decisions when the outcomes of the funded research reverberate through the health care system" (Gaus, 1975).

Involvement of the private sector in biomedical R&D varies according to the stage of research. Industry supports very little fundamental bioscience, concentrating rather on applied research and, especially, development. This is consistent with the theory of public goods, since the economic benefits of development work are both more certain and more appropriable than those deriving from basic research. Thus, private industry contributes relatively little to the creation of new basic bioscience knowledge but plays a major role in bioengineering and the development and production of hardware.

Both for-profit firms and non-profit researchers have incentives to work toward the solution of unsolved medical problems. There are few incentives to search for less expensive means of accomplishing an existing task, which is the goal of much of private industry's conventional research. The bias toward "new-solution" technology results from the professional prestige associated with developing and using a "new solution" and a reimbursement environment (discussed below) in which adoption and use decisions are effectively free to the decision makers. The consequence, many observers suggest, is that the bulk of the technological innovations that issue from biomedical R&D increase costs; relatively few save costs.

46

The biomedical R&D enterprise continually presents health care providers with a wide array of innovations. The medical professional environment encourages the adoption and use of innovations. Physicians, it has frequently been claimed, are driven by a "technological imperative" instilled during medical training where the image of high quality medicine is predicated on a scientific approach to problems, with modern technology constituting the instruments with which that approach is practiced. Furthermore, the existence of high-cost, hospital-based technology is considered a factor in the trend toward increasing physician specialization, which in turn reinforces the hospital's growing importance as a source of care and increases the demand of physicians for still more technology. Possession of modern, sophisticated technology confers prestige on physicians, and it often contributes to their economic well-being. As a result, hospital administrators want to acquire sophisticated equipment and facilities, both for their own prestige and to attract and hold high caliber physicians on their staffs. Finally, the public's growing faith in the power of science in general and of curative medicine in particular accelerates the demand for technologically advanced methods of care. In short, technological sophistication is viewed by many—patients, physicians, and administrators—as a surrogate for high-quality care.

The "social contract" binds physicians to provide the "best possible care." This acts as an additional pressure to adopt and use new technology. In medically desperate situations—*i.e.*, where the prognosis is poor and reasonable therapeutic alternatives few—physicians are often encouraged to use experimental innovations in nonexperimental settings.This may result in widespread diffusion of innovations well before their medical efficacy, toxicities, costs, and so on are understood (Warner, 1975), although early diffusion is not restricted to medical crisis situations (Altman and Eichenholz, 1976; Gaus, 1976).

Direct governmental involvement can promote the development and diffusion of technology, as does its support of research, but it can also restrict production and use, principally through regulatory policies. The overall effects of regulation on technology adoption and use are uncertain, although the available evidence is not encouraging: regulation intended to limit the spread of medical capital appears to have been reasonably ineffective (Needleman and Lewin, 1977). For example, where CON has succeeded in limiting growth in hospital bed supply, purchase of other equipment has increased, resulting in no overall savings in capital expenditures (Salkever and Bice, 1976). In contrast, the new medical device regulation procedures (U.S. Congress, 1976), which are intended only to assure the safety and efficacy of medical services, have raised the fear that "over-regulation" will stifle entrepreneurial initiative and thus reduce the discovery and production of new safe and efficacious devices. Certainly the regulatory effects of a ceiling on capital expenditures might be quite significant.

The economic environment of medical care provides some positive incentives and few disincentives to adopt the newest technology. Beginning with the subsidization of research and development, the government pumps considerable money into medical schools and elsewhere to encourage development of new knowledge and technical innovations.

But the most salient feature of the medical technology market is the mixture of the sellers' profit incentive and buyers' relatively unconstrained positions. The sellers' profit incentive has been cited as motivating the rapid and indiscriminate adoption of technology (Fuchs, 1973), but such adoption can occur only because technology buyers and users do not discriminate on the basis of all costs as well as benefits. This applies to each of the groups that buy or use medical technology: physicians, consumers, and hospitals.

As buyers and users of technology, cost-reimbursed physicians are indifferent to costs that are not borne by themselves or by insured patients. As suppliers of services in a fee-for-service setting, physicians often have a positive economic incentive to overutilize tests and other services that can generate personal profit.

Consumers find that increasing insurance coverage and affluence have significantly reduced the real direct (out-of-pocket) cost of much medical care, especially that provided in hospitals. Patients now pay less than one-eighth of the average hospital bill directly, compared with one-half in the early 1950s. In addition, increases in real income over the period mean that patients must now work fewer hours to pay the direct cost of a day of hospital care (Feldstein and Taylor, 1977). The lower real direct cost has increased the demand for care, particularly for the "style" and "high quality" of care (Feldstein, 1971, 1977). The hospital administrators' response has been "improvements," including the acquisition of the "latest" technology, which have driven costs up. Completing the circle is the consumers' response to the higher costs—namely, to buy more insurance (Russell, 1977):

> Thus, as third party payment has increased over the years, the benefit required to justify a decision in the eyes of doctors and patients has declined. This has led to the increased use of resources in all sorts of ways — including the introduction of technologies that otherwise might not have been adopted at all and, more often, the more rapid and extensive diffusion of technologies that had already been adopted to some extent.

Cost or cost-plus reimbursement has two direct influences on hospitals *qua* technology purchasers. First, reimbursement of interest payments lowers the effective cost to hospitals below the true interest rate, encouraging overinvestment in marginal projects. Overinvestment is further encouraged by the relative ease with which hospitals can borrow, a result of the tax-exempt status of many bond issues and the safety associated with third party reimbursement. Thus, hospitals are not forced "to experience the real discipline of the capital market" (Silvers, 1974). This is particularly important if, as some observers argue, the availability of financing governs the rate of adoption of high-cost technology, with the technology's medical efficacy being of secondary importance (Rice and Wilson, 1975), as may be demand or costs (Ginsburg, 1972). Second, the reimbursement mechanism fails to distinguish resource-saving from quality-enhancing or service-expanding projects. Hence the economic system does not counter the non-economic forces that favor adoption of sophisticated and generally costly technology. Both of these consequences are reinforced by the fact that frequent upgrading of existing services and addition of new ones give providers greater leeway in the allocation of overhead, and most cost-based reimbursement schemes probably allow considerable latitude in this area (Silvers, 1974).

"In short, when those making the decisions pay none of the costs, resources are used as though they cost nothing" (Russell, 1976). All of the elements come together here to produce a situation in which the binding constraint may be the state of the art, *i.e.,* the technology itself, and not, as elsewhere, considerations of all costs and benefits.

Likely Effects of Hospital Cost Containment on the Development and Use of Medical Technology

Hospital cost containment is not a panacea in the battle against the rapidly rising costs of medical care. Even if it were thoroughly successful, hospital cost containment would only address the inflation problem in one component of the medical care sector. Medical inflationary pressures might continue unabated outside of hospitals. Indeed, there is considerable concern that hospital cost containment will transfer inflation problems—and technology—to non-hospital settings, conceivably exacerbating overall inflation and making containment of costs within hospitals a Pyrrhic victory. In addition, of course, is the real possibility that a program of hospital cost containment will not work. The ability of such a program to succeed in its principal objective—containing costs—is not the focus of this paper; neither are other, non-technology effects (*e.g.,* effects on employment in hospitals). These concerns are left to other authors (*e.g.,* Congressional Budget Office, 1977; Reinhardt, 1977; Silver, 1977; Zelten, 1977) but are mentioned here to keep the ensuing discussion in perspective.

The immediate target of hospital cost containment is decision-making on resource allocation within hospitals. Changes in the mix of resources within hospitals and in the frequency of their use are the first-order effects of cost containment. The effects on other health care delivery institutions and on the development and advancement of technology—in essence, on public and private sector R & D— are mainly derivative or second-order consequences. We shall examine separately both first- and second-order consequences for each of a general inpatient revenue limit and a ceiling on capital expenditures.

Limit on Total Inpatient Revenues

First-Order Effects: The most direct impacts of an inpatient revenue limit relate to the acquisition and use of technology within hospitals. The following first-order effects can be anticipated:

1. Decreased use of technology already in place. Staff physicians would be discouraged from ordering procedures perceived to have only marginal value. The recent trend toward more and more laboratory tests per illness (Scitovsky and McCall, 1976) can be expected to be reversed. Increasing input intensity—that is, inputs used per patient with a given diagnosis—has been cited as a major source of hospital cost inflation (Feldstein, 1971; Feldstein and Taylor, 1977; Redisch, 1974).

2. Substitution of existing lower-cost alternatives to tests or procedures of choice. The cost factor would join the convenience, versatility, or other attributes of procedures that currently dictate preferences.

3. Reduction in the flow of new cost-increasing technology into the practice of medicine, particularly in hospitals. This reduction would result from both supply and demand factors. Under pressure to contain costs, hospitals would reduce their orders (demand) for new cost-increasing technology. A second-order effect, expanded upon below, would be a reduced supply of cost-increasing innovations unless demand outside of hospitals grows sufficiently to compensate for the loss in hospital-based demand.

4. Increased interest in and consumption of new cost-saving technology. Obviously, this has implications for R&D, as discussed below.

5. Decreased diffusion of existing technology.

6. Increased hospital and area-wide cooperation and coordination. This is an obvious desirable outcome of a hospital cost containment program. Empirical studies provide evidence that many service areas currently have unnecessary excess technology and duplication of facilities (Abt, 1975; Roche and Stengle, 1973; U.S. DHEW, 1971).[2] Reimbursement mechanisms foster adoption of such excess capacity, and apparently regulatory efforts have not demonstrably inhibited it (Needleman and Lewin, 1977). Cost containment would put a significant price on duplication of facilities, and should therefore encourage hospital administrators to seek

---

[2]Excess capacity may be justified on the basis of option demand. That is, we are willing to pay a price (*i.e.*, the costs of unutilized capacity) in exchange for the certainty of the ready availability of the technology whenever it might be needed. While option demand is a legitimate basis for unused capacity, the amount of excess capacity often documented considerably exceeds that which option demand would recommend.

means of reducing duplication and excess capacity. An obvious means is the coordination of area-wide facilities planning, which is much more likely to be effective with the support, rather than opposition, of hospitals.[3] In major cities, this might result in specialization in the services offered by hospitals.

Second-Order Effects on Other Health Care Delivery Institutions: The derivative effects of an inpatient revenue ceiling on other health care delivery institutions reflect incentives to shift resource-intensive care to these other settings:

1. The "dumping" of expensive cases on other institutions. Since financially catastrophic cases would reduce the hospital's resources for treating other patients, the hospital would have an incentive to send expensive cases to other institutions, including public (*e.g.,* state) hospitals and nursing homes. While this might be within the letter of the law, it would certainly violate the spirit, since the cost would have been transferred, not contained. Whatever technology must be applied to expensive cases — and expensive cases are often technology-intensive — would probably move with the patients to these alternative institutions.

2. Shift in the use of cost-increasing technology from hospitals to private physicians' offices. As long as cost containment is limited to hospitals, there would be incentives for technology suppliers and physicians to locate technology in private practices. Both public and private organizations have called for extension of regulatory authority (especially for CON) to private non-hospital settings (Iglehart, 1977b; Institute of Medicine, 1977). Needless to say, such an extension would be politically difficult, but without it some cost problems might simply be transferred from hospitals to other delivery settings. Indeed, with physicians having a greater financial interest in the use of such technology in their own offices, additional unnecessary uses of technology might result. The danger of transfer

---

[3]Area-wide planning has met with limited success. The Comprehensive Health Planning Agencies, which preceded the new Health Systems Agencies (HSAs), were viewed as generally ineffective in this capacity. The National Health Planning and Resources Development Act of 1974 (PL 93-641) put some teeth into the HSAs created by the Act. However, active and cooperative involvement of hospitals and the medical profession in area-wide planning would certainly facilitate this process. Hospital cost containment would appear to encourage such constructive involvement.

of technology is exacerbated by the growth of Medical Service Plans (MSPs), groups of private physicians who contract with hospitals to staff specific services. Such groups are not covered in most hospital cost containment proposals, yet they are in an ideal position to purchase and use technology normally employed only in hospitals. Thus, hospital cost containment raises the spectre of the following scenario. Cost containment makes technology usage in hospitals "expensive" to medical decision-makers; *i.e.,* it limits the resources available for other inputs. Consequently, it provides an incentive to remove such technology use from the hospital's class of costs that are subject to the revenue ceiling. Private groups (*e.g.,* MSPs) then form, leasing or purchasing the technology in question, charging patients for its use, independent of their hospital bills, despite the fact that the technology is employed in the hospital in the care of in-patients. The cost of the technology is transferred through an ac-counting trick—it is not contained—and as observed above, use and hence cost actually increase with private groups now possessing a profit motive. This is not a certain consequence of an inpatient revenue ceiling, but neither is it a logical impossibility.

3. Shift in the use of technology from an inpatient to an outpatient basis. With the revenue limit applying only to inpatient care, there might be a wholesale shifting to outpatient care, according to op-ponents of this form of hospital cost containment. However, the question of the net effects of such shifting on both technology use and cost remains unresolved. Much hospitalization and inpatient use of technology result from an insurance system that favors these over ambulatory care. Thus, the cost containment incentive favoring out-patient care may simply balance the insurance system's inpatient bias.

Second-Order Effects on Development of New Technology: The effects of an inpatient revenue ceiling on the development of new technology derive from the effects on the use of technology by health care providers. The greater the distance between the stage of development and the application of technology, the less consequen-tial should cost containment be. Thus, in general, basic research should be little affected, while some applied research and develop-mental work might respond significantly. The differential effects on private and public sector activity relate principally to the R&D

stages upon which these sectors focus their efforts and on the financial dependence of the sectors' R&D on the use of technology.

The most profound consequences are likely to be experienced by private firms engaged in applied R&D, where most private sector R&D activity is concentrated. The dependence of such firms on the successful marketing of their R&D products is clear. If a revenue cap diminishes the market for cost-increasing technology,[4] one would expect to see:

1. Reduction in private sector R&D activity directed toward cost-increasing technology; decrease in the production of cost-increasing technological innovations; reduction in the number of firms engaged in the development and supply of such medical technology. This is a simple and direct response to the change in market conditions.

2. Greater price competition among suppliers and lowered hospital costs. With the economic discipline imposed on hospitals, administrators and department heads would be forced to shop around. Hence cost containment would have a double-dose effect on hospital costs, inducing price competition among suppliers and encouraging frugality in the use of existing resources within hospitals.

3. More R&D and production of cost-saving technologies. Hospitals' incentive to constrain costs would create a significant new demand for cost-saving technology. Coupled with decreased demand for cost-increasing technology, this new demand would provide a powerful incentive for private firms to aggressively enter this new market. It is conceivable that hospitals' demand for cost-saving technology and the potentially large, relatively untapped reservoir of research ideas would combine to produce an even more robust medical technology market than currently exists. To be sure, the character of that market and its product would differ substantially from that which exists today, but the possibility remains that there would be active, imaginative R&D into a wealth of technological possibilities yet to be unearthed simply because the system has not previously offered professional or economic rewards for such

---

[4]The "if" relates to the question of how much technology demand would be transferred to non-inpatient settings rather than simply "drying up."

products. If this accurately characterizes the situation, applied R&D might prove extremely productive in an era of cost containment.[5]

4. Little effect on basic bioscience research. As noted above, the amount and nature of basic research are principally a function of federal funding. The incentive for researchers is to produce new knowledge, not to develóp and sell a physical product. If anything, there has been a concern that fundamental biomedical research and medical practice are so dissociated that the fruits of research are not diffused sufficiently rapidly or widely into practice (Gordon and Fisher, 1975). If cost containment did have an undesirable effect on this most basic stage in the advancement of medical technology, research funding policies could be adjusted to compensate. Because there is likely to be a limited effect on basic research and a more significant effect on targeted R&D, one might anticipate a relative shift away from big capital-intensive technology toward knowledge-intensive "soft" technology. Much of the cost-increasing equipment embodied technology—the centerpiece of the current cost of technology debate—arises from the applied R&D work of the private sector. If this work declines due to a hospital cost containment program, the product of biomedical R&D will shift toward that which is least affected by the program, namely, the outcomes of basic science research.

A revenue limit program will not take place in what is otherwise a regulatory vacuum. Changes in the regulatory environment may have as much effect on the development of technology as do the explicit cost containment provisions. In addition to professional ethics, government policy and regulation are the only major hindrances to

---

[5]This theoretical conclusion is supported by the analysis of a major private sector supplier of hospitals. Becton Dickinson, a firm with nearly $600 million in sales last year, believes that the struggle to hold down costs "can open up a relatively new area of product opportunity in the hospital for supplies primarily designed to reduce the cost of procedures. Historically, most new supply items have been sold on the basis of improvement in medical care . . . . The system . . . has not been receptive to cost reduction as a sales tool.

"Given a receptive, cost conscious environment, cost-reducing supplies represent a truly new class of products. Such items will be less expensive to develop and market and involve significantly less regulatory delay and risk than the medically more innovative products." (Blue Sheet, 1978)

the development, adoption, and use of technology.[6] Cost containment could replace or eliminate the need for certain types of regulation that have had a repressive effect on the advancement of technology due to the maze of bureaucratic red tape they have constructed. Any diminution of such regulation would encourage exploration of new technological possibilities, even cost-increasing ones, thus partially offsetting the deterrent effects of cost containment *per se*.

Ceiling on Capital Expenditures

A ceiling on total capital expenditures would have many of the same effects as that on total revenues, but it would also have some quite distinct impacts resulting from concentration on a particular class of inputs, with exclusive focus on the capital costs of those inputs. The latter differentiates a dollar spent on acquisition of technology from one devoted to its use. Under a capital limit, a hospital faces real penalties for acquiring high-cost capital equipment, but virtually none for using equipment once it is in place.[7]

Were high-cost capital-intensive technology perceived to be simply another input responsive to the same incentives as other inputs, there would be no reason to have a ceiling on capital expenditures in addition to one on overall revenue if the revenue ceiling were applied to both equipment acquisition and all operating activities. The economic discipline inherent in the revenue limitation would be relied upon to produce a rational allocation of the limited

---

[6]Regulation can retard or prevent development, adoption, or use, either directly or indirectly. Examples of direct effects include: on development, restrictions on recombinant DNA research; on adoption, CON for high-cost technology; and on application, FDA approval of drug uses. Indirect effects are illustrated by the development penalties of added delays and other costs in the research-to-market process due to medical device certification of safety and efficacy. Policy decisions not to reimburse for use of a technology for specified purposes obviously will have strong deterrent effects.

[7]To the extent that physical depreciation of equipment is positively associated with use, increasing usage leads to an earlier need for replacement, and hence to capital expenditure. This would seem to be a very minor consideration relevant to frequency of use, particularly given that much medical equipment is scientifically obsolete well before it has physically deteriorated to the point where replacement is necessary.

resources across all inputs. The fact that major legislative proposals include a separate capital expenditure ceiling suggests that policy makers do perceive a distinct "technology problem," and do believe that, under a general revenue limit alone, high-cost technology would continue to flow into the hospital sector at rates disproportionate to the true relative value of such technology. Although politically prominent, this view is far from universally accepted in academic circles. Indeed, a separate capital ceiling might be considered counterproductive, for reasons suggested below.

First-Order Effects: The direct results of a capital expenditure ceiling on the acquisition and use of technology within hospitals would include the following:

1. Decrease in the acquisition by hospitals of expensive capital-intensive technology. Both acquisition of new technology and diffusion of established high-cost technology would decrease. Furthermore, the ceiling would not distinguish between cost-increasing and cost-decreasing technology. Unlike the general revenue limit, which would encourage acquisition of the latter, the capital expenditure ceiling would discourage all forms of capital acquisition, irrespective of ultimate operating cost. Implicit in the incentive to avoid high-cost capital technology is decreased use of such technology in the aggregate, with the possibility of more intensive use of acquired technology. Obviously, a capital expenditure ceiling would combat the purported unnecessary duplication and consequent underutilization of capital-intensive facilities. The danger is a reversal of the problem: a very restrictive ceiling might lessen the optimal availability of facilities and impose excessive burdens on existing technology, leading to reliance on second-best alternatives instead of capital-intensive technologies.

2. Search for diagnostic and therapeutic alternatives with lower component prices.

Second-Order Effects on Other Health Care Delivery Institutions: The derivative effects of a capital expenditure ceiling on other health care delivery institutions are similar to those associated with the overall limit. One would anticipate some shifting of capital-intensive technology and associated care to non-hospital settings, including to the offices of private medical group practices.

Second-Order Effects on Development of New Technology: The effects of the capital ceiling on the development of medical technology are also similar to the effects of the revenue limit, although certain effects are exacerbated by the capital ceiling and at least one effect is quite distinct:

1. Decrease in technology-oriented applied R&D. This effect is exacerbated by the capital ceiling.

2. Decrease in the development of all high capital cost technology. This impact is distinctive because it will occur irrespective of the technology's implications for hospital operating costs. Unlike the general limit on inpatient revenue, the capital expenditure ceiling will work against the search for capital-intensive cost-saving technologies. This has obvious implications for the medical technology industry.

3. Little effect on basic bioscience research. Like the revenue limit, the capital ceiling should have little impact on fundamental research.

Conclusions

Hospital cost containment will restrict the flow of resources into medical care, assuming that "contained" costs are not transferred *in toto* to non-inpatient medical care. Containment may inhibit research into and the development of cost-increasing technology; a capital expenditure ceiling would also discourage R&D related to certain cost-decreasing technologies. Evaluation of the desirability of these consequences may ultimately rest on one's subjective opinion, but an informed judgment will include appreciation of the economic context in which such changes will take place. These are not changes from a position of social optimality. If they were, there would be no need to consider a policy of containing hospital costs.

The fundamental economic truism is that resources are scarce and have alternative uses. The true cost of an activity is the benefit that the resources consumed would have produced in their best alternative use(s). In a market economy, prices reflect these opportunity costs: to acquire a resource or commodity, one must be willing to pay at least what that good is worth to others. The assurance of the value of the good lies in the sacrifice the purchaser must make: by willingly sacrificing the price of the good — and hence foregoing alternative purchases — the buyer is demonstrating that the benefit of the good is at least commensurate with its cost and exceeds the benefits that would have been derived from the alternative purchases.

In medical care, the absence of direct financial liability for the consumption of many services implies that neither patients nor providers need be concerned with the economic value of the medical resources consumed. Hence, the true social cost of utilizing the resources can exceed the benefit that induced their consumption. Providers' profit incentives may exacerbate the situation. The logical outcome is excess and possibly inappropriate use of resources. The problem is most acute where the vast majority of costs are assumed by third party payers, as in the case of hospital care.

The existence of widespread and deep insurance coverage reflects a variety of factors. In the private sector, both the depth of coverage—the small deductibles and low copayments—and the extensiveness of employer provision of coverage reflect in part the preferential tax treatment of medical insurance premiums (Ehrbar, 1977; Havighurst, 1977). In addition to performing the true insurance function—providing protection against unforeseen financial catastrophes—relatively complete coverage becomes a form of prepayment, significantly lowering the out-of-pocket cost of care and hence encouraging increased consumption. Increased demand leads to higher prices, which in turn increase the demand for insurance.

Public insurance programs are a positive reflection of the nation's social conscience in general and specifically of the attitude that money should not be a barrier to the receipt of necessary high-quality medical care. The inflationary implications of Medicare and Medicaid are the price society has been paying for the equity these programs have delivered. Herein lies the problem: in both the private and public sectors, we have been attempting to implement the principle that health care is a right, by incrementally decreasing the out-of-pocket cost of care. In essence, we have been "freeing up" and "nationalizing" the demand side of the economic equation while struggling to preserve the free enterprise character of the supply side. Any student of elementary economics could predict the effects; any literate citizen can read about them daily.

Cost containment represents an attempt to preserve the distributional equity gains of the past decade while reintroducing an economic discipline into the provision of care, at least in hospitals. The objective is to counteract the consequences of the removal of financial barriers to care: inflation and the less understood problem that excess resources devoted to medical care deprive people of greater benefits from alternative uses of the resources. Conceptually, cost containment is a step in the right direction, attuning decision makers in the health care system to the cost implications of resource consumption. Furthermore, one group of hospital cost containment proposals—those which constrain overall revenues or expenditures but leave individual resource decisions to physicians and administrators—forces knowledgeable decision makers to confront alternatives directly: purchase of a CAT scanner would no longer simply require CON approval; now it would imply that a hospital could *not* purchase machines X, Y, and Z.

Many health care professionals argue that putting a cap on hospital revenues will unduly restrict the provision of services, possibly decreasing both the quality and quantity of care (Silver, 1977). If it is assumed that physicians and administrators will learn to make wise choices, damage can be minimized. Services of marginal effectiveness should be the ones reduced, and decision makers should learn to provide services more efficiently. Again, from the social perspective, resources not consumed in medical care will be used in other activities, possibly with more beneficial implications for health (*e.g.,* pollution control). Indeed, if the previous characterization of the medical market is accurate—namely, that the relative absence of economic constraints has led to an overproduction of services, to excessive and inefficient use of resources—then an absolute *decrease* in resources devoted to medical care might actually be socially desirable. However, hospital cost containment calls only for *relative* belt-tightening, *i.e.,* a decrease in the rate of growth of hospital expenditures.

Needless to say, it is a long way from the concept of cost containment to the implementation of an effective program. Regulation is pervasive in health (Iglehart, 1977a); based on past experience in this and other fields (Havighurst, 1977; Noll, 1975), one should not feel entirely sanguine about the prospects for success. Hospital cost containment is not synonymous with medical care cost containment. As noted above, a principal concern is that costs intended to be contained will simply be shifted from inpatient to outpatient status or from hospitals to other delivery settings. To the extent that this occurs, the predicted effects on the development and use of technology would be diminished.

The discussion above should place in perspective the effects on technology development and use of two major cost containment proposals. A ceiling on capital expenditures appears to be a means of supplementing relatively ineffective regulatory apparatus (*e.g.,* CON) with some policy muscle. A truly restrictive ceiling, such as that proposed by the Carter Administration, would have clear and strong implications for both the development and use of capital-intensive medical technology, particularly if combined with equipment- and service-specific national guidelines on appropriate maximum supplies, as defined in the Administration's bill (HR 9717, Sec 302). Put simply, the acquisition of such technology would be discouraged and hence so would be related research and development. Unfortunately, the ceiling fails to distinguish cost-saving from cost-increasing capital expenditure. Thus, to the extent that cost-saving capital-intensive technologies might be developed, the proposal is partially self-defeating.

The general inpatient revenue limit might adequately serve the cost containment objective independent of the capital expenditure ceiling, assuming that the revenue limit was structured to relate to reimbursement for all costs and not simply operating costs. This is especially true if, as suggested earlier, excess investment in and use of technology are simply a reflection of the general problem of excess use of resources in medical care. Even if sophisticated technology is currently treated preferentially, the revenue limit's imposition of an effective budget constraint would force reevaluation of such preferential treatment.

Under a general inpatient revenue limit, the demand in hospitals for certain types of technology would slacken, and overall demand would cease to grow as rapidly as it has in recent years. Both of these factors could be viewed as deterrents to the development and adoption of technology. However, both can also be viewed as bringing the demand for cost-increasing technology, and hence for related research, more into line with the reality of the opportunity costs associated with them. Significantly, under a revenue limit, the new economic environment for hospital-based care would produce incentives for technology researchers and developers to channel their creativity into the search for and development of cost-saving technology. Such technology could expand the capability of the health care industry to deliver care with a given amount of resources. The relative absence of research effort in this area suggests the possibility that it might have a high and rapid pay-off. A shift in the mix of technology from cost-increasing toward cost-saving would represent a significant change in the delivery of medical care, and it might augur a new golden age of medical technology.

Much of the impact of cost containment on the improvement of health through new technology depends on the research origins of real breakthroughs. If future medical progress lies in the development of sophisticated capital equipment, with the private sector playing a leading role in the design and production of such equipment, hospital cost containment could significantly slow the advancement of medical science. If, by contrast, the true high technology of medicine is simple, inexpensive, and derived from basic research, cost containment seems unlikely to jeopardize medical scientific progress.

Hospital cost containment represents an attempt, albeit imperfect, to reduce or compensate for the discrepancy between the private decision-making costs and the social costs of medical care. Any serious and effective cost containment policy will have a substantial impact on the quantity and use of resources devoted to hospital-based care. The likely effects on medical technology are numerous and significant, although as a price to pay for controlling the ever-inflating costs of care, they do not necessarily appear to be intolerable. Some, in fact, should prove to be desirable.

References

Abt Associates, Inc. 1975. Incentives and Decisions Underlying Hospitals' Adoption and Utilization of Major Capital Equipment. HRA contract no. HSM 110-73-513. Cambridge, Mass.

Altman, S., and Eichenholz, J. 1976. Inflation in the Health Industry—Causes and Cures. In Zubkoff, M., ed., *Health: a Victim or Cause of Inflation?*, pp. 7-30. New York: PRODIST.

Blue Sheet, The Drug Research Reports. 1978. Hospital Supply Firm Sees New Sales Opportunities in Cost Control Effort; Shift to Preventive Medicine, Use of Paraprofessionals to Open New Markets? Washington, D.C. 21 (January 11): 6-7.

Committee on Interstate and Foreign Commerce, U.S. House of Representatives. 1977. Selected Hospital Cost Containment Proposals: Major Provisions (September 9). Washington, D.C.: U.S. Government Printing Office.

Congressional Budget Office. 1977. *The Hospital Cost Containment Act of 1977: An Analysis of the Administration's Proposal.* Report prepared for the Subcommittee on Health and Scientific Research of the Committee on Human Resources, U.S. Senate. Washington, D.C.: U.S. Government Printing Office.

Ehrbar, A. 1977. A Radical Prescription for Medical Care. *Fortune* XCV (February): 164-172.

Feldstein, M. 1971. *The Rising Cost of Hospital Care.* Washington, D.C.: Information Resources Press.

———. 1977. Quality Change and the Demand for Hospital Care. Paper written for the Council on Wage and Price Stability, Executive Office of the President.

Feldstein, M., and Taylor, A. 1977. *The Rapid Rise of Hospital Costs.* Staff Report of the Council on Wage and Price Stability, Executive Office of the President. Washington, D.C.: U.S. Government Printing Office.

Fuchs, V. 1973. Health Care and the U.S. Economic System. In Collen, M., ed., *Technology and Health Care Systems in the 1980's,* National Center for Health Services Research. DHEW Pub. No. (HSM) 73-3016. Washington, D.C.: U.S. Government Printing Office.

Gaus, C. 1975. Biomedical Research and Health Care Costs. Testimony of the Social Security Administration before the President's Biomedical Research Panel.

———. 1976. What Goes into Technology Must Come Out in Costs. *National Leadership Conference on America's Health Policy,* April 29-30, pp. 12-13.

Gaus, C., and Cooper, B. 1976. Technology and Medicare: Alternatives for Change. Background Paper for Conference on Health Care Technology and Quality of Care, Boston University Health Policy Center, November 19-20, at Boston, Mass.

Ginsburg, P. 1972. Capital Investment by Non-Profit Firms: the Voluntary Hospital. East Lansing: Michigan State University, Econometrics Workshop Paper No. 7205.

Gordon, G., and Fisher, G., eds. 1975. *The Diffusion of Medical Technology: Policy and Research Planning Perspectives.* Cambridge, Mass.: Ballinger.

Havighurst, C. 1977. Controlling Health Care Costs: Strengthening the Private Sector's Hand. *Journal of Health Politics, Policy and Law* (Winter) 1: 471-98.

Iglehart, J. 1977a. The Cost and Regulation of Medical Technology: Future Policy Directions. *Milbank Memorial Fund Quarterly/Health and Society* (Winter) 55: 25-59.

———. 1977b. Stemming Hospital Growth—the Flip Side of Carter's Cost Control Plan. *National Journal* 9 (23): 848-52.

Institute of Medicine. 1977. *Computed Tomographic Scanning—a Policy Statement.* Washington, D.C.: National Academy of Sciences.

National Academy of Sciences. (Forthcoming). Report of the Committee on Technology and Health Care. Washington, D.C.

Needleman, J., and Lewin, L. 1977. Impact of State Health Regulation on the Adoption and Utilization of Equipment-Embodied Medical Technology. Paper prepared for Committee on Technology and Health Care, National Academy of Sciences. (Forthcoming in the Committee's Report.)

Noll, R. 1975. The Consequences of Public Utility Regulation of Hospitals. In *Controls on Health Care,* pp. 25-48. Washington, D.C.: National Academy of Sciences.

Office of Technology Assessment, U.S. Congress. 1978. Efficacy and Safety of Medical Technology. Draft Report.

President's Biomedical Research Panel. 1976. Report of the President's Biomedical Research Panel. Washington, D.C.: U.S. Government Printing Office.

Redisch, M. 1974. Hospital Inflationary Mechanisms. Paper presented at Western Economics Association Meetings, Las Vegas, Nevada, June 10-12. Revised October, 1974.

Reinhardt, U. 1977. The Role of Health Manpower and Education in Cost Containment. Paper prepared for Project HOPE Committee on Health Policy Meeting, Washington, D.C., October 30-November 1.

Rice, D., and Wilson, D. 1975. The American Medical Economy— Problems and Perspectives. Paper prepared for International Conference on Health Care Costs and Expenditures, Fogarty International Center, Bethesda, Maryland, June 2-4.

Roche, J., and Stengle, J. 1973. Facilities for Open Heart Surgery in the United States: Distribution, Utilization, and Cost. *American Journal of Cardiology* 32 (August): 224-28.

Russell, L. 1976. Making Rational Decisions about Medical Technology. Paper presented at meeting of the AMA's National Commission on the Cost of Medical Care, Chicago, Ill., November 23.

———. 1977. How Much Does Medical Technology Cost? Paper presented at Annual Health Conference of the New York Academy of Medicine, New York, April 29.

Salkever, D., and Bice, T. 1976. The Impact of Certificate-Of-Need Controls on Hospital Investment. *Milbank Memorial Fund Quarterly/Health and Society* 54 (Spring): 185-214.

Schroeder, S., and Showstack, J. 1977. The Dynamics of Medical Technology Use: Analysis and Policy Options. Health Policy Program Discussion Paper. San Francisco: University of California, School of Medicine.

Scitovsky, A., and McCall, N. 1976. Changes in the Costs of Treatment of Selected Illnesses 1951-1964-1971. Washington, D.C., National Center for Health Services Research, DHEW Pub. No. (HRA) 77-3161.

Silver, G. 1977. Hospital Cost Control: Implications for Access and Quality for the Poor. Paper prepared for Project HOPE Committee on Health Policy Meeting, Washington, D.C., October 30-November 1.

Silvers, J. 1974. The Impact of Financial Policy and Structure on Investments in Health Care. In Abernathy, W., Sheldon, A., and Prahalad, C., eds., *The Management of Health Care*. Cambridge, Mass.: Ballinger.

Thomas, L. 1974. The Technology of Medicine. In *Lives of a Cell*, pp. 31-36. New York: Viking Press.

U.S. Congress. 1976. Medical Device Amendments of 1976. *Congressional Record-House*, March 9, pp. H1719-H1759.

Wagner, J., and Zubkoff, M. 1978. Medical Technology and Hospital Costs. In Zubkoff, M., Raskin, I., and Hanft, R., eds., *Hospital Cost Containment: Selected Notes for Future Policy*. pp. 263-289. New York: PRODIST.

Warner, K. 1975. A "Desperation-Reaction" Model of Medical Diffusion. *Health Services Research* 10 (Winter): 369-83.

———. 1977. The Cost of Capital-Embodied Medical Technology. Paper prepared for Committee on Technology and Health Care, National Academy of Sciences. (Forthcoming in the Committee's Report.)

Zelten, R. 1977. Hospital Cost Containment and Hospital Fiscal Management. Paper prepared for Project HOPE Committee on Health Policy Meeting, Washington, D.C., October 30-November 1.

This is a revised version of a paper submitted to the Project HOPE Committee on Health Policy and does not necessarily express the views of that organization, nor those of Project HOPE or its cooperating organization, the University of Southern California Center for Health Services Research.

The helpful comments of the referees are gratefully acknowledged.

Address correspondence to: Kenneth E. Warner, Ph.D., School of Public Health, University of Michigan, Ann Arbor, Michigan 48109.

II Technology and the Health Cost Spiral

The Cost and Regulation
of Medical Technology:
Future Policy Directions

JOHN K. IGLEHART

Contributing Editor, National Journal
and Consultant, Health Staff Seminar, Washington, D.C.

"I don't really know how much is enough technology; I can tell you this, when we're dealing with patients and when we're dealing with a patient's family, their response to this would be, 'as much as is necessary to get our loved one restored to normal life.' And that's about the only answer I can give."

> *Dr. Michael E. DeBakey, heart surgeon,*
> *speaking at theNational Leadership Conference*
> *on America's Health Policy, April 29, 1976*

A decade after the federal government plunged into the financing of health care, it has emerged not only as the system's major purchaser, but also as the major influence on health policy directions of the future. The traditional Washington dictum of "he who pays the piper calls the tune," is becoming a reality in health care, albeit not without a struggle. As a result, the new administration of President Carter will have to confront a range of difficult health issues and decide how best to balance the conflicting forces that call for different answers.

The Carter administration, though, will hardly be dealing with a clean slate. Indeed, the health policy stewards of Carter's team will have to recognize that the government already is well on its way to casting an imposing regulatory net over the health care system. The net is incomplete, but the political forces that have nurtured it to this point were put in a more commanding position with the election of Carter. To generalize, these forces lean to the liberal side of the political spectrum and believe that government should be used as

M M F Q / Health and Society / *Winter 1977*
© Milbank Memorial Fund 1977

a tool of action, and not as a benign force that has only limited reign, such as President Ford favored.

As the Carter administration moves to address the major health issues before it, no issue will be more complex or far-reaching than how government should seek to influence the cost and diffusion of medical technologies. Modern medicine is pictured in the public's mind, more times than not, as a stunning breakthrough, a result of the miraculous intervention of man and machine. The government has fostered this technological imperative through its attention to and funding of research that leads to the development of life-saving and life-prolonging technologies. And well it should, based on the public's expectations. If the tax-paying public expects anything from the government's investment in medical research, it is eventual relief from diseases that have so far proven incurable, even in the face of a massive federal commitment.

This fascination with technology, though, is giving way to new concerns over its cost and efficacy, in political, social, economic, and ethical terms. Government policy makers are beginning to recognize that the technologies developed by publicly subsidized research are increasing at an uncontrollable rate. And, perhaps more important, these officials are drawing links between this research and what it costs the government as a major purchaser of care. The fear in some quarters is that this trend, if left unchecked, will lead to a public investment in health care that knows no limits.

This article will cover some of the cost implications of medical technology and directions the government is headed in to deal not only with the question of cost, but also of whether existing and emerging technologies are worth the money and the risk to patients and society. Many of the issues are not new, but they are pressing upon the government. The answers will not be for all time either. As in the past, the government will strike temporary balances and eventually move on to cope with problems that emerge from the policy responses.

Technology: Its Cost

The diffusion of technology in the health care system, and particularly in hospitals, is recognized as a primary element fueling the medical cost spiral. That spiral is forcing a commitment of more and more of the nation's resources to finance health care, with a return that is increasingly being called into question in terms of its effect on the nation's health status. Moreover, the cost explosion has led to a volatile policy-making climate.

The dimensions of the cost spiral were underscored in December 1976 when the Social Security Administration released its estimate of public and private spending for health care in fiscal 1976—$139.3 billion, or an increase of 14 percent over the previous year. The new total represents 8.64 percent of the Gross National Product, up from 8.3 percent in the previous year. In a study three months earlier, Trapnell (1976) estimated that national health expenditures will total $180.2 billion by fiscal 1980 under existing policies.

Technological advances are a major factor in the rising cost of health care. McMahon, a hospital industry spokesman, testified to this in public hearings before the House Ways and Means Committee in 1976:

> The third factor affecting hospital cost increases is the changing nature of the output of the hospital. As a result of continuing research and new technology, services provided by hospitals are constantly improving in terms of treatment methods and the expansion of capability for dealing with conditions previously untreatable or untreated. Renal dialysis, laser surgery, total blood replacement, cancer therapy, and a host of new diagnostic approaches to diseases are but a few of the many examples of the costly improvements and expansion of hospital services.

Technology, in McMahon and in this article, is defined very broadly. As Russell (1976) suggests, medical technology refers to the ways in which resources are combined in a hospital to produce medical care, and to changes in those combinations, regardless of whether the change is simply a new mix of well-known resources and services or an innovation like the computerized tomography scanner.

Modern technology has made hospitals into capital-intensive institutions. Plant assets in community hospitals totalled some $20 billion at the end of the 1960s and averaged more than $20,000 per bed, Foster (1976) said. In 1975, such assets were worth $31.7 billion (AHA, 1976), or $33,400 per bed. Technology in the health field has demonstrated a unique characteristic. In virtually all other industries, new technology has the effect of reducing manpower and production costs. But in health care, new technology usually increases both labor and capital costs, a fact which the government is recognizing increasingly (Hastings, 1976; Council on Wage and Price Stability, 1976).

Butler and Lee (1975) make a similar point in their preface to an updated study by Scitovsky.

> In 1967 when Anne Scitovsky published her original work comparing the costs of treatment of selected illnesses in 1951 and 1964, it was recognized as an outstanding piece of technical data collection and analysis. What was not as clear then, but stands out strikingly now, is the great significance of her findings for public policy. This update by her and Nelda McCall of the earlier work confirms where cost increases have occurred. It suggests that the net effect of changes in medical treatment, that is, of changes in technology, tend to be cost-raising rather than cost-saving. The message needs to be heard by everyone interested in health policy.

The shape of this technological change has been altered dramatically in the last decade, as Rice and Wilson (1975) point out. A previous focus was on the use of new antibiotics and drugs that called for no new equipment, but incurred primarily research, development, and marketing costs. Now, the emphasis is on new techniques that are usually resource intense, requiring hospitalization of the patient. Examples of this trend are chemotherapy, open heart surgery, organ transplant, intensive care units for heart attack, burns, and traumatic shock.

It is mostly in the last several years that the impact of this technology and the intensity with which it is applied has begun to win recognition among federal health decision makers. Perhaps the first real attempt by the government to cope with this phenomenon on a national basis came in the Phase IV health cost controls of the economic stabilization program. In this phase, the Cost of Living Council adopted controls that sought to influence the intensity factor by placing limits on expenditures per patient admission. This would have compelled hospital administrators to seek to influence the rate at which technology is applied. The controls never were implemented because the Economic Stabilization Act expired April 30, 1974, and organized labor applied strong pressures on the Congress not to extend it. Nevertheless, disclosure of the controls policy prompted the American Hospital Association[1] to file a lawsuit in an effort to block the plan.

[1]The cost explosion after the demise of the economic stabilization program's health cost controls is causing legislators to be very wary of industry's claims that it will

Gaus and Cooper (1976) refer to intensity as the "technology factor." Using the estimates of the American Hospital Association, they say expense per patient per day in community hospitals rose from $49 to $147 between 1967 and 1976. More than half of this increase went for increases in wage rates and prices paid by hospitals to maintain the same level of service. The remainder, though, represents the cost of changes in service through new equipment and supplies and more or different levels of employees. This "technology factor," they estimate, represented 47.3 percent of the nine-year increase, or $46 of today's per diem cost. Placing this estimate in the context of the Medicare program, Gaus and Cooper estimate that this federal program for the elderly spent $4 billion in fiscal 1976 for technology that has been implemented since 1967.

In an illuminating comment which reflects the lack of information available to federal policy makers on the impact of this technology, Gaus and Cooper asked:

> What did we get for our $4 billion that year and what will we get every year in the future? We are not quite sure. We do know that many new procedures were introduced and many new facilities added. For example, the proportion of community hospitals with electroencephalographs rose from 30 percent in 1969 to 43 percent in 1974; mixed intensive care rose from 42 percent in 1966 to 66 percent in 1974; inhalation therapy from 48 percent to 76 percent; and the list goes on. But has technology improved the health of the aged? And if so, how much? Again, we do not know. Death rates are down, but so are the number of smokers. We have no way of knowing whether improved hospital care is responsible for the improved mortality statistics or whether

hold the line in the future. For example, Sen. Jacob K. Javits, R-N.Y., said in an opening statement April 2, 1976, at a Senate Labor and Public Welfare Subcommittee on Health hearing on medical cost inflation: "Mr. Chairman, it is indeed unfortunate that the promises made to the committee on March 20, 1974, by the American Medical Association and the American Hospital Association with respect to holding the line on increased cost have proven inaccurate. At that time, Mr. McMahon, president of the American Hospital Association, said: 'In sum, we do not think the allegations that Dr. [John] Dunlop [Chairman, Cost of Living Council] has made about the health industry are fair or supportive of the need for continuation of health controls, and that . . . [the absence of control] will not lead, as he is suggesting, to a huge mushrooming of prices and costs in the health industry.' Unfortunately, we all know . . . the litany of the seemingly unending upward spiral. . . . It seems that the sky is the limit. If massive health spending is not regulated we shall have sown the seeds of our own destruction."

improved life style, access to care, etc., has caused the change. We do not even know whether or not many of the specific technologies are efficacious since procedures and equipment often enter the medical marketplace before adequate testing for efficacy.

Gaus, director of the Division of Health Insurance Studies in the Social Security Administration's Office of Research and Statistics, represents a school of thought within HEW that worries more about the economics of emerging technologies than about the potential for improving health status. On the other side, Dr. Theodore Cooper, who, on January 20, 1977, resigned from the post of Assistant Secretary for Health, HEW, leans in favor of considering health questions as more important than costs. These two schools often are in conflict within the department on many policy issues.

Cooper (1976) testified to the cost-benefit of one technology to stress that the added costs apparently are worthwhile:

> . . . the average cost for the treatment of heart attacks in hospitals rose from $1,450 in 1964 to $3,280 in 1971, some of which can be accounted for by inflation and some by increasing sophistication of technology and medical knowledge; fortunately, accompanying this increase in the cost of care has come an apparently continuing trend of reduced morbidity and mortality from heart attacks for the last 10 years.

There have been many reasons cited for the rapid diffusion of costly technologies, many of which attack disease after the fact and largely at a symptomatic level. But the reason cited most often (Rice and Wilson, 1975; Russell, 1976) is the nature of the hospital reimbursement system, which provides little incentive for either the hospital administrator or attending physician to favor the purchase of resource-saving technology. On average, more than 90 percent of the cost of hospital care is paid for through this cost-plus, third-party reimbursement method.

The Tale of a Single Technology

No single new technological device has had a more profound effect on Washington's health policy community, nor drawn the link between innovation and cost more distinctly, than the computerized tomography (CT) scanner. Government is concerned about its high cost, but perhaps its chief worry is the rapid diffusion of the scanner, caution and rational planning seemingly having been thrown to the four winds. The medical professions, and particularly the specialties of radiology and neurology, are far more enthusiastic about its potential as a diagnostic tool than worried about questions of cost and diffusion.

Developed in 1967 by G. Housfield, an engineer working for Emitronics (EMI) Ltd. in Britain, the CT scanner is hailed generally as the greatest advance in radiology since the discovery of the x-ray. Ironically, Banta and Sanes (1976) report that two scientists, Oldendorf and Cormack, working in the United States in the 1960s, constructed tomographic devices that embodied some of the principles later used in the CT scanner, but they were unable to generate any interest for their development in either the medical or industrial sectors.

The scanner is a new diagnostic device that combines sophisticated x-ray equipment with an on-line computer to produce images of sections of the human body. The first machines were head scanners, designed to diagnose abnormalities within the skull, such as brain tumors. More recently, though, scanners have been produced which are capable of detecting lesions throughout the body. By August 1976, Banta and Sanes had identified 321 scanners in use in the United States. Of these machines, nearly two-thirds were head scanners and the remainder were body scanners.

In addition to those scanners already in use, at least 330 scanners have been ordered from manufacturers and/or approved for purchase by planning agencies. Two hundred applications are awaiting planning agency approval for the purchase of scanners. By population, the national average is about one scanner per 664,000 population. When those CT units now approved and/or on order are installed, the national average will be one scanner per 327,000 population. Georgia will then have the largest number of scanners per population—one unit per 130,000 people (Banta and Sanes, 1976).

At this point in the evolution of CT scanning, one's view usually is formed by one's relation to the technology. Radiologists, for instance, have no reservations about the scanner. In their view, it is a breakthrough of sweeping proportions. Dr. Thomas F. Meaney, chairman of the Cleveland Clinic Foundation's Division of Radiology, reflected his enthusiasm in a letter written to Otha W. Linton, Director of Governmental Relations of the American College of Radiology, dated December 1, 1976. Meaney wrote:

I believe it is well acknowledged by all that computerized tomography of the brain has been an unqualified success, both from the medical and financial standpoints with respect to patient care.

In government circles, though, the view of the scanner and its rapid proliferation is more circumspect. The Department of Health, Education, and Welfare recognizes the substantial cost implications of this one procedure for the public treasury. Banta and Sanes (1976), who, incidentally, accumulated far better information on the scanner than was available at HEW, estimated that the 320 scanners now in operation would generate revenue of $207.4 million a year on the basis of 3,000 scans per unit. The estimated costs would total $127 million, leaving a surplus of $80.4 million.

But even more than the immediate cost considerations, what HEW and legislators are fretting about is their inability to influence the placement of scanners through the planning process created by the National Health Planning and Resources Development Act of 1974. Rep. Paul G. Rogers, D-Fla., Chairman of the House Interstate and Foreign Commerce Subcommittee on Health and the Environment, pointed out the problem when speaking before the National Leadership Conference on America's Health Policy. Rogers (1976) said:

> ... Now we're going through this business with the scanner. What's it cost? $300,000 to $600,000 to purchase and install. And the Society of Neuroradiologists, a group that probably would not necessarily err on the side of too little, has estimated that there ought to be six or seven scanners in the Washington area. ... We already have three and a dozen more on order right here in the nation's capital. This cost will run from about $4–7 million. That's at today's prices. And in England, do you know how many they have? Two, and I think that's where they invented it.

Rogers, who represents an affluent Florida district just north of Miami, has been particularly distressed by the way in which physicians in Dade County have circumvented the planning process there to purchase scanners. The Comprehensive Health Planning Council of South Florida, subsequently renamed the Health Systems Agency of South Florida, concluded in mid-1974 that Dade County's health system could support three brain scanners. Today, Dade County is supporting seven scanners and William C. McCue, the agency's executive director before he resigned at the end of 1976, said that requests to approve the acquisition of six more scanners "are waiting in the wings" (Iglehart, 1976a).

Two of the seven scanners were placed in an ambulatory care facility and a physician's office. The planning agency has no authority under the 1974 law to veto the placement of scanners in such places. McCue said (Iglehart, 1976a):

> If we stop the institutions from purchasing the equipment, the doctors turn around and install it in their own offices.

Although the government has not yet taken direct policy action affecting the scanner and its diffusion, it has displayed its concern in a variety of ways. The Senate Finance Subcommittee on Health, on March 5, 1976, directed the Office of Technology Assessment (OTA), an arm of the Congress, to undertake

> a study of the computed tomography scanner, covering such aspects as its usefulness, its costs, its effects on medical care delivery patterns, and ways to improve planning affecting such devices.

The OTA's study by Banta and Sanes (1976) has become a ready reference for information on the uses of scanners, their distribution, utilization, and economics, and on health policy issues raised by the proliferation of this technology.

HEW's health planning program has sought to alert the new national network of health systems agencies to the importance of carefully reviewing all requests for scanners under authority provided by the 1974 law. Harry P. Cain II, the program's director, told the agencies in a memorandum:

> Of all the planning and regulatory issues currently before you . . . perhaps none has attracted more public interest than the increase in the number of computerized tomography scanners throughout the nation. . . . Recently we have heard many calls for federal action to limit increases in scanners in order to prompt their appropriate and economical use. We have been asked, for example, to support a national moratorium on the purchasing of scanning units, until more information is available upon which to assess the need for these very expensive machines. Several states, under their planning or regulatory authority, already have declared such moratoriums. While a national moratorium seems to us to be insupportable, we think it is advisable, and important, that we ask you to examine each scanner proposal with considerable care.

A month later, Cooper, HEW's Assistant Secretary for Health, called a meeting of representatives of agencies in the Public Health Service with an interest in scanners to discuss the health policy implications of such technology. Cooper said in a memorandum announcing the meeting:

> . . . this has been an area of intense interest among the Congress, the public, professional groups, manufacturing interests, public interest groups, and the department.

The department's interest in the scanner ranges widely, as does its interest in many other major pieces of new technology. In the Public Health Service alone,[2] there are six agencies with a legitimate policy interest in brain and body scanners. And this does not include Medicare and Medicaid, the two major health financing programs which pay for scans on individuals eligible for services. Such diversity makes it difficult for HEW to shape a policy that balances the competing interests of the several agencies.

The health planning program has a responsibility under the 1974 planning act to develop a regulatory framework that will provide for the orderly diffusion, but not expensive duplication, of the scanner. The Health Services Administration's Bureau of Quality Assurance serves as the medical advisor to Medicare and Medicaid on whether these programs should reimburse for scans. The brain scanner has been approved for payment, but the body scanner remains, in the bureau's judgment, an experimental device and thus not eligible for reimbursement under the federal programs. The Food and Drug Administration's Bureau of Radiological Health has major regulatory responsibilities for devices such as CT scanners, including standards for personnel who work with such equipment. The FDA's Bureau of Medical Devices and Diagnostic Products and Bureau of Drugs also have a regulatory interest in scanners.

The National Institutes of Health (NIH) has four operational

---

[2]The Office of Technology Assessment found, when it surveyed the government to determine interest in the CT scanner, eight agencies outside of the Department of Health, Education, and Welfare with some direct involvement in the device. Those agencies were the Department of Defense, the Department of Commerce, the Energy Research and Development Administration, the Environmental Protection Agency, the National Aeronautics and Space Administration, the National Bureau of Standards, the National Council on Radiation Protection and Measurements, and the Veterans Administration.

scanners it uses with patients clinically. The NIH also is supporting some one hundred research projects which use CT scanning; the largest number of these are funded by the National Cancer Institute. The cancer institute also is funding a major clinical trial to determine the effectiveness of CT scanning. The National Institute of Neurological and Communicative Disorders and Stroke held an International Symposium on Computerized Axial Tomography on October 12–15, 1975.

But the government is not alone in its concern over the scanner. As Phillips and Lille (1976) noted, the innovation has thrown hospitals into "technological shock." They added:

> Surprised by its immediate success and acceptance but stunned by its cost, hospital administrators find themselves in a quandary over the purchase of this expensive equipment—balancing institutional demands versus budgets on one hand, and community needs versus restrictions on the other.

The Blue Cross Association also has taken steps which reflect its concern. The association contracted with the Institute of Medicine in late 1976 to undertake a short-term policy appraisal of the scanner to provide recommendations to Blue Cross on how they may set up payment systems for scanning procedures. Charles A. Sanders, M.D., General Director of Massachusetts General Hospital, Boston, chaired the institute's scanner study group, which planned to deliver its recommendations in early 1977.

In Maryland, the state medical society is drafting guidelines to regulate the number of private practice head and body scanners and how much doctors can charge patients to cover the cost of the procedure. John Sargeant, Executive Director of the Maryland Medical and Chirurgical Faculty, said in a newspaper interview (Miller, 1977) that, according to the American Medical Association, the Maryland doctors' group is the only one in the nation that is attempting to regulate the use of the scanner in physicians' offices.

Policy Directions: More Regulation

The government has abandoned past notions that it should strive to repair the medical marketplace, rather than impose more regulation, as the best way to deal with inequities in the health system. The market advocates made their most forceful effort with the 1971 drive by President Nixon to dot the medical landscape with health maintenance organizations through the provision of public subsidies. Today, HEW's health maintenance organization program is but a tiny outpost in the department's vast bureaucracy, a standing that reflects the lack of enthusiasm in the agency for any renewed efforts to bolster the market.

The trend favoring regulation already has resulted in the enactment of laws that will affect the development and diffusion of technology. At this point, many federal officials view this regulatory network as incomplete. Thus, future policy efforts will concentrate on imposing more regulation by beefing up laws already enacted and fashioning new laws and policies which depend on direct government regulation.

Recent major laws that have an effect on technology are the Social Security Amendments of 1972, the Health Planning and Resources Development Act of 1974 and the Medical Device Amendments of 1976. These laws, enacted after prolonged debate, underscore the government's willingness to opt for regulation to monitor the cost and quality of medical care, allocate the system's resources, and screen the introduction of new technologies.

This sharp turn toward government regulation is a phenomenon which has picked up considerable steam in the 1970s, as these laws illustrate. The government finds direct regulation appealing for two reasons. Most policymakers now agree that there really is no viable medical market. Congressman Rogers (1976) made this point:

> The AMA (American Medical Association) maintains that the marketplace is going to take care of all this specialty maldistribution. But I think that the marketplace really is leaning not toward a solution but to a complication of the problem, because people are paying more for the specialist to go to the urban setting. So the Congress is moving in here because the leadership won't be assumed by the profession to do something about it. The problem, I guess, is pretty well set out by now. I think we have problems because the marketplace in health care is unique. It is not competitive. And the incentives are for over-utilization, over-mechanization, over-medication, with a tendency to over-balance.

Secondly, direct government regulation is very appealing to politicians when matters are not going well. As Ball (1974) so perceptively predicted:

> Regulation seems to be the approach that addresses itself most directly to the perceived problem. If prices are too high, set rates; if desired services are not available in some area or for some people, fix the responsibility on some institution or organization to see that they are made available; if the quality of service is too low, set standards. Alternatives that involve incentives for performance seem indirect and do not have the appeal of an immediate solution, whereas goals and requirements can be written into law and into regulations giving the appearance, at least, of having solved the problem. We sometimes don't stop to realize that ordering a man to jump ten feet in the air doesn't make it possible for him to do so.

And how right he was. We now have the economic stabilization program, the Health Professions Educational Assistance Act of 1976, and the Professional Standards Review Organizations.

There are two provisions in the Social Security Amendments of 1972 that are having a regulatory effect on medical technology. A third provision, which authorized HEW to finance the treatment of most individuals suffering from end-stage renal disease, will be discussed later. The lesser of the two regulatory provisions, Section 1122, empowered HEW, and through it Medicare and Medicaid, to withhold reimbursement to hospitals for depreciation, interest, and return on equity capital in cases where institutions make capital expenditures in excess of $100,000 without first winning the approval of the state planning agency.

The capital outlays can be for plant and equipment in excess of $100,000, for changes in bed capacity of an institution, and for substantial changes in the services provided by an institution. The purchase by a hospital of a large piece of capital equipment such as a CT scanner is, for instance, subject to review and approval by a state planning agency under Section 1122, although this provision has not been aggressively enforced by HEW or the states. Erwin Hytner, a professional staff member of the House Ways and Means Committee and Medicare's former Deputy Director of Program Policy, described Section 1122 in a private interview with the author as:

> sloppily drafted and with little teeth. Moreover, it never really has been effectively applied.

Hytner's view squares with a study by Lewin and Associates, Inc. (1975) which found that (1) states approve 90 percent of the dollar expenditures proposed; (2) there is little opposition to expanding facilities; and (3) proposals to purchase equipment and add new hospital services are almost always approved. Few state agencies were found to have adequate need projections, review criteria, or data resources with which to conduct review functions. The problem, Lewin concluded, is quite often "a lack of management leadership and commitment. . . ."

Even if Section 1122 was effective, however, the capital investment in new equipment only accounts for part of the cost of new technology. Another recent study (Abt Associates, Inc., 1975), showed that equipment purchases alone account for only nine percent of total hospital inflation. The new personnel and supplies required by the equipment add significant costs, yet they are not covered under this provision of the Social Security Act. The study also found that new equipment had a use rate of only 50—60 percent; the equipment had a five to eight year obsolescence rate and little attempt was being made by hospitals to measure the effectiveness of equipment in improving care.

Although state planning agencies are not required under Section 1122 to deal with noncapital costs related to equipment, several state rate-setting agencies are striving to do so. Gaus and Cooper (1976) report that in Washington, Connecticut, and, to some extent New York, regulatory commissions are conducting cost-impact studies in order to determine whether or not they will reimburse for particular equipment. They are looking at all costs connected with equipment in their determination, not just purchase price. This effort is new, but the presumption is, Gaus said in a private interview, that if it proves effective federal policy makers would seriously consider broadening the scope of Section 1122 to include these noncapital costs.

Professional Standards Review Organizations

The Professional Standards Review Organization (PSRO) network has been evolving slowly since enactment of the 1972 amendments. Physicians in many regions have resisted the federally sponsored movement which requires that doctors monitor the cost and quality of federally financed medical care. In part, the concern of physicians stems from a belief that the government would only step up its regulatory demands if medicine rushed to implement the statutory requirements of the new law.

The effect of PSROs on the use of medical technologies would be great, were these physician-dominated organizations to establish norms of diagnosis and treatment of diseases as the law dictates. A PSRO will be compelled to address the issues spawned by the highly technological health care system. It will have to consider the appropriate use of coronary and intensive care units, coronary artery bypass procedures, oral hypoglycemic agents and antibiotics, as well as the efficacy of Papanicolaou smears and alternative treatments of breast cancer. Welch (1973), a respected spokesman for surgeons, said:

> The public has long believed that medicine has continued to be a cottage industry. The PSROs for the first time would begin to create a single system that is quite in contrast with present disorganized methods. . . . Physicians will of necessity become cost conscious, a feature that at present is woefully lacking. No longer can they use expensive bed space for ambulatory workups or procrastinate with indicated treatment. Sooner or later they will become involved in risk-sharing with health underwriters.

At this point, Congress is following implementation of the PSRO program rather casually, except for a few professional staff members who were a party to its creation. The father of the program, Sen. Wallace Bennett, R-Utah, retired in 1974 and no legislator has replaced him as a prime overseer. The Senate Finance Committee did hold two days of oversight hearings in May 1974, while Bennett still was active, but the program has sparked no major inquiries since.

The most visible flap involving PSROs in the last two years has been its level of funding. The PSRO program is a creature of the tax committees and mostly the Senate Finance Committee, of which Bennett was the ranking Republican member when he retired. Thus, the appropriations committees feel no keen interest in strongly supporting PSROs with funds that could be used for a range of health-related purposes which enjoy more popular appeal.

Congress has not been quick to judge the performance of the PSRO program, although in some quarters a movement is afoot to create a competing mechanism that is less dominated by private physicians. This movement will be discussed later. Other observers, though, are beginning to question whether PSROs, as self-regulatory organizations of physicians, can be expected to render tough judgments on the use of technology. Havighurst and Blumstein (1975) raised this doubt when they argued that:

although originally conceived by Congress primarily as a cost-control device, physician-dominated PSROs as now structured will systematically exaggerate the value of expensive, high-quality care. As a result, they are likely to perpetuate, if not exacerbate, the allocative biases which already characterize the health care system.

Health Planning

With enactment of the health planning law in 1974, Congress put in place a regional network of health systems agencies that it hopes will improve the process of allocating resources in the health field, including technology. The program's mandate, though, of containing costs while at the same time improving access to care reflects the sharp conflicts confronting Congress as it seeks to fashion the future health system.

HEW designated 196 health systems agencies (HSAs) to serve as the regional planning units in their respective areas. The HSAs, as a part of their vast statutory mandate, must develop short- and long-range health plans based, in large part, on priorities set out in the law. Of more relevance, though, are provisions of the law that will have an effect on technology. These provisions involve the role of states under the act. All states must designate state health planning agencies which will be charged with administering the planning and regulatory responsibilities granted to these jurisdictions.

States also must enact certificate of need (CON) laws by 1980, or suffer the loss of funds authorized under the act. These state CON laws and the federal planning act would serve as the statutory base for a regulatory program intended to influence the diffusion of technology by requiring hospitals to seek state approval before acquiring major pieces of equipment, such as scanners. Hospitals and other institutional providers, including health maintenance organizations, also would be required to seek state approval before adding beds or engaging in a major renovation or modernization program.

Some thirty states already have enacted CON laws. Most were approved before the 1974 federal law became a reality. For the last decade, many state hospital associations have pressed their legislatures to enact CON laws, calculating that such laws would restrict the entry of new health care providers while leaving the public impression that hospitals were striving to contain needless expansion. The CON laws also force into the public eye requests for new technology and beds. And traditionally, the public has favored such development (Lewin, 1975) because of the absence of a direct and negative economic impact on it.

The impact of these CON laws on the diffusion of technology is a question for the future, but the question of the breadth of scope of these laws ignited an intriguing internal struggle at HEW. The dispute serves well to illustrate a continuing conflict between health professionals, who tend to favor more rather than less technology, and other officials whose biases lean toward limiting resources for economic reasons. The conflict revolves around an issue that very likely will be dealt with early in the Carter administration.

The conflict became apparent during the process which led to the publication on March 19, 1976, of proposed regulations intended to serve as guidelines for the development of state health planning and development agencies. The regulations also outlined minimum requirements for states to follow when enacting their CON statutes.

The CON regulations generated heated debate between the offices of Cooper, Assistant Secretary for Health, and William A. Morrill, Assistant Secretary for Planning and Evaluation. At issue was whether HEW should subject to CON review organized ambulatory care facilities that generated annual revenues of more than $1 million. The acting director of the health planning program at that time, Eugene J. Rubel, recommended that such facilities be required to seek CON approval if they planned to expand or add a piece of high-cost technology.

Rubel was supported by Stuart H. Altman, who at the time was HEW Deputy Assistant Secretary for Planning and Evaluation, and by Altman's boss, Morrill. Rubel favored a strong degree of regulation in the planning program generally, but Altman and Morrill based their view more squarely on the knowledge that physicians were purchasing CT scanners for placement in ambulatory care facilities without planning approval, at a time when health maintenance organizations were subject to CON review under the law.

Cooper flatly opposed subjecting organized ambulatory care facilities to such review, arguing that it was an inappropriate federal intrusion into the practice of medicine. Cooper was backed strongly by the American Medical Association, which considered the prospect of subjecting ambulatory care facilities to CON review as by far the most objectionable element of the proposed regulations because it would bring "the federal government into the doctor's office," one AMA spokesman said (Iglehart, 1976a).

After a prolonged internal debate, Morrill came around to Cooper's view in opposition to subjecting ambulatory care facilities to CON review. Cooper defended his position in a private interview at the time by saying that the department's thinking was not well enough advanced to set such specific regulation.

> I recommended that the preamble [to the regulations] say coverage of ambulatory care facilities needs to be developed, but to just put out regulations based on billings of $1 million as a criterion, I think is the kind of peremptory judgment that begins to prejudice a constructive and acceptable approach to this issue.

Rubel's successor as health planning director, Harry P. Cain II, rekindled the issue in the fall of 1976 when he recommended that the department seek an amendment to the 1974 law which would explicitly declare that ambulatory care facilities are covered under CON review. Cain's move was based on a concern that the proliferation of scanners in free-standing facilities was seriously eroding support for the new planning effort. "The CT scanner has forced the ambulatory care issue to the fore," Cain said in a private interview. In an internal and confidential program memorandum which sought to justify expanding the scope of the CON provision it was said that:

> This modification is necessary so that we can require state programs to provide for review to expensive medical equipment in ambulatory care settings. This equipment often duplicates the services provided by traditional inpatient facilities and can, thus, contribute substantially to increasing health care costs.

Cooper again rejected the planning program's policy overture on ambulatory care facilities. On January 21, 1977, HEW published the final CON regulations, which did not cover ambulatory facilities, much to the displeasure of Congressman Rogers and Senator Kennedy.

In early 1977, Congress will likely move to extend the 1974 health planning law for one year, in accordance with President Carter's decision that short extensions be granted to expiring programs so the administration is afforded some time to cast its policy recommendations. Congress, though, could very well extend the CON requirement to ambulatory care facilities. And the Carter administration, with its plans to emphasize cost containment, might go along.

The Office of Technology Assessment's report on scanners will provide legislators with a compelling argument that ambulatory care facilities have become, in some instances, centers of high-technology equipment. The report said that about one-sixth of all CT scanners now in use in the United States are in private physicians' offices or ambulatory care clinics. Moreover, the American Hospital Association (1976) and several Blue Cross and Blue Shield plans (1975, 1976) have advanced arguments against the maintenance of CT scanners outside of hospitals.

Although Congress rejected ultimately a highly prescriptive regulatory approach to health planning when it fashioned the 1974 law, the committee staff professionals who pressed for such an approach are still around pushing. In addition, many of the health officials in the Carter administration advocate an active government role, a posture that leads in many instances to direct government regulation. Finally, there are just not enough powerful forces at work to halt the government's relentless drive toward more regulation, a direction that inevitably will make the public sector a more imposing factor in the development and diffusion of technology.

Medical Device Law

The Medical Device Amendments of 1974, signed into law by President Ford on May 28 of that year, represents another significant addition to the government's regulatory phalanx. The amendments create a pervasive, government-dominated regulatory program that will place all medical devices in three classifications, the most stringent requiring pre-market clearance of a product.

Advances in technology in recent years have transformed the manufacture of medical devices into a major industry, with sales the Health Industry Manufacturers Association estimates will total between $6 and $8 billion in 1977. The Food and Drug Administration (FDA) defines a medical device as any instrument, apparatus, machine, contrivance, or implant used to diagnose, prevent, treat, or cure a disease. Medical devices range from surgeon's gloves to jelly-filled teething rings, cardiac pacemakers, hypodermic needles, oxygen units, kidney dialysis machines, surgical sponges, prophylactics, air purifiers, crutches, and tongue depressors.

The federal government embarked on its first regulation of medical devices in 1939; in the next three years, the FDA removed from the market a hundred which were deemed dangerous or were obviously defective. The rapid expansion of technology in the years after World War II produced hundreds of new devices and greatly complicated the FDA's regulatory task. During the 1950s and 1960s, for instance, the agency found it far more difficult to recall products because the increasing number of device manufacturers began regularly to challenge FDA actions in courts, thus forcing it to develop extensive evidence to back up its proposed actions.

While continuing to review products already on the market, as a strict interpretation of its statutory mandate allowed, the FDA also began to conduct pre-market clearance reviews, claiming that the devices in question were in fact drugs and thus could be regulated under pre-market clearance provisions of the drug laws. These actions, in turn, were challenged in the courts by manufacturers. Two court decisions in recent years, though, upheld the FDA's authority to determine which products in the legally grey area between drugs and devices could be considered drugs and hence subject to pre-market clearance.

The court decisions prompted the Nixon administration to launch a "Study Group on Medical Devices" at HEW, following the President's declaration (1969) that:

> certain minimum standards should be established for [medical] devices; the government should be given additional authority to require pre-market clearance in certain cases. The scope and nature of any legislation in this area must be carefully considered.

In focusing presidential attention on this issue, Richard M. Nixon followed in the footsteps of his two predecessors, Lyndon B. Johnson and John F. Kennedy, both of whom had called for medical device legislation when each occupied the White House.

After years of debate, Congress finally enacted legislation in the spring of 1976. The law includes a broad definition of a device,[3]

---

[3]The new law defines a device as an instrument, apparatus, implement, machine, contrivance, implant, in vitro reagent, or other similar or related article, including any

thus its impact on manufacturers of medical technology will be quite broad, too.

The medical device law was fashioned in large part by four lawyers who met privately on a number of occasions in 1974. Involved were Peter Barton Hutt, who, at the time, was general counsel of the FDA; Stephan E. Lawton, counsel to the House Interstate and Foreign Commerce Subcommittee on Health and the Environment; David Meade of the Office of Legislative Counsel, and Rodney R. Munsey of the Pharmaceutical Manufacturers Association. A fifth lawyer, Anita Johnson, of Ralph Nader's Health Research Group sat in on some of the later sessions after she protested that the group lacked a consumer representative.

The House Interstate and Foreign Commerce Committee, reflecting the conflicting interests of these lawyers and others who were less intimately involved in the policy process, said in its bill report:

> . . . the committee has developed a balanced regulatory proposal intended to assure that the public is protected from unsafe and ineffective medical devices, that health professionals have more confidence in the devices they use or prescribe, and that innovations in medical device technology are not stifled by unnecessary restrictions.

Before enactment of the legislation, the FDA's Bureau of Medical Devices and Diagnostic Products focused its regulatory effort on maintaining vigilance against unsafe devices, as the agency's recently retired commissioner, Schmidt (1976), said:

> . . . in recent years, FDA has had to deal with intrauterine devices that would perforate a uterus, poorly designed and manufactured artificial heart valves, faulty cardiac pacemakers, heart monitors that electrocuted or wouldn't work, improperly designed respirators, electric beds that killed people, a cobalt therapy unit that crushed a woman to

---

component, part or accessory, which is (1) recognized in the official National Formulary, or the United States Pharmacopoeia, or any supplement to them; (2) intended for use in the diagnosis of disease or other conditions, or in the cure, mitigation, treatment, or prevention of disease, in man or other animals, or (3) intended to affect the structure or any function of the body of man or other animals, and which does not achieve any of its principal intended purposes through chemical action within or on the body of man or other animals and which is not dependent upon being metabolized for the achievement of any of its principal intended purposes.

death, others that broke ribs; we've dealt with contaminated catheters, unsterile intraocular lenses resulting in the removal of eyes, unsafe x-ray machines, inaccurate thermometers, unsterile disposable surgical sets, unsafe anesthesia machines, unsafe pump-oxygenators, and the list goes on. Each year, we require hundreds of medical device recalls, and may seek injunctions, product seizures and prosecutions.

The law, as Baram (1976) noted, reinforces the FDA's emphasis on safety, but it also requires the agency to measure devices for their efficacy. The FDA, though, is not required to determine whether one device is more efficacious than another which is manufactured to perform the same task. Baram described the law's major significance to the device industry as "single-mindedness."

> Consumer health protection is repeatedly set forth as the primary basis for setting standards and for making other regulatory decisions. Nowhere in the act is mention made of regulating medical technologies on the basis of "economic feasibility" or "technological practicability."

The emphasis on safety and efficacy is consonant with the strong feelings of one of the law's prime sponsors, Rep. Paul G. Rogers, D-Fla., who leaned in this legislation and most other measures[4] he has championed in favor of consumer protection and safety, rather than questions of cost.

Baram suggested that it is premature to speculate on the implications of the law for the development and diffusion of technology. Other observers, though, have been less reticent to comment on the potential impact of the new law. Nobel (1976), a respected expert in the device field, said:

> Over the next decade, health care institutions can look forward to the following undesirable effects: (1) Fewer new devices will be developed and enter the marketplace. (2) Some smaller companies will go out of business, sell out to larger companies, or go into other areas. (3) As the larger companies need to diversify and grow stronger, they will acquire the smaller companies. (4) The diversity of suppliers and competition will be reduced. (5) The price of medical devices and supplies will increase.

[4]The Clean Air Act Amendments of 1976, which failed to become law, was another major instance where Rogers put health considerations before cost questions, to the consternation of the automobile manufacturers.

No interest group involved in the medical device debate disputed that there will be new costs attached to the tighter regulation. The FDA, for instance, told Rogers in a private communication that the estimated costs of scientific review of such devices as prosthetic heart valves, arrhythmia detectors and alarms, and air fluidized beds were, respectively, $225,000, $10,000 to $160,000, and $4,000 to $14,500. The agency further estimated that clinical investigations concerning heart pacemakers may be more costly than those for heart valves.

Lawton, the House subcommittee counsel, said in a private interview on January 10, 1977, that Congress took steps in the law to prevent the effects Nobel speculates the Act will have on devices but he conceded:

> Regulation is expensive. The important thing is that the committee determined that the need to insure safety and effectiveness of medical devices was paramount to the considerations Dr. Nobel mentioned, including cost. When one speaks in terms of the unnecessary deaths and injuries that have occurred because of less than satisfactory testing of devices, safety and effectiveness considerations just have to take precedence. Beyond this, though, the committee made a conscious effort to avoid the effects that Nobel predicts. The thesis of the legislation is, for example, that the least regulation necessary in order to insure safety and effectiveness is all that is required. Unlike drug law, where all new drugs must face pre-market clearance, fewer than half of all new devices will be subjected to this test, which is expensive. Secondly, the product development protocol procedure is an attempt to speed the approval process as well as an attempt to cut the cost of research by essentially merging FDA's processes for determining safety and effectiveness. Third, the law mandates that FDA extend assistance to small manufacturers of devices in complying with it. It's true, though, that after enactment of the 1962 drug amendments smaller drug companies were gobbled up by the corporate giants. This phenomenon supports Dr. Nobel's thesis of what may happen to some of the smaller device manufacturers, although it is our hope that it won't.

Catastrophic Health Insurance

The legislation which is perhaps most likely to compel Congress to address policy questions surrounding technology, its cost and regulation, on a more comprehensive basis revolves around the politically appealing notion of protecting all Americans against the economic consequences of catastrophic illness. Such legislation has gained increasing favor with federal policy makers, even though its implications span many social, ethical, and economic fronts.

Sens. Russell B. Long, D-La., Chairman of the Senate Finance Committee, and Abraham Ribicoff, D-Conn., a senior member of that committee, introduced the first major catastrophic health insurance bill in October 1973. This measure attracted 23 other Senate sponsors. Since then, President Ford proposed a catastrophic benefit for Medicare beneficiaries and other key legislators have advanced their own prescriptions, including Rep. Dan Rostenkowski, D-Ill., Chairman of the House Ways and Means Subcommittee on Health. The plans advanced all have been different and no consensus has emerged, but it is clearly an issue that will come before the 95th Congress.

Congress already has enacted one program that extends substantial benefits to individuals afflicted with one catastrophic illness—end-stage renal disease. Although it is difficult to generalize on the basis of HEW's experience with the kidney program, it does provide some insight into how the government has sought, through direct regulation, to implement this effort. Congress initially provided HEW with sweeping powers to finance and regulate the treatment of kidney disease, a reflection of its concern over the potential cost of the program. Looming on the legislative horizon is a new effort to impose tighter regulations in a way that would seek to encourage more renal disease patients to undergo dialysis at home or in less costly institutional settings.

The concern over the cost of financing what Lewis Thomas, M.D., has described as a "half-way technology" was well placed, although it did not stop the Congress from acting. During the 1972 Senate floor debate on the kidney amendment, program cost estimates for fiscal 1976 and 1977 were $198 million and $252 million, respectively. Today, revised program cost estimates for the same fiscal years are $400 and $500 million, respectively. HEW now projects that after a decade of operation, the kidney disease treatment program will cost $1 billion, as a result of higher unit costs and a growing number of renal disease patients.

The House Ways and Means Subcommittee on Oversight has been conducting a continuing series of hearings on the kidney program. In a report (1975), the subcommittee expressed its concern over the cost projections:

>The subcommittee is deeply concerned with these high costs, which place a heavy burden on the trust funds and general revenues. These costs also limit options to provide protection for the cost of treating equally deserving patients confronted with other forms of catastrophic disease such as hemophilia, stroke, cerebral palsy, cancer, and so forth.

Congress is under heavy pressure from interest groups representing these disease categories to extend its catastrophic coverage to other illnesses. HEW already has funded seventeen comprehensive diagnostic, evaluation, and treatment centers for hemophilia, which are intended to provide information and guidance on the disease to other hospitals. A next step could be financing treatment for hemophilia.

The debate over financing kidney treatment spanned almost a decade, as Rettig (1976) depicts so well in recounting it, although 1972 Senate action stemmed from a hastily drawn, little discussed floor amendment. Congress specified kidney treatment coverage for all renal disease patients covered by social security, about 97 percent of the population afflicted with this disease, and then authorized HEW to say where the treatment could be rendered and how much care these facilities had to deliver to be eligible for reimbursement. Further, Congress directed HEW to create a mechanism to decide who should receive the care.

In the history of federal involvement in medicine, these measures were revolutionary when compared with the degree of intervention that Congress accorded HEW in the administration of Medicare, according to Wolkstein (Iglehart, 1976b). But now the House Ways and Means Subcommittee on Health is preparing legislation that would carry government intervention a good deal farther in an effort to contain costs. Although the measure is still under development, its principal author, Erwin Hytner, of the Ways and Means staff, outlined its major purposes in a private interview on December 6, 1976.

>The costs of the kidney treatment program have gotten out of hand. The program has been loosely administered in these first years, in part because Medicare's top priority was putting it in place; financing treatment was the priority. Now we want to seriously consider some rather sweeping changes that we envision could have two major impacts: one, reducing program expenditures by redirecting the place of treatment away from free-standing proprietary kidney facilities, which are making substantial profits, if not abusing the program. And

two, injecting financial incentives that would encourage physicians to urge their patients to use home dialysis or self-treatment in a supervised institutional setting. In other words, the government would be applying in a very direct way its financial leverage to get doctors and hospitals to change a course of behavior they have been following. Also, we will propose shifting Medicare's basis for payment to facilities from charges to costs. And we want to look closely at empowering medical review boards that were created under the original act with making the determination of whether a patient could appropriately use self-care. This decision, then, would not be left solely to a patient and his or her physician. These proposals will stir up a hornet's nest, but we really need to get a very tight handle on costs. The free-standing proprietary facilities are taking over the field of kidney treatment.

Technology and the Biomedical Research Community

Traditionally, there has been little appreciation in the political world for the binding relationship between the development of technology and the government's massive investment in biomedical research. Increasingly, though, as medical costs have increased and public demands have grown for science to account for its government subsidies, legislators and executive branch officials have been raising new questions about the link between technology and research.

No such statement was more compelling, nor drew more attention, than that offered by Gaus in 1975 in testimony before the President's Biomedical Research Panel. Gaus outlined the reasons why Medicare, as a financier of health services, is deeply interested in biomedical research funding and priorities.

> Medicare does not finance or engage in biomedical research. It does, however, finance the results of this research. The diffusion and adoption of health care innovations often results in the utilization of far more resources than was initially expended in the research effort and the process plays a major role in the dramatic increases in the open-ended budget levels of the Medicare and Medicaid programs.

In expressing concerns over the impact of new technology on cost, Gaus articulated a view that no other top-level official of Medicare or its parent agency, the Social Security Administration, has stated publicly. Besieged by other concerns deemed as more pressing,

94

SSA's hierarchy has left to Gaus the issue of Medicare and technology, although Thomas Tierney, director of the Medicare program, said in a private interview that officials must recognize that the idea of controlling technology has enormous implications for public policy.

> In a public program, you must have the best as long as the government asserts that the covered population will get the best.

Other voices, though, are starting to be heard. One of the most forceful among them is that of Sen. Edward M. Kennedy, D-Mass., who, as Chairman of the Senate Labor and Public Welfare Subcommittee on Health, is responsible for overseeing the National Institutes of Health, which dispenses $2.5 billion a year in funds for biomedical research and allied purposes. Another is Dr. Donald S. Fredrickson, Director of the NIH.

Kennedy's keenest interest is in creating a government-sponsored mechanism to assess the value of medical technologies. And he deeply believes that academic medical centers, which received 46 percent of NIH's biomedical research monies in fiscal 1974 (Morgan and Jones, 1976), have a major role to play in such an exercise. In a public hearing on June 17, 1976, Kennedy signalled his strong interest in creating such a mechanism when he asked Cooper, HEW Assistant Secretary for Health:

> Is it possible for us to formulate some kind of panel or mechanism or institution which will evaluate what is going on in terms of the medical technique or practice which will include the clinicians and researchers and also a public dimension?

Cooper replied: "I think it is possible to do that."

From the outset of what Kennedy described as a year-long examination of federal biomedical research policies, which he launched with public hearings in June 1976, the senator and his staff assumed that the NIH and its clients would resist addressing questions of assessment, questions which extend far beyond the traditional role of the research community. Kennedy's view was colored in good part by the work of the President's Biomedical Research Panel in 1976, which concluded that the research community had no major responsibility in the interface between research and delivery. The panel also endorsed, without reservation, the job the research community was doing. Officials at the NIH who followed the panel's work also sensed that the panel's failure to address these broader issues was a significant shortcoming. Seymour Perry, M.D., an aide to Frederickson, said in a private interview, "I think it really hurt the research community."

Unlike the panel, though, Fredrickson was more sensitive to the strong political currents that surrounded the issues of the biomedical research community's mission, on the one hand, and its strong dependence on public support, on the other. Fredrickson sensed that the winds of change were blowing and, unless NIH began to show some commitment to examining technologies produced by the research community, the federal health policy makers might react in ways that could only be detrimental to research. Fredrickson expressed the essence of his thinking at a hearing before Kennedy in 1976:

> I think that there are some new social imperatives for science. They include a full measure of responsibility for what should not be in the doctor's bag, for the rate of transfer of new knowledge into practical use, a sharper concern for matters of ethics and due process in clinical research, technology assessment and public involvement in such decisions.

In an interview subsequent to his congressional testimony, Fredrickson said (Iglehart, 1976c) that he has come to recognize that NIH and the research community it subsidizes have a taller order than simply generating knowledge.

> There are new interventions. By this I mean, traditionally we have been laissez-faire. We have created scientific opportunities, but left their execution to a conglomerate of health-care vendors and the voluntary sector. Very often we have done that without making an authoritative assessment of the value of the technology or rendering a judgment on the cost-benefit relationship. We have to get more deeply involved in that process. Some kind of collective authority is needed, because once you have created a piece of new technology, there are forces pushing diffusion that press for its maximum use . . . the profit motive among health vendors and the concept, almost legal, that everybody should have access to what is perceived as the best care available.

Soon after delivering his testimony last June, Fredrickson moved aggressively to create at NIH a policy that underscored what he believed should be the biomedical research community's new commitment to more actively focus its energies on broader health problems in the future. One political reality pressing upon him was that, as an appointee of a Republican president, Fredrickson had to demonstrate to his new Democratic stewards that there were compelling reasons why he should be retained as NIH director.

Fredrickson surfaced at NIH, two weeks before the November 1976 election, a draft issue paper entitled, "The Responsibilities of NIH at the Health Research/Health Care Interface." In a cover letter to the proposal, Fredrickson said:

> The issue addressed is one of exceptional importance to the NIH and the larger biomedical research community: what should be the responsibility of NIH be in assuring effective introduction into the health care system of knowledge pertinent to disease prevention, detection, diagnosis, treatment and rehabilitation? How should the NIH organize, what processes must be put into place, to discharge these responsibilities?

In the paper, which NIH distributed among only its institute directors on a "confidential basis," Fredrickson proposed that the agency and the scientific community:

> assume a greater responsibility in the selection and use of that knowledge pertinent to disease diagnosis and treatment, which is to become accepted health practice.

Further, Fredrickson proposed that this function be carried out through a mechanism created in each of NIH's research institutes that would:

> identify and foster evaluation of appropriate new knowledge on the verge of transfer to the health care community.

These mechanisms would function under the aegis of the NIH, but representatives of nongovernmental professional and lay organizations would be parties to the process.

Fredrickson's proposal generated a good deal of controversy at the NIH. Several of the institute directors argued privately that the new processes could come to dominate the research institutes, sap funds from their on-going research activities and engage the agency in running disputes with organized medicine. On Capitol Hill, though, where word of the proposal soon leaked, the reception was far more positive, particularly from the Kennedy camp. The senator's chief health aide, Jones, said in an interview:

> I'm surprised by the paper, surprised that Fredrickson has gone so

far. I think it's fantastic. Fredrickson has taken the lead in asking questions of the research community that we want to press, but within that community his voice has far more real influence than does ours.

The creation of a government-sponsored mechanism to assess technologies and treatment practices would, in some ways, compete with the PSROs. In Kennedy's view, PSROs are too dominated by private physicians, individuals he fears may have a vested interest in a process of treatment assessment and therefore may have a hard time being objective. The assessment process that Kennedy and Fredrickson envision would more nearly be a set of public bodies, set up under the aegis of the government, but also engaging academic researchers, practicing physicians, medical specialists, and other experts.

What Fredrickson is driving at in this early cut at assessment is developing a mechanism through which knowledgable experts could strive to reach a consensus on what technologies are most effective. For example, the NIH recently completed such a process for the treatment of hypertension. In an interview on December 16, 1976, Robert L. Ringler, M.D., Deputy Director of the National Heart and Lung Institute, said that the Joint National Committee on Detection, Evaluation, and Treatment of High Blood Pressure:

> attempted to build a consensus on the treatment of hypertension that would avoid putting everybody with high blood pressure in the hospital for a week. The group set down guidelines for the treatment of this particular disease.

The committee plans to disseminate its findings widely, hoping that physicians who treat individuals with hypertension will embrace the recommendations of the group. The findings will be published in the *Journal of the American Medical Association*.

Fredrickson believes that eventually HEW will link such research findings to stricter guidelines on what services its health financing programs will pay for. He said in an interview on December 16, 1976:

> I think it is inevitable that the fiduciary, either government or outside third parties, will begin slowly to make decisions about what it will and will not pay for [on the basis of government-sponsored judgments on what medical practices are the most effective.] They do that now but only in the most general sort of way. I would expect that trend to increase.

The NIH will not be alone in its interest in undertaking medical assessments, if the government decides to plunge into such exercises in a big way. HEW's National Center for Health Services Research and the Center for Disease Control both have strong interests in this area, as do members of the Institute of Medicine of the National Academy of Sciences and its president, David Hamburg, M.D. Indeed, it was the Institute of Medicine that the Blue Cross Association turned to when it sought some quick guidance on the CT scanner. Walter J. McNerney, the president of Blue Cross, said in an interview on December 23, 1976:

> How the institute steps up to the plate on this one will have a lot to say about its future usefulness in this area. If the institute performs well, then I will move to an on-going strategy of getting early advice on emerging technologies.

Summary

The federal government's entry into the financing of medical services has spawned a multitude of activities that are affecting every element of the health system. Rising medical costs have become the No. 1 problem for the government because this phenomenon absorbs limited dollars needed to finance many other worthy social goals. In Medicare alone, the costs have jumped from $5.3 billion in 1968, to $9.5 billion in 1973, to $26.1 billion in 1978, to an estimated $30.4 billion in 1979. As long as medical costs climb at a rate faster than other elements of the Consumer Price Index, the government will be seeking to stem this tide, regardless of the uproar it generates among health care practitioners.

A central facet of this cost spiral, as industry spokesmen acknowledge, is the changing nature of the medical product, particularly within hospitals. The product is becoming more technologically complex and more expensive. Not only are the new machines themselves more expensive, but they require more manpower and additional space. The government has fostered this technological imperative through its massive financial commitment to biomedical research, which generates new knowledge and, thus, new technology. The cost-plus hospital reimbursement system also has served as a powerful force stimulating this imperative.

In the last five years, as Medicare and Medicaid have evolved into big ticket cost items, federal decision makers have begun to recognize more clearly vital links in the system which drive it; links between the manner of reimbursement and the amount of technology deemed as essential; the development of technology and the degree to which it is regulated; and the effect of this equipment on patients and the quality of care delivered.

The government has begun to intervene in these linkages, principally through new laws that seek to constain costs, insure quality and influence the system's growth. Major new laws that reflect this trend are the Social Security Amendments of 1972, the Health Planning and Resources Development Act of 1974, and the Medical Device Amendments of 1976. All of these laws include new threads of direct government regulation of the health industry, the central federal health policy theme of the 1970s. Looming ahead is more regulation effecting clinical laboratories, kidney treatment, and perhaps costs on a general basis.

Government control of technology is a touchy issue. And the federal policy process sometimes has a hard time dealing decisively with such sensitive matters. Federal decision makers certainly do not want to inhibit the orderly diffusion of life-saving technology. Nor do they favor imposing arbitrary restraints on the use of sophisticated diagnostic equipment, like the brain scanner. But their credulity is taxed when the proliferation of a technological device like the scanner is so rapid and so without rational planning that there seems no limit to the number that ultimately may function in the system.

A new dimension of government activity in the health field is emerging—an interest in the value of medical technologies. This effort, though only in its earliest stages, could stamp even more firmly the government's imprint on the field. The movement stems from a slowly evolving belief at the National Institutes of Health that the biomedical research community must relate more closely to the clinical practice of medicine. The chief political stalwart of this movement is Sen. Edward M. Kennedy, D-Mass.

This effort, plus the many other health regulatory activities that are engaging the government, guarantee that the system will remain unsettled and tension-filled. The government's policy-making mechanisms are imperfect, often slow to react and often lacking in precision. But in most instances, sooner or later—government acts to protect the public's investment. And there is no reason to believe that it won't take the steps it deems necessary to do just that.

References

Abt Associates, Inc., 1975. Incentives and decisions underlying hospitals' adoption and utilization of major capital equipment. Executive summary.

American Hospital Association. 1976. Status report on computerized axial tomography. Chicago.

Ball, Robert M. 1974. Background of regulation in health care. In *Controls on Health Care.* pp. 3−22. Washington, D.C.: National Academy of Sciences.

Banta, H. David, and Sanes, Joshua R. 1976. How the CAT got out of the bag. Background paper for Conference on Health Care Technology and Quality of Care, Boston University Health Policy Center, 19−20 November, at Boston, Mass.

Baram, Michael. 1976. Medical device legislation and the development and diffusion of health technology. Background paper for Conference on Health Care Technology and Quality of Care, Boston University Health Policy Center, 19−20 November, at Boston, Mass.

Blue Cross Association. 1975. Memorandum—a certificate of need update and BCA health planning information clearinghouse. Chicago.

———. 1976. Computerized axial tomography—CAT scanners. Chicago.

Blue Cross, Blue Shield. 1976. News release. New York.

Butler, Lewis H., and Lee, Philip R. 1975. Preface to health policy program discussion paper: The costs of treatment of selected illnesses, 1951−1964−1971. pp. i−vii. University of California School of Medicine, San Francisco.

Cooper, Theodore. 1976. Testimony before the Senate Labor and Public Welfare Subcommittee on Health on subject of inflation of health care costs. April 2. Washington, D.C.

Council on Wage and Price Stability. 1976. The problems of rising health care costs. Staff report (April). Washington, D.C.

Foster, Richard W. 1976. *The financial structure of community hospitals: impact of Medicare.* Chicago: Hospital Research Educational Trust.

Gaus, Clifton R., and Cooper, Barbara S. 1976. Technology and Medicare: alternatives for change. Paper presented at the Conference on Health Care Technology and Quality of Care, Boston University Health Policy Center, 19−20 November, at Boston, Mass.

Hastings, James F. 1976. Keynote address published in conference proceedings of the National Leadership Conference on America's Health Policy. pp. 8−10. Washington, D.C.

Havighurst, Clark C., and Blumstein, James F. 1975. Coping with quality/cost trade-offs in medical care: the role of PSROs. *Northwestern University Law Review.* 70 (No. 1): 6–68.

Iglehart, John K. 1976a. HEW takes final step down road to local health planning network. *National Journal* 8 (No. 14): 436–439.

———. 1976b. Trial for national health insurance. *National Journal* 8 (No. 26): 895–900.

———. 1976c. Is it time for biomedical researchers to hunt for new fields? *National Journal* 8 (No. 35): 1217–1221.

Lewin and Associates, Inc. 1975. Evaluation of the efficiency and effectiveness of the Section 1122 review process. Washington, D.C.

Miller, Sue. 1977. Med-chi plans to draft policy on scanners. In *The Evening Sun.* (Baltimore, Md.) January 10.

Morgan, Thomas E., and Jones, Daniel D. 1976. Trends in dimensions of biomedical and behavioral research funding in academic medical centers, 1964–1974. Submitted to the President's Biomedical Research Panel by the Association of American Medical Colleges, Washington, D.C.

Nobel, Joel J. 1976. Medical device act; impact on hospitals and industry. *Hospital Progress* 57 (No. 10): 54–56.

Phillips, Donald F., and Lille, Kenneth. 1976. Putting the leash on the CAT. *Journal of the American Hospital Association* 50: 45–49.

Rettig, Richard A. 1976. *Valuing lives: the policy debate on patient care financing for victims of end-stage renal disease.* Washington, D.C.: The Rand Corporation.

Rice, Dorothy P., and Wilson, Douglas. 1975. The American medical economy—problems and perspectives. Paper prepared for the International Conference on Health Care Costs and Expenditures sponsored by the Fogarty International Center, Department of Health, Education, and Welfare, 2–4 June, at Bethesda, Md.

Rogers, Paul G. 1976. Before national health insurance: some points to consider. In conference proceedings of the National Leadership Conference on America's Health Policy. pp. 64–65. Washington, D.C.

Russell, Louise B., and Burke, Carol S. 1975. Technological diffusion in the hospital sector. Study prepared for the National Science Foundation under grant no. RDA75-14274. Washington, D.C.

Russell, Louise B. 1976. Making rational decisions about medical technology. Paper presented at meeting of the National Commission on the Cost of Medical Care, 23 November, Chicago.

Schmidt, Alexander M. 1976. Medical device regulation without interference. In fourth annual Hans M. Hecht Memorial Lecture, University of Utah, Salt Lake City.

Trapnell, Gordon R. 1976. A comparison of the costs of major national health insurance proposals. Prepared for the Office of the Secretary, Department of Health, Education, and Welfare under contract no. HEW-0S-74-138.

U.S. Congress, Committee on Ways and Means. 1975. Report on the administration of the end-stage renal disease program established by public law 92-603 (with additional views). p. 3. Washington, D.C.: Government Printing Office.

Welch, Claude E. 1973. Professional standards review organizations—problems and prospects. *New England Journal of Medicine* 289 (No. 6): 291−295.

Address reprint requests to: John K. Iglehart, 12008 River Road, Potomac, Md., 20854

Medical Technology

and Hospital Costs

JUDITH L. WAGNER
AND MICHAEL ZUBKOFF

Introduction

Medical technology, particularly the kind found in hospitals, has undergone a curious shift in public acceptability over the past five years. Those who influence and shape national health policy have shown increasing alarm over the way in which new technologies are developed and introduced into the health care system. With few exceptions, the present concern is with the proliferation of new technologies in hospitals.[1] New equipment, procedures, or systems appear to be introduced by hospital decision makers often without knowledge of or concern for their relative effectiveness or efficiency. Technology purportedly follows its own imperative, eluding effective control by regulatory or financing agencies (Rabkin and Melin, 1976). Most important, new hospital technologies have allegedly raised health care costs, and herein lies the major source of

---

[1] The exceptions are important. Some observers have noted the low development or implementation of technologies for use in primary care that would allow the substitution of low-cost for high-cost manpower (see White, Murnaghan, and Gaus, 1972). Barriers to development and diffusion of technologies that would be very useful to the handicapped have been noted in a recent report by the National Research Council (1976).

In *Hospital Cost Containment: Selected Notes for Future Policy*, edited by Michael Zubkoff, Ira E. Raskin, and Ruth S. Hanft. New York: PRODIST, 1978.

alarm. Clifton Gaus of the Social Security Administration recently stated:

> The long-term cumulative effect of adopting new health care technologies is a major cause of the large yearly increases in national health expenditures and in total Medicare and Medicaid benefit levels [Gaus, 1975:12-13].

Technology has clearly acquired a bad name; increasingly, policies to assess, evaluate, or control the introduction of new technologies on the federal and state levels have been suggested as cost-containment strategies (see, for example, Russell, 1976; Rabkin and Melin, 1976; Gaus and Cooper, 1976; Weiner, 1976). Debates over the nation's ability to continue to pay for new technologies as it has in the past have flourished (DeBakey and Hiatt, 1976).

The obvious question arises as to why technology, and particularly hospital technology, has been singled out at this time as a particular problem of hospital behavior. The answer lies in the convergence of three lines of criticism of the health care system.

First, recent studies decomposing hospital cost inflation into its constituent parts have provided some circumstantial evidence linking technology to increased hospital costs. In 1972, Waldman estimated that increases in real inputs accounted for 50 percent of the annual changes in per diem hospital costs between 1951 and 1970. Similar findings by Worthington (1975) and, most recently, Feldstein and Taylor (1977) have demonstrated the changing nature of the hospital product. Feldstein and Taylor found that about 75 percent of the rise in hospital costs relative to the general economy can be attributed to increases in labor and nonlabor inputs per patient day. Although there is no one-to-one correspondence between the increasing level of intensity of care (as measured by increasing inputs) and the rate of technological change, a clear implication of these studies is that the introduction of new technologies is responsible for much of the trend.

The second factor leading to the assault on hospital technology is the mounting evidence that many health services, indeed perhaps *all* medical care, have made little difference in health outcomes. Nonmedical factors appear to have been more important in reducing mortality and morbidity rates over the past fifty years than has medical care. The works of Cochrane (1972) and McKeown (1976) have raised considerable doubt 'about the efficacy of many medical procedures. It has become increasingly clear that clinical research is not organized to provide definitive information on the effectiveness of existing or new medical procedures. In the absence of hard scientific proof, several observers have suggested that we should avoid heavy investments in technologies that enhance the delivery of dubious services (see, for example, White, Murnaghan, and Gaus, 1972; Banta and McNeil, 1977). Arguments for redistribution of health dollars to areas of health promotion and prevention are based on an acceptance of this thesis (Lalonde, 1972).

A third source of concern lies in the disappointing record of programs designed to control hospital capital expenditures. State certificate-of-need laws and state programs for approval of large capital expenditures under Section 1122 of the 1972 Social Security Amendments have been in existence long enough for some evidence to be accumulated about their effectiveness in controlling the proliferation of expensive pieces of capital equipment. The record has been dismal. Not only have health planning agencies proved to be unprepared to make appropriate judgments about new technologies, but certificate of need appears to have shifted the composition of capital spending from investments in new beds to investment in sophisticated equipment (Salkever and Bice, 1976). Capital equipment expenditures should not be unequivocally equated with adoption of new technologies, but the lack of effective control over this aspect of hospital expenditure has raised the question whether any control over decisions of hospitals to adopt new and expensive technologies exists.

The convergence of these three separate types of evidence has created an environment of cynicism about the value of new technologies to the delivery of health care. If health care services make so little difference to the community's health level, then investments in an increasing level of sophistication embodied in new technology become especially suspect. As the major repository of the visible symbols of sophisticated technology, the hospital is a natural target for criticism. Sensitive to this emerging anti-technology trend, the authors of DHEW's 1976 *Forward Plan for Health* defended technology's contribution to the well-being of the nation:

> During the past 30 years, national investment in biomedical and behavioral research has been enormously productive and has revolutionized clinical care. It is true that it is not yet possible to prevent many of our most frequent and costly illnesses, but that is not because such "high technology" (in Lewis Thomas' concept) is not a goal of research; rather, it is that research progress has not yet permitted the kind of definitive interventions that antibiotics brought for many infectious diseases. . . . Nevertheless, 30 years and billions of dollars of public funds have been invested in this progress against disease, and the public believes it has a right to the benefits of its investment whether such benefits are "half way" or not [pp. 93–94].

Because the issue of technology is so visible at present and the policies that have been suggested to deal with problems of technology are so varied and in some cases extreme,[2] it is important to differentiate among the kinds of "technology problems" that have been identified. As the previous discussion indicates, inferences about the improper use of technology by the health care system have been drawn from very different kinds of evidence, including the volume of inputs devoted to the production of hospital services and the level of capital expenditures undertaken by hospitals. For the most part, critics have not distinguished among the particular problems that they address. Confusion stems partially from the broad scope of hardware and software activities that are often thought of as technology. According to the definition offered by the U.S. Congressional Office of Technology Assessment (OTA), medical technologies include techniques, drugs, procedures, or systems combining these elements, used in the practice of medical care (U.S. Congress, OTA, 1976a). The very comprehensiveness of this definition blurs some of the critical policy problems currently under consideration. More important, however, is a general failure to

[2] See, for example, Bogue and Wolfe (1976), calling for the establishment of a moratorium on the purchase of CAT scanners.

107

distinguish between problems associated with the improper use of existing technologies and the process by which new technologies are developed, introduced, and diffused into the medical care system. Often, the two problems are lumped together, as in a recent article by Banta and McNeil (1977), focusing on problems associated with new and existing diagnostic technologies. Policy recommendations often involve combined strategies to control both the use of existing capabilities and the introduction of new technology. As a result, exactly which problems specific policies address and how these policies will affect different aspects of the "technology problem" are often unclear.

For the purpose of this chapter, the technology problem can be divided into two subproblems, each with its own policy implications. The first is the problem of the way in which the health care system allocates resources to and uses existing technologies. The second is the problem of technical change involving the introduction of new equipment, systems, or procedures into the health care system. Each of these problems must be defined separately, although it is obvious that the way in which existing technologies are used has immense impact on the direction and speed of technical change in the health care system.

Problems Involving Existing Technology

If we accept the OTA definition of medical technology, the problem of existing technology becomes synonymous with the more general problems of resource allocation and use of health care services. And if, as Perrow has claimed (1965), the hospital itself is the technological instrument of the medical profession, then all problems of utilization of hospital services and allocation of resources to hospitals are inherently problems of the inappropriate use of existing technologies. Most frequently, critics of "existing technology" focus on particular elements of hospital behavior or resources that are "technological" by nature, such as equipment (U.S. Congress, OTA, 1976b), capital-intensive facilities (Russell and Burke, 1975), diagnostic tests (Rushmer, 1976; and Banta and McNeil, 1977), or surgical procedures (Orloff, 1976). These particular elements are identified as sources of abuse of existing technology because they represent the "sophisticated" element of medical care. The tendency of the health care system to bias the allocation and use of resources toward these more sophisticated elements is often referred to as the "technological imperative" (Rushmer, 1976). To the extent that the tendency to overinvest in and overuse sophisticated services is just part of a larger tendency to overuse health services or to invest too many labor or nonlabor resources in the production of hospital services, the problem is not related to technology itself and should not be singled out as one of technology. The impact of present reimbursement and regulatory policies on hospital resource allocation, particularly on decisions to overinvest in capital assets and overuse services, should be viewed as a problem of cost control and not of technology per se.

However, insofar as decisions to invest in or use certain equipment, procedures, or drugs are made on the basis of their level of technical sophistication, the existence of the "technological imperative" must be accepted. A number of arguments have been put forth to justify the view that technology is a problem in its own right. Changes in medical education have purportedly placed increasing emphasis on objective tests and precise measurement when less technologically advanced methods might still be adequate for diagnosis and treatment (Gellman, 1971). Medical students and residents, trained in the most sophisticated institutions, expect and depend upon the availability of diagnostic and therapeutic assists in the form of instrumentation and facilities. Thus, clinical decision makers may be functionaries of the technological imperative.

Several economists have theorized that patient demand for medical care is, among other things, a function of the perceived quality of care (Feldstein, 1976). Others postulate that the objective of the hospital is to maximize a weighted function of the quality and quantity of the services it produces (Newhouse, 1970). How quality is perceived by patients and hospital decision makers thus has a major influence on the behavior of the health care system with respect to technologically sophisticated procedures and services. Feldstein (1976) hypothesizes that hospital decision makers' perceptions of quality depend on the amount of labor and nonlabor inputs devoted to the production of medical care. However, perceived quality may be correlated as much with the level of sophistication of those inputs as with their absolute amounts.[3] If, too, patients perceive quality in terms of high levels of sophistication in the delivery of services, including the application of many and frequent diagnostic tests, performance of equipment-bound procedures (such as respiratory therapy), and increases in the number and training level of health care personnel, then physicians and hospitals will respond by emphasizing those inputs. Similarly, if an important element of the patient's perception of hospital quality were the efficiency of its billing procedures, then the hospital would invest capital and labor resources to improve these. Thus, to the extent that it does exist, the source of the technological imperative rests largely on the value that patients and hospital decision makers place on technological sophistication for its own sake.

Newhouse (1970) has posited that under a predominantly charge- or cost-based system of third-party payment, the hospital decision maker could conceivably push both quality and quantity to the point where the additional utility to the hospital is zero. If quality is equated with the availability and use of sophisticated services, then this hypothesis implies a level of sophistication much beyond that which would result were marginal utility equated with the marginal cost of these services.

The problem of existing technology can thus be related to three factors: structural changes in the nature of medical education, which stresses dependence on scientific instrumentation; patient demands for technological sophistication as a surrogate for high "quality" care; and the failure of the cost-reimbursement system to constrain hospitals from increasing their investment in expensive and sophisticated technological capabilities. On balance, these factors create powerful incentives for the hospital to invest in the showpieces of technological sophistication, including clinical instrumentation, special care units, specialized facilities for complex procedures (for example, cardiac catheterization and cardiac surgery), and automated clinical laboratory systems.

[3] See for example, Grimes and Moseley (1976), relating hospital characteristics with indices of their performance.

The implications for public policy to deal with these sources of abuse of the existing armamentarium of equipment and procedures available to hospitals and physicians are fairly clear. First, the present reimbursement system as it is currently structured needs a major overhaul. Either detailed regulation of the investment decisions of hospitals and health care facilities must be undertaken, or reimbursement systems must be so structured as to provide different incentives to hospitals and health care facilities. Certificate-of-need programs represent one regulatory approach, but these laws generally fail to require the approval of capital purchases under some threshold level or to apply to all health care settings. Furthermore, the separation of the responsibility for regulation of health care expenditures from the responsibility for paying for the services produced creates an institutional weakness in the certificate-of-need arrangements.

Rate setting on a prospective basis is also a potential solution for the bias toward the use of sophisticated technology, but as Bauer's paper in this book points out, rate setting may not lead to the cost control results that many expect of it. Rate setting does not apply to decisions to use sophisticated services. These decisions remain for the most part the exclusive domain of physicians. Thus, rate setting may keep unit costs low, but it cannot be expected to control the utilization of services effectively. Also, hospital rate setting would not alter the internal bias within the hospital decision-making structure toward technologically advanced services. Because the hospital administrator views quality as related to sophistication, the tendency to invest in these services will still remain.

Ellwood (1975) has suggested that a system of competing prepaid group practices would provide the incentives to health care providers to make resource allocation decisions in the light of the relative cost effectiveness of each decision. With appropriate information on measures of performance of such prepaid plans, patients could trade off quality against cost in a fashion that would approach a more conventional market decision.

A second policy implication arising from the tendency to equate technological sophistication with quality of care is the need for a reexamination of the efficacy of medical practices, particularly those involving the use of expensive equipment, facilities, or personnel. Furthermore, the results of this reexamination must be transmitted or communicated to physicians and patients so that a more informed set of demands can be made for quality. Indeed, the results could also be used to control utilization of sophisticated services.

The organization of such deliberate and ongoing research into efficacy requires the delegation of a new set of responsibilities to some federal agency or the establishment of an agency to perform this role. At present, no federal health agency has the specific charge of evaluating the efficacy of existing medical practices.

The third policy implication argues for changes in methods of medical education, including incorporation into the educational process the information on efficacy produced through research efforts. Some critics of the medical education system have noted that medical schools do not provide any training in statistical decision theory to enable medical students to evaluate the relative information content of diagnostic tests (Schwartz, 1976). Of course, if the reimbursement system were altered so that hospitals and physicians had to choose among alternative uses of limited economic resources and if appropriate information on efficacy were produced by a research organization, medical education would be likely to reflect the new incentives and knowledge.

The Problem of Technical Change

Technical change refers to the complex and not well understood process by which new capability is developed and brought into use. New technical capability in health care refers to the ability to produce new products or services that did not previously exist or to produce existing products or services in a new way, with greater reliability or less cost. Because the nature of the hospital product is so poorly defined, these two kinds of capability are often difficult to distinguish from one another. For example, was gastric freezing a new service, or was it a "better" way to perform an old service—the treatment of ulcers? The most important distinction for policy purposes is between changes that at least theoretically enhance the quality of care and changes that lower the cost of providing care. Gastric freezing was clearly intended to fall into the former category.

Technical change implies that the new capability has resulted from scientific progress, not from changes in the hospital's economic environment. For example, if the hospital reorganizes previously scattered services into a separate respiratory therapy unit for economic reasons, it has not introduced a new technology, as some would claim (see, for example, Russell, 1976), but has merely adjusted methods of providing services. However, the introduction of intermittent positive pressure breathing (IPPB) as a new service clearly represents the adoption of a new technical capability, as would the replacement of existing laboratory methods with new automated laboratory equipment.

Technical change is a dynamic process that involves several identifiable but somewhat overlapping phases. The process has been classified in a number of ways (U.S. Congress, OTA, 1976a), but it can be summarized in terms of four major phases: (1) generation of clinically useful knowledge; (2) prototype development; (3) testing; and (4) diffusion. The first phase can be equated with scientific and biomedical research, or in some cases with technological development outside of health care. The development phase may occur as part of the first or may involve a significant time lap (President's Biomedical Research Panel, 1976a). Testing in the clinical environment is likely to be concurrent with development activities to some extent. Diffusion represents the final phase in which a technology is adopted for nonexperimental use by individual or organizational decision makers.

The dependence of diffusion of new technology on the outcome of scientific and biomedical research has complicated the policy problems associated with the process. Two major strains of criticism appear to be in direct conflict with each other. The first is that the process of technological change has raised health care costs too high; the second is that the pitfalls in each step of the process of technical change render it extremely delicate and in need of assists at critical points, particularly in the research and development phase. The first criticism implies that too much technology is emerging from the process; the second that too little results.

The result of this schism is a spate of policy recommendations that on their face appear contradictory. Those whose focus and experience lie in the early phases of the process are extremely sensitive to the obstacles that must be overcome to reach the testing and diffusion phases and the high mortality rate of ideas and inventions along the way (see, for example, Anderson, 1976). Among the obstacles cited are biomedical research funding policies that bias the kinds of clinically useful knowledge that develop (RAND Corp., 1976); property rights policies that provide inadequate incentives to developers of new technologies (U.S. Federal Council for Science and Technology, 1975); the small size and disaggregated nature of the potential markets (National Research Council, 1976); inadequate networks for communicating the results of clinically useful research to the health care community (U.S. DHEW, 1977) and the host of regulatory processes required before new technologies can reach their markets (Noll, 1975).

Those whose primary concern is the cost of new technologies cite the failure of those who test new technologies to consider the important concepts of efficacy and effectiveness in a complete or consistent fashion (Hiatt, 1975); the willingness of hospital decision makers to serve as an easy market since they bear no risk if the technology proves to be inadequate or quickly outmoded (Brown, 1972); the apparent bias in the system toward the development of hospital technologies instead of ambulatory or home setting (Hiatt, 1975); and the lack of any responsibility for early assessment of the impact of new technologies on costs or effectiveness (Arnstein, 1976).

The first set of arguments would call for public policy to facilitate the development and diffusion of new technologies and the elimination of bureaucratic and regulatory barriers. The second set would imply the intensification of public efforts to shape and control the process through research funding and regulatory avenues. The recent passage of the medical device amendments, which will require significantly new devices to obtain clearance prior to entry in the market is an interesting example of the conflict. Critics cite the impact that new drug regulation has had on both the rate of introduction of these new technologies and the structure of the drug industry (U.S. Congress, 1973). Supporters point to the need for intervention in a field that poses ever increasing safety and efficacy questions, and to the savings that have resulted from the inability of unsafe or ineffective new drugs to reach the market.

The source of the conflict expressed in this context arises from the paucity of information now available about several critical aspects of the process of technical change. First, the empirical evidence on the impact that new technology has had on medical and social costs and effectiveness is fragmentary and inconclusive. We need to know the extent to which the process has worked inefficiently and whether new technologies have indeed raised costs as so many claim. Some recent research efforts have been devoted to this question. The results of that research are summarized in a subsequent section of this paper.

Second, we know very little about the way in which new medical technologies are developed. We do not even have a clear picture of who the developers are and what environments produce what kinds of technologies. The impact of government funding of biomedical research on the development of different kinds of technology is also unclear. The settings for development of different kinds of technology unquestionably vary. Considering the many different procedures, techniques, equipment, and systems that have come into being in the past ten years, it is reasonable to assume that the patterns of development among these will be highly varied. Research and development can occur in universities, hospitals, medical schools, large or small research and development laboratories, manufacturing firms, and even in physicians' offices; frequently, the process involves a combination of these settings. Although it is easy to theorize about the motivations of various kinds of participants in the development process, there is very little evidence to support a model to explain the determinants of technology development. The background studies commissioned by the President's Biomedical Research Panel (1976b) made a start in this direction, but they did not focus on the different kinds of developers and the differences among them. A frequently described model is the "advocacy" theory (Anderson, 1976). The individual scientist, engineer, or clinician has a strong personal faith in the value of his idea and mothers it through the paths of development. The success of a technology at least to the prototype state is said to be a function of the degree of advocacy it engenders as well as its usefulness. But we know so little about who actually does research and development and how they interact, that it is virtually impossible to diagnose failures in the development process.

Third, the evidence on how hospital decision makers adopt new medical technologies is scattered among several research disciplines with different approaches; consequently, the results are somewhat equivocal. It is important to identify not only the early adopters of new technologies and the time and spatial patterns of diffusion, but also how these factors differ among different classes of medical technologies. Unfortunately, the research has not looked directly at these questions; rather, individual studies have focused on a single technology or a specific type of hospital behavior, such as capital equipment purchases. Nevertheless, some tentative conclusions can be drawn from this literature. Indeed, there appears to be more systematic analysis of the process of medical technology diffusion than of any other important policy-related question in the area. The major findings of the literature on this question are summarized in a subsequent section.

The Economic Costs of New Technology

A number of studies have attempted to estimate the economic impacts of new technology. These studies measure different concepts of cost, including hospital costs, total costs of medical care, and net social costs. They also vary in the operational definition of technological change. These variations render objective comparison difficult; nevertheless, the results do provide some insight into the relation between technology and health care costs.

In a study of the impact of new technology on the cost of hospital care, Davis (1974) used data from approximately 200 non-profit hospitals for the period 1962 to 1968. Using time as a proxy for technological change, Davis found that when demand and supply variables had been taken into account, hospital expenses per admission rise about 2 percent annually. The time trend variable is an imperfect proxy since it also includes effects due to gradual changes that influence demand, including changing attitudes about hospital care, improved methods of ambulatory care, or other changes in behavior over time that are not accounted for by explicit variables in her model. Davis suggests that the time estimate provides an upper limit for an estimate of the effect of technological change on hospital costs, but the other influences represented by the time variable could have had a negative effect, leading to an understatement of technology's effect on hospital costs.

Several researchers have studied the impact of technical change on total medical care costs. Mushkin et al. (1976) analyzed the total impact of biomedical research on health expenditures from 1930 to 1975. Using a time residual as a proxy for biomedical advances, they found that this factor was responsible for an annual reduction in total health expenditures of 0.5 percent. This result compared favorably with a twenty-year study by Fuchs (1972), which found that technology and biomedical change had a positive residual effect on total health care expenditures in the amount of 0.6 percent annually. The difference in these studies may be attributable to differences in the study periods (Fuchs' study compared the years 1947 to 1967) and to other effects included in the studies. These longitudinal studies include the effects on medical care costs of the significant advances in the treatment of communicable diseases during the period under study. They also include the net effect of shifting disease patterns of the population. Thus, the relatively favorable outcome with respect to the role of technology and biomedical research over the entire study period obscures some of the changes in the health of Americans. The pattern of cost changes in the recent past may not be consistent with long-run trends.

Scitovsky and McCall (1975) have analyzed the changes in cost of medical care associated with selected illnesses. Between 1964 and 1971, the net increase in the average cost of treatment of an episode of illness was calculated for eight conditions: otitis media; forearm fractures; appendicitis; maternity care; cancer of the breast; pneumonia; duodenal ulcer; and myocardial infarction. In almost every instance, there were cost-raising and cost-saving changes in treatment. However, Scitovsky and McCall noted that "the costs of treatment of conditions requiring hospitalization rose at a considerably faster rate than those of conditions treated on an ambulatory basis" (p. 15). Cost-raising sources were found to include shifts to more expensive drugs, an increase in the number of laboratory tests per case, and an increase in the number of miscellaneous inpatient and outpatient services. However, the most dramatic cost increases occurred in the treatment of myocardial infarction; these changes were traced principally to the increasing use of intensive care units. Thus, we see that sources of medical cost increases reflect an epidemiological shift from diseases requiring outpatient to those requiring inpatient care, and a shift of setting of care within the hospital from less specialized services to more specialized units. Unfortunately, the analysis does not permit any comparison of cost-increasing conditions with cost-decreasing conditions because of the selected nature of the conditions considered. Combined with Mushkin's results, these findings show that the ultimate impact of technological change on medical care costs is not clearly cost-increasing. A more selective approach to analysis is required. Cooper (1976) has observed that the important policy issues lie not in the total impact of technological change across all diagnoses and settings of care but in the misallocation of resources in whatever settings they occur. However, if the overall effect of the introduction of technology does not clearly lead to inordinate increases in the cost of medical care, then the impact of an elaborate system to control the introduction of new technologies may not be worth the administrative costs involved.

Although the application of benefit-cost analysis to health programs has a long history (see Klarman, 1974), only one study has attempted to measure the "social" costs of a broad class of technological developments. This study, by Orloff (1976), estimated the net contribution to medical and nonmedical social costs of research in surgery over the study period. Using the life-cycle earnings approach to valuation of changes in morbidity and mortality, this study found that the most significant research contributions had resulted in a net saving of $2.8 billion for the year 1970. The study suffers from the bias of dealing only with selected surgical advances, but there was some attempt to consider the leading advances in the period under study as identified by a panel of surgeons. It is possible that the surgical advances not considered would have shown systematic increases in hospitalization and total social costs.

Although the studies described here represent significant advances in the economics of technological change in medical care, they fall short of providing policy guidance. New technologies appear to be raising hospital costs, but it is not altogether clear that these increases are not offset by savings in other sectors of the health care delivery system or by nonmedical benefits to society.

A major problem with these analyses is the lack of a normative base for comparison. The real question is not how much total health care costs increased or decreased, but how far that change differed from what would be possible under an ideal system of technical change, that is, a system in which development and adoption decisions were made with full information and with the maximization of social benefits as the objective.

The Diffusion of New Hospital Technologies

In order to devise good policies to control the introduction of new technologies, it is necessary to know a great deal about how they find their way into hospitals and into the practice of medicine. What factors determine whether and when a hospital adopts a new technology? How do these factors differ among classes of hospital technologies? What are the characteristics of early adopters and of late adopters? How do they differ? What determines the speed with which new technologies are introduced? And, most important, how does the process diverge from patterns of diffusion that would occur in an ideal situation?

The literature offers answers to some of these questions but leaves the central question of the ultimate effectiveness of the diffusion process unanswered. What we do know must be synthesized from several independent bodies of research, representing different disciplines. Economists have studied the economic characteristics of the adopting unit and the new technology; sociologists have studied the attributes of organizations and individuals determining their propensity to adopt new technologies; political scientists have considered the political environment in which change takes place.

Definitional problems pose significant barriers to comparison of research studies. Not only do operational definitions vary because of constraints on data available to various researchers, but there are also basic conceptual differences in various approaches. In order to avoid confusion, we must define some terms commonly used in this literature. First, the adoption of a new technology refers to a decision by an adopting unit (defined as an individual or organization) to make use of the technology's capability. Adoption is often confused with utilization of a new technology. For many hospital technologies, adoption is synonymous with the purchase or lease of equipment, construction of a facility, or decision to offer a new service. When, however, the adopting unit is likely to be the physician (as is the case with new drugs or surgical procedures not requiring extraordinary equipment), then adoption cannot be easily distinguished from the first use of the technology. Because so many hospital technologies require a decision to make capital expenditures, the determination of whether and when a hospital has adopted a new technology is often based on the time of the commitment of capital resources.

Diffusion refers to the pattern of adoption decisions over time and sometimes space. The diffusion process is often expressed as the number of units adopting a new technology as a function of the time or distance from its first availability on the market. Diffusion studies often differentiate early adopters from late adopters and attempt to characterize them. The time path of adoption of new medical technologies may be either too fast or too slow depending on the real social value of the change.

Many studies focus on the determinants of "innovation" by individuals or organizations. Innovation is defined as the first use of a product or program by a given adoption unit.[4] The adoption of a new technology is, then, one kind of innovation possible within the hospital. Innovations can include program or organizational changes

<hr>

[1]See Mohr (1969) for a discussion of alternative definitions of innovation.

as well. Much of the literature on innovation in health care organizations has involved the study of these nontechnological innovations. Using these studies to make inferences about the determinants of technological innovations may be dangerous, as the external validity of such studies across innovation types has not been demonstrated in the literature.

Economic studies of technological diffusion outside of health care have provided empirical support for the hypothesis that the rate of innovation is a function of the profitability of the innovation and the resources required for adoption relative to the size of the firms in the industry (see Mansfield, 1961, 1968). To apply these findings to technological innovation in health care, it would be necessary to redefine "profitability" to be more consistent with the objectives of hospitals. In fact, it is the generalization of this concept that most studies of the diffusion of medical technologies address. Substitutes for profitability must be found to explain differences in the way that particular technologies are adopted by hospitals. As discussed above, these substitutes are most often postulated to be some combination of quantity and quality of services provided by the hospital, where quality may be perceived in different ways by hospital decision makers. Economic studies of diffusion of hospital technologies relate adoption of specific technologies to variables believed to be related to these objectives and to the resources available to the hospital.

In a recent study of nuclear medicine facilities, Rapoport (1976) used statewide data to regress the speed of diffusion over different time periods against a number of factors, including the ratio of the state's population in urban centers, state income, availability of physicians, hospital size, percent of hospitals affiliated with medical schools, and the variation in size among hospitals. Depending on the time period under study, these variables explained between 50 and 75 percent of the total variation in diffusion rates across states. The most interesting result was the strong negative relationship between the medical school affiliation variable and the diffusion rate in all time periods. Rapoport offers the explanation that in areas with many affiliated hospitals, which acquired nuclear medicine early, the nonaffiliated groups may not have considered themselves capable of competing in this arena and thus did not adopt this new technology as rapidly as hospitals in states with few such medical school affiliations. Thus, regionalization of this service may have occurred by default.

Cromwell et al. (1975) have studied the relationship between the existence of particular high technology facilities in a state and a number of explanatory variables. Their results show that the diffusion of equipment-intensive hospital services such as intensive care units, open heart surgery, x-ray therapy, cobalt therapy, radium therapy, diagnostic radioisotope, and therapeutic radioisotope services is significantly and positively related to per capita income, age, total per capita number of physicians in the state, the ratio of specialists to total physicians, and for certain facilities, the existence of a certificate-of-need law.

Studies of innovation in health care organizations have related adoption of innovations to factors such as organizational size, wealth, or access to resources; organizational structure; the nature of the environment facing the organization; and attributes or attitudes of individual decision makers within the organization. In a study of respiratory therapy technologies, Gordon et al. (1974) showed that innovation in hospitals is a function of several structural characteristics of the organization, including the degree of decentralization of decision making, the visibility of consequences of medical care within the organization, and the complexity of the medical staff resources of the hospital. This study looked only at respiratory therapy services which were judged by an expert panel to be elements of "good" medical care. Whether these factors would remain important as determinants of adoption of technologies of questionable efficacy is uncertain; the study also failed to include any technologies requiring substantial capital resources.

Resource availability has surfaced as the leading determinant of innovation in health departments and other public health agencies (see Gordon and Fisher, 1975). Studies of innovations in these agencies have concentrated on program changes rather than on the adoption of new medical technologies; therefore, their external validity for the adoption of medical technology in hospitals is suspect. However, evidence from the economics literature tends to support this finding. In a study of capital expenditure decisions by hospitals, Ginsburg (1972) showed that the availability of capital funds and hospital size were important determinants of the overall level of capital investment, whereas composition of investment depended on demand factors. In a more recent study of capital equipment expenditure decisions by fifteen hospitals, in the greater Boston area, Cromwell et al. (1975) found that larger hospitals spend proportionately more on capital equipment than smaller hospitals, but the relationship between capital expenditures and the availability of financial resources was found to be insignificant.

Taken together, these studies show that hospitals are likely to adopt new technologies when they are large, complex, and wealthy institutions. Medical centers and teaching hospitals can be expected to be the early adopters of new technologies, although there is no information on how well these early adopters differentiate between "good" and "bad" technologies.

The diffusion literature has provided virtually no information on the channels of communication responsible for the dissemination of information on new technologies. What role early adopters such as medical schools play compared with suppliers in communicating information on new technologies has not been studied. Nor have researchers studied at what stage in the process of diffusion new technologies become standards of medical practice, virtually guaranteeing their ultimate penetration of the health care system. The impact of the emergence of health planning and concepts of regionalization on different patterns has also not been assessed.

If, as one might expect, medical centers offering a full array of services and training are the early adopters of new medical technologies, followed by the rest of the hospitals, then it would be useful to focus policy development on these units. The impact of recent experimental reimbursement policies on adoption decisions may be perverse. Many hospital prospective reimbursement systems group hospitals according to certain characteristics for the purposes of rate setting. Often these include teaching status, bed size, case mix, or "service intensity." By so doing, these formulas are likely to compare the costs of early adopters with one another and thus ensure the continued resource availability to future adoption of new technologies by these hospitals. As other groups of hospitals respond to the new standards of medical practice developed in these centers, their costs get pulled upward as well.

Conclusion

The one clear implication of this discussion is that there are major gaps in what we know about the real impact of hospital technologies, new or existing, on social costs and benefits. We do not fully understand the nature of the development process, nor do we know how sensitive that process is to changes in the health care delivery or financing system.

This lack of knowledge does reveal that there needs to be increasing federal attention paid to the generation of valid information on the efficacy of medical procedures, particularly those involving the use of new and existing "sophisticated" services (that is, capital-intensive, equipment-oriented, requiring a high level of staff capabilities). That such information is not currently generated is reflected in our inability to determine the extent to which the hospital industry makes appropriate adoption decisions. We do not even know to what extent we are wasting our health care dollars on relatively ineffective but technically sophisticated services.

In the long run, the problem facing policy makers will be where on the trade-off curve between health care costs and benefits we should be and how to ration the availability of expensive technologies whose benefits are clear. To date, we have shown that the health care system as it works today cannot ration such technologies effectively (witness the renal dialysis program). Up to now we may have wasted resources, but we have been able to offer the benefits of new technologies to an ever wider class of beneficiaries. In the future, we may not be able to do so.

Refernces

Anderson, N.
1976   "Critical steps in the development of new health technology."
        Paper prepared for the Conference on Health Care Technology

and Quality of Care, Boston University, November 19–20, 1976. Boston: Boston University, Program on Public Policy for Quality Health Care.

Arnstein, S.
1976   Statement by Sherry Arnstein, Senior Fellow, Intramural Research Section, National Center for Health Services Research, U.S. DHEW, at the Conference on Health Care Technology and Quality of Care, Boston University, November 19–20, 1976. Boston: Boston University Program on Public Policy for Quality Health Care.

Banta, H.D., and B.J. McNeil
1977   "The costs of medical diagnosis: The case of the CT scanner." Photocopy. Washington, D.C., Office of Technology Assessment.

Bogue, T., and S.M. Wolfe
1976   "CAT scanners: Is fancier technology worth a billion dollars of health consumers' money?" Washington, D.C.: Health Research Group.

Brown, R.E.
1972   "Managing the mushrooming growth of America's hospital system." In Regulating the Hospital, a report of the 1972 National Forum on Hospital and Health Affairs. Durham, N.C.: Department of Health Administration of Duke University.

Cochrane, A.L.
1972   Effectiveness and Efficiency: Random Reflections on Health Services. London: The Nuffield Provincial Hospitals Trust.

Cooper, B.
1976   Statement by Barbara Cooper, Office of Research and Statistics, Social Security Administration, at the Conference on Health Care Technology and Quality of Care, Boston University, November 19–20, 1976. Boston: Boston University Program on Public Policy for Quality Health Care.

Cromwell, J., et al.
1975   Incentives and Decisions Underlying Hospitals; Adoption and Utilization of Major Capital Equipment. Cambridge, Mass.: Abt Associates.

Davis, K.
1974   "The role of technology, demand and labor markets in the determination of hospital costs." In Mark Perlman, ed., The Economics of Health and Medical Care. New York: John Wiley & Sons.

DeBakey, M.E., and H.W. Hiatt
  1976   "Medical technology: How much is enough?" In Proceedings of
          the National Leadership Conference on America's Health Policy.
          Washington, D.C.: National Journal.

Ellwood, P.M., Jr.
  1975   "Alternatives to regulation: Improving the market." In Institute
          of Medicine, Controls on Health Care. Washington, D.C.: Na-
          tional Academy of Sciences.

Feldstein, M.S.
  1976   Quality Change and the Demand for Hospital Care. Discus-
          sion Paper No. 475, Harvard Institute of Economic Research,
          Cambridge, Mass.

Feldstein, M.S., and A. Taylor
  1977   "The rapid rise of hospital costs." Discussion Paper No. 531,
          Harvard Institute of Economic Research, Cambridge, Mass.

Fuchs, V.
  1972   Essays on the Economics of Health and Medical Care. New
          York: Columbia University Press.

Gaus, C.R.
  1975   "What goes into technology must come out in costs." Excerpt
          from testimony of the Social Security Administration before the
          President's Biomedical Research Panel, September 29, 1975, in
          The National Leadership Conference on America's Health Pol-
          icy. Washington, D.C.: National Journal.

Gaus, C.R., and B.S. Cooper
  1976   "Technology and Medicare: Alternatives for change." Paper
          prepared for the Conference on Health Care Technology and
          Quality of Care, Boston University, November 19-20, 1976.
          Boston: Boston University, Program on Public Policy for Quality
          Health Care.

Gellman, D.D.
  1971   "The price of progress: Technology and the cost of medical
          care." Canadian Medical Association Journal 104 (March 6):
          401–406.

Ginsburg, P.B.
  1972   "Resource allocation in the hospital industry: The role of capital
          financing." Social Security Bulletin 35 (August): 20–30.

Gordon, G., and G.L. Fisher, eds.
  1975   The Diffusion of Medical Technology. Cambridge, Mass.: Bal-
          linger Publishing Co.

Gordon, G., et al.
1974   "Organizational structure, environmental diversity and hospital adoption of medical innovations." In A.D. Kaluzny, J.T. Gentry, and J.E. Veney, eds., Innovations in Health Care Organizations: An Issue in Organizational Change. Chapel Hill, N.C.: School of Public Health, University of North Carolina.

Grimes, R.M., and S.K. Moseley
1976   "An approach to an index of hospital performance." Health Services Research 11 (Fall): 294.

Hiatt, H.H.
1975   "Protecting the medical 'commons'—who has the responsibility?" The New England Journal of Medicine 293 (July): 235–241.

Klarman, H.E.
1974   "Application of cost-benefit analysis to health systems technology." In Morris F. Collen, ed., Technology and Health Care Systems in the 1980's. DHEW Publication No. HRA-74-3016. Rockville, Md.: National Center for Health Services Research and Development.

Lalonde, M.
1972   A New Perspective on the Health of Canadians: A Working Document. Ottawa: Government of Canada.

McKeown, T.
1976   The Role of Medicine. London: The Nuffield Provincial Hospitals Trust.

Mansfield, E.
1961   "Technical change and the rate of imitation." Econometrica 29 (October): 741–766.

1968   Industrial Research and Technological Innovation: An Econometric Analysis. New York: W.W. Norton & Co., Inc.

Mohr, L.B.
1969   "Determinants of innovation in organizations." American Political Science Review 63 (March): 111–126.

Mushkin, S.J., L.C. Paringer, and M.M. Chen
1976   "Returns to biomedical research 1900–1975: An initial assessment of impacts on health expenditures." Photocopy. Washington, D.C.: Georgetown University, Public Services Laboratory.

National Research Council
1976   Science and Technology in the Service of the Physically Handicapped. National Research Council, Assembly of Life Sciences, Division of Medical Sciences, Committee on National Needs for

the Rehabilitation of the Physically Handicapped. Washington,
D.C.: National Academy of Sciences.

Newhouse, J.P.
1970 "Toward a theory of nonprofit institutions: An Economic Model
of a hospital." American Economic Review 60 (March): 64-74.

Noll, R.G.
1975 "The consequences of public utility regulation of hospitals." In
Institute of Medicine, Controls on Health Care. Washington,
D.C.: National Academy of Sciences.

Orloff, M.J.
1976 "Contributions of research in surgical technology to health care."
Paper prepared for the Conference on Health Care Technology
and Quality of Care, Boston University, November 19-20, 1976.
Boston: Boston University, Program on Public Policy for Quality
Health Care.

Perrow, C.
1965 "Hospitals: Technology, structure, and goals." In J.G. March,
ed., Handbook of Organizations. Chicago: Rand McNally.

President's Biomedical Research Panel
1976a Report of the President's Biomedical Research Panel, Appendix
B: Approaches to Policy Development for Biomedical Research:
Strategy for Budgeting and Movement from Invention to Clinical Application. DHEW Publication No. (OS) 76-502. Washington, D.C.: Government Printing Office.
1976b Report of the President's Biomedical Research Panel, Supplement 1: Analysis of Selected Biomedical Research Programs:
Case Histories. DHEW Publication No. (OS) 76-506. Washington, D.C.: Government Printing Office.

Rabkin, M.T., and C.N. Melin
1976 "The impact of technology upon the cost and quality of hospital
care, and a proposal for control of new and expensive technology." Background paper prepared for the Conference on Health
Care Technology and Quality of Care, Boston University,
November 19-20, 1976. Boston: Boston University, Program on
Public Policy for Quality Health Care.

RAND Corporation
1976 "Policy Analysis for Federal biomedical research." In President's
Biomedical Research Panel, Appendix B: Approaches to Policy
Development for Biomedical Research: Strategy for Budgeting
and Movement from Invention to Clinical Application. Washington, D.C.: Government Printing Office.

Rapoport, J.
1976   "Diffusion of technological innovation in hospitals: A case study of nuclear medicine." Photocopy. South Hadley, Mass.: Mount Holyoke College.
Rushmer, R.F.
1976   "The technological imperative." Editorial, American Journal of Roentgenology 127 (August): 356–357.
Russell, L.B.
1976   "Making rational decisions about medical technology." Paper presented at the National Commission on the Cost of Medical Care, November 23, 1976, Chicago, Ill. Photocopy. Washington, D.C.: L.B. Russell.
Russell, L.B., and C.S. Burke
1975   Technological Diffusion in the Hospital Sector. Washington, D.C.: National Planning Association.
Salkever, D.S., and T.W. Bice
1976   "The impact of certificate-of-need controls on hospital investment." Milbank Memorial Fund Quarterly/Health and Society 54 (Spring): 185–214.
Schwartz, William
1976   Statement by William Schwartz, Vannevar Bush University Professor, Tufts University School of Medicine, at the Conference on Health Care Technology and Quality of Care, Boston University, November 19–20, 1976. Boston: Boston University, Program on Public Policy for Quality Health Care.
Scitovsky, A.A., and N. McCall
1975   Changes in the Costs of Treatment of Selected Illnesses 1951–1964–1971. San Francisco: Health Policy Program, University of California School of Medicine.
U.S. Congress
1973   Senate, Select Committee on Small Business, Subcommittee on Monopoly, Present Status of Competition in the Pharmaceutical Industry: Hearings. 93d Congress, 1st Session, February 5–8 and March 14, 1972. Washington, D.C.: Government Printing Office.
U.S. Congress, Office of Technology Assessment
1976a   Development of Medical Technology: Opportunities for Assessment. Washington, D.C.: Government Printing Office.
1976b   The Computerized Tomography (CT or CAT) Scanner and Its Implications for Health Policy. Draft. Washington, D.C.

Judith L. Wagner and Michael Zubkoff

U.S. Department of Health, Education, and Welfare
  1976   Public Health Service, Forward Plan for Health: FT 1978–82.
          DHEW Publication No. (OS) 76-50046. Washington, D.C.:
          Government Printing Office.
  1977   National Institute of Health, "The responsibilities of NIH at the
          Health Research/Health Care interface." Draft. Bethesda, Md.:
          National Institute of Health.
U.S. Federal Council for Science and Technology
  1975   Executive Subcommittee of the Committee on Government
          Patent Policy, University Patent Policy Ad Hoc Subcommittee,
          Report. Photocopy.
Waldman, S.
  1972   The Effect of Changing Technology on Hospital Costs. Research
          and Statistics Note No. 4, DHEW Publication No. (SSA) 72-
          11701 (February 28).
Weiner, S.M.
  1976   "State regulation and health technology." Paper prepared for the
          Conference on Health Care Technology and Quality of Care,
          Boston University, November 19–20, 1976. Boston: Boston Uni-
          versity, Program on Public Policy for Quality Health Care.
White, K.L., J.H. Murnaghan, and C.R. Gaus
  1972   "Technology and health care." The New England Journal of
          Medicine 287 (December): 1223–1227.
Worthington, N.L.
  1975   "Expenditures for hospital care and physicians' services: Factors
          affecting annual changes." Social Security Bulletin 38 (Novem-
          ber): 3–15.

III Hospitals and the Diffusion Process

Innovation of Health Services:
A Comparative Study of Hospitals
and Health Departments

ARNOLD D. KALUZNY

JAMES E. VENEY

JOHN T. GENTRY

This paper investigates the differential contribution of various organizational variables affecting the innovation of high-risk versus low-risk health service programs in two types of health care organizations: hospitals and health departments. It was found that variables are differentially related to both the type of program and the type of organization. Organizational size was a critical factor in program innovation as it relates to high-risk services in hospitals and low-risk services in health departments. Excluding size, characteristics of the staff, such as cosmopolitan orientation and training, were prime predictors for both high- and low-risk programs in health departments and low-risk programs in hospitals. The degree of formalization was the primary predictor of innovation of high-risk programs in hospitals. Cosmopolitan orientation of the administrator was a critical factor in the innovation of high-risk programs in both hospitals and health departments.

The assessment of change in health care organizations, and particularly program innovation, has received increasing attention by social scientists. Using a wide range of explanatory variables, research, with few exceptions, has tended to concentrate on explaining variation in the innovation of a single program or that of aggregate change. For a review of these studies see Kaluzny (1972). While this represents progress, it is important to consider two underlying problem areas. First, it is necessary to inquire into the general area of programmatic change and whether factors associated with program innovation differ by type of program innovated. Essentially, this exploration involves assessment of a set of services and activities that have common characteristics, making possible generalization from known determinants of innovation of one program to other programs with similar characteristics. Secondly, explanation of differences by type of organization is necessary to provide insight into the specific organizational setting under which

M M F Q / Health and Society / *Winter 1974*

various factors are most appropriate. Thus, the introduction of a comparative study of organizational innovation permits an assessment of the generalizability of findings and provides an evaluation of the impact of organizational variables on concrete operational programs. Insight into these aspects is critical to the development of effective intervention strategies that may be used systematically to administer organizational innovation.

In an attempt to address these problems, the present study will provide a comparative analysis of organizational factors affecting the innovation of selected health services with a specific set of characteristics in two types of health care organizations: hospitals and health departments. The objective is to assess the differential contribution of organizational variables relating to the innovation of selected health services with specific characteristics as implemented within and between hospitals and health departments. To meet this objective, two specific questions are examined. First, is there a difference in organizational variables which accounts for innovation of services having different characteristics? Second, are there differences between organizational variables for hospitals as one type of health care organization and those for health departments as a distinctively different type of health care organization?

Method

Data for the study are based on questionnaires and interviews conducted in all organized county and city health departments in New York State excluding New York City ($n = 23$) and a sample of general acute hospitals ($n = 59$) located in the respective health department jurisdictions. Within each health department jurisdiction at least two hospitals were selected, unless only one hospital was available. The selection of hospitals was based on their innovative status and number of beds. Hospitals with three or more of the six program areas under study were considered innovative; all other hospitals were considered low innovators. Hospitals in each of the two innovation groups were further classified into those with more than 500 beds and those with 500 or fewer beds. Final selection of hospitals included all high-innovation hospitals regardless of number of beds and all hospitals of over 500 beds regardless of innovative status. One-fourth of the low-innovator hospitals with 500 or fewer beds were randomly selected. These hospitals were evenly divided on the basis of whether they had more or fewer than 300 beds.

Within sample organizations, four sets of respondents were selected. For hospitals, the list included (a) the administrator, (b) assistant-associate administrators and all department heads, (c) executive directors of the boards of trustees and a randomly selected sample of trustees, (d) chairmen of medical staff and a sample of physicians on the staff of the respective hospitals. For health departments, the respondents included (a) the director of the health department, (b) deputy and all department heads, (c) executive officers of the board of health and a sample of board members, and (d) a sample of staff public health nurses. Non-professionals and non-supervisory personnel were excluded because they were less directly involved in decision-making processes within the organization.

Administrators of both organizations were interviewed. In addition, questionnaires were sent to all personnel including the administrator. For hospitals, responses were received from 48 administrators (81 percent), 343 associate and assistant administrators and department heads (85 percent), 529 physicians (61 percent), and 366 hospital trustees (70 percent). In health departments, responses were received from 23 health officers (100 percent), 112 department heads (89 percent), 96 members of boards of health (61 percent), and 176 public health nurses (82 percent). Analysis of data from hospitals and health departments excluded from this analysis and non-respondents from within participating organizations indicates that the non-participants are not significantly different from organizations and respondents that did participate in the study.

Within participating organizations, attention focuses on the innovation of selected health services and activities associated with six program areas: home health, family planning, rehabilitation, mental health, medical social work, and chronic-disease screening. The specific services within each program area are shown in Table 1. These services were selected because of their association with the comprehensiveness and continuity of community health services. As the table indicates, the most commonly provided service for hospitals is physical therapy within a rehabilitation program, and, for health departments, home nursing within home health programs. Less commonly provided services for both hospitals and health de-

TABLE 1

Proportion of Hospitals and Health Departments
Implementing Services and Activities

Services and Activities	Proportion of Hospitals Implementing	Proportion of Health Departments Implementing
Home health		
Social services	11.7	20.9
Home nursing	9.6	66.3
Physician services (for coordination and planning of patient care)	7.7	28.8
Homemaker or health aide	5.4	43.4
Home-delivered food	2.3	1.5
Transportation	5.4	7.3
Patient care conferences	7.1	43.4
Physical therapy	11.9	51.7
Speech therapy	5.2	25.4
Family planning		
Provision as separate entity	11.7	41.5
Provision in conjunction with other services	20.2	43.4
Case-finding activities	14.2	26.3
Systematic follow-up procedures	13.3	49.8
Community case-finding activities using indigenous workers	4.6	28.8
Rehabilitation		
Routine evaluation of all patients	20.8	23.9
Standard nursing procedures	38.3	42.4
Physical therapy	67.9	41.5
Occupational therapy	31.7	16.6
Speech and hearing therapy	27.5	32.2
Mental health		
Outpatient diagnostic and treatment	26.3	23.4
Inpatient diagnostic and treatment	40.6	7.3
Use of indigenous workers for case-finding and information dissemination	8.5	8.8
Integration with other health services	20.8	36.7
Follow-up care after hospitalization	20.0	44.9
Medical social work		
Psychological and social consultation	29.6	22.9
Information and referral	42.7	29.3
Predischarge planning (hospitals)	40.0	
Assist families with legal problems (health departments)		7.3
Chronic disease screening		
Cervical cytology	36.3	53.7
Ocular tonometry for glaucoma	18.9	26.8
EKG cardiac anomaly	17.3	11.7
Multiple blood chemistry	36.0	19.5
Self-administered health questionnaire	4.8	5.9

partments are generally within the home care programs, with home-delivered food the least commonly provided.

Organizational Innovation

In using the concept of innovation, a number of alternatives have been considered for the classification of the dependent variable, i.e., degree of innovativeness of the organizations under study. Most of the classification schemes have various shortcomings. The least complex score which has been used with these data is classification of organizations on a scale of innovativeness using a simple sum of the 32 study services provided by each organization while controlling for the date of innovation. If innovation is considered as the simple adoption of services, the more services adopted the more innovative is the organization.

However, the gross services-provided score has several drawbacks. First is the fact that an organization providing a large number of services may have implemented them at some point in the fairly distant past but may not currently be undergoing substantial change. In essence, an organization, innovative in the past and hence receiving a high innovation score, may no longer be innovative. Another related problem is the difficulty of relating explanatory organizational variables based on cross-sectional data to retrospective data on innovation.

A partial solution to these problems has been to consider only programs implemented within the five-year period prior to the study in developing a score of innovation. This tends to limit the effect of extensive early adoption of services and also the possibility that early innovators may no longer be innovative. The use of data for the last five years does, however, produce one conceptual problem. Because a finite number of services are under consideration, some highly innovative organizations may have implemented all or most of the services prior to the five-year period and then moved off into other even more innovative areas which our data do not tap. A partial control for this possibility can be developed using the number of services provided at the beginning of the five-year period.

A second major difficulty in developing an index of innovation based on the 32 services under study is the diversity of the services. As Table 1 shows, a score based on the total 32 services combines a large number of fairly diverse activities. On the face of it, no logical reason exists to assume that homemaker services are comparable to routine cervical cytology, or that speech and hearing rehabilitation are comparable to family-planning case finding. A logical procedure for assuring a greater degree of consistency within an innovation score using the 32 services is to generate a score for each of the six program areas. Such scores, however, seem unsatisfactory for two reasons. On the one hand, services such as family-planning case finding and mental-health case finding may have more in common with one another than with other family-planning or mental-health services. Speech therapy within the home and in-hospital speech therapy, family-planning case finding and mental-health case finding, or integration of either family-planning services or mental-health services with other routine activities of the institution represent similar examples. Consequently, it is difficult even to evaluate the meaning of specific program scores.

At the same time, the services under study do not represent an exhaustive list of activities or services a health establishment might provide. Despite the fact that a real effort has been made to include all services considered to be critical to the successful operation of the six program areas, a legitimate case might be made for other services, or, indeed, for other programs as the focus of study in innovation. Because specific services analyzed leave little potential for generalization to other unstudied services and little potential for discussing the attributes or underlying commonalities of services rather than the services themselves, a means must be found to classify services on some logical basis relative to the nature or effect on the organization.

Fliegel and Kivlin (1966), in a study of the adoption of innovative practices among farmers in the state of Pennsylvania, discuss a number of attributes of practices such as cost, payoff, social approval, and divisibility which may be used to describe such practices. Using judgments by various experts about the attributes of farm practices, they are able to find high correlations between the attributes of a particular practice and the degree of adoption of that practice.

Drawing on the work of Fliegel and Kivlin, a set of potential attribute categories was devised. To arrive at a rating for each of these attributes, a group of judges, all having relevant administrative experience, was asked to rate each of the 32 health care services under study on a set of 10 nine-point scales. The 10 attributes, their definition, the overall mean rating and standard error for both hospitals and health departments are shown in Table 2. While the specifics are discussed in a previous paper (Kaluzny and Veney, 1973), Table 2 shows that the ratings for both hospitals and health departments are quite similar for all attributes. The two possible exceptions are rate of cost recovery where the mean differs by as much as the standard error of the hospital measure, and association with the major activities of the enterprise where the mean differs by half of the standard error. The standard errors of the ratings for both hospitals and health departments are also relatively similar with the exceptions being in initial cost, continuing cost, and social approval where there was slightly more variation among the services for health departments than for hospitals.

For the purposes of this paper the question is whether attribute judgments for each service can be used to classify services into logically related categories. A factor analysis, carried out for each of the 32 services and the mean value of all judgments on the ten attributes, produced two major factors for both hospitals and health departments. The respective factor loadings for the 32 services are shown in Table 3 along with the proportion of variance accounted for by both factors.

Analysis of the two separate factors for hospitals and health departments reveals some interesting characteristics. When the mean attribute score for services with high factor loadings on each factor was compared to the mean attribute score for services with low factor loadings, a pattern emerged. The mean attribute judgment appears in Table 4. Those services which generate high factor loadings in factor 1 for hospitals tend to be judged low in initial and continuing costs and high in payoff, social approval, complexity, clarity of results, association with major activities, and pervasiveness. Those services which generate high factor loadings for factor 1 in health departments tend to be the same types of services as appeared for hospitals. At the same time, the attributes tend to remain quite similar. This includes low initial and continuing cost and high payoff, clarity of results, and association with major activities of the enterprise.

The comparison of mean attribute judgments of those services with high loadings on factor 2 in both hospitals and health departments produces almost a mirror image of factor 1, except for the fact that certain services load high on both factors and certain ones

TABLE 2

Mean and Standard Error of Attribute Ratings
for Hospitals and Health Departments

Attributes	Hospitals		Health Departments	
	$\bar{X}$	S.E.	$\bar{X}$	S.E.
Initial cost: cost to initiate the use of this particular service or activity in a hospital (health department)	4.96	1.00	4.80	1.40
Continuing cost: cost to provide this service or activity on a continuing basis within a hospital (health department)	5.48	0.87	5.39	1.10
Rate of cost recovery: length of time it takes to return the investment cost of implementing this service or activity in a hospital (health department)	4.68	0.52	5.20	0.65
Payoff: impact the service or activity has in terms of improving the quality and or continuity-comprehensiveness of overall services or activities provided in a hospital (health department)	7.11	0.71	7.00	0.71
Social approval: amount of increased community recognition gained by the hospital (health department) in providing this service or activity	6.30	0.71	6.45	1.01
Divisibility: feasibility of implementing part of the service or activity on a trial basis in a hospital (health department)	6.04	0.70	6.65	0.93
Complexity: ease with which the objectives of the service or activity can be explained or understood	6.55	0.62	6.58	0.74
Clarity of results: visibility of the implemented service or activity relative to objectives	6.34	0.83	6.46	0.79
Association with major enterprise of hospital (health department): degree to which service or activity has to do with direct patient care of the hospital/preventive services of health departments	6.71	1.00	7.18	1.00
Pervasiveness: degree to which the provision of this service or activity requires other changes in the hospital (health department)	5.98	0.74	5.58	0.64
Percentage which have service	20.46	15.14	28.95	16.17

TABLE 3

Factor Loadings for Each Study Service or Activity

SERVICE AND ACTIVITIES	HOSPITALS		HEALTH DEPARTMENTS	
	Column 1 Low Risk	Column 2 High Risk	Column 3 Low Risk	Column 4 High Risk
Home health				
Social services	.6924	.6117	*.6036	.5449
Home nursing	*.8747	.4560	*.9161	-.3048
Physician services (for coordination				
and planning of patient care)	*.8892	.3768	*.7632	.3571
Homemaker or health aide	.5922	*.7348	*.7341	.5235
Home-delivered food	.6230	.6401	.6313	.7259
Transportation	.7328	.6187	.6366	.7207
Patient care conferences	.2675	*.8741	-.0373	*.6466
Physical therapy	*.8229	.4714	*.9448	-.0312
Speech therapy	*.7629	.5629	*.8482	.4679
Family planning				
Provision as separate entity	*.8673	.4709	*.9201	-.0538
Provision in conjunction with other				
services	.5454	*.7770	*.6473	.4622
Case-finding activities	.3098	*.9123	.1274	*.8243
Systematic follow-up procedures	.2133	*.9580	.0015	.4164
Community case-finding activities				
using indigenous workers	.2616	*.8968	.0582	*.9100
Rehabilitation				
Routine evaluation of all patients	*.7374	.4794	.6837	.6179
Standard nursing procedures	.4674	.4555	.4772	.5733
Physical therapy	*.6320	-.4443	*.9673	.1100
Occupational therapy	*.8795	.2161	*.8429	.5136
Speech and hearing therapy	*.8564	.2660	*.9416	.3004
Mental health				
Outpatient diagnostic and treatment	*.9352	.1727	*.9287	.2581
Inpatient diagnostic and treatment	*.9261	.0122	*.8722	.3197
Use of indigenous workers for case-				
finding and information				
dissemination	.2895	*.8964	.1793	*.9646
Integration with other health services	.5597	*.7027	.5779	*.6697
Follow-up care after hospitalization	*.8355	.4388	*.8614	.3323
Medical social work				
Psychological and social consultation	*.8072	.3703	*.7862	.4376
Information and referral	4553	.4441	.3179	*.8265
Predischarge planning (hospitals)	.3702	.5295		
Assist families with legal problems				
(health departments)			.3549	*.8853
Chronic disease screening				
Cervical cytology	*.6957	.3589	*.8561	.0448
Ocular tonometry for glaucoma	*.7437	.5197	*.6413	.6110
EKG cardiac anomaly	*.8063	.4433	*.8670	.4751
Multiple blood chemistry	*.8466	.1661	*.8108	.5178
Self-administered health questionnaire	.0781	*.9538	-.0437	*.9375
Pct. Variance explained	82.0	13.7	73.5	18.9

* Indicates those services used in computation of high- and low-risk scores.

TABLE 4
Mean Attribute Ratings by Factor: High versus Low Loading

	HOSPITALS				HEALTH DEPARTMENTS			
	Factor 1		Factor 2		Factor 1		Factor 2	
	Loading		*Loading*		*Loading*		*Loading*	
	High	*Low*	*High*	*Low*	*High*	*Low*	*High*	*Low*
Initial cost	4.3 <	6.0	5.7 >	4.5	4.3 <	6.1	5.8 >	4.2
Continuing cost	4.9 <	6.3	6.2 >	5.0	5.0 <	6.5	6.3 >	4.9
Rate cost recovery	4.8	4.4	4.6	4.7	5.1	5.6	5.5	5.0
Payoff	7.4 >	6.7	6.5 <	7.5	7.0	7.0	6.9	7.1
Social approval	6.6 >	5.8	6.0	6.4	6.8 >	5.3	5.8 <	6.9
Divisibility	6.0	6.1	6.0	6.0	6.5	7.0	6.5	6.8
Complexity	6.8 >	6.2	6.1 <	6.8	6.7	6.3	6.4	6.7
Clarity of results	6.7 >	5.7	5.8 <	6.7	6.7 >	5.9	6.3	6.6
Association with major enterprise of hospital (health department)	7.2 >	5.8	5.8 <	7.2	7.4 >	6.5	6.5 <	7.6
Pervasiveness	6.3 >	5.4	5.4 <	6.3	5.6	5.5	5.3	5.7

load high on neither. In general, however, those programs which load high on factor 2 in hospitals are characterized by judgments of high initial and continuing cost, low payoff, low complexity, low clarity of results, low association with the major activities of the enterprise, and low pervasiveness; while in health departments, they are high on judgments of initial and continuing cost and low on social approval and association with the major activities of the enterprise.

Except for the fact that separate factors in this type of analysis are conceptually and statistically assumed to reflect different underlying dimensions, one is tempted to view the services with high loadings on the first factor as primarily low-risk services and those with high loadings on the second factor as high-risk services. Because a substantial proportion of the total variance is contained in factor 1, both for hospitals and health departments, this course takes on additional appeal. While any number of names could be devised to differentiate between factor 1 and factor 2 in each case, it was decided to consider the critical underlying dimension to be the judges' assessment of risk involved in attempting to provide the services. On the basis of this information, two separate measures of innovation were devised for hospitals and health departments.

The first measure for hospitals, the level of implementation of low-risk services (those services marked by asterisks in column 1, Table 3) is a summation of all such services, i.e., home nursing, home physician services, physical therapy, and so on, implemented by each hospital. The second measure for hospitals, the level of implementation of high-risk services (those marked by asterisks in column 2, Table 3) is a summation of all such services, i.e., homemaker, patient care conferences, implemented by each hospital. Similar measures were constructed for health departments using data from columns 3 and 4 of Table 3. Those services with high loadings on both factors were eliminated from consideration as well as those with low loadings, in order to avoid confounding the results.

In accepting these measures of organizational innovation, there is some concern that organizations which had implemented numerous services prior to the last five years would be limited in the amount of innovation they would be able to record in the last five-year period simply because of the limit on the number of programs under study. If, for example, the organization had innovated most of the study services prior to the last five-year period, it would not be able to obtain a high innovation score by the measure being used no matter how innovative the organization actually was during the more recent period. By the same token, an organization having done nothing prior to the last five-year period could potentially implement a number of services during the last five-year period and be classified as highly innovative.

Consequently, before accepting the services implemented in the last five years as a measure of innovation, it was desirable to examine the relationship between that score and both an overall measure of innovation and a measure of the services provided by the organization prior to the last five years. An examination of these data, however, indicates that the measure of services implemented in the last five years as the innovation score is not artificially reduced by the finite limit to the number of services under study.

Table 5 shows the relationship between those services provided in the last five years and the total number of services provided as well as those services provided in the last five years as compared to those provided prior to the last five years. Only with

TABLE 5

Relationship of High- and Low-Risk Services of Hospitals and Health
Departments by Overall Innovation and Innovation Prior to the
Five-Year Study Period

| | INNOVATION WITHIN LAST FIVE YEARS | | | |
| | Health Departments | | Hospitals | |
	Low-risk	*High-risk*	*Low-risk*	*High-risk*
Overall innovation				
Low-risk	.717	—	.756	—
High-risk	—	.848	—	.901
Innovation prior to last five years				
Low-risk	0.48[a]	—	.138[a]	—
High-risk	—	.415 (.05)	—	.226[a]

[a] Not Significant

high-risk programs in health departments is there a significant correlation between those services provided in the last five years and those provided prior to the last five-year period. This correlation, moreover, is positive, which indicates that the more high-risk services provided prior to the last five years, the more such services an organization is likely to innovate within the most recent five-year period. This finding eliminates our initial concern that the finite number of services would reduce the number any organization could innovate over a five-year period relative to those begun prior to that period. Moreover, the relatively high correlations between total scores and the scores for the last five years, ranging from .901 for high-risk services within hospitals to .717 for low-risk services within health departments, lead to the conclusion that the finite number of services under study will not artificially decrease the innovation score assigned to any one organization. Thus, the number of services innovated in the last five years in each of these areas is the operating definition of innovation in this study.

Factors Influencing Organizational Innovation

Selection of the set of explanatory variables used in the analysis was guided by the Pugh et al. (1963) scheme of conceptually distinct

144

levels of analysis in the behavior of organizations: (1) context within which the organization is found, (2) organizational structure and function, (3) organizational composition, (4) individual personality and behavior. The last level for our purposes was specified as selected personality and behavioral aspects of the administrator of the hospital or the director of the local health department.

The findings of the major studies of organizational innovation were a second important influence in designating specific factors that might account for variation in the innovation of the respective programs in the two types of organizations. In fact, the empirical analysis reported in this paper was primarily oriented toward considering variables within the conceptual levels of analysis for which some theoretical and/or empirical evidence had alreay been elaborated.[1] Thus, the major emphasis is not only to replicate and test relationships where possible, but, more important, to assess the generalizability of these propositions and/or empirical evidence to the innovation of high- versus low-risk programs in hospitals and health departments.

Organizational Context. Pugh et al. (1963) posit that the socioeconomic context of the organization has primary influence on its structure and function and thus on its innovative activity. Two contextual variables are considered. Size of organization is important to any analysis of organizational innovation simply because it connotes a summary of factors that constitute various organizational resources, complexities, etc. However, there is less agreement as to which aspects of size are related to program innovation and to the differential relationships between type of organization and type of program. Mytinger (1968) finds various indices of health department size, e.g., number of staff, size of budget, and characteristics of the jurisdiction, strongly influencing the innovation of various types of health care programs. Contrariwise, Mohr (1969), in a similar assessment of program innovation in health departments, notes that resources available as a consequence of size have no impact on the proportion of total increase of resources devoted to instituting or expanding innovative health care services. In this

---

[1] Variables already eliminated because of the minimal contribution and/or high correlation with other variables include rule observation, hierarchy of authority, organizational member's values toward change, and professional activism and professional training of the administrator.

analysis, organizational size for hospitals was defined simply as the number of beds within the organization. For health departments, size was defined as the population within the department's jurisdiction. In both cases, we expect organizational size to be positively related to program innovation.[2]

Other contextual variables considered relevant and obviously part of the general composite of variables involved with size are resources and specifically organizational slack. The latter is defined as the existence of uncommitted money or manpower available to the organization (March and Simon, 1964). Although this variable has received limited empirical documentation within health care organizations (Mohr, 1969), the notion as presented by March and Simon suggests that if slack resources exist, various specializations arise with respect to commitment to new programs or program elaboration. Thus, to the extent that variation exists between organizations, the availability of slack resources may differentially influence the amount and type of program innovation.

Two different measures of slack are utilized relative to the type of organization. For hospitals, slack is measured by the ratio involving the number of assistant-associate administrators per bed. It is inferred that the larger the ratio the greater the slack. A comparable measure was not available for health departments; however, as an approximation for this type of organization, slack was measured by the ratio of dollars to population coverage.

Organizational Structure and Function. Organizational structure and function in this analysis include three variables: (a) centralization as defined by the degree of participation in organizational decision making;[3] (b) formalization as defined by the degree to which

[2] Data for hospitals were obtained from the 1969 Hospital Guide Issue. The size of health department jurisdiction was based on data available in the City-County Data Book (1968).

[3] The index of participation in decision making was based on the extent to which individuals indicated participation in decisions concerning the following items: (a) allocation of total organizational income, (b) adoption and implementation of new organization-wide programs and services, (c) development of formal affiliation with other organizations, (d) appointment and promotion of administrative personnel, (e) appointment of medical staff members, and (f) long-range planning for new hospital-wide programs and services. Response categories involved (a) considerable participation, (b) some participation, and (c) no participation. The data were obtained from all respondent groups in both types of organizations.

rules define the person's activity within the organization;[4] (c) perceived performance as defined by the membership's satisfaction with the ability of the organization to meet community health needs and with the organization's reputation in the community.[5]

Although no available data exist on a comparative assessment of these variables in different types of health care organizations or as they relate to programs having different characteristics, there is a fair amount of agreement that both centralization and formalization are negatively related to innovation. Hage and Aiken (1967), in their study of sixteen health and welfare organizations, find that a high degree of participation and low formalization are highly associated with a high rate of program change. Palumbo (1969), in his assessment of health departments, presents similar findings. In a study of a single innovation, i.e., adoption of new drugs in hospitals, Rosner (1968), using a measure comparable to formalization, finds a negative relationship between the degree to which members of the organization follow procedures specified by superiors and that of innovation.

There has been no empirical attention given to performance satisfaction as a factor in organizational innovation. However, following March and Simon (1964), performance satisfaction refers to the amount of satisfaction with the organization's achievement relative to its changing environment. The underlying theory is that the lower the satisfaction with the organization's performance, the

[4] Formalization was based on scales developed by Hall (1963) and was measured by the individual's response to two questions: (1) Are how things are done here left up to the person doing the job? (2) Do most people here make their rules on the job? Response categories involved (a) basically true, (b) basically false, and (c) no opinion. Data were obtained from the administrators, assistant/associate administrators, and all department heads in hospitals and from the director, deputy, all department heads, and a sample of staff public health nurses in health departments.

[5] Organizational reputation was measured by a single question with five response categories: "To the best of your knowledge, what kind of reputation does this hospital (health department) have in the community?" (1) excellent; (2) very good; (3) good; (4) fair; (5) poor. Perceived need was similarly measured: "On the whole, how well do you feel this hospital (health department) is meeting the needs of the community as compared to similar hospitals (health departments) in this area of the country?" (1) extremely well; (2) very well; (3) adequately; (4) not well enough; (5) poorly. For both questions responses were received for all respondent groups within the organization.

greater the probability that programs will be innovated in an attempt to increase the level of satisfaction.

Organizational Composition.[6] Two variables are presented under this category: cosmopolitan-local nature of the staff[7] and the degree of training.[8] Both of these may be considered as a measure of organizational complexity and as such present a direct relationship with the rate of program change (Hage and Aiken, 1967). Empirical data on both health departments and general health and welfare organizations suggest that both these measures have a positive association with program innovation (Mytinger, 1968; Mohr, 1969).

Characteristics of the Administrator. Two basic characteristics of the administrator are considered. The first involves his values toward change and in this sense represents an index of his ability to

[6] Organizational composition variables are what Lazarsfeld and Menzel (1961) term analytical properties of collectivities, i.e., properties of collectives which are obtained by performing some mathematical operation upon some property of each single member.

[7] Index of cosmopolitanism-localism was based on the extent to which individuals within respective respondent groups participated in various professional activities. In hospitals, trustees and administrative staff responded to the degree to which they participated in (a) American College of Hospital Administrators and (b) American Hospital Association. Physicians responded as to their activities in the American Medical Association. In health departments, the members of the board of health, department heads, and staff nurses responded as to their participation in the (a) American Public Health Association and (b) the New York State Public Health Association. Response categories involved (1) attend meetings regularly; (2) have presented paper at meetings; and (3) currently hold or have held office.

[8] We used an organizational complexity scale developed by Hage and Aiken (1967). The index was scored as follows: (a) an absence of training beyond a college degree and the absence of other professional training received a score of 0; (b) an absence of training beyond a college degree and the presence of other professional training received a score of 1; (c) a presence of training beyond a college degree and the absence of other professional training received a score of 2; (d) a presence of training beyond a college degree and the presence of other professional training received a score of 3. Data were obtained for all assistant-associate administrators including department heads in both hospitals and health departments.

accept new concepts and ideas.[9] The second variable is the extent to which the administrator is cosmopolitan in his orientation.[10] Studies which have included the administrator as a unit of analysis strongly support the inclusion of both these variables in any consideration of innovation. Becker (1970), for example, notes that more cosmopolitan administrators tend to be early adopters of programs classified as having high adaptive potential. Similarly, Kaplan (1967), in an assessment of aggregate change, notes that administrators who manifest psychological flexibility have a higher proportion of program innovation. Finally, Mytinger (1968), in his study of health departments, finds the cosmopolitan orientation of the administrator strongly associated with program innovation.

Data Analysis and Findings

Before launching into the analysis of the data, it is necessary to give special attention to organizational size as one of the major variables under study. Organizational size, which has been discussed previously, was measured in hospitals by the number of beds the hospital reported in our interview. The measure of size for health departments was considered to be the number of people within the geographical area served by the health department. In a number of previous analyses of data from a national survey of hospitals and

[9] Index of values toward change was based on scales developed by McClosky (1958). Four questions from the original nine-item scale were selected: (1) I prefer a practical man any time to a man with ideas; (2) if something has existed a long time, there is very likely much wisdom in it; (3) I'd want to know that something would really work before I would be willing to take a chance on it; (4) groups can live in harmony in this country without changing the system in any way. Respondents were asked to "agree" or "disagree" with each of these four items. An "agree" response is a conservative response.

[10] The administrator's cosmopolitan orientation was based on the degree to which he was involved in professional groups. For hospital administrators this involved the American Hospital Association and the American College of Hospital Administrators. For health department directors, this involved the Public Health Association and the New York State Public Health Association. The response categories were the same as those presented in footnote 7.

health departments (Veney et al., 1971) and the New York data, size, either as measured by beds or by population served, has shown itself to be an influential variable. However, some question exists as to whether size per se is a causal variable. Size by its very nature stands as a proxy for a number of other characteristics of the organization. Examining national data, it was found that size of the organization was highly correlated with such things as population density, region of the country, urban/rural locations, and even with mean income and education of the population.

In a simple stepwise multiple regression in which these types of variables are permitted to enter the equation in order of explained variance, size generally serves to eliminate most of the variance which may be attributed to the characteristics of the region in which the organization is located. At the other end of the spectrum, we also found size to be highly correlated with the characteristics of the organization's structure and characteristics of the personnel of that organization. In the data under study, size correlates more highly with overall innovation for both high- and low-risk services and for both organizations than does any other variable with the exception of staff training within the high-risk programs in health departments (refer to Tables 6–9).

Because we believe that size is essentially a proxy for other characteristics of the organization, there are two ways in which size might be viewed. Size can be considered first as essentially a prior causal variable which is in part largely a characteristic of the region of the country in which the organization is located. Thus, densely populated urban areas tend to produce larger hospitals and larger health departments, which in turn attract more capable administrators and more capable staff, and produce a structure which is more favorable and amenable to change. This view of size suggests that the effect of the other variables under study could not be evaluated until the variance attributable to size had been eliminated from the innovation score. Under this assumption, size is an essentially uncontrollable external constraint.

The alternative view of size is as an emergent variable. From this view, growth is a part of the whole host of organizational characteristics, some of which can be manipulated and some of which cannot. Even from this view, size may be in part an uncontrollable external constraint, particularly as it is a function of location. However, size can also be seen as a characteristic of the structure and organization of the hospital, including the characteristics of the administrator.[11]

Given these two alternative views of size, the analysis was carried out both with size included, in which case it is considered to be a prior variable, and with size eliminated from the analysis. In the latter case, size itself is considered to be partly a function of the independent variables under study. Interestingly enough, as may be seen from the column marked R^2 in Tables 6–9, there appears to be an interaction effect between type of service, i.e., high- or low-risk, the organization which is doing the innovating, and the variable size. Table 6 shows that size is independently important to the innovation of low-risk services within health departments, and Table 9 shows that, alternatively, size is important to the innovation of high-risk services within hospitals. In health departments, as shown in Table 6, the over-all significant regression equation allows the prediction of 55 percent of the variance in low-risk innovation score with size included, but only 42 percent of the innovation score with size eliminated. By the same token, in Table 9, the significant regression equation allows a prediction of approximately 31 percent of the innovation score for high-risk services within hospitals, but, with size eliminated, the overall significant regression equation allows only the prediction of 21 percent of the variance in the innovation score for high-risk services.

However, as Tables 7 and 8 show, size is not a critical variable in the prediction of high-risk services within health departments or prediction of low-risk services within hospitals. Fifty-nine percent of the variance in the innovation score for low-risk services can be predicted using size within health departments and about 57 percent can be predicted without size. Similarly, as Table 8 shows, 31 percent of the variance in the low-risk innovation score can be

---

[11] This view of size as an emergent variable does gain some support from the data of the study itself. Thirty-nine of the 59 hospitals under study indicated that they had increased their number of beds in the five years prior to the study date. Twenty of these hospitals indicated that they had changed their size as much as 60 beds or more. At the same time 11 of the 23 health departments under study indicated that they had merged with another health department in the previous five years. These findings lead to an interesting direction for further research—the extent to which the set of independent variables under study here can predict change in size of health organizations over time. This examination remains for further analysis, however.

TABLE 6

Multiple Regression of Health Department Factors in Innovation of Low-Risk Services

Variable	Multiple R	R^2	Simple R	B	Std. B	Beta
Organizational size	.6273	.3935	.6273	.0053	.0024	.6939
Staff—professional training	.6962	.4847	.3928	.4231	.1856	.4349
Org—cosmopolitanism	.7075	.5005	.4543	.5712	.4425	.2891
Administrator—cosmopolitanism	.7301	.5331	.3817	-.0514	.0431	-.3076
Formalization	.7380	.5446	-.3812	.6813	.8622	.1682
Centralization	.7417	.5501	.1804	-.1990	.3506	-.1202
Slack Resources	.7436	.5529	.1134	-.1548	.4467	-.0619
Administrator—change values	.7442	.5538	.3249	.0739	.4121	.0384
(Constant)				-.5401		

Variable [a]	Multiple R	R^2	Simple R	B	Std. B	Beta
Org—cosmopolitanism	.4543	.2064	.4543	.8381	.3510	.4242
Staff—professional training	.6038	.3645	.3928	.4690	.1944	.4821
Administrator—change values	.6284	.3941	.3249	.5657	.4147	.2938
Centralization	.6458	.4171	.1804	.3372	.3522	.2036
Organizational performance	.6485	.4205	.2878	-.2392	.6828	-.0707
(Constant)				-16.1713		

[a] Organizational size excluded.

TABLE 7

Multiple Regression of Health Department Factors in Innovation of High-Risk Services

Variable	Multiple R	R²	Simple R	B	Std. B	Beta
Organizational size	.5518	.3045	.5518	.0012	.0008	.3554
Staff—professional training	.7591	.5763	.5984	.2259	.0735	.5041
Slack resources	.7659	.5866	-.0634	.1817	.1846	.1578
Administrator—cosmopolitanism	.7719	.5946	.4656	.0102	.0162	.1331
Centralization	.7732	.5978	.3263	.0580	.1277	.0760
Formalization	.7742	.5994	-.4601	-.1008	.3561	-.0540
(Constant)				-2.6349		

Variable [a]	Multiple R	R²	Simple R	B	Std. B	Beta
Staff—professional training	.5984	.3581	.5984	.2343	.0894	.5225
Administrator—cosmopolitanism	.6066	.4852	.4656	.0210	.0179	.2723
Formalization	.7191	.5171	-.4601	-.3141	.3454	-.1687
Slack resources	.7378	.5443	-.0634	.2014	.2127	.1749
Administrator—change values	.7503	.5630	.3020	.1230	.1865	.1396
Org—cosmopolitanism	.7526	.5664	.3176	.0687	.1948	.0755
Organizational performance	.7536	.5680	.3286	-.0634	.3311	-.0407
Centralization	.7539	.5684	.3263	.0223	.1691	.0293
(Constant)				-4.1420		

[a] Organizational size excluded.

TABLE 8

Multiple Regression of Hospital Factors in Innovation of Low-Risk Services

Variable	Multiple R	R²	Simple R	B	Std. B	Beta
Organizational size	.3426	.1173	.3426	.0016	.0021	.1174
Staff—Professional training	.4212	.1774	.3165	.3038	.1820	.2211
Org—cosmopolitanism	.4624	.2139	.3403	.4562	.2377	.2906
Administrator—change values	.4893	.2394	.2330	.2757	.1768	.1929
Organizational performance	.5091	.2592	.0893	.5506	.3601	.1989
Centralization	.5363	.2876	-.0034	-.2922	.2184	-.1729
Administrator—cosmopolitanism	.5519	.3046	-.0050	-.0246	.0262	-.1152
Slack resources	.5554	.3085	.1779	.0015	.0023	.0910
Formalization	.5586	.3120	.3018	-.3991	.7784	-.0758
(Constant)				-5.1151		

Variable ª	Multiple R	R²	Simple R	B	Std. B	Beta
Org—cosmopolitanism	.3403	.1158	.3403	.4905	.2319	.3131
Staff—professional training	.4129	.1705	.3165	.3089	.1811	.2248
Organizational performance	.4497	.2023	.0893	.6365	.3397	.2299
Administrator—change values	.4865	.2367	.2230	.2846	.1757	.1998
Centralization	.5179	.2682	.0036	.2945	.2174	.1743
Slack resources	.5339	.2851	.1779	.0024	.0020	.1423
Formalization	.5442	.2962	-.3018	-.5851	.7342	-.1111
Administrator—cosmopolitanism	.5518	.3045	-.0050	-.0201	.0255	-.0945
(Constant)				-4.3318		

ª Organizational size excluded.

154

TABLE 9

Multiple Regression of Hospital Factors in Innovation of High-Risk Services

Variable	Multiple R	R²	Simple R	B	Std. B	Beta
Organizational size	.4851	.2353	.4851	.0037	.0014	.4241
Formalization	.5111	.2613	-.3159	-.4271	.5062	-.1244
Slack resources	.5247	.2754	.0709	.0014	.0015	.1335
Staff—professional training	.5356	.2868	.2006	.1344	.1184	.1500
Centralization	.5430	.2949	.0225	.1361	.1420	.1235
Organizational performance	.5516	.3042	.1481	.2132	.2342	.1181
Administrator—cosmopolitanism	.5574	.3107	.1865	.0117	.0171	.0837
Administrator—change values	.5598	.3134	.0442	-.0458	.1150	-.0491
Org—cosmopolitanism	.5616	.3154	.2472	.0607	.1546	.0594
(Constant)				-.9499		

Variable [a]	Multiple R	R²	Simple R	B	Std. B	Beta
Formalization	.3159	.0998	-.3159	-.8204	.4897	-.2390
Administrator—cosmopolitanism	.3702	.1371	.1865	.0211	.0172	.1520
Organizational performance	.4136	.1711	-.1481	.4286	.2289	.2374
Staff—professional training	.4392	.1929	.2097	.1497	.1177	.1670
Org—cosmopolitanism	.4484	.2011	.2472	.1544	.1560	.1512
Centralization	.4629	.2143	.0225	.1408	.1478	.1278
(Constant)				.6468		

[a] Organizational size excluded.

predicted using size in hospitals and 30 percent can be predicted without size.

These data, then, do not give us a firm mandate for eliminating size as a predictive variable. However, because we wish to examine those characteristics of the organiaztion which may be subject to change and their predictive power in determining organizational innovation, the remaining discussion will be limited primarily to that analysis in which size is not included.

Low-Risk Services

Tables 6 and 8 show the predictive equations for low-risk services within health departments and hospitals, respectively. Forty-two percent of the variance in innovation score for low-risk services within health departments may be attributed to the cosmopolitan orientation of organizational members, training of the staff, values of the administrator toward change, participation of organizational members in decision making, and their perceived performance of the organization. At the same time, 30 percent of the variance in innovation scores for low-risk services within hospitals can be accounted for by the cosmopolitanism of organiaztional members, training of the staff, perceived performance of the hospital, the values of the administrator toward change, participation of organizational members in decision making, available slack in the organization, formalization, and the cosmopolitanism of the administrator. Within both these organizations, the innovation score in low-risk services can best be accounted for, once size is removed, by the degree of cosmopolitanism on the part of organizational members. This variable accounts for 20 percent of the variance within health departments and 11 percent of the variance within hospitals.

The second most important variable in each case is staff training, which accounts for an additional 16 percent of the variance in health departments and an additional 6 percent of the variance in hospitals. Within both organizations, these two variables entered the equations in one-two order. In the ultimate prediction equation, cosmopolitanism of organizational members and training of the staff have the largest beta weights in each instance except within hospitals where performance satisfaction of the organization has a beta weight slightly stronger than the ultimate beta weight of training. The administrator's values toward change, with a beta weight of .29 in health departments and .20 in hospitals, is also important to over-all prediction. However, the perceived performance of the health department, with a beta weight of $-.07$, is not an important variable in predicting innovation of low-risk services, whereas perceived performance recorded a strong beta weight in hospitals.

Nevertheless, the conclusion might be safely reached from Tables 6 and 8 that the innovation of low-risk services, both within hospitals and health departments, may be attributed substantially to the same basic set of characteristics. Thirty-nine percent of the variance in the innovation of low-risk services may be accounted for in health departments by the cosmopolitanism of organizational members, training of the staff, and administrator's values toward change, in that order. The ultimate significant prediction is 42 percent. Twenty-four percent of the variance in innovation score for low-risk services within hospitals can be predicted by cosmopolitanism of organizational members, training of the staff, preceived performance of the organization, and administrator's values toward change, in that order. The significant overall prediction is 30 percent.

High-Risk Services

Within the scores for innovation of high-risk services, there is less obvious consistency than appeared in the case of low-risk services. The predictor equations for high-risk services are shown in Tables 7 and 9. As Table 7 shows, training of the staff is again critical to innovation of high-risk services in health departments. Training entered the equation first and accounts for about 36 percent of the variance explained. The second variable to enter the equation was cosmopolitanism again—in this case not the cosmopolitanism of organizational members but the cosmopolitanism of the administrator himself.

Examining the predictor equation for hospitals in Table 9, one finds a similar result. While formalization, reflecting the extent to which rules do not define individual activity within the organization, is the first and most important variable in the innovation of high-risk services in hospitals, accounting for about 10 percent of the variance, the cosmopolitanism of the administrator again comes in as the second most important variable in the equation and accounts for an additional approximate 4 percent. In this latter case the proportion of variance accounted for is fairly small, and it may be safe to suggest that while it is sufficient to have a highly sophisticated staff for the innovation of low-risk services either within hospitals or health departments, the sophisticated administrator is the critical element in the innovation of high-risk services. Though considerable agreement exists that low-risk services should be provided and that the structure of the organization itself may be sufficient to promote this provision of services, the highly sophisticated administrator essentially provides leadership in regard to the high-risk services if these are to be innovated. This conclusion based on the data at hand may be overly strong but certainly suggests an area for further study.

Further examination of Tables 7 and 9 shows that formalization enters the predictor equation third for health departments, reflecting the same variable in hospitals, whereas the third variable into the equation for prediction of high-risk services in hospitals is again the perceived performance of the organization. Training of the staff and cosmopolitanism of the administrator are the two most critical variables in predicting overall innovation of high-risk services in health departments as indicated by their beta weights, .52 and .27, respectively. In the final overall significant equation, formalization and perceived performance of the organization are the most important in predicting the R^2 for hospitals as reflected by their beta weights, $-.239$ and .237, respectively.

One conclusion that might be drawn from these data is that while there are definite commonalities between hospitals and health departments in the characteristics which lead them to innovate either low-risk or high-risk services, it is at the same time important to hospitals that they maintain a high degree of perceived performance. It is possible, of course, to view performance as a dependent variable itself and a function of the number of services provided. However, if one assumes that an organization perceiving itself as having high performance will strive to maintain this performance by continuing to be innovative in the area of health services, performance can be seen as a causal variable. In that sense, performance appears to be much more important to hospitals than to health departments.

The two most critical variables in predicting the overall R^2 for health departments in the high-risk area are training of the staff and the cosmopolitanism of the administrator. Together these account for about 49 percent of a total 56 percent predicted variance. Formalization, cosmopolitanism of organizational members, and the perceived performance of the organization account for 17 percent of an overall predicted 21 percent of the variance and are the three most important predictor variables in hospitals.

Discussion and Conclusions

What can be said about program innovation in a comparative set of hospitals and health departments? Were there differences between the types of organizational variables that affect the innovation of high-risk versus low-risk programs? Were differences in innovation largely a function of the fact that the organization was a hospital or a health department?

The results indicate that organizational size is a critical variable in program innovation as it relates to high-risk services in hospitals and low-risk services in health departments. However, surprisingly enough, size was not a critical factor in the innovation of high-risk services in health departments and low-risk services within hospitals.

While the role of organizational size is not well understood, the above would suggest that the very nature of the two organizations is different vis-à-vis the community. Health departments implement high-risk programs such as patient care conferences, case finding, and information and referral services regardless of department size because their traditional role is to provide services only where such services are not already provided by other community resources. Since these high-risk services are usually not provided by other health agencies, it thus becomes the responsibility of even small health departments to provide such services. In contrast, these high-risk activities are not traditional hospital functions. It is therefore only the large hospitals, where sufficient resources are available, that undertake high-risk types of activities.

The designation of such programs as occupational therapy, speech and learning therapy, and mental-health inpatient services as low-risk reverses this pattern. Hospitals, for example, are more likely than health departments to have such services regardless of size. It is with this type of services that health department size is important because size tends to provide the necessary economies of scale for implementation. For example, only a large health department can justify the inclusion of an occupational therapist in its staff.

In a sense, health departments, by implementing high-risk programs independent of size, suggest a more community-focused organization responding to the particular health needs and demands of the community. Hospitals, on the other hand, take the opposite position and develop a floor of low-risk services that are provided independent of organizational size and implement high-risk programs only in large-scale organizations where sufficient resources are available to support such activities. These findings are consistent with other findings (Kaluzny et al., 1971) in which it is shown that, unlike those of hospitals, the health care programs implemented by health departments do not demonstrate any systematic pattern of implementation, but tend to reflect individual community circumstances.

When we focus on variables within organizations (excluding size), composition variables represented by cosmopolitanism and training of the staff are critical to the innovation of low-risk services in both hospitals and health departments. This variable set is again important to the innovation of high-risk programs in health departments; however, personal variables of the administrator as measured by his own cosmopolitan orientation are an added ingredient to program innovation. A similar pattern is presented for hospitals, except that structure as reflected by less formalized rules defining individual activity within the organization replaces the composition variables, and satisfaction with organizational performance is added as the significant variable.

Thus, it would appear that a pattern emerges for both types of organizations and for both types of innovative services. Composition variables are central to innovation in both hospitals and health departments for low-risk services. These variables are also important to the innovation of high-risk services in health departments except that the personal variables of the administrator become critical for this type of service. On the other hand, structural variables replace composition variables as the primary factor in innovation of high-risk programs in hospitals while again the personal characteristics of the administrator present themselves as a critical variable.

These findings add to the growing body of literature that assesses factors affecting organizational innovation. However, as with most research, more questions are raised than are answered. Several are suggested here as implications for further research. First, empirical attention needs to be given to the concept of innovation as a process. It is quite likely that the process will be influenced by a number of variables on a differential basis. For example, as Wilson (1966) suggests, organizational complexity may positively affect the degree to which innovative concepts are conceived and proposed, but it may have a negative influence on actual implementation. Thus, the nature of the causality must be explicitly introduced, making necessary the conduct of longitudinal studies on a number of organizations.

Second, the study of innovation needs to be broadened to include other predicting variables outside the organization as well as the consequences of such innovation. While this analysis has focused primarily on the organization as the unit of analysis, it is important to consider in greater detail the context of that organization. This research would focus on community and interorganizational variables such as political climate, community decision-making patterns, and the nature and number of interorganizational programs. With regard to the implications of program innovation, consideration also needs to be given to their effect on organizational structure and function. For example, does innovation affect the perception of organizational performance? Do the rate and kind of innovation affect the structure of decision making within the organization?

Third, the study of attributes needs further attention. Although the current data point out the utility of such study in analyzing innovation, attention needs to be given to further methodological refinement in measurement procedures and in the consideration of relevant attributes (Zaltman and Lin, 1971). Moreover, the perception of attributes by organizational participants and how it affects organizational innovation at various points in time is also in need of research.

Finally, while we have been primarily concerned with assessing variables that relate to different types of program innovation and various types of organizations, our findings have obvious bearing on the development and application of change strategies in health care organizations. The results strongly argue against any view of organizational change and/or innovation as a relatively homogeneous phenomenon. The data presented here seem to indicate that factors tend to have a differential effect for different types of programs and for various types of organizations. Any efforts to intervene in an attempt to introduce new programs must take into account these variations.

Arnold D. Kaluzny, PH.D.
Department of Health Administration
School of Public Health
University of North Carolina
Chapel Hill, North Carolina 27514

James E. Veney, PH.D.
Department of Health Administration
School of Public Health
University of North Carolina
Chapel Hill, North Carolina 27514

John T. Gentry, PH.D.
Department of Health Administration
School of Public Health
University of North Carolina
Chapel Hill, North Carolina 27514

This research was supported by Health Services Research Center of the University of North Carolina through Research Grant HS–00239 from the National Center for Health Services Research and Development, Department of Health, Education, and Welfare.

References

Becker, M.
   1970   "Sociometric location and innovativeness: reformulation and extension of the diffusion model." American Sociological Review 35 (April): 267–282.

Fliegel, F. C., and J. E. Kivlin
   1966   "Attributes of innovations as factors in diffusion." American Journal of Sociology 72 (March): 503–519.

Hage, J., and M. Aiken
   1967   "Program change and organizational properties." American Journal of Sociology 72 (March): 503–519.

Hall, R. B.
1963   "The concept of bureaucracy: an empirical assessment." American Journal of Sociology 69 (July): 32–40.

Kaluzny, A. D.
1972   "Innovation in the health system: a selective review of system characteristics and empirical research." Paper prepared for the National Institutes of Health Conference on Medical Innovation, Cornell University, Ithaca, New York.

Kaluzny, A. D., and J. E. Veney
1973   "Attributes of health services as factors in implementation." Journal of Health and Social Behavior (June): 124–133.

Kaluzny, A. D., J. E. Veney, J. T. Gentry, and J. B. Sprague
1971   "Scalability of health services: an empirical test." Health Services Research (Fall): 214–223.

Kaplan, H. B.
1967   "Implementation of program change in community agencies." Milbank Memorial Fund Quarterly 45:3 (July): 321–331.

Lazarsfeld, P. F., and H. Menzel
1961   "On the relation between individual and collective properties." Pp. 422–440 in A. Etzioni (ed.), Complex Organizations: A Sociological Reader. New York: Holt, Rinehart & Winston.

March, J. G., and H. A. Simon
1964   Organizations. New York: John Wiley & Sons.

McClosky, H.
1958   "Conservatism and personality." American Political Science Review 52 (March): 27–45.

Mohr, L. B.
1969   "Determinants of innovation in organizations." American Political Science Review (March): 111–126.

Mytinger, R. E.
1968   Innovation in Local Health Services. Washington, D.C.: Government Printing Office, Public Health Service Publication No. 1664-2.

Palumbo, D. J.
1969   "Power and role specificity in organizational theory." Public Administration Review XXIX:3 (May-June): 237–248.

Pugh, D. S., D. J. Hickson, C. R. Hinings, K. N. MacDonald,
C. Turner, T. Lupton
  1963   "A conceptual scheme for organizational analysis." Administrative Science Quarterly VIII: 289–319.

Rogers, E., and F. F. Shoemaker
  1971   Communications of Innovation: A Cross-Cultural Approach. New York: Free Press.

Rosner, M. M.
  1968   "Administrative controls and innovation." Behavioral Science 13: 36–43.

Veney, J. E., A. D. Kaluzny, J. T. Gentry, J. B. Sprague, and
D. P. Duncan
  1971   "Implementation of health programs in hospitals." Health Services Research 6:4 (Winter): 350–361.

Wilson, J. Q.
  1966   "Innovation in organizations: notes toward a theory." Pp. 195–218 in J. D. Thompson (ed.), Approaches to Organizational Design. Pittsburgh: University of Pittsburgh Press.

Zaltman, G., and N. Lin
  1971   "On the nature of innovations." American Behavioral Scientist: 651–673.

Hospital Costs
and Quality of Care:
An Organizational Perspective[1]

EDWARD V. MORSE

GERALD GORDON

MICHAEL MOCH

Based on survey data gathered from 388 government non-federal and voluntary general service hospitals, this study examines the impact of several dimensions of organizational structure on indicators of hospital efficiency and level of adoption of new medical technology. Attention is focused on the degree to which resource allocation decision making is centralized and levels of visibility of medical and economic consequences. The evidence presented suggests that, in terms of efficiency, organizational structure is an important factor in determining whether gains in effectiveness outweigh expenses associated with the adoption of new medical technology.

Within a predictive framework this paper will deal with the relationships among several dimensions of organizational structure and performance and their impact upon the quality and cost of care provided by hospitals. An assumption often made is that modern medical technology is costly. Clearly hospital medical costs are rising with a large percentage of the rise due to increased delivery of new and improved medical services made possible by advances in medical technology.

However, it is less clear that new medical technology increases the cost for care. Indeed, the argument can be made that by increasing the ability to treat illness, technology which facilitates higher quality care may be reducing patient care costs. A major problem in dealing with the effect of technology on efficiency is the difficulty in employing econometric methods to non-profit areas such as health. Lave and Lave (1970b:294) state, "The difficulties in estimating hospital costs and production functions are overwhelming. . . ." As a result of the difficulties in assessing quality of care from an

[1]This research was supported, at different times, by U. S. Public Health Service Contract No. 8667268 and Social Security Administration Grant No. 10-P-56076/2/-02.

M M F Q / Health and Society / *Summer 1974*

economic perspective, many investigators have discussed medical cost reduction with little reference to the level of care provided. A consideration of both efficiency and quality measurements is necessary if we are to adequately deal with the question of the utility of expenditures for health care.[2] Further, to our knowledge little large-scale empirical research has been conducted on the impact hospital structure has on quality of care and efficiency. Two structural factors, the degree of centralization of decision making and the levels of visibility of medical and economic consequences in a hospital, are seen as having predictable impact on both quality of care and efficiency. Before presenting our theoretical framework, it will be useful to specify how both the independent and dependent variables have been conceptualized for purposes of this paper.

Quality of Care

Quality of care is an elusive factor to measure. It would appear at first easy to compare hospitals in terms of the morbidity and recidivism rates of a representative sample of patients. However, comparisons of hospitals in terms of mortality, morbidity, and recidivism cannot be related directly to quality of care.

First of all, hospitals differ in the facilities and services they offer to patients. Some have emergency rooms, intensive care units, outpatient units, etc., while others have none of these facilities. This complicates the comparative process, for the hospital with an intensive-care unit may receive many victims of accidents, heart attacks, etc., and consequently show a high mortality rate.

A second consideration implicit here is that hospitals are likely to develop exchanges of patients. The consequence of this is that one partner in such an exchange relationship may appear to obtain better results in its treatment of patients, but this is only because difficult cases are sent elsewhere.

Third, it is clear that medical science has made great advances

---

[2]Here efficiency is only being considered in terms of process. Ultimately it is felt a single index which considers both quality and process efficiency must be developed. Understanding how various organizational factors are related to both process efficiency and effectiveness is viewed as a first and necessary step in the development of such an index.

in the knowledge and technology used for diagnosing and treating disease, yet hospitals differ widely in the extent to which they have incorporated these new techniques into patient care. Acquisition of these techniques may alter the clientele of the hospital considerably, possibly increasing or decreasing the numbers of patients with serious illnesses.

An alternative to direct, comparative measurement of quality and, we believe, at the present a more viable strategy is to develop a set of criteria for an "effective" hospital. By an effective hospital, we mean one which has the ability to deliver high-quality patient care. Once variability in effectiveness has been specified, factors which help explain it can be isolated and anlyzed.

In attempting to provide a proxy measure or indicator of quality of care to meet our definition, we have developed a scale of institutional adoption of specific innovations in modern medical technology rated by a panel of experts as important for high-quality medical care within a defined area.[3] We have labeled this scale "adoption."

The fact that a hospital can treat the whole patient means that, in general, patients do not have to be transferred in order to receive emergency treatment and that facilities are available for handling complications associated with a particular disease; this appears to be fundamental to the concept of an effective hospital. Similarly, a hospital that lacks medical innovations deemed important by medical experts simply cannot deliver high-quality (i.e., effective) care by current standards.[4] Finally, because medical care involves economic goods or scarce resources, cost inefficiencies may function to deny services to those who need them and hence limit a hospital's effectiveness.

It is recognized that availability of technology is no insurance that it will be properly employed. However, without appropriate technology the potential quality of care delivered is likely to be at a lower level.

---

[3]We recognize this measure may not be appropriate for use with hospitals individually in determining effectiveness. However, we feel it does have validity on an aggregate analysis basis.

[4]These statements are made with reference to medical technology basic to the normal practice of medicine in a hospital and not with regard to technology required for the diagnosis and management of esoteric diseases which present themselves far less frequently.

Efficiency of Operation

While there are few who would disagree with the idea that all
hospitals should have up-to-date facilities and deliver a high quality
of medical care, economic realities of the nation's health care
system necessitate considering quality of care in relation to efficiency of hospital operations. Given cost constraints, from a policy
perspective the question becomes how to provide modern
technology at the lowest possible cost. Before proceeding, it is important to explicate clearly the term "efficiency."

In asking how efficient a hospital is, three different and distinct
questions are really being raised:

1. To what extent is the hospital utilizing the capacity of its
   physical plant?
2. How much *time* does it take to process a patient?
3. How much *money* does it cost to process a patient?

An indication of the extent to which a hospital is utilizing its
physical plant can be inferred from its occupancy rate. A hospital's
occupancy rate may be affected by a number of factors (Rafferty,
1971; Ingbar and Taylor, 1968; Lave and Lave, 1970a). But given
that an unoccupied hospital bed producing no revenue costs about
three fourths as much to maintain as one which is filled, underutilization of a facility clearly results in diseconomies (Lave and
Lave, 1970a; Feldstein, 1961). These diseconomies must eventually be borne by the patient and third-party payers.

The second question is directed at the time dimensions of efficiency, a sense of which can be gained by calculating the average
length of stay for a hospital's patients. Once again, it must be recognized that a number of factors not controlled for, particularly a
hospital's case mix, may play a significant part in determining a
hospital's average length of stay. Still, how long a patient remains
in the hospital is not wholly determined on the basis of medical ex-
igencies and thus is amenable to being affected by administrative as
opposed to purely medical decisions. One example is the informal
practice of some hospitals of holding patients over to reduce the
likelihood of malpractice suits.

A third question raised deals with the expenses incurred by a
hospital to process patients. How much a hospital expends to process a patient is a highly significant question—much more easily
asked than answered. The difficulties stem basically from whether
expenses should be measured in terms of admissions or patient
days. Conceptually, using either unit of analysis would entail mak-

ing a series of erroneous assumptions noted by Lave and Lave (1970b:295). Though seemingly an unlikely choice, the total expenses of a hospital were chosen to measure the monetary dimensions of efficiency. The rationale for using total expenses and the method of calculation are discussed in a later section of the paper.

Keeping in mind how quality of care (adoption) and efficiency have been conceptualized, the next thing to consider is how organizational factors affect both quality and efficiency. It is to this matter the paper now turns.

Organizational Variables

Centralization/Decentralization

We believe that certain organizational factors affect both adoption and efficiency. Our perspective derives from the work of Becker and Gordon (1966) who postulate that formal organizations are developed to coordinate scarce resources to achieve given goals in as efficient a manner as possible. Coordination, however, limits the organization's ability to change. All organizations thus face a dilemma posed by the desire to maximize the benefits of coordination and the necessity for change in response to environmental demands. According to this perspective, the best organizational structure reflects a balance between the gains to be accrued from coordination and the need to adjust to environmental changes. The general premise is that the lower the level within an organization at which procedures are specified, the less requirements for coordination inhibit organizational change.

For example, in assembly-line manufacturing, specified procedures are spelled out to determine the flow of resources from the time the raw materials enter the plant gate to the end of the assemblage process. The end product (e.g., in automobile production) is highly standardized, with limits placed on the variation allowed to meet unique demand requirements. Highly coordinated centralized authority structures are postulated as most effective when external conditions are relatively stable and uniform.

Most organizations, however, deal with heterogeneous environments. Often, as a means of handling diverse environments, multiple authority structures will be established within the same organization. The occurrence of units with different authority patterns within the same organization can best be understood in terms of what we have referred to as the organizational dilemma: the desire to maximize the gains of coordination and yet respond to environmental demands. One way to resolve this dilemma is to divide the organization into component elements, some with centralized authority patterns facilitating coordination and others with decentralized authority patterns responsive to change.

Hospitals are prime examples of organizations with multiple organizational structures. Characteristically the administrative group in a hospital operates under a different authority pattern from the doctors: the administrators have an executive authority pattern while the doctors operate on a collegial basis with some degree of unit autonomy. By decentralizing decision making in the larger organization to smaller semi-autonomous units, each having responsibility for dealing with a limited sector of the environment, coordination can be accomplished with fewer hierarchical levels. This not only reduces the number of hierarchical levels that must decide upon change but permits independent unit change.

As with all administrative structures, advantages gained in one area incur costs in other areas. Decentralization through the development of semi-autonomous units leads to duplication of administrative functions, difficulties in over-all coordination, and limits economies of scale. On the other hand, decentralization facilitates resource change—that is, the introduction of new and different resources into the organization.

Thus, if the board of directors of a hospital retains most decision-making prerogatives over resource allocation (indicating a centralized structure), the benefits of coordination would be maximized. On the other hand, to permit maximal response and resource flexibility, a hospital would decentralize decision making down to the lowest possible level. However, for most organizations, moving to either extreme compromises overall ability to perform.

This has specific bearing on the question of the impact of organizational structure on adoption and cost. Adoption reflects the ability of an organization to change. But if the ability to change is associated with a lack of coordination in areas in which such coordination is desirable, costs associated with change will be high.

Visibility of Consequences

Given these assumptions, the fundamental question is what factors tend to lead to a hospital structure with a balance between coordination and responsiveness to change? One of the most important factors affecting organizational structure is the basis upon which decisions are made. The assumption underlying this postulate is quite simple, namely that knowledge of cause and effect in terms of goal attainment (e.g., quality of care) leads to the selection of organizational practices that facilitate goal achievement at lowest costs. Going one step further, it is predicted that in the absence of knowledge about goal-related cause and effect, organizational structure will reflect whatever criteria are used to assess performance. Often, where information regarding goal performance is lacking, the organization assesses performance in terms of relative costs (Thompson, 1967).

Visibility of consequences is considered to range from highly visible, where an organization gathers information on the results of its past performance, to low visibility, where it is not possible or no information on performance is gathered. In the case of hospitals, it is useful to distinguish between two different types of visibility, one related to medical consequences, the other to economic consequences of the hospital's behavior. The sheer presence of either type of information would not be expected to have a direct relation with either a hospital's level of adoption, or its efficiency, since information in and of itself is assumed to have little or no impact until acted upon. The relation of centralization of resource decision making to a hospital's level of adoption and efficiency is expected to be affected by the type and level of information available upon which to base decisions.

Data Base

To collect data to test the relationship between cost and adoption as well as other organizational variables, a random sample of 1,021 hospitals was drawn from the population of United States hospitals for detailed study. Separate questions were sent to each hospital's chief administrative officer and medical officer.[5] Sixty-seven per-

[5]This not only enabled us to obtain a wide range of information but also provided two sources of data on which to base an analysis of the reliability of the instruments. Although space limitations preclude a delineation of our reliability analyses, we can say that, for each hospital, the amount of agreement between the medical officers, the administrative officers, and, for the intensively studied hospitals, our field site researcher, was high. For the questions concerning the presence or absence of each technological item within the hospital, for example, the medical and administrative officers agreed 75 percent of the time. Furthermore, for these items, the administrative officer agreed with study researchers who performed 17 intensive case studies 77 percent of the time and the medical officers agreed with our researchers 79 percent of the time.

cent of the administrative officers ($N = 678$) and 67 percent of the medical officers ($N =669$) returned the questionnaire. Forty-seven percent of the hospitals returned both questionnaires, and 86 percent responded with at least one of the two instruments.

We also compared our data with the 1968 American Hospital Association annual survey data to determine possible sources of bias. Aside from a tendency for proprietary and federal hospitals to be slightly under- and overrepresented respectively, the two populations appeared similar. In an effort to reduce introduction of factors which might obscure testing the principle thrust of the analysis, the study was limited to a sample of government non-federal general service hospitals and voluntary general service hospitals. Limiting our frame to these hospitals enables us to perform our analysis in the context of hospitals with similar functions. The primary function of these hospitals is to treat a wide range of diseases without limitations due to profit motive or social characteristics of the patient. Since voluntary and government non-federal general service hospitals account for 60 percent of the hospitals in the United States, to a large degree generalizability is not compromised. Limiting our analysis to these classes of general service hospitals leaves us with a sample of 388 hospitals.

Operationalization of Variables

In selecting a measure of adoption it was decided, for purposes of comparison, to concentrate on a limited area of medical care. The criteria in selecting the area for study were:

- a. That the medical area be relatively broad and relevant to the over-all quality of medical care provided in a hospital;
- b. That the area be one where significant progress has occurred, but where serious problems remain;
- c. That the innovations in the area reflect many different aspects of medical technology (e.g., drugs, equipment, operating procedures);
- d. That the area include a large group of medical experts competent to evaluate the innovations.

The area selected was respiratory disease. Modern technology in this area seemed sufficient to provide a general measure of technological innovativeness. Besides occurring fairly frequently, respiratory disease often complicates other illnesses. Furthermore, respiratory technology is very often applied in anesthesiology and in postoperative-care illnesses entirely unrelated to respiratory disease itself. It was felt that the ubiquitous nature of respiratory disease technology in health care delivery made it an appropriate focus for study.

To measure the level of adoption of a hospital, a scale was constructed by counting the number of items from a list of twelve innovations[6] each hospital reported having purchased, leased, or rented. The scale constructed can take on values ranging from "0" (no adoption) to "12" (high adoption).[7]

The three dimensions of efficiency are measured using data taken from the 1968 American Hospital Association annual survey. The dimensions of physical plant utilization and time are operationally defined in terms of average occupancy rate and average length of stay respectively. Directly measuring the third dimension, expenses incurred to process patients, gives rise to some conceptual difficulties as previously discussed. An indirect indication of hospital expenses, however, can be constructed. It was reasoned that a hospital's total expenses are affected by both the number of patients it admits and its number of patient days. In turn, both of these factors should be a function of hospital bed size. Analysis of the data showed that size was correlated + .98 with number of ad-

---

[6]In order to identify technological innovations in this disease area, Dr. Robert Anderson, then Medical Director of the American Thoracic Society, and Dr. Lewis B. Clayton, Director of Medical Statistics for the National Tuberculosis Association, selected from the ranks of the American Thoracic Society 75 physicians who were thought to be experts on respiratory disease. The experts were split into two panels, one to generate a list of technical innovations, the other to rate these innovations in terms of various criteria including the initial and current importance of the innovation for diagnosis and treatment. From the initial list generated of over 200 ideas and discoveries, 12 items were selected for study. Many factors, such as importance, availability of records, and risk, influenced the selection of the 12 items. In each case, however, the items selected were rated to be of at least some importance for the diagnosis or treatment of respiratory disease. An additive index, we felt, was justifiable in this case because the items form a Guttman Scale.

[7]The items selected for inclusion were: Macroaggregated[131], Venti Mask, Blood Gas Electrode, Esophageal Balloon, Plethsmograph, Spirometer, Ethambutol, Nacetylysteine, Ultrasonic Nebulizer, IPPB Unit, Mediastinoscope, and LDH Determination. For the sample the 12 form a Guttman Scale with a coefficient of reproducibility of .92.

missions and + .95 with number of patient days. The high correlation with size means that if the effects of size were controlled for in the data analysis, variation in the hospital's total expenses attributable to its number of admissions and patient days would also be controlled for. This is done for the analysis presented by mathematically regressing each independent variable on the variable bed size and extracting the residual for each independent variable. Hence, it should be noted that in the presentation of findings, the independent variables will all be residuals of the variable size. The mathematical treatment of the measure results in it being independent of size and, therefore, analogous to hospital expenses per bed.

Measures of the extent of centralization-decentralization and visibility of consequences were derived from responses to the questionnaires sent to the chief of medicine and hospital administrator.

The survey questionnaire sent to each hospital included an item designed to determine the locus of discretion for five representative resource allocation decisions. To build an index of centralization/decentralization, the responses given for each of the five decisions were coded to reflect the relative frequency with which each decision was made by the board of the hospital, the chief subunit officer (hospital administrator or chief of medicine), or lower levels of the medical staff. Responses were combined to provide an over-all measure of the number of decisions made at each of the three organizational levels. The final measure constitutes an index ranging from ''0'' (decentralized) to ''10'' (centralized) which is taken as an indicator of the extent to which the locus of resource allocation decision making is predominantly situated at the board level, the chief officer level, or at the level of the medical staff.

The index of visibility of medical consequences is based on four factors: a hospital's autopsy rate, the number of times a year a hospital's credentials committee met, the percentage of time the chief of medicine devoted himself to the administration of the medical staff, and the percentage of time the hospital administrator devoted to administration of the medical staff. The index of medical visibility was constructed by first ipsitizing the responses to correct for response set. The standardized responses were then weighted by their respective factor loadings generated by a principal components analysis and summed for each hospital.

The index of economic visibility was built by summing the numerical responses hospitals made to two questions regarding the extent to which the governing body of the hospital was actually involved in decisions about how money is to be spent (i.e., specifications of budget categories) and examination of expenditures within budget categories.

Other Factors Included for Analysis

Although the primary thrust of this study focuses on the impact of centralization-decentralization and visibility of consequences on hospital adoption behavior and efficiency, a series of other factors felt likely to affect either adoption behavior or efficiency was introduced into the analysis as control variables. The series of factors includes: demographic (rural-urban) location of hospital, affiliation with medical schools, presence of outside funds for research, number of full-time non-medical personnel, number of full-time physicians, and number of services available in the hospital. Since, however, a multiple-regression technique will be employed in analyzing the data, an advantage is gained in that any control variable can also be examined in terms of its independent impact on the dependent variables.

The Relationship Between Efficiency and Adoption

As a first step in understanding the impact of organizational structures on efficiency and adoption, it is essential to examine the nature of the relationship between the three measures of efficiency and adoption. From the statements made in the introduction to the paper, two contradictory hypotheses may be advanced:

1. Modern technology is expensive and increases the costs of care in an absolute sense.
2. The costs associated with adoption of modern technology are more than offset by the savings resulting from higher-quality (i.e., more efficient) treatment associated with such technology.

If the first hypothesis is correct, we would expect costs of processing a patient to increase with adoption. A finding that adoption is associated with lower costs would not, in and of itself, indicate that the costs associated with adoption are offset by an increase in efficiency. However, if such a decrease were associated with a reduc-

TABLE 1
Zero-Order Correlations Between Adoption
and Three Measures of Efficiency

Total expenses (per bed)[a]	.18[b]
Average length of stay	−.12[b]
Average occupancy rate	.04

a   Each variable is a residual of the variable bed size
b $<.05$

tion of time spent in a hospital, support would increase for the
second hypothesis. If, in addition, the occupancy rate were found
to be associated with adoption, there would be some indication that
where choice is possible the medical profession is channeling its patients to what it feels are better hospitals. Controlling for bed size,
the following zero-order correlations were found:

Although the relationships are not large, the findings provide
support for both hypotheses—there is a relationship between cost
and adoption, but there is also support for the effectiveness
hypothesis. The smallness of the relationship and its contradictory
nature leads one to suspect that other factors may be affecting the
efficiency/adoption relationships.

Centralization, Adoption, and Efficiency

Following from the "organization dilemma" discussed earlier, decentralization of decision making was associated with adoption and
increased effectiveness, and centralization with increased efficiency. Thus, two hypotheses are posited:

1. The less centralized a hospital's decision-making struc-
    ture, the greater its rate of adoption of medical
    technology.
2. The more centralized a hospital's decision-making
    authority structure, the more efficient it will be in its
    health care delivery as measured by average length of
    stay, average occupancy rate, and total expenses.

To investigate the impacts of centralization on adoption and the
three measures of efficiency, a series of multiple regressions was

TABLE 2

Regression Estimates of the Impact of Centralization
and Other Organizational Factors on Adoption

Explanatory Variables	Adoption [a]
Centralization of decision making	−.13[b]
Urban/rural (urban = 1, rural = 0)	.36[b]
Hospital affiliated with medical school	.08
Years since founding	.09
Outside funds for research	.26[b]
Other assets	−.09
Number of full-time physicians	−.01
Number of different specialists on staff	+.06
Number of full-time non-medical personnel	−.02
Number of services	.07
Visibility of economic consequence	.00
Visibility of medical consequence	−.07

$MR = .64$ $N = 388$.
[a] Values reported are Beta weight.
[b] Beta greater than twice its standard error, significant at .05 level.

performed. Turning to the data presented in Tables 2-5, it is seen that when the direct effect of centralization is taken into account, hospitals which adopt more modern technology have higher occupancy rates, lower average lengths of stay, and no higher level of total expenses. Table 2 presents the results of the multiple regression of adoption on a series of variables. The negative Beta = − .13 supports the hypothesis that centralization of decision making has an inverse effect on a hospital's level of adoption. This finding supports the proposition that concentration of decision making, with regard to resource allocation, tends to result in the hospital's incorporating fewer advances in medical technology. Conversely, when the discretion to make resource decisions is held by members of the medical staff, the hospital is more likely to acquire technological advances in medicine and thus have more up-to-date medical facilities.[8] If, as stated earlier, having a modern medical facility is a prerequisite to delivery of a high quality of medical care, then the data suggest that consideration be given to developing mechanisms which increase physician participation in the resource allocation decisions of hospitals. The positive and negative consequences which might arise as a result of involving

[8]In the 10 percent of hospitals where the hospital administrator is a physician, it is expected that the impact of centralization on adoption would be modified.

TABLE 3

Regression Estimates of the Impact of Centralization
and Other Organizational Variables on Occupancy Rate

Explanatory Variables	*Average Occupancy Rate* [a]
Centralization of decision making	$-.10$[b]
Adoption	.13[b]
Urban/rural (urban = 1, rural = 0)	.10[b]
Delay in admission	.34[b]
Hospital affiliation with medical school	.05
Other assets	$-.04$
Number of full-time physicians	.00
Number of different medical specialists on staff	.06
Number of full-time non-medical personnel	.02
Number of services	$-.04$
Visibility of economic consequence	$-.01$
Visibility of medical consequence	$-.14$[b]

$MR = .46$ $N = 388$.
[a] Values reported are Beta weight.
[b] Beta greater than twice its standard error, significant at .05 level.

physicians in the process of resource allocation decisions are important considerations worthy of empirical study.

Given the second hypothesis, though, an equally critical problem is posed: what happens to the level of efficiency with which care is delivered if decision making is decentralized? Tables 3, 4, and 5 show the impact of centralization-decentralization and the organizational factors on the three dimensions of efficiency: the average occupancy rate, average length of stay, and total expenses.[9] A hospital's level of adoption is retained in the analyses of efficiency, since interest lies with the impact of centralization on the efficiency with which a hospital processes patients at a given level of quality.

Table 3 shows that centralization of resource decision making has a negative relation (Beta $= -10$) to occupancy rate, indicating that utilization of a hospital's physical facilities is not facilitated where decision-making powers rest with the head of the organization, as hypothesized. On the contrary, the data suggest that more

[9]Although our primary theoretical concern is with the effect of centralization on adoption, significant impact of geographic location and outside funds for research can also be seen. Further comment on the independent impact of these factors will be deferred until a later point.

complete use of beds occurs where physicians at the patient-care level are themselves directly involved in the administration of resource allocation decisions in the hospital. Why this is the case is possibly clarified if one notes that the relation of level of adoption to occupancy rate is significant and positive (Beta = .13), keeping in mind that centralization of decision making was found to have a negative relation to adoption. This suggests that hospitals which adopt more medical innovations tend to experience higher rates of utilization of their facilities. A possible explanation for this finding is that hospitals with modern medical facilities are more medically attractive to both patients and physicians and thus experience greater demand for their beds. The plausibility of this explanation is supported in part by the significant relation between delay in admission and occupancy rate (Beta = .34). Thus, contrary to what might have been expected, having modern medical facilities may in fact lead to greater efficiency of health care delivery in terms of the more complete utilization of the facility. The direction of causality could, however, work in the opposite direction. That is, fully utilized hospitals would be more likely to have the resources needed to adopt new medical technology. Obviously, longitudinal data are required to determine directionality. However, regardless of the direction of causality, the analysis suggests that the nature of the association of adoption and occupancy rate does not directly contribute to hospital inefficiency.

It can be seen from Table 4 that centralization does not have a significant impact on a hospital's average length of stay, as hypothesized. Taking account of other variables, whether the owner of the hospital maintains tight control over decisions himself or lets the medical staff make decisions has little impact on expediting the process of treating patients. As was the case in Table 3, however, a hospital's level of adoption does appear to bear significantly on the average time it takes to treat a patient (Beta = −.11). To the extent that a hospital's level of adoption can be taken as an indicator of the hospital's over-all ability to provide modern medical facilities, the data suggest that adoption contributes to efficiency by reducing the average length of time taken to treat patients.

Of further interest, it is noted from Table 4 that while the number of non-medical personnel (presumably available to treat patients) appears to have the effect of reducing average length of stay (Beta = − .14), the magnitude of a hospital's outside funds for research (Beta = .10) and its number of full-time attending physi-

TABLE 4

Regression Estimates of the Impact of Centralization
and Other Organizational Factors
on Average Length of Stay

Explanatory Variable	*Average Length of Stay* [a]
Centralization of decision making	.05
Adoption	−.11[b]
Urban/rural (urban = 1, rural = 0)	.01
Delay in admission	.01
Hospital affiliated with medical school	.01
Outside funds for research	.10[b]
Other assets	.00
Number of full-time physicians	.18[b]
Number of different medical specialists on staff	−.06
Number of full-time non-medical personnel	−.14[b]
Number of services	−.03
Visibility of economic consequence	.05
Visibility of medical consequence	−.02

$MR = .29$ $N = 388$.
[a] Values reported are Beta weight.
[b] Beta greater than twice its standard error, significant at .05 level.

cians (Beta = .18) are related to an increasing average length of stay. These fundings raise the question of whether teaching hospitals, which normally have both large numbers of full-time attending physicians and large quantities of outside research funds, tend to keep patients for longer periods of time. It would be of interest to examine the implications of these findings with regard to the relation between the quality of patient care received and the use of patients for teaching purposes in such hospitals.

Finally, Table 5 shows that centralization of decision making appears to have an inverse effect on a hospital's total expenses (Beta = − .08), as predicted.[10] If the causal sequence is as predicted, in terms of monetary dimension of efficiency, this means that greater cost savings are realized by hospitals which have resource decision-making authority vested at the top than in hospitals

[10]The reader is reminded that by using variables in the analysis where the effect of hospital bed size, total number of admissions, and total number of patient days have been controlled for, the variable "total expenses" can be taken as a measure of expenses per bed.

TABLE 5

Regression Estimates of the Impact of Centralization
and Other Organizational Factors on Total Expenses

Explanatory Variables	Total Expenses [a]
Centralization of decision making	−.08[b]
Adoption	.03
Urban/rural (urban = 1, rural = 0)	.27[b]
Cost of manpower	.03
Delay in admission	.17[b]
Hospital affiliated with medical school	.14[b]
Years since founded	.16
Outside funds for research	.33[b]
Average occupancy rate	.03
Average length of stay	.08[b]
Other assets	.04
Total visits—outpatient services	.03
Number of full-time physicians	−.04
Number of different medical specialists on staff	−.16[b]
Number of full-time non-medical personnel	.18[b]
Number of services	−.09[b]
Visibility of economic consequence	−.05
Visibility of medical consequence	−.03

$MR = .81$ $N = 388$.
[a] Values reported are Beta weight.
[b] Beta greater than twice its standard error, significant at the .05 level.

where responsibility for resource allocation decisions lies with the medical staff.

Further, it is seen from Table 5 that a hospital's level of adoption does not, as is often assumed, appear to exert any influence on total expenses.[11] Care must be taken, however, in interpreting this finding. It would be in error to conclude from this that the costs of operating a modern medical facility are not increased, particularly where, in conjunction with adoption of a new innovation, a hospital must hire technical support personnel to operate it. Analysis by Andersen and May (1972) of factors contributing to increasing costs of hospital care strongly suggests that increased labor costs are a major cause of rising hospital expenses. Looking at the impact of the number of full-time non-medical personnel on total expenses (Beta = .18) would appear to support such a contention. For this argu-

[11]Since staff size is an independent variable in our multiple regression, the effect of adoption on total expenses is independent of its contribution to increases in staff size.

ment to hold, though, there would have to be a strong relation between level of adoption and number of full-time non-medical personnel. The correlation between adoption and number of full-time non-medical personnel, however, is only $r = .03$ (data not shown), suggesting that the relation between adoption of medical technology, labor costs, and total expenses is much more complex than previously conceived of in the literature. Insight into the nature of this series of relationships will be presented in Table 9.

Total expenses, however, are only one way of looking at monetary efficiency. As has already been reported in Tables 2 and 3, hospitals with high adoption rates have a shorter average length of stay and a higher occupancy rate. Thus, while the technologically modern hospital may have higher costs per patient day, it processes more patients in fewer days, with the result that the cost per patient stay may be lower for higher-quality care.

Thus, from Tables 2-5 it is seen that while the impact of centralization-decentralization of resource decision making on a hospital's level of adoption is as was predicted, its impact on efficiency is not as clear. It was hypothesized that centralization would facilitate efficiency of health care delivery, but this appears to be the case only with regard to total expenses. In terms of the time it takes the hospital to process patients, it seems to make little difference at which level resource allocation decisions are made in the organization. On the other hand, hospitals with decentralized decision-making authority do show a higher rate of utilization of bed capacity. Taken together, these findings emphasize the underlying complexity of factors which must be understood in order to deal with the problems of increasing hospitals' efficiency of health care delivery.

Further, in Table 5 it can be seen that geographical location (urban), delay in admissions, affiliation with a medical school, age of facility, amount of outside funds for research, average length of stay, and number of full-time non-medical personnel all contribute to higher total expenses for hospitals. However, as will be seen shortly, the impact of some of these factors is variable when the availability of information to decision makers (as measured by visibility of consequences) is taken into account.

Having examined the effect of who in the hospital makes decisions (centralization), the next question to raise is how the presence or lack of information (medical/economic visibility of consequences) concerning the organization's activities modifies the impact of adoption on efficiency under varying degrees of centralization-decentralization of decision-making authority.

The Basis of Decision

The data presented thus far provide support for the contention that who makes decisions in a hospital has differential effects on how well the organization is able to handle the problem of keeping down the cost of care and maintaining up-to-date medical facilities. Following this lead, the next thing asked is whether having available information or knowledge of past consequences on which to base decisions facilitates these trends.

Distinguishing between medical and economic visibility of consequences led to the formulation of two hypotheses:

1.   Decentralized hospitals with high visibility of medical consequences would adopt more new medical technology than decentralized hospitals having low medical visibility.
2.   Centralized hospitals with high visibility of economic consequences would be more efficient than centralized hospitals with low visibility.

Further, it was expected that the predicted relations between adoption and centralization of resources decision making and the three measures of efficiency and centralization would be enhanced when either type of visibility was high. Operating under conditions of high visibility of either type, it was felt, would have the general effect of facilitating decision makers' awareness of issues, thus enabling them to find ways to improve the hospital's quality of care when resource decision making was decentralized and improve efficiency of delivery when decision making was centralized.

To test the hypotheses, it is necessary to dichotomize hospitals twice: first on the basis of high or low visibility of medical consequences, and second on high or low economic visibility.[12] Tables 6-9 display the results of this analysis.[13]

A comparison of the beta values for centralization across conditions of visibility of consequences in Table 6 indicates two points.

---

[12]The correlation between economic and medical visibility of consequences is $r = -.05$.

[13]For reasons already explained, the variables used are corrected for hospital bed size.

TABLE 6

Regression Estimates of the Impact of Centralization and Other Organizational Factors on Adoption Controlling for Levels of Economic and Medical Visibility of Consequence

	ADOPTION [a]			
	Visibility of Economic Consequence		Visibility of Medical Consequence	
EXPLANATORY VARIABLE	*High*	*Low*	*High*	*Low*
Centralization of decision making	-.20[b]	-.11[b]	-.20[b]	-.09[b]
Urban/rural (urban = 1, rural = 0)	.28[b]	.45[b]	.31[b]	.30[b]
Hospital affiliated with medical school	-.03	.16[b]	.05	.09
Outside funds for research	.22[b]	.31[b]	.30[b]	.29[b]
Other assets	-.17[b]	-.02	-.03	-.08
Number of full-time physicians	.20[b]	-.08[b]	.02	-.03
Number of different medical specialists on staff	.02	.09[b]	.14[b]	.03
Number of full-time non-medical personnel	-.16[b]	.01	.09[b]	-.17[b]
Number of services	.10[b]	.06	.07	.02
Visibility of economic consequence			-.09[b]	.03
Visibility of medical consequence	.03	-.13[b]		
MR =	.64	.72	.67	.64
N =	205	170	156	184

[a] Values reported are Beta weight.
[b] Beta greater than twice its standard error, significant at the .05 level.

First, the negative signs of all four beta weights for centralization mean that, regardless of the type or level of visibility of consequences present in a hospital, centralization of resource decision-making authority has a negative relation to a hospital's level of adoption. Conversely, in situations where authority has been delegated to the medical staff, the hospital tends to keep the facility up to date medically. Secondly, the decentralized structure appears to facilitate adoption more when visibility of either medical or economic consequences is high. This finding tends to support the general contention that having information regarding the past performance of the hospital provides a basis for assessing anticipated courses of action and acts as an impetus on decision makers to improve medical performance.

Relevant to the above point are findings from a further analysis done on the same data base (Gordon, Tanon, and Morse, 1974). There hospitals were categorized into one of four groups on the basis of whether they exhibited high or low economic and medical visibility of consequences. A comparison of the mean level of adoption of each group supported the prediction that hospitals having a high level of medical visibility and a low level of economic visibility would adopt more medical innovations ($\bar{X} = 5.9$) than hospitals having high economic visibility and low medical visibility ($\bar{X} = 4.5$).

Returning to the present analysis, however, a more complex picture emerges when the direct effects of economic and medical visibility of consequences are examined. Under the condition of low economic visibility of consequences, the higher the level of medical visibility the lower the level of adoption (Beta $= -.13$). Similarly, under conditions of high visibility of medical consequences, the higher the level of economic visibility the lower the adoption. Further examination of the impact of other variables indicates that geographic location (urban) and amount of outside research funding have the most significant and consistent impacts on adoption. The differential impact of the number of full-time physicians and number of full-time non-medical personnel under different types and levels of visibility of consequences is a further indication of the complex relationship among information, structure, and adoption. The interrelationship among these variables clearly indicates that further research is warranted in this area.

Turning to the impact of centralization on efficiency, for occupancy rate, under all conditions of visibility (Table 7), the negative beta weights suggest that centralized decision making is associated with underutilization of a hospital's bed capacity.

TABLE 7

Regression Estimates of the Impact of Centralization and Other Organizational Factors on Average Occupancy Rate Controlling for Levels of Economic and Medical Visibility of Consequence

EXPLANATORY VARIABLE	AVERAGE OCCUPANCY RATE [a]			
	Visibility of Economic Consequence		Visibility of Medical Consequence	
	High	Low	High	Low
Centralization of decision making	-.10	-.17b	-.11b	-.04
Adoption	.08	.20	.05	.16b
Urban/rural (urban = 1, rural = 0)	.07	.12b	.07	.10
Delay in admission	.40b	.28b	.40b	.30b
Hospital affiliated with medical school	.01	.09	.03	.05
Other assets	-.07	-.02	.01	-.16b
Number of full-time physicians	.01	.03	.00	-.03
Number of different medical specialists on staff	.03	.07	.11b	.06
Number of full-time non-medical personnel	.00	.03	.02	.08
Number of services	.01	-.13b	-.06	-.06
Visibility of economic consequence				
Visibility of medical consequence	-.05	-.26b	+.01	-.13
MR =	.47	.52	.53	.45
N =	205	170	156	184

a Values reported are Beta weights.
b Beta greater than twice its standard error, significant at the .05 level.

Further, this tendency is facilitated somewhat when the staff is operating in a situation where medical performance is being evaluated (high medical V of C) (Beta $= -.11$) or when the governing body of the hospital is not as cognizant of the hospital's economic circumstances (low economic V of C) (Beta $= -.17$). These patterns in the data suggest, contrary to the hypothesis, that allowing physicians more freedom in and responsibility for determining how and when to utilize the bed capacity of the hospital facilitates use of the physical plant.

Looking at the direct effect of adoption on average occupancy rate under different types and levels of visibility of consequences, it appears that adoption only has a positive influence when either economic or medical visibility is low. It also seems apparent from looking at the other variables in Table 7 that a hospital's delay in admission is most directly interrelated with its occupancy rate.

Table 8 shows the relation of centralization and other factors to the second dimension of efficiency, average length of patient stay. It was predicted that under the condition of high visibility of economic consequences, centralization would have a significant influence on reducing patients' average length of stay. The exact opposite is evidenced in the data.

The importance of introducing the factor of visibility of consequences into the analysis is made particularly evident in this instance. The reader will recall that Table 4 indicated that who made decisions had no significant impact on a hospital's average length-of-stay statistics. However, a very different conclusion is drawn when comparing the relation of who makes decisions under conditions of high and low economic visibility to average length of stay. Centralization of authority has the impact (Beta $= .08$) of increasing the average length of stay when visibility is high. There is a suggestion in the data, although not significant (Beta $= -.07$), that centralization only facilitates a lower average length of stay where awareness of the hospital's economic state is low. Why might this be the case?

The measure of economic visibility, it will be recalled, is based on the extent to which the governing body of the hospital participates in the budget allocation and review processes. Given this fact, the data indicate that if persons at the top of the organization retain administrative control over the hospital's activities, they are more apt to establish procedures and follow courses of action which give priority to economic rather than medical considerations when they are cognizant of the economic state of the system

TABLE 8

Regression Estimates of the Impact of Centralization and Other Organizational Factors on Average Length of Stay Controlling for Levels of Economic and Medical Visibility of Consequence

EXPLANATORY VARIABLE	AVERAGE LENGTH OF STAY [a]			
	Visibility of Economic Consequence		Visibility of Medical Consequence	
	High	*Low*	*High*	*Low*
Centralization of decision making	.08[b]	-.07	.03	.08
Adoption	-.12[b]	-.13[b]	-.12[b]	-.07
Urban/rural (urban = 1, rural = 0)	-.02	.09	.08	.02
Delay in admission	-.02	.08	.06	-.04
Hospital affiliated with medical school	-.02	.06	.06	-.10[b]
Outside funds for research	.13[b]	.07	.13[b]	.20[b]
Other assets	-.02	.04	.02	-.05
Number of full-time physicians	.22[b]	.24[b]	.21[b]	.18[b]
Number of different medical specialists on staff	-.04	-.10[b]	-.08	-.15[b]
Number of full-time non-medical personnel	-.21[b]	-.13[b]	-.11[b]	-.17[b]
Number of services	-.02	-.07	-.04	.03
Visibility of economic consequence			-.04	.05
Visibility of medical consequence	-.03	-.06		
MR =	.33	.39	.40	.33
N =	205	170	156	184

[a] Values reported are Beta weight.
[b] Beta greater than twice its standard error, significant at the .05 level.

than when they are not. This is not meant to imply that in such instances persons intentionally made decisions disregarding the medical needs of the hospital's patients. However, the economic realities of delivery of hospital care, if given priority over medical considerations, are less likely to result in decisions favorable to the patient.

For the most part, hospitals follow a policy of billing patients a fixed charge per day, regardless of how many days they remain in the hospital. In reality, though, a hospital incurs more expenses to process a patient at the time of admission and for a period thereafter than it charges the patient. As the patient stays longer, however, the price charged exceeds the expenses of services delivered, enabling the hospital to recover its costs. Thus as it now stands, given the billing policies which hospitals must presently follow if they are to be reimbursed by the major third-party payers, the economically aware rational head is likely to favor decisions which extend or do not reduce the average length of time a patient stays in the hospital.

A change in the present nationwide billing policy to allow hospitals to charge patients on the basis of a decreasing sliding scale would reduce or eliminate the economic constraints now operating and thus encourage hospitals to keep patients for a shorter period of time. Though such a policy would not presumably reduce the total charged a patient, by lowering the hospital's average length of stay, a hospital would be able to serve more patients with the same number of beds. Given the expanding demand for hospital inpatient care and the high cost of building new bed facilities, such a change seems warranted.

Returning to Table 8, it may be seen that, as was the case in Table 4, the number of non-medical personnel has the effect of reducing average length of stay, whereas the magnitude of a hospital's outside research funds and its number of full-time attending physicians have the effect of increasing average length of stay. It would appear then that the trends previously discussed remain even under different conditions of visibility of consequences.

The final dimension of efficiency considered, total expenses (Table 9), is seen to be inversely influenced by centralization under all four types and levels of visibility of consequences. Looking at the impact of other factors, it can be seen that geographic location, the time since the hospital was founded, and amount of outside research funds all have a positive impact on a hospital's total expenses. Adoption of medical technology has a differential impact on total expenses, depending upon the nature of a hospital's visibility of consequences. Under conditions of low economic visibility or high medical visibility, adoption has a positive impact on total expenses; but when economic visibility is high or medical visibility is low, a hospital's level of adoption has no effect. The interrelationship between types and levels of visibility of consequences as they impinge upon the impact of adoption on total expenses warrants further investigation. In line with this, there are several other indications from the data in Table 9 of the differential impact of various organizational factors on total expenses under varying conditions of availability and use of information in the hospital (i.e., visibility of consequences). For example, with high visibility of economic consequences, the greater the number of full-time nonmedical personnel the lower the total expenses. However, the reverse is true under conditions of low economic or high medical visibility of consequences. Thus, in reference to the previous discussion of the relation among level of adoption, labor, and total expenses, it can be seen that whether labor has an impact on total expenses depends upon the nature of the organization's information system. Similarly, where visibility of economic consequences is low, medical school affiliation has a positive relation to total expenses, whereas when economic visibility is high, such an affiliation appears to have no effect on total expenses. Interestingly, with high visibility of medical consequences, the use of outpatient services has a positive relation to total expenses but holds no relation under other conditions of visibility.

Looking at the effects of economic visibility of consequences itself on total expenses, only when visibility of medical consequences is low does it have a negative effect. On the other hand, there is no effect of visibility of medical consequences on total expenses under either level of visibility of economic consequences. These findings raise the serious question of the circumstances under which various medical and economic information systems contribute to improved performance of the hospital.

To a large extent, information regarding past performance can be thought of as value-free. While it can form the basis of a series of decisions, it does not determine the nature of the decisions themselves. Today, top officials of hospitals face myriad pressures from the public and private sectors of society to keep costs down. Thus it is understandable that their decisions would reflect a

TABLE 9

Regression Estimates of the Impact of Centralization and Other Organizational Factors
on Total Expenses Controlling for Levels of Economic
and Medical Visibility of Consequence

	TOTAL EXPENSES [a]			
	Visibility of Economic Consequence		Visibility of Medical Consequence	
EXPLANATORY VARIABLE	*High*	*Low*	*High*	*Low*
Centralization of decision making	-.13[b]	-.14[b]	-.21[b]	-.04[b]
Adoption	-.03	.12[b]	.08[b]	-.02
Urban/rural (Urban = 1, rural = 0)	.21[b]	.31[b]	.19[b]	.22[b]
Cost of manpower	.04	.00	.02	.00
Delay in admission	.19[b]	.14[b]	.16[b]	.19[b]
Hospital affiliated with medical school	-.03	.27[b]	.14[b]	.12[b]
Years since founding	.16[b]	.14[b]	.16[b]	.13[b]
Outside funds for research	.43[b]	.28[b]	.32[b]	.37[b]
Average length occupancy rate	.06	-.01	-.07	.06[b]
Average length of stay	.04	.03	.01	.10[b]
Other assets	.13[b]	-.09	.05	.00
Number of full-time physicians	.06	-.05	.04	-.38[b]
Total visits—outpatient services	.06	-.04	.11[b]	.01
Number of different medical specialists on staff	.00	-.32[b]	-.10[b]	-.17[b]
Number of full-time non-medical personnel	-.09[b]	.26[b]	.30[b]	.00
Number of services	-.01	-.16[b]	-.12[b]	-.14[b]
Visibility of economic consequence	.00	-.03		
Visibility of medical consequence			.02	-.08[b]
MR =	.84	.89	.86	.91
N =	205	170	156	184

[a] Values reported are Beta weights.
[b] Beta greater than twice its standard error, significant at the .05 level.

stronger concern for the monetary aspects of health care delivery. On the other hand, physicians are more likely to concern themselves with the quality of care they deliver to their patients. Thus simply increasing the level of awareness of economic and medical past performance in a hospital as a means of improving the quality and efficiency of health care delivery without concern for who is going to use the information is likely to result in wasted efforts. While this may appear to be a rather obvious point, it is the case that hospitals have in the past and are presently being pressed to institute programs and procedures for evaluating both their economic and medical performance. In at least two instances, findings of this study suggest that information-collecting programs have, as yet, little positive impact on hospital behavior. Specifically, we are referring here to a hospital's accounting system, and second, to whether a hospital participates in the Medical Audit Procedures (M.A.P.) program.

Though developing and maintaining an elaborate accounting system necessarily requires a sizable expenditure of funds, pressure at a national level has been placed on hospitals to improve their accounting practices. One possible rationale behind doing so is that having a sophisticated accounting system will provide a hospital with the kind of financial information needed to effectively control, if not reduce, its costs of delivering care. In a similar vein, encouraging hospitals to utilize the services of M.A.P. can be seen as a way a hospital can gain an increased awareness of its medical staff's performance relative to other hospitals. Conceivably, such information could provide a strong impetus to improve the quality of care they deliver. One indicator of this would be the frequency with which they adopt new medical technology. Since there is a great variation in the sophistication of hospitals' accounting systems, and less than half of them subscribe to M.A.P., it was possible to test whether in fact these two mechanisms for raising levels of visibility were having any effect.

The relation between hospitals' sophistication level of accounting techniques and the three dimensions of efficiency was found to be almost nil. Similarly, whether or not a hospital participated in M.A.P. showed no relation to the frequency with which it adopted new technology.

Hence, using the criteria of increasing efficiency on the one hand or stimulating the adoption of new medical technology on the other, neither of these techniques appears to work. But why shouldn't they, at least potentially, lead to increased information being available in the organization upon which to base decisions?

The answer may lie with a point raised earlier. Simply increasing the quantity and/or quality of information a hospital has concerning its past performance with regard for who is going to make use of the information may be a fruitless endeavor. Without question, an elaborate accounting system can provide decision makers with a great deal of information, but effective use of it can only be made if a hospital has someone on hand with the expert knowledge of accounting theory to interpret the figures. To the extent that decision makers in the hospital lack such expertise or access to it, a more sophisticated accounting system is only producing information which no one knows how to apply. It might be more judicious in terms of reducing expenses to refrain from pressuring hospitals any further on this front until such time as they are also required to retain on their administrative staffs the experts needed to adequately interpret the information.

Likewise, a hospital which participates in M.A.P. receives aggregated information regarding its past medical performance. While such information could be potentially useful, in the hands of individuals who are not oriented to it and who work in an environment which requires them to deal with one patient at a time, it may have no significant value. It is likely that such information can only be effectively utilized by persons sensitive to the complex issues involved in organizing health care delivery systems. Suffice it to say, it is unlikely physicians in most cases are prepared to use the statistics generated by M.A.P.

To the extent that what has been found in the two instances can be generalized to other mechanisms for generating information in hospitals, it would seem imperative to evaluate more fully the circumstances surrounding the intended use of the information produced before requiring hospitals to invest money and manpower to institute such mechanisms.

Conclusion

As stated in the introduction to the paper, our major concern was with clarifying the effects of various organization factors surrounding the relationship between level of adoption of new medical technology and the costs of hospital services. The data presented support the contention that who makes decisions in a hospital has a differential effect on how well the organization is able to handle the problem of keeping down the costs of care and maintaining up-to-date medical facilities. Decentralization of decision making appears to facilitate a hospital's adoption of modern medical technology. Conversely, centralization of decision making is associated with lower total expenses. Further, contrary to what is often thought, it was found that a high level of adoption has the effect of reducing average length of stay and increasing average occupancy rate while having little direct impact on a hospital's total expenses. The evidence indicates that in terms of efficiency, organizational structure is an important factor in determining whether gains in effectiveness outweigh expenses associated with the adoption of new technology.[14]

When the level of economic and medical information available (visibility of consequences) in hospitals is taken into consideration, the impact of centralization on adoption behavior and efficiency is found to be far more complex than initially predicted. These findings, in concert with the lack of effect of a hospital's sophistication level of accounting techniques on total expenses and the lack of effect of participation in M.A.P. on adoption behavior, suggest the importance of increasing our understanding of the relationships between information systems, decision making, and organizational structure in hospitals.

[14]While this paper has focused on the impact of internal organizational structure on hospital efficiency and effectiveness, a relatively consistent relation of hospital location (rural-urban) to the dependent variables is also apparent. Though only a global indicator of the nature of a hospital's external environment, the data suggest that a more refined examination of the impact of environmental characteristics on hospital behavior may be fruitful.

Edward V. Morse, PH.D.
Department of Sociology
Tulane University
New Orleans, Louisiana 70118

Gerald Gordon, PH.D.
New York State School of Industrial and Labor Relations
Department of Sociology
Cornell University
Ithaca, New York 14850

Michael Moch, PH.D.
Department of Sociology
University of Michigan
Ann Arbor, Michigan 48104

References

Andersen, Ronald, and J. Joel May
1972   "Factors associated with increased costs of hospital care." The Annals of The American Academy of Political and Social Science (January):62-72.

Becker, S., and G. Gordon
1966   "The entrepreneurial theory of formal organizations, part I: patterns of formal organization." Administrative Science Quarterly, 2, number 3:315-344.

Carr, J., and P. Feldstein
1967   "The relation of hospital cost to size." Inquiry 4:45-65.

Feldstein, M.
1967   Economic Analysis for Health Service Efficiency. Chicago: Markham.

Feldstein, P.
1961   An Empirical Investigation of the Marginal Cost of Hospital Services. Chicago: University of Chicago Press.

Gordon, G., C. Tanon, and E. Morse
1974   "Professional power, hospital structure, and innovation." Paper prepared for the American Sociological Association Meeting, Montreal, Canada.

Ingbar, Mary Lee, and Lester Taylor
1968   Hospital Costs in Massachusetts. Cambridge: Harvard University Press.

Klarman, H.
1965   The Economics of Health. New York: Columbia University Press.

Lave, J.
1966   "A review of the methods used to study hospital costs." Inquiry 3:57-81.

Lave, Judith R., and Lester B. Lave
1970a   "Hospital cost functions." The American Economic Review (June): 379-395.
1970b   "Economic analysis for health service efficiency: a review article." Applied Economics 1:293-305.

Mann, J., and D. Yett
1968   "The analysis of hospital costs: a review article." Journal of Business 41:191-202.

Rafferty, John
1971   "Patterns of hospital use." Journal of Political Economy 79 (January-February): 154-165.

1972   "Hospital output indices." Economic and Business Bulletin 24 (Winter): 21-27.

Rogers, Everett M.
1962   Diffusion of Innovation. New Yori: Free Press of Glencoe.

1967   Bibliography on the Diffusion of Innovation. East Lansing, Michigan: Michigan State University.

Rosner, Martin M.
1968   "Economic determinants of organizational innovation." Administrative Science Quarterly 12 (March): 614-625.

Thompson, James D.
1967   Organizations in Action. New York: McGraw-Hill.

A Contingency Model for the Design
of Problem-Solving Research Programs:
A Perspective on Diffusion Research

GERALD GORDON

ANN E. MacEACHRON

G. LAWRENCE FISHER

Employing relevant research findings of the administration of research, we have developed guidelines for the effective administration of problem-solving research. Using the problem of the diffusion of medical technology as a case in point we sought to identify relevant steps in the research process. The initial step is to provide a bridge between practical and theoretical concerns. For example, the increasing federal role in health care delivery and the public demand for improvement of health care have led to the question of how social science may assist in the diffusion of medical technology and, therefore, improve further the quality of health care delivery. Only recently, however, has social science research in the diffusion of technology area begun to provide some information on potential inter- and intra-organizational factors that affect diffusion and that may facilitate the "reasoned" implementation of social policy. One way to view the lack of theoretical information relevant to policy issues is by understanding the nature of the problem-solving process. In this regard, a six-stage classification scheme for evaluating research sophistication and problem-solving capability was proposed.

This led to a conclusion that social science in general and diffusion research in particular were in a "pre-paradigm" stage of development and raised the question of what could be done to improve the quality of future research. The principal factors considered were internal and external evaluation criteria, disciplinary versus interdisciplinary research, types of institutional settings, and types of funding patterns. Given the constraint of limited knowledge in this area, it was suggested tentatively that institutes with an emphasis on interdisciplinary and group research and funded through contracts may be more appropriate for the further development of applied or mission-oriented research while continuation of individual research projects characteristic of university settings and funded through grants may be more appropriate for the development of discipline-centered research.

A contingency model for research administration was proposed to suggest more specific ways in which the effectiveness of problem solving in diffusion research could be improved. The concepts of urgency (the social need for rapid, applicable research results) and predictability (the extent to which researchers can predetermine the steps needed to reach their objectives) were used to develop administrative guidelines as well as predict the probability of tangential research, the emergence of anomalies, the probable sources of conflict, and the personality attributes required by researchers in different research settings.

M M F Q / Health and Society / *Spring 1974*

An underlying assumption of this paper is that social science can and should play an important role in regard to social problems. Yet there is reason to question the effectiveness of such research. All too often social research in general, and health-related social research in particular, has reflected the whims and vagaries of social fad, social pressure, and changing support patterns. This has often resulted (as we shall show in regard to studies of the diffusion of medical technology) in research findings which are noncumulative, conceptually noncomparable, and of questionable relevance to social policy.

We feel that the relevance of social research to policy decisions would be increased if long-range systematic research programs aimed at specific social problem areas, such as the delivery of health care, were developed. Critical to the success of such programs is the fostering of cumulative research accomplishment. This objective, we believe, would be furthered if policy administrators and social scientists were encouraged to discuss science policy and administration not solely in terms of immediate concerns, but also from the perspective of the growing body of research on science administration policy.

The opportunity to implement this approach was created when the National Institutes of Health (NIH) asked us to plan a conference directed toward the development of policy in regard to research on the diffusion of medical technology. The conference was held in September 1972, at Cornell University. The eighty participants included government officials, physicians, and social scientists.

This paper follows our approach to the conference in that we first examine diffusion research from the perspective of policy imperatives and then present the issues and problems of medical diffusion research, assessing accomplishments to date, and outlining future objectives.

In the second part of the paper we review work on the general question of the administration of research which can facilitate the achievement of these objectives. In the third part we develop a contingency model for research administration and relate that model to diffusion research and the objectives of the conference.

Policy Issues in Studying the Diffusion of Medical Technology

The interest in examining diffusion of technology represents a widening of federal concern with the health system. Historically, the federal government has stressed the importance of establishing a scientific base for improving medical care. Consequently, a large share of federal health funds has been allocated to the development of medical technology and the support of research- and training-based institutions.

In recent years, however, the public has demanded a greater federal role, and, as a result, Congress has passed legislation to promote increased governmental intervention in health care delivery. This concern was summed up by a government participant at the conference (Tilson and Carrigan, 1972:2):

> The ever-enlarging Federal role, and the powerful public demand that this role be exercised to improve health care for all of the people, raises the question of whether conventional wisdom should continue to be the sole guide in designing Federal programs to intervene in the health system or whether systemic study of the diffusion of medical innovations might yield knowledge that could be used to make Federal health programs more effective.

The trend toward a greater federal role in health care is reflected in the development of the National Institutes of Health. In 1945, for example, the NIH annual budget was approximately $3 million; by 1972, it has reached $1.5 billion (Tilson and Carrigan, 1972:9). The growth of NIH is largely attributable to its broad mandate: it is responsible for developing new medical technology, and it shares responsibility with other federal agencies for facilitating the application of this technology. The Institutes' expanding role and their success in developing viable medical technologies have led to a concern within NIH with optimal diffusion and use patterns for the technologies already developed, as well as for future technologies. It was recognized that, if facilitating activities were to be planned, knowledge regarding diffusion in general and, more specifically, the manner in which technology is diffused among the organizations and individuals in the health care delivery system, is necessary.

The Conference on Diffusion had as its mandates to develop guidelines for a research thrust which would provide this information and also to provide the basis for a judgment as to whether such a thrust is warranted. This meant multiple concerns by participants with substantive questions and potential research strategies.

While our immediate task related to research on the diffusion of medical technology, our broad concerns and the programmatic design problems we encountered have implications for other problem-oriented social science research programs. In particular, since the bulk of the illustrations and supporting data relate to health research, we feel that our discussion bears directly upon many social problem areas and the delivery of care.

During the last four decades, interest in the development and use of innovations in medical technology has increased, primarily because medical science has been successful in solving problems, delineating new problems to explore, and discovering new areas where technology can be applied. These successes have led to the allocation of large sums of money and other resources for research on medical technology. Commenting on the need for such resources, Weinberg (1967:101) has said:

> We are, or ought to be, entering an age of biomedical science and biomedical technology that could rival in magnitude the richness of the present age of physical science and physical technology . . . of all the bases for claiming large-scale public support for a scientific activity, the possibility of alleviating human disease through such activity is obviously one of the most compelling.

The extent of funding for these research efforts is currently being questioned. One reason for questioning current and projected support levels is an uncertainty about the social effectiveness of biomedical research. This uncertainty is one of the factors leading to a concern to learn more about the diffusion of medical technology. But the question of the diffusion of technology transcends funding concerns. Given that the ultimate aim of medical research and development is improved medical care, evaluating technology's impact on care is, in and of itself, a central concern. If medical technology is presumed to be generally beneficial, access to the technology is one important way to improve the quality of care. The diffusion problem may be seen as the gap between the number of users who have adopted desirable technological innovations and the universe of appropriate users. Conversely, the problem may be seen in terms of premature acceptance, or the number of users who have adopted undesirable innovations. Both views imply the need for a high degree of quality control over the adoption of technologies, and stress the relationship between diffusion and the quality of medical care.

Research Problems

In any research area definitions pose a problem. What is meant by diffusion, innovation, technology, and quality of care? These are value-laden terms whose connotations are complex and diverse. Such terms are never completely adequate. The following definitions are offered as sensitizing rather than definitive.

Diffusion is the dispersion, or rate of dispersion, of ideas, techniques, practices, knowledge, information, and products to adopters at various distances from the innovation's point of origin. The literature defines *technology* in many different ways, but two elements are common to all the definitions: physical techniques, procedures, or programs to achieve desired goals; and a broad knowledge or skill base to achieve the goals. Medical technology which results from basic and applied biomedical research is a scientific body of knowledge underlying the techniques, procedures, or programs needed for effective medical diagnosis, therapy, or prevention. *Innovation* is a significant technological change. *Quality of care* refers to the continued upgrading of health facilities, the increased training of health professionals and paraprofessionals, and the coordination of health services to improve medical care. These definitions, in turn, create an awareness of several interrelated questions:

1. How do we select criteria for deciding whether a specific technological item should be diffused?
2. How much research evidence do we have on the types of diffusion patterns and the factors which cause them?
3. How can we identify the institutional and individual factors that lead to optimal diffusion?

The first problem, selection of criteria, is a matter of critical judgment, because there is neither an appropriate model nor a competitive marketplace to help us decide whether a specific item should be diffused. Given this situation, can a functional decision-making model be developed? Is it possible to evaluate current innovations, to reassess earlier innovations that are at various diffusion stages, and to examine the basic decision-making criteria on which the diffusion of these innovations were based? To be effective, the criteria must take into account judgments of experts in many fields, and must also be based on innovation characteristics that apply to many innovations, so that effectiveness can be measured, and diffusion rates can be accurately predicted, for a wide variety of innovations.

The second problem involves examining the currently available information on factors that affect diffusion patterns and adoption rates in medical organizations. Research is available on: (1) environmental pressures which encourage organizations to adopt innovations—

Rogers and Shoemaker (1971), for example, report on the effects of legislation and persuasion, and Thompson (1967) on power-dependence relationships with the task environment; (2) factors which determine adoption rates in different organizations—Aiken and Hage (1968) have studied the relationship between organizational diversity, resources, and diffusion, and Gordon et al. (1974) have approached the diffusion problem in terms of the locus of decision making in organizational structure; (3) innovation characteristics which facilitate rapid adoption—Thio (1971) has reported on the relationship between the characteristics of innovations and diffusion patterns, and Fliegel and Kivlin (1966) examined diffusion patterns in terms of the economic factors associated with innovation. Though one can point to other studies which contribute to our knowledge base, the research on factors that affect diffusion patterns in medical organizations is sparse. Not only do we need more knowledge, but that which we already have must be coordinated before viable intervention strategies can be developed to improve diffusion patterns.

A third problem is how to identify the institutional and individual factors that can lead to optimal diffusion. Given Perrow's (1965) suggestion that hospitals, as organizational structures, are dependent on medical technology, it is possible to use technology as a reference point and then determine the organizational structures and resource characteristics necessary for its effective use. Organ transplant technology, for example, is impossible in the absence of organizational structures that allow coordination of skilled personnel, necessary equipment, and operating rooms. Scarcity of specialized manpower, limited funds for technology, and lack of organizational support are assumed to limit diffusion. However, we have very little hard knowledge about the impact that each kind of scarcity (separately and in conjunction with one another) has on diffusion of technology.

The potential impact of organizational and individual factors can be seen in the relationship between practitioners and administrators within a hospital. Hall (1968:92–104) in his study of professions, found that problems resulted from different views of authority and autonomy held by professionals and administrators. These problems are exacerbated when, as in the case of medicine, the profession has a history of self-administration. For example, the AMA has played an important role in evaluating and certifying competency; through activities such as publishing acceptable medical practices, it has helped increase coordination within the medical profession while retaining authority over its membership. Furthermore, physicians have historically had sole responsibility for the coordination of patient care. But, as Glaser points out, the coordination, scheduling, and regulation of hospital resources have been increasingly determined by hospital administrators rather than practicing 'physicians, and this has led to tension between the two groups (see Glaser, 1963; Gordon and Becker, 1964). The question researchers must ask is: What is the effect of this tension on diffusion patterns?

Diffusion and the Health Care System

There is some movement toward an understanding of these problems. Rogers (1972) points out that the classical diffusion model has been of limited use in health field studies, because its treatment of organizational structures is inadequate. The classical model emphasized individual adopters (Coleman et al., 1966) and ignored organizational characteristics which affect either the diffusion process or the adoption process.[1] Recently, however, productive information exchanges have occurred between researchers in the diffusion and organizational fields.

In recent review of the literature on program changes in organizations, Aiken and Hage (1968) argue that a systems approach is needed for understanding the intra- and inter-organizational process of change. They say that changes occur at different organizational levels, and, in order to cope with multiple levels of analysis, we must view the basic organizational dimensions and their relation to performance in terms of social resources (e.g., technology), social structure (e.g., specialization), integration processes (e.g., communication), and social environment (e.g., inter-organizational linkages).

Currently, findings in the health and organizational fields are converging. Hospitals, like most organizations, have a complex network of relations with other organizations and individuals. Government agencies, national associations, regulatory bodies, local health organizations, community interest groups, and many individuals influence the hospital's functioning (see Glaser, 1963; Elling, 1963). Some research suggests that the relation of the hospital to outside groups influences its capacity to provide medical care; hospitals associated with community leaders, through the hospital's governing body, have better access to resources for expanding their services and adopting

---

[1]The *diffusion process* "refers to the spread of new product from its manufacturer to ultimate users or adopters. To model a diffusion process, the analyst works with a few macroparameters that will locate a curve to describe the spread of the innovation over time." The *adoption process* "refers to the mental sequence of stages through which a consumer progresses from first awareness of an innovation to final acceptance."

new technologies. Other researchers have demonstrated that the attributes of an innovation affect its diffusion. The more compatible an item is with an existing social system, for instance, the more rapidly it will spread.

Research results make it clear that inter- and intra-organizational factors, the nature of the delivery system, and the technology itself are all centrally related to medical diffusion. Facilitating optimal diffusion, therefore, requires the cooperation of experts in at least four distinct research disciplines: medicine, formal organization, medical sociology, and diffusion. This poses problems of communication and coordination among researchers with different orientations and research traditions, and it also raises a series of important questions. What problems need to be solved in each field? What facts do we need to solve them? What further knowledge would provide a bridge between theoretical concerns and practical applications? Are the problems and methodologies of each field well enough developed for interdisciplinary work to produce comprehensive directions, or would it just create a quagmire of misunderstandings? Do some fields need separate treatment in order to focus problems and tools and stimulate further growth? Can we use current knowledge and methodologies for diffusion and intervention purposes? Finally, what problems do we face, if we attempt to use interdisciplinary research to expand our predictive power in diffusion? Answers to these questions relate directly to the nature of problem-solving research.

The Problem-Solving Process

The term "problem-solving" implies fixed objectives and a relatively natural progression of activities aimed at achieving those objectives. This process can be analyzed in terms of six interdependent research stages, which, along with the research methodologies associated with each stage, are present in Table 1.

The first stage, *problem delineation,* involves determining which areas of concern can be fruitfully researched. Before we can develop effective research programs, we must assess certain factors, including, for instance, the diffusion patterns of current medical technologies, and techniques which are overdiffused or underdiffused. After this assessment, it is necessary to have a preliminary policy statement, highlighting relevant issues and available data, and defining the range and scope of the research problems. While statistical studies and secondary data sources are important, assessments are qualitative and relate to social judgments. In delineating a problem, the data selected for re-

TABLE 1.
A Classification of Social Science Research

Research Stages	Research Purpose	Research Mode
1. Problem delineation	To define what we are looking for and the extent to which it is a problem	Qualitative analysis
2. Variable identification	To identify variables which might be linked to the problem, and describe possible interconnections between these variables	Exploratory case studies
3. Determination of relations among variables	To determine the clusters of relevant variables required for prediction and to analyze their patterns	Cross-sectional studies
4. Establishment of causality	To determine which factors are critical in promoting or inhibiting the problem	Longitudinal studies, small-scale experiments
5. Manipulation of causal variables	To determine the correspondence between a theoretical problem solution and the controllable technical factors	Field experiments
6. Evaluation	To assess the advantages, as well as unanticipated consequences, of various programs before and after they are applied on a large scale, and to determine the effectiveness of such programs in overall problem solution	Controlled field comparisons

view, the weight given to a body of data, and interpretation are, more than in any other stage, the resultant of qualitative assessments.

The next stage is *identifying important variables.* This is an exploratory step taken to discover what variables are systematically linked to diffusion and to describe interconnections among them. The major research technique employed is the case study. Questions that arise during this phase include: What areas in the health care system are critical to understanding the diffusion problem? At what points do effective and ineffective innovations enter the health system, and how do these entry points affect diffusion and health care? What characteristics of potential adopting units affect adoption rates? How do those characteristics vary? What are the users' concerns about various technological innovations? How is the type of adopting unit related to the type of innovation? Do innovations spread outside, among, or only within medical centers? Who are the gatekeepers in the diffusion process, and what influences them? What roles do the media, voluntary associations, and government agencies play in medical diffusion?

The third stage involves *determining the relations among variables.* At this stage, researchers determine the strength of relationships among variables that have been associated with diffusion patterns.

This requires a shift in research mode, from case studies to cross-sectional techniques, in order to extend the comparative range of our research. The research range and results, however, will vary according to the level of analysis used and the field that furnishes the theoretical guidelines. Social scientists concerned with the individual level of analysis, for example, might examine the characteristics of adopters or the degree to which potential adopters are socially isolated from a professional group (see, for example, Coleman et al., 1966; Shepard, 1967; Schron, 1963). Social scientists concerned with structural variables, on the other hand, might examine the ways that organizational slack influences innovation (see Cyert and March, 1963). Differences among fields also exist. Researchers in the organizational field might assume that organizations resist innovations, whereas researchers in economics might assume that organizations have a common mechanism that allows them to adapt to their environment and adopt innovations. Despite differences in orientation the research has a central focus—the relation of a given factor to diffusion patterns.

At the fourth level, *establishment of causality,* research is directed toward systematic predictions. Most work conducted in the diffusion, health, and organizational fields has produced cross-sectional or case study material, so the data base consists primarily of correlated gross variables. Consequently, we know more about adoption patterns than we do about the factors that cause the pattern. Longitudinal studies are critical if we are to identify the behavioral or social factors that are causally related in the diffusion of medical technology. Longitudinal studies, however, are both expensive and time-consuming, which accounts for the dearth of longitudinal studies in the social sciences. This is a matter of concern, because understanding causal relationships is an important precursor of successful intervention. Unfortunately, many health and other types of social programs have been initiated on the basis of untested assumptions about causality. Experience has taught us the inherent perils of such assumptions. Recently, for example, the National Institutes of Mental Health sponsored two programs aimed at developing community mental health centers and regional medical programs, but, as Tilson and Carrigan (1970:2) state:

> . . .the [health centers] concept was launched by NIMH on a wholesale basis without pilot testing or evaluation of a model. The regional medical program concept sprang from the observation that, on the whole, better medicine was being practiced at the academic medical centers than in nonacademic settings, and that additional resources and new organiza-

tional arrangements could reduce this quality gap. There is at least some preliminary evidence that neither of these intuitive judgments—on the basis of which very large sums were committed—was based on an adequate appreciation of the complexity of the factors involved.

The fifth research stage, *manipulation of causal variables,* involves identification of causal factors that can be manipulated relatively easily. To illustrate this, let us assume that diffusion is causally related to the growth rate of the gross national product. Changing the GNP is not feasible, however, so we must find other, manipulable variables that affect diffusion. The level of available medical skills might be such a variable. Another concern related to the manipulation of variables is an understanding of the system implications of a given intervention. Field experiments, which enable investigators to introduce various changes into a part of a system, represent an effective way to study both concerns.

The Tavistock studies of British coal mines are illustrative of the field-experiment approach and provide a classic example of how technological change may be ineffective unless it is integrated with the existing social patterns of organizational groups. When technical changes were introduced into the coal-mining process, the traditional division of labor was changed from independent work groups responsible for a series of coordinated tasks, to individuals assigned to simple, singular tasks. Productivity and job satisfaction dropped, even though the new task divisions were supposed to be more efficient. The Tavistock researchers found that the cohesiveness, autonomy, and self-regulation of traditional work groups had produced "behavior which goes beyond specified role requirements and . . . advances the organization towards its goals" (Katz and Kahn, 1966: 441), but the social changes generated by the new arrangement had discouraged such productive behavior. When the traditional social organization was retained and the new arrangement was integrated into it, the expected benefits were derived; but this integration could not be sustained (Katz and Kahn, 1966:441):

> The thrust of the Tavistock group toward developing the best fit between the technological system and the social system met with only partial success. Its efforts were limited by its inability to gain entry to the top-power circles in the industry, the difficulty of communicating the research results to groups who had not themselves been involved in the experimental comparisons, and the threat to the larger social system of the implications of a thorough rational reform.

While the Tavistock experiments failed in implementation, the potential viability of integrating new methods into traditional structures was illustrated in a recent replication study of industrial organizations. The study found that "technological sophistication seems to operate as a conditioning variable in social change efforts directly through situational constraints on worker behavior, and indirectly through affecting interconnectedness of social subsystems" (Taylor, 1971).

No similar studies have been done on health organizations, but we can assume that such studies would offer many research payoffs, since similar problems are created when technological change is introduced into medical institutions. Hospital adoption of certain items, for example, will necessitate new kinds of social organization. The Tavistock research indicates that the benefits of change can be realized only if the changes are integrated with existing work procedures.

The phenylketonuria program illustrates how medical programs can gain large-scale acceptance and yet prove ineffective because of insufficient testing and control. Phenylketonuria (PKU) is a hereditary, metabolic disorder which "inhibits the synthesis of the liver protein . . . (so that) . . . mental impairment appears" (Bessman and Swazey, 1971: 49–76). After researchers discovered PKU's etiology and developed a dietary treatment program, forty-one states passed laws regulating or requiring tests and treatment for PKU and other metabolic disorders in newborns. In 1963, Massachusetts was the first to pass such laws, and, in the next four years, forty other states followed suit. In 1967, two federal bills, Kennedy-Prouty and Moss, were proposed in committee to standardize PKU testing and extend its principle to detect "other inborn errors of metabolism leading to mental retardation or physical defects" (Bessman and Swazey, 1971: 58–63). The scientific validity of PKU testing and treatment programs has not yet been established, however; and, according to Bessman and Swazey (1971:49–76), four major but false assumptions are made about PKU: (1) there are reliable, inexpensive mass-screening procedures; (2) the higher the level of phenylalaine in the blood the greater the degree of mental retardation; (3) dietary treatment programs effectively prevent PKU retardation; and (4) PKU generally produces retardation. Thus, the proprietary of making PKU testing and treatment compulsory is highly questionable. Yet the availability of techniques and the claims made for their effectiveness evidently precluded testing of the techniques themselves (Bessman and Swazey, 1971:64–71):

These laws are better characterized as symptomatic of the conflict between the scientific commitment to unfettered research and the public
commitment to social betterment, however construed. . . .In the case of
PKU the ideological and the economic play almost no part, yet we find
that the dilemmas of the scientists, the policy maker, and the citizen
remain much the same . . . the doleful story of PKU teaches us that
political methods are more likely to achieve conformity than knowledge,
that consensus is not truth, and that action is not always better than inac-
tion.

The final level in the research scheme, *evaluation,* involves controlled assessment of programs aimed at solving particular problems in
order to understand their advantages as well as their unanticipated consequences. Evaluation, although often the most important, is the most
neglected research stage. Even when evaluations are conducted, Weiss
(1972: 332) points out: "they are beset by conceptual and methodological problems, problems of relationship, status, and function, practical
problems of career and reward. To add to the perils . . . evaluation is
now becoming increasingly political." Accordingly she notes that
most evaluation studies stress discrepancies between initial and accomplished goals in single programs, rather than emphasizing the differences among programs or program components. The former is an
all-or-nothing approach to isolated phenomena, whereas the latter involves a systems perspective in which goals are the sum of the sub-
goals (March and Simon, 1958) and are a function of the "effectiveness of other functions, such as recruiting resources, maintaining the structure [and] achieving integration into the environment" (Weiss, 1972:334). Moreover, failure to attain a goal may result from many factors (e.g., social science theory, a program's
historical background, or the fragmented nature of program structure), and all those factors should be analyzed before any program
is considered a total failure, discarded, and replaced by a quick
substitute (Weiss, 1972:340).

As Suchman (1967: 152) noted, the administration of an evaluation program is very important. Public demand and cooperation, the
available resources, the problems caused by role relationships and
value conflicts, the definition of evaluation objectives, the evaluation
research design and execution, and the use of research findings all
affect the administrative structures and the outcomes of evaluative research.

The Administration of Problem-Solving Research

We are not implying that the progression of stages is deliberate or that the stages necessarily follow one another in sequence. We are suggesting that most research dealing with problem-related questions falls into one or another of these categories. Moreover, a prima facie case can be made that success in later stages is to some extent dependent upon adequate development in early stages. What we are seeking to do in this discussion is to make explicit the framework that we feel most research administrators have been implicitly employing. By doing so we hope to provide a focus for understanding the conference deliberations and for raising a number of questions bearing on research accomplishment. An initial question, for instance, is whether social scientists such as those attending the Conference on the Diffusion of Medical Technology can agree on the research level currently held by each discipline. Researchers in any given field may ask: Are we at the problem-defining stage? Are we seeking causal relationships? Are we ready to run field experiments? If we know the problems and the important variables, do we have the appropriate methodology for establishing causality, for experimenting, and for evaluating? How adequate is our data bank for developing appropriate research programs? In short, at what stage are we as we attempt to intervene in medical diffusion?

We have suggested that the nature, range, and certainty of a field's conceptual schemes reflect its level of development. What, then, is the developmental level of the social sciences as they relate to the study of diffusion? Barber (1962:37–38) offers the following evaluation:

> As for the social sciences, they tend to be still in quite an empiricist tradition, with few if any general conceptual schemes that are widely accepted . . . the fundamental cause of the difficulty is the high degree of indeterminancy in most social science knowledge. . . .

Barber made this statement in 1952, and again in 1962. Others have made similar comments about social science progress (Kuhn, 1970; Masterman, 1970). Their criticisms indicate an increasing desire to maximize research success. Success is more likely when we accept the early stage of social science development, and recognize the factors that hinder progress.

Although we can evaluate the level of social science development by Barber's criteria, major problems remain. Assuming that a science with sophisticated conceptual schemes (and, thus, a high degree of certainty in its predictions) facilitates problem solving, how can we move social science, especially diffusion research, toward this goal? With a limited conceptual scheme, or no scheme at all, how do we proceed with scholarly work? Here, Kuhn's concepts of *paradigm* and *normal science* are most helpful.

According to Kuhn (1970:11–12, 59–60), a *paradigm* is an implicit body of law, theory, application, and instrumentation which is learned through example and practice. A paradigm guides scientific research by encouraging expert consensus on what problems and facts are important, what methods and techniques are appropriate, and what scientific standards determine proof of findings. Paradigms gain status through their promise of success in directing the search for solutions to acute problems; and *normal science* (Kuhn, 1970:24) is the

> actualization of that promise, an actualization achieved by extending the knowledge of those facts that the paradigm displays as particularly revealing, by increasing the extent of the match between those facts and the paradigm's predictions, and by furthering the articulation of the paradigm itself.

The maturity of a science, then, depends on the nature of its paradigm (Kuhn, 1970: 10). Research can and does occur without a paradigm, but in the absence of paradigm criteria for measuring relevance or importance, research very often resembles random fact-gathering. In pre-paradigm science, or in subfields with competing paradigms, the selection, evaluation, and criticisms of relevant facts is possible through "intertwined theoretical and methodological belief" (Kuhn, 1970:17) but the interpretation of these facts differs: (Masterman, 1970:74):

> Here, within the sub-field defined by each paradigmatic technique, technology can sometimes become quite advanced and normal research puzzle-solving can progress. But each sub-field as defined by its techniques is so obviously more trivial and narrow than the field as defined by intuition, and also the various operational definitions given by the techniques are so grossly discordant with one another, that discussion on fundamentals remains, and long-run progress (as opposed to local progress) fails to occur.

The development of normal, paradigm-based science is "usually caused by the triumph of one of the pre-paradigm schools which, because of its own characteristic beliefs and preconceptions, emphasized only some special part of the two sizable and inchoate pool of knowledge'' (Kuhn, 1970: 15–17). This triumph is based on a concrete scientific accomplishment which a scientific community acknowledges for a time as supplying the foundation for its further practice'' (Kuhn, 1970: 10). According to Kuhn (1970:178, 179) the social sciences are now at the pre-paradigm stage of development, while the natural and physical sciences are at more advanced paradigm stages.

Recent research supports Kuhn's concepts of paradigms and paradigm development. Studying the structure of scientific fields and the functioning of university graduate departments, Lodahl and Gordon (1972: 57–72) investigated the assumed differences in paradigm development between the physical and social sciences by asking faculty members from eighty departments to rank seven fields. The results were as follows: physics (higher development), chemistry, biology, economics, psychology, sociology, and political science (lower development). They further report that intrafield consensus in regard to teaching and research was much greater in fields ranked high in paradigm development.

Why has social science in general and diffusion research in particular remained in a pre-paradigm stage? To say a field must wait for a ''triumph'' based on ''concrete scientific accomplishment'' is somewhat self-defeating. We suggest that triumphs have been limited because social scientists tend to use internal referents or field-centered criteria in assessing research. Such criteria tend to reinforce prevailing research traditions.

The need for a scientific perspective that transcends a given field is supported by Ben-David's discussion of scientific growth and activity during the seventeenth, eighteenth, and nineteenth centuries. Ben-David (1964:475) found that growth and innovations in medicine occurred more frequently when scientific systems were open, diversified, and free to ''defenses against any external influences.'' He also reported that major conceptual breakthroughs during this period tended to occur from problem-oriented research. In a similar vein, Weinberg (1968:26–38) argued that resource allocation among fields should be based on external rather than internal criteria because:

> no universe of discourse can be evaluated by criteria that are generated solely within that universe. Means are established within a universe of

discourse: ends—that is, values—must be established from outside the universe.

Internal criteria reflect the competence of scientists in terms of the standards of a given field, whereas external criteria measure the field's social importance. Weinberg (1964) claims that internal criteria constitute a necessary condition for potential scientific growth and external criteria constitute a sufficient condition.

The need for external criteria is reflected in the fact that in the 2,000-odd research studies on diffusion we reviewed in preparation for the conference we could find relatively little policy applicability. The lack of applicability was especially evident in the specific area of the diffusion of medical technology. Of the 2,000 studies, there were only eight that were both concerned with technology diffusion in medical organizations and had a sample size sufficient to permit generalization. At the time of the diffusion conference these eight studies constituted the core of our knowledge in the specific area of diffusion of medical innovation in health care organizations. Yet none of the studies is experimental in nature; one study is longitudinal and the rest are cross-sectional. Moreover, because of design or sampling limitations, imputations of causality are questionable.

The limitations of this research are a cause for concern and raise the question of what can be done to improve the quality of the data base. We believe that in stressing the external criteria implicit in problem solving, both research accomplishment and the social relevance of findings can be increased. In contrasting disciplinary criteria with problem-solving criteria, Coleman (1973:6) stated: "The criteria of parsimony and elegance that apply in discipline research are not important [in applied or policy-oriented research]; the correctness of the predictions or results is important [in applied research], and redundancy is valuable." The extent to which one or the other criterion is followed is contingent in part upon whether research is disciplinary bound or interdisciplinary, the setting of the research, and the patterns of funding research as well as its level of paradigm development.

Interdisciplinary Research

The problem of collaboration between researchers with different perspectives occurred often during the conference. The issue of interdisciplinary versus discipline-centered research had been approached by a number of researchers. Analyzing sixty-two major advances in the social sciences since 1900, Deutsch et al. (1971:450–459) found that since 1930 over half of the significant contributions have come from team research and that nearly two-thirds have come from interdisciplinary work. They concluded, as did the conference members, that teamwork and interdisciplinary work would become increasingly important during the next decade. Predicting the future of science, Dobrov (1966: 229) reached a similar conclusion:

> Science must nowadays combine the knowledge and efforts of scientists from several (often remote) specialized disciplines, utilize increasingly powerful and complex equipment, process a tremendous amount of information from various branches of knowledge and in various languages. All this can only be done by teams of scientists.

More philosophically, Campbell (1969) has argued that the ethnocentrism of disciplines, which results from present training and reward systems as well as present departmental decision-making and communication patterns, has precluded an "integrated and competent" social science. To achieve integration, Campbell suggests developing narrow but overlapping interdisciplinary specialists that together form a comprehensive whole.

Institutional Settings

Researchers have also examined the research setting and its effect on accomplishment. Ben-David (1964) found that decentralization and competition, among and within universities, were strongly associated with scientific discovery during the seventeenth, eighteenth, and nineteenth centuries. Decentralization avoided the inefficient monopolization of research facilities and resources, and competition encouraged creative approaches to difficult or tangential problems. The twentieth-century growth of science and the pressure for large-scale research have produced different organizational imperatives. Rossi (1964) examined the evolution of university-based research institutes and noted that large-scale research often requires an elaborate, hierarchical division of labor as well as a large resource investment. He concluded that the traditional departmental structure of the university, which rewards individual research and teaching, is organizationally incompatible with large-scale research. It promotes narrow disciplinary concerns and the reward system discourages long-term research. Doctoral research, for example, is usually planned to yield a completed product in one year, or, in rare cases, two years. Also, the tenure and promotion systems create pressure for publishable results every two to three years. Research institutes were established to promote the benefits of large-scale research as well as to alleviate the strain between individual and team-oriented approaches. (It is important to note that similar observations were made by members of the diffusion methodology panel.) Weinberg (1965: 1–14) agrees with Rossi and adds that, between universities and mission-oriented research institutes, the institutes should have the prior claim on resources, because they can coordinate interdisciplinary efforts to solve social problems. Thus, when large resources and applied interdisciplinary solutions are required, research institutes seem to be the most appropriate setting.

Funding Patterns

Members of the conference questioned the relationship between type of funding and research accomplishment. In the past, however, researchers have paid little attention to the ways in which social science research is funded. Deutsch et al. (1971), Rossi (1964), and others have observed that the cost of doing effective research will increase as social science develops its methodologies and the range of behavior it can predict. Lodahl and Gordon (1972) have found that, in university departments, research quality is ''not associated as strongly with levels of funding in the social as in the physical sciences.'' We have no evidence, however, on the funding levels and mechanisms which are most appropriate for different types of research. It would seem that funding levels should depend on criteria like scientific potential and social applicability, no matter what level of research activity is undertaken. The choice of funding mechanisms is more difficult. Reviewing national biomedical research agencies, Grant (1966:484) suggested that the NIH pattern of using grant review committees to determine ''scientific excellence on a project-by-project basis'' is satisfactory for discipline-centered problems, but does not ''coincide with judgments on the most effective way to reach a particular scientific goal.'' Particular goals could be reached most effectively by establishing priorities among research problems and then contracting with scientists who can solve them. The funding mechanism issue cannot be completely resolved here, but we suggest that the interdisciplinary, applied work of university and other research institutes may warrant contract or similar funding mechanisms; while the individualistic, discipline-centered research characteristic of universities may call for funding through nonrestrictive mechanisms such as grants.

A Contingency Model

Administrative Perspectives

The question remains of how to systematically apply these findings so as to increase the effectiveness of problem solving in general and diffusion research in particular. In effect, we are stressing the need for developing a perspective to facilitate the application of the above and other findings to the administration of problem-solving research programs.

In attempting to develop a perspective for research administration, we ignored the distinction between basic and applied research, which refers to use or intent, and instead emphasized the research process and social imperatives. The importance ascribed to the basic/applied dichotomy is a deeply entrenched preconception in science, but it hinders our investigations of the relationship between organizational structure and scientific accomplishment. The dichotomy offers no clear-cut basis for categorization. More important, it is not directly related to the research process, and it discourages the recognition that all research activity is aimed at some type of problem solving.

The mystique which has grown up around the terms "basic" and "applied" has encouraged patterns of research administration based on misconceptions rather than empirical fact. Research findings indicate, for instance, that the following widespread beliefs are questionable:

1. Most scientific breakthroughs occur in universities, whereas exploitations of the breakthroughs occur in industrial and other applied research settings.
2. Basic researchers tend to be more creative or innovative than applied researchers.
3. Because basic researchers are highly dedicated, administrative controls over their work are unnecessary and tend to inhibit innovation.
4. The university structure is an optimal setting for all types of research activity.

Ben-David's (1960:828–843) findings challenge the first two assumptions. Noting the breakthroughs of Koch, Pasteur, Villemin, Devaine, Freud, and others, Ben-David has argued that, historically, breakthroughs have tended to occur in applied settings. Pelz (1964) and others have challenged the third belief by finding that certain organizational controls, particularly those associated with sources and evaluation, promote innovation. Kaplan (1964:463) has also questioned the assumption that universities are always optimal research settings:

> However adequate is the research environment in some universities, it is usually the top ten or perhaps even the top twenty that we are thinking about. And even in these top schools there is little question any more that everything is the best in the best of all possible worlds. Yet this . . . is what some observers would have all of industry or government transpose to their own environment.

The distinction between basic and applied research might have been appropriate in the day of the lone researcher, but it is misleading when applied to modern research, which depends on expensive tools controlled by organizations and requires extensive teamwork. Modern research should be analyzed using concepts that refer to the research process itself and its organizational setting.

Two concepts which we found particularly valuable in analyzing patterns of research administration are *urgency* and *predictability*. *Urgency* is the social need for rapid, applicable research results, and it implies that large expenditures are justified to achieve these results. *Predictability* is the extent to which researchers can predetermine the steps needed to reach their research objectives. Predictability depends on the degree of paradigm development and the degree of involvement in paradigm-based, normal science. In Weinberg's terminology, urgency reflects social and scientific "importance," while predictability reflects a discipline's degree of "competence." By dichotomizing these concepts, we can construct four ideal situations:

$U-P-$ Little urgency, little predictability
$U-P+$ Little urgency, great predictability
$U+P-$ Great urgency, little predictability
$U+P+$ Great urgency, great predictability

Of course, research is always somewhat predictable, and there is always some urgency for the results. Also, the urgency and predictability associated with a research problem can change over time. Thus, the ideal types can be precisely matched with only a small range of studies. They are approximated in most studies, however, and using them can clarify design problems. Combining the ideal types with some findings from group dynamics and from the sociology of science produces the research administration guidelines that are outlined below.

Research Findings

1. Groups generally solve problems with predetermined answers (e.g., crossword puzzles) better than individuals; but individuals solve problems without predetermined answers (e.g., constructing crossword puzzles) better than groups (see Hare, 1962; Taylor et al., 1958).

2. In terms of absolute time, groups solve problems faster than individuals; but, in terms of man minutes per hour, individuals solve problems faster than groups (Hare, 1962).

3. Administrative control over resources stimulates scientific accomplishment. Nonpredictable research is stimulated by an administrator's evaluation of results and is hindered by an administrator's specification of research procedures (see Pelz, 1964; Gordon et al., 1966). Predictable research, however, is stimulated by administrative guidance in research procedures.

4. Effective organization of a group of research projects depends on the stage of research development. Highly developed research is facilitated by one or two concentrated projects; less developed research is facilitated by many dispersed projects (Sayles and Chandler, 1971).

Administrative Guidelines

1. Groups should be responsible for predictable (P+) research; individuals should be responsible for nonpredictable (P−) research.

2. Groups should suggest research approaches for urgent research (U+); individuals should suggest approaches for less urgent (U−) research. Also, when urgency is great (U+), different approaches should be tested simultaneously; when urgency is low, different approaches should be tested sequentially. This is especially true for nonpredictable (P−) research.

3. For nonpredictable research (P−), evaluative administrative control is advisable; for predictable research (P+), executive control is advisable.

4. Organizations should sponsor multiple projects for nonpredictable research (P−) but only a single project for predictable research (P+), because the procedures for goal attainment are predeterminable.

Classifying research in terms of urgency and predictability not only helps us develop administrative guidelines, but also allows us to predict the probability of tangential research, the emergence of anomalies, probable sources of conflict, and personality attributes required by researchers in different research settings.

Innovation

The pursuit of interesting tangents has long been considered a source of scientific innovations. A researcher's tendency to pursue a tangent is partly determined by the urgency and predictability of his research. In nonpredictable research, the procedures are determined by accepting or rejecting a series of alternatives. This selection process stimulates interest in areas tangential to the initial problem. In predictable research, procedures are usually specified in advance, which reduces tangential investigations. The urgency of the research also affects its sponsor's willingness to support tangential research: greater urgency leads to less support. We would therefore expect the $U-$ $P-$ situation to encourage tangential research, and the $U+$ $P+$ situation to discourage it. The $U+$ $P+$ and $U+$ $P-$ situations should involve moderate constraints against tangential research. Another factor related to innovation is the anomalous finding. An anomaly is a finding that does not conform to paradigm-based expectations (Kuhn, 1970:52, 62):

> Normal science does not aim at novelties of fact or theory and, when successful, finds none. New and unsuspected phenomena, are, however, repeatedly uncovered by scientific research . . . [thus] research under a paradigm must be a particularly effective way of inducing paradigm change. . . . [Change] characteristics include: the previous awareness of anomaly, the gradual and simultaneous emergence of both observational and conceptual recognition, and the consequent change of paradigm categories and procedures often accompanied by resistance.

The probability of recognizing anomalies is greatest in the $U+$ $P+$ situation. Given social urgency and high predictability, the research paradigm is subject to external testing, which, as we have noted, increased the likelihood of uncovering anomalies. The recognition of anomalies may, in rare instances, induce a research crisis that "provides the incremental data necessary for a fundamental paradigm shift" (Kuhn, 1970:89) as well as the redefinition of the degree of research predictability.

Sources of Conflict

Administrator-researcher conflicts are more likely to occur in some situations than in others. One source of conflict that we have already noted involves organizational tolerance of tangential research. In the U+P− situation, where the researcher tends toward tangential investigation and the organization resists it, the potential for conflict concerning tangential research is high.

Resource allocation and procedure specification are also major sources of conflict in research settings. In the U−P− situation (where procedures are conceived of as nonpredictable by management) conflict between management and researcher over procedures should be minimal. On the other hand, since urgency is not great, support of the project might be limited. In this situation, therefore, more conflict would occur over resource allocations than over procedures. Conversely, where urgency is great and research considered predictable, much more conflict could be expected over procedures than over resources. In the U−P+ situation, conflict would tend to occur over both procedures and resources, and one would probably find a great deal of discontent among researchers.

Personality Attributes

The last predictions concern the personality attributes of the researchers. When procedures are not predictable, the researcher would seem to need a high tolerance for ambiguity; when urgency is great, he would need a high tolerance for pressure. Thus, it could be predicted that, for research personnel, the least psychologically demanding situation would be the U−P+ situation and the most demanding the U+P− situation.

The evidence we have presented to support our model is inferential in the sense that the studies cited were not designed specifically to test the assumptions implicit in the use of the predictability and urgency concepts for administrative purposes. In our study of research projects concerned with the social aspects of disease, we sought to directly examine whether urgency did affect outcome and whether predictable research (which we termed productive research) is fostered by a different administrative environment than unpredictable (innovative) research.

In our study, data were obtained by mail questionnaires sent to the directors of 245 projects (Health Information Foundation, 1954–1960). Questionnaires for 223 (91 percent) of the projects were returned. Detailed information was obtained on various aspects of the organizational structure within which each project was conducted. To determine research performance, a panel of experts was asked to evaluate specially prepared summaries of the major reports resulting from these projects.[2] The projects were evaluated in terms of both the innovativeness and productivity of the research:

> Innovation—the degree to which the research represents additions to our knowledge through new kinds of research or the development of new theoretical statements or findings which were not explicit in previous theory.

> Productivity—the degree to which the research represents an addition to knowledge along established lines of research or an extension of previous theory.

The panel consisted of 45 persons chosen as leaders in medical sociology by the members of the Section of Medical Sociology of the American Sociological Association. The summaries were standardized in form and efforts were made to conceal identities and publication sources.

Each evaluator was given 25 randomly selected and ordered studies to evaluate in terms of their innovativeness and productivity. The average number of panel members evaluating a project was 4.5. According to their ratings, the projects were divided into fifths—quintile 1 indicating the lowest 20 percent of the ratings and quintile 5 the highest 20 percent of the ratings on a given scale.[3]

One hypothesis following Ben-David and Barber was that in pre-paradigm sciences such as medical sociology, external pressures

---

[2] The decision to use summaries rather than major reports was based upon the recognition that time pressures upon rater would have precluded us getting multiple ratings for a given study if we used the major reports. To examine the tenability of using summaries in place of major reports, an experiment was run in which ratings based on summaries were compared with ratings based on major reports. The extent of agreement greatly exceeded change. For further information see Gordon (1963).

[3] As the interpretation of the intervals on the rating scale was found to differ from evaluator to evaluator, the 25 ratings for each evaluator were converted to *t* scores. The mean *t* score for each project was determined. According to the ranking of the mean *t* scores, the projects were divided into quintiles numbering 43, 43, 42, 43, 43. Nine of the projects which had no findings at the time of the evaluation, during a follow-up two years later, were found to have publications then available. Feeling that the evaluations of the projects therefore were inaccurate, they were removed from all analyses using the dependent variables.

(i.e., social urgency) were an important impetus to innovative research. We found, based on the assessments of 40 leading medical sociologists, that the research conducted in applied settings (hospitals, medical schools, health agencies), under conditions of evaluative administration (freedom in research decision and evaluation) was three times more innovative than similar research conducted in academic settings (university social science departments) under similar administrative conditions and was two times more innovative than research in applied institutions under conditions of executive administration.

Relating to our concepts of evaluative administration we found that where administrative practices were evaluative (i.e., gave researchers responsibility for research procedures but assessed outcomes) the extent of innovation was three times greater than where administrative superiors prescribed research procedures for project directors (Gordon et al., 1962:201).

The question remains, do the factors which stimulate innovative research also stimulate productive research? Judging from our study of research projects dealing with social aspects of disease, the answer is no. In that study, as we mentioned earlier, information was obtained both on the productivity and innovativeness of the research.

TABLE 2.
Percentage of Projects for Urgency and Authority Patterns
in Most Innovative (Fifth) Quintile

Setting	AUTHORITY PATTERN			
	Evaluative*		Executive	
	N	%5Q	N	%5Q
Applied setting	62	31	45	13*
Academic setting	21	10	35	9

*Visibility + freedom

Significance of Differences (z—Tests)

	P
1. Academic—Evaluative versus Applied—Evaluative	0.03
2. Academic—Executive versus Applied—Evaluative	0.006
a. Academic—No discussion versus Applied—Evaluative	0.02
b. Academic—little freedom versus Applied—Evaluative	0.05
3. Applied—Executive versus Applied—Evaluative	0.02
a. Applied—no discussion versus Applied—Evaluative	0.05
b. Applied—little freedom versus Applied—Evaluative	0.06

Freedom to determine research procedures, hire staff, etc., which we found positively related to innovation, has a 0.31 negative correlation with productivity (Gordon et al., 1962). Decker (1967), in a further examination of how administrative factors affected productivity and innovation, found there was a significant relationship between administrative perceptions of their participation in allocation of research funds and the quality of professional administrative relationships. She concludes that:

> The factors correlated with productivity seem to be concerned more with the amount of administrative influence over the project director, either in the management of the project (allocation of funds) or the design of the research than with the conduct of the research, and they are also quite sensitive to the personal relations between the two levels of supervision. We have consistently seen this emphasis in productivity, especially in its need for strong administrative ties to management.

Decker's findings support the argument that predictable research is fostered by direct administrative control and support our assumptions in regard to predictive and nonpredictive research. This evidence in conjunction with prior evidence lends further viability to the categorization of research in terms of social urgency and predictability.

A Contingency Model for Research Administration

We have emphasized the need for a coherent framework to facilitate a unified approach to research administration. If the administrative guidelines are used in combination with the problem-solving approach, they may provide the beginning of such a framework. The interface between the problem-solving approach and administrative guidelines involves the predictability of procedures. The problem-solving approach is based upon the assumption that in the earlier stages of the research process, procedures are relatively unstructured (i.e., case study procedures) and that, as we learn more about the problem, procedures become more predictable. For example, once causality has been established, procedures for field experiments are relatively straightforward. Consequently, guidelines related to low predictability (P−) of procedures apply more in the early stages of problem solving, and guidelines associated with high predictability (P+) are more applicable in the later steps. For instance, individual-based research teams which facilitate nonpredictable research are more appropriate in the early stages of problem solution, whereas institutional structures

TABLE 3.
Contingency Model for the Administration of Problem Solving

Research Classification			Initial Problem-Solving Stages	Research Administration	
*Degree of Predict-ability**	*Problem-Solving Stage*	*Prime Research Mode*	*Guidelines*	*Little Urgency* (U−)	*Great Urgency* (U+)
Low	1. Problem delineation	Qualitative analysis	*Administrative*		
			Suggestion of approaches	Individual	Group
			Number of approaches	Multiple sequential	Multiple simultaneous
			Responsibility for research decisions	Individual	Individual
			Administration authority pattern	Evaluative	Evaluative
			Funding	Nonrestrictive	Nonrestrictive
P−	2. Variable identification	Exploratory case studies	*Innovation*		
			Toleration of tangents	High	Moderate
			Stimulation to tangential research	High	High
	3. Determining of relations among variables	Cross-sectional studies	Recognition of an anomaly	Low	Low
			Personality characteristics		
			Tolerance for ambiguity	Needed	Needed
			Ability to tolerate pressure	Not needed	Needed
Moderate			*Prime Conflict Areas*	Resources	Tangential research

Later Problem-Solving Stages

Stages			
4. Establishment of causality	Longitudinal studies small-scale experiments		
5. Manipulation of causal variables	Field experiments		
6. Evaluation	Controlled field comparisons		

Administrative			
Suggestion of approaches		Individual	Group
Number of approaches		Single	Single
Responsibility for research decisions		Group	Group
Administrative authority pattern		Executive	Executive
Funding		Restrictive	Highly restrictive
Innovation			
Toleration of tangents		Moderate	Low
Stimulation to tangential research		Low	Low
Recognition of an anomaly		Moderate	High
Personality characteristics			
Tolerance for ambiguity		Not needed	Not needed
Ability to tolerate pressure		Not needed	Needed
Prime Conflict Areas		Resources Procedures	Procedures

Moderate → High (P+)

*The degree of predictability is the resultant of paradigm level and problem-solving stage.

facilitate research in the more predictable later stage. Thus, research funds may be channeled primarily through grants during earlier stages of development of a problem and through other, more restrictive research support mechanisms after immediate objectives have been articulated.

It is important to note that the presence of a viable paradigm not only leads to increased predictability throughout the problem-solving stages, but also may enable researchers to skip certain stages in the process. For example, the manned space program had to solve a number of problems involving heat transfer. Since many of the factors affecting thermal quality of materials are known, all that was necessary in many instances were evaluations of promising solutions. We are, in effect, advancing not an absolute, but a contingency model of research administration that is dependent on social urgency, problem-solving stage, and paradigm development. The contingency model and the administrative recommendation derived from it are presented in Table 3.

To use the contingency model viably, we must be able to determine degrees of urgency and predictability. We can never be completely sure of research predictability, but experts in given disciplines can assess the state of the art in their respective fields and, in conjunction with a determination of the problem stage, they should be able to estimate predictability with some accuracy. Determining urgency is more difficult, since urgency varies with social values. This can be seen in the attitudinal change regarding availability of medical technology. Medical care, or access to a specific medical technique, can be considered a privilege, a right, or a mandate. When access to a technique is considered a privilege, the technique is not available to everyone, and special considerations (e.g., money) are prerequisites for access. Types of care which are considered a matter of right are available to everyone, so use depends primarily on individual choice. Techniques that are mandated involve little or no individual discretion; under a positive mandate, a procedure is imposed on people (e.g., no abortions after six months). Before 1900, medical care was considered a privilege except in some cases of communicable disease, and governmental resources were only marginally involved in medical care. During the last seventy years, however, we have increasingly come to think of medical care as a right rather than a privilege. This attitude change has been accompanied by a dramatic increase in governmental involvement in health activities as reflected in increased public expenditures for health. The government has become directly involved in providing services, training professionals, and developing new techniques. Today, no one would deny the right of all people to have the best medical treatment available. But, in competition with other rights, how much of our scarce resources should be allocated to providing the best available medical technology? Moreover, how much do we expend on improving technology and how much on the distribution of existing technology? While some of these questions require a determination of the extent to which diffusion of medical technology is a problem, the ultimate decision is a political one relating to social values and aspirations. It has to be recognized that, given its political nature, perceptions of urgency vary over time.

We expected that the diffusion conference, in addition to determining problem stage and assessing the "state of the art," would provide a dialogue between governmental representatives and potential diffusion researchers on the nature of the diffusion problem and its perceived urgency. Before determining guidelines for research on medical diffusion, conference participants had to consider several questions: Is diffusion of some medical innovations more important than diffusion of others? Can we establish criteria for evaluating the level of urgency? The contingency model for research administration which we have presented is only a starting point in a dialogue that we hope will focus discussion for the diffusion and similar conferences. Ideally, the model will also provide a thrust for the systematic application of existing knowledge to the development and administration of research programs.

Admittedly, the base upon which to apply such knowledge is sketchy and identification of relevant factors is incomplete. Even employing such relatively simple distinctions as predictability and urgency presents major problems. Research urgency tends to change in response to success and failure, and projects may require state-of-the-art methodologies at one stage and innovative procedures at another stage. Though difficult, such decisions will have to be made; and we should recognize that the same types of decisions are constantly being made under such rubrics as "basic" and "applied," "fundamental" and "problem-oriented." In making such distinctions, we have too often failed to treat social research as a problem-solving process. Consequently, we have emphasized men and organizational structures, but neglected the prerequisites of science. By prerequisites of science, we mean more than just a determination of the nature of the problem; rather, we are referring to a broad view of the science system including the steps necessary for problem solution. Instead of treating research as a continually changing process, we have too often applied rules and precepts about research willy-nilly to all projects within an institution or program.

In conclusion, we raise this question: Would the 2,000 diffusion studies we reviewed have yielded more compelling findings if they had been done in the context of unifying administrative and support structures designed to facilitate the various phases of diffusion research? Given increasing funding pressures and social needs, it is becoming imperative that this question be dealt with in a systematic fashion by research and policy makers.

Gerald Gordon, PH.D.
New York State School of Industrial and Labor Relations
Cornell University
Ithaca, New York 14850

Ann E. MacEachron, M.S.W.
New York State School of Industrial and Labor Relations
Cornell University
Ithaca, New York 14850

G. Lawrence Fisher, PH.D.
National Institute of Neurological Diseases and Stroke
Bethesda, Maryland 20014

This is a revised version of two chapters of a report, prepared for the National Institutes of Health, titled, "The Diffusion of Medical Technology—Policy & Research Planning Perspectives, 1974," edited by Gerald Gordon and G. Lawrence Fisher.

Opinions expressed in this article are those of the authors in their private capacities and do not necessarily reflect the opinions, views or policies of the National Institutes of Health or the United States Department of Health, Education and Welfare.

References

Aiken, Michael, and Jerald Hage
    1968   "Organizational interdependence and intraorganizational structure." American Sociological Review 33 (December): 912–930.

Barber, Bernard
    1962   Science and the Social Order. Revised ed. New York: Collier Books.

Ben-David, Joseph
    1960   "Roles and innovations in medicine." American Journal of Sociology 65:828–843.

    1964   "Scientific growth: a sociological view." Minerva 2:475.

Bessman, Samuel P., and Judith P. Swazey
1971   "Phenylketonuria: a study of biomedical legislation." In Mendelsohn, Swazey, and Taviss (eds.), Human Aspects of Biomedical Innovation. Cambridge, Massachusetts: Harvard University Press.

Campbell, Donald T.
1969   "Ethnocentrism of disciplines and the fish-scale model of omniscience," In Sherif, M., and C. Sherif, (eds.), Interdisciplinary Relationships in the Social Sciences. Chicago: Aldine Publishing Co.

Coe, Rodney, and Elizabeth A. Barnhill
1967   "Social dimensions of failure in innovation." Human Organization 26 (Fall):149–156.

Coleman, James
1973   "Ten principles governing policy research." APA Monitor (February):6.

Coleman, James, Elihu Katz, and Herbert Menzel
1966   Medical Innovation: A Diffusion Study. Indianapolis: The Bobbs-Merrill Company.

Cyert, Richard M., and James G. March
1963   A Behavioral Theory of the Firm. Englewood Cliffs, New Jersey: Prentice-Hall, Inc.

Decker, Anne Folger
1967   Relations Between Scientific Accomplishment and Hierarchical Conflict in Research Organizations. Ph.D. dissertation, Department of Sociology, New York University (October).

Deutsch, Karl W., John Platt, and Dieter Senghaas
1971   "Conditions favoring major advances in social science." Science, 171:450–459.

Dobrov, G. M.
1968   "Predicting the development of science." Minerva 4:229.

Elling, R.
1963   "The hospital support game in urban center." In Freidson, Eliot (ed.), The Hospital in Modern Society. New York: The Free Press.

Fliegel, Frederick C., and Joseph E. Kivlin
1966   "Attributes of innovations as factors in diffusion." American Journal of Sociology 72 (November):235–248.

Glaser, W.
1963   "American and foreign hospitals: some sociological comparisons." In Freidson, Eliot (ed.), The Hospital in Modern Society. New York: The Free Press.

Gordon, Gerald
1963   "The problem of assessing scientific accomplishment: a potential solution." IREE Transactions on Engineering Management EM-10, No. 4: 192–196.

Gordon, Gerald, and Selwyn Becker
1964   "Changes in medical practice bring shifts in the patterns of power." The Modern Hospital 2 (February): 102–106.

Gordon, Gerald, Sue Marquis, and Odin W. Anderson
1962   "Freedom and control in four types of scientific settings." The American Behavioral Scientist 6 (4): 39–42.

1966   "Freedom, visibility of consequences, and scientific innovation," The American Journal of Sociology 72, No. 2 (September): 195–202.

Gordon, Gerald, Edward V. Morse, Sue Marquis Gordon, Jean de Kervasdoue, John R. Kimberly, Michael K. Moch, and Donald G. Swartz
1974   "Organizational structure, environmental diversity, and hospital adoption of medical innovations." In Kaluzny, Arnold D., John T. Gentry, and James E. Veney (eds.), Innovation in Health Care Organizations. Chapel Hill: University of North Carolina, Department of Health Administration.

Grant, Robert P.
1966   "National biomedical research agencies: a comparative study of fifteen countries." Minerva 4:484.

Hage, Jerald
1974   "A systems perspective on organizational program change." In Kaluzny, Arnold D., John T. Gentry, and James E. Veney (eds.), Innovation in Health Care Organizations. Chapel Hill: University of North Carolina, Department of Health Administration.

Hall, Richard H.
1968   "Professionalization and bureaucratization." American Sociological Review 33 (February):92–104.

Hare, A. P.
1962   Handbook of Small Group Research. New York: Free Press of Glencoe.

Health Information Foundation
1954–1960 An Inventory of Social and Economic Research in Health, New York, Editions III–IX. New York: Health Information Foundation.

Kaplan, Norman
1964   "Organization: will it choke or promote the growth of science?" In Hill, (ed.), The Management of Scientists. Boston: Beacon Press.

Katz, Daniel, and Robert L. Kahn
1966   The Social Psychology of Organizations. New York: John Wiley and Sons.

Kuhn, Thomas
1970   The Structure of Scientific Revolutions. Second ed. Chicago: University of Chicago Press.

Lodahl, Janice Beyer, and Gerald Gordon
1972   "The structure of scientific fields and the functioning of university graduate departments." American Sociological Review 37 (February):57–72.

March, James G., and Herbert A. Simon
1958   Organizations. New York: John Wiley and Sons.

Masterman, Margaret
1970   "The nature of a paradigm." In Lakatos, Imre, and Alan Musgrove (eds.), Criticism and the Growth of Knowledge: Proceedings of the International Colloquium in the Philosophy of Science. London: Cambridge University Press.

Pelz, Donald C.
1964   "Freedom in research." International Science and Technology: 33.

Perrow, Charles
1965   "Hospitals: technology, structure, and goals." In March, James G. (ed.), Handbook of Organizations. Chicago: Rand McNally and Co.

Robertson, Thomas S.
1971   Innovation Behavior and Communication. New York: Holt, Rinehart and Winston.

Rogers, Everett M.
1972   Research on the Diffusion of Innovations: Applicability to the Diffusion of Medical Technology in the Health Field. Paper presented at the Conference on the Diffusion of Medical Technology, Cornell University, Ithaca, New York, September.

Rogers, Everett M., and Floyd F. Shoemaker
1971   Communication of Innovations: A Cross-Cultural Approach. New York: The Free Press.

Rosner, Martin M.
1968   "Administrative controls and innovation." Behavioral Science 13: 36–43.

Rossi, Peter H.
1964   "Researchers, scholars and policy makers: the politics of large scale research," Daedalus 93:1142–1161.

Sayles, Leonard R., and Margaret K. Chandler
1971   Managing Large Systems: Organization for the Future. New York: Harper and Row.

Schron, Donald A.
1963   "Champions for radical new inventions." Harvard Business Review (March-April): 77–86.

Shepard, Herbert A.
1967   "Innovation-resisting and innovation-producing organizations." Journal of Business 40 (October): 470–477.

Suchman, Edward A.
1967   Evaluative Research: Principles and Practice in Public Service and Social Action Programs. New York: Russell Sage Foundation.

Taylor, D. W., P. C. Berry, and C. R. Black
    1958   "Group participation, brainstorming, and creative thinking." Administrative Science Quarterly 3: 5.

Taylor, James C.
    1971   Technology and Planned Organizational Change. CRUSK, Institute for Social Research. Ann Arbor: The University of Michigan.

Thio, Alex O.
    1971   "A reconsideration of the concept of adopter-innovation compatibility in diffusion research." The Sociological Quarterly 12 (Winter):56–58.

Thompson, James D.
    1967   Organizations in Action. New York: McGraw Hill Book Company.

Tilson, David, and William T. Carrigan
    1972   The NIH Interest in Research on the Diffusion of Innovation in Medicine. Paper presented at the Conference on the Diffusion of Medical Technology, Cornell University, Ithaca, New York, September.

Weinberg, Alvin M.
    1964   "Criteria for scientific choice." Physics Today 17 (March):44.

    1965   "Scientific choice and biomedical science." Minerva 4 (Autumn):1–14.

    1967   Reflections on Big Science. Cambridge, Massachusetts: The M.I.T. Press.

    1968   "The Philosophy and Practice of National Science Policy." Pp. 26–38 in de Reuck, A., M. Goldsmith, and J. Knight (eds.), Ciba Foundation and Science of Science Foundation Symposium on Decision-Making in National Science Policy. London: J. and A. Churchill Limited.

Weiss, Carol H. (ed.)
    1972   Evaluating Action Programs: Readings in Social Action and Education. Boston: Allyn and Bacon, Inc.

From "Promising Report" to "Standard Procedure": Seven Stages in the Career of a Medical Innovation

JOHN B. McKINLAY

Boston University

> If men could learn from history, what lessons it might
> teach us! But passion and party blind our eyes, and
> the light which experience gives us is a lantern on
> the stern, which shines only on the waves behind us!

S.T. Coleridge, 18 December 1831,
in T. Alsop, *Recollections*, 1836.

I N 1972, IN AN EDITORIAL FOR THE *Annals of Thoracic Surgery*, Tom Chalmers (1972:323–327), a highly respected contributor to this special issue, provided examples of widely advocated and commonly used therapies that either had never been established to be effective by adequate clinical trials, or in a number of instances had actually been shown to be without merit (Chalmers, 1972: 326). The editorial concluded with the question, "Can we learn from our mistakes of the past?" That question is as poignant today (perhaps even more so) as it was when posed by Chalmers nearly a decade ago. This paper is a response (admittedly belated) to this question and is divided into two main sections. The *first* describes some types of mistakes by outlining the typical career of a medical innovation. How do medical innovations (diagnostic techniques, surgical procedures, and medical interventions) become part of established medical practice? What stages do they typically pass through? What

Milbank Memorial Fund Quarterly/*Health and Society*, Vol. 59, No. 3, 1981
© 1981 Milbank Memorial Fund and Massachusetts Institute of Technology
0160/1997/81/5903/0374-38 $01.00/0

admission requirements (if any) must be satisfied before innovations gain privileged access to the House of Medicine? What types of evidence are employed, when, and by whom, in support of which innovations? Having outlined the typical career of an innovation, the *second* section describes an alternative approach, based upon evidence derived from randomized controlled trials (RCTs), to the allocation of ever scarcer public funds to health care. This alternative approach takes account of some past mistakes and the wastefulness and irrationality associated with the ways that things are done at present.

On the basis of a review of many studies of diffusion and the careful examination of the careers of several different types of innovation, it is considered useful to break the diffusion process into the seven distinct stages outlined below. Several aspects of the career approach to the diffusion of medical innovations should be highlighted here in order to minimize misunderstandings. There is, *first,* no suggestion here that every innovation passes through each of the seven stages in the exact order in which they are discussed. The concept of a career, with its seven stages, is simply a heuristic device employed to highlight particular issues and possible points of intervention. The following discussion is intended to identify the typical or usual stages in the career of an innovation—the pattern that is followed more often than not. There are situations in which, as in the case of tragedies like thalidomide, some of the typical stages are circumnavigated, or telescoped, but the career of an innovation has at least a beginning point (the promising report) and an ending (established procedure, or erosion and discreditation). The heuristic advantages of this notion of a typical career are fairly obvious: it enables one to break fairly complex social behavior and political processes into a manageable form, identifies possible points of intervention, and bestows a semblance of order on the present chaotic state of diffusion studies. Therein, however, lies a major disadvantage: it suggests that more order and coherence exist than is actually the case.

Second, every effort is made to avoid the suggestion that the medical establishment is only self-interestedly involved in the diffusion of innovations. The ideological basis of much recent research on medical technology appears to require a villain to whom responsibility can be ascribed: hospitals, and more particularly physicians, are highly visible targets. This paper represents an attempt to move beyond this superficial level to a consideration of the activities of hospitals, physicians, and other interest groups in relation to more basic structural processes that impinge upon them.

Third, there is obviously variation within, and between, medical specialties in the sponsorship of innovations, and the willingness to undertake proper evaluations. Spodick (1973) argues that there is a double standard in the acceptance of reports of surgical versus medical treatments, and that this arises from professional and lay attitudes. After reviewing some 70 reports in specialty journals appearing during 1971, to compare the methods used for evaluating medical versus surgical treatments for cardiovascular disease, he found that 9 of 16 qualifying studies evaluating medical treatments were controlled. None of the 49 studies of surgical intervention involved a controlled study. Cochrane (1979) considers it not unreasonable to judge the medical profession, and its specialties, by the use they have made of the RCT technique. He rather humorously awards first prize (the "Bradford" in praise of Sir Austin Bradford-Hill) to the tuberculosis chest physician, with almost unlimited praise. After considering psychiatry, surgery, and cardiology, he awarded the wooden spoon to obstetrics and gynecology, with the following explanation:

> The specialty missed its first opportunity in the sixties when it failed to randomize the confinement of low risk pregnant women at home and in the hospital. This was followed by a determined refusal to allow "Pap smears" to be randomized, with disastrous results for the whole world. Then having filled the emptying beds by getting nearly all pregnant women into the hospital, the obstetricians started to introduce a whole series of expensive innovations into the routines of pre- and post-natal care and delivery, without any rigorous evaluation. The list is long but the most important were induction, ultrasound, fetal monitoring and placental function tests. The specialty reached its apogee in 1976 when they produced 20 percent fewer babies at 20 percent more cost. G and O stands for gynecologists and obstetricians but it could also stand for GO ahead without evaluation! (Cochrane, 1979:11)

1. The Stage of the "Promising Report"

Many studies of the diffusion of innovations resemble those frustrating occasions when one arrives late at the theater, after a performance has commenced, and is forced to leave before the final curtain. One is never really on top of what occurs, finds it difficult to unravel the relationships between the various actors, and is left wondering how the whole thing ended anyway. Diffusion studies tend to cover what can be termed the midpoints in the career of some new procedure, drug, machine, or whatever (Gordon and Fisher, 1975; Russell, 1978). They provide useful information on the most publicly visible stages, but give inadequate attention to either their points of origin, or where they eventually end. By failing to trace innovations back to their points of origin in order to identify the interests and processes that launched them, such studies have limited utility for social policy (McKinlay, 1977a, 1977b). And without some understanding of the final stages, social policy upon the allocation of resources cannot be properly informed by the successes and failures of the past.

The careers of most medical innovations seem to be launched with the appearance of an enthusiastic report on some promising performance, increasingly in the mass media. One reads, almost daily, of startling "scientific" breakthroughs and new weaponry for the battle against illness and death (Sontag, 1978). A few examples will vividly illustrate the point. The *Boston Globe* (1980) recently reported that a doctor at Johns Hopkins University *is* extending the lives of patients suffering from inoperable liver cancer by making them temporarily radioactive. In 7 of 8 patients treated, tumor size has been drastically reduced from 70 to 18 percent of the liver in one case, and from 50 to 5 percent in another. To quote this report:

> The new technique floods the liver with continuous radiation for days or weeks, rather than brief bursts, which is the usual treatment. To do this, a protein made by liver cancers is extracted, purified and injected into rabbits. The rabbits then make antibodies—disease fighting proteins—against the cancer protein. The rabbit antibodies are then heavily dosed with radioactive iodine and injected into the patient. The antibodies then attach themselves to the liver cancer, and the radioactive material begins its destructive work.

A similarly optimistic report of a different type of innovation recently appeared in the *New York Times* (1980a):

> Researchers at the Mayo clinic have developed an advanced X-ray machine that displays organs in three-dimensional moving images that may then be electronically dissected without ever touching the

patient with a scalpel. The device, known as the Dynamic Spatial Reconstructor or DSR, has been built at a cost of approximately $5.2 million with grants from the National Institutes of Health. The DSR is regarded by many scientists as the most significant technological advance in diagnostic medicine since the invention of computerized axial tomography, known as CAT. . . . The main component of the DSR is a 15 foot circular gantry that supports 14 X-ray tubes (the final model will have 28 tubes) aimed at the gantry's center. To obtain a DSR scan, a prone patient is inserted into the gantry, which spins around his body once every four seconds. The X-ray tubes take 60 X-ray photographs a second, with each pulse of radiation lasting 350 millionths of a second. . . . [the DSR] stands 15 feet high and weighs 17 tons.

While on acronyms, one must not overlook the *Newsweek* (1980:63) report on the PET, or positron-emission tomography—a machine that detects changes in chemical physiology:

In a PET scan, the patient first receives an injection of deoxyglucose, a compound chemically related to glucose. The compound contains radioactive fluorine. Then the patient lies with his head inside the scanning device. The radioactive deoxyglucose—which has been absorbed by the brain cells—emits positively charged particles called positrons. These immediately collide with negatively charged electrons normally present in the cells. Each positron-electron collision produces high energy particles called photons, and PET's detector records their path and speed. This information is processed by a computer that runs out a composite color picture on a display screen.

Various shades of color in the PET image indicate levels of glucose metabolism. A region of high activity might show up as light beige, while a low area would be deep russet. In their most significant preliminary studies, researchers have found altered glucose metabolism in schizophrenia and manic-depressive psychosis.

It is understandable that the media should seize upon these promising reports, since they are highly newsworthy for a public conditioned to expect miracle cures for the diseases that plague it. Many magazines and newspapers regularly devote a section or column to promising reports, and have a staff of medical reporters constantly looking for the latest newsworthy innovation in professional journals and through contact with the researchers directly. These promising media stories usually report activities that meet no methodological criteria whatsoever. Moreover, it is not always possible to obtain information on the specifics of the unpublished "preliminary studies," the results of which frequently form the basis of the promising report. Certainly, the association of a promising report with "respected scientists," and with prestigious institutions, serves to arouse public interest (especially if, as is usually the case, it concerns a life-threatening problem such as heart disease or cancer).

A second, but not exclusive, source of promising reports may be found in major medical journals, some of which set aside space for accounts of the management of a few, or even solitary, cases. Dr. A, from a respected institution, may describe how he successfully treated Mrs. B, who was suffering from X, by employing Y. Medical journals, along with those in other fields, tend to publish only reports of "successful" interventions. One seldom reads of *un*successful interventions, even though their frequency may be equal to, and probably greater than, those purported to be successful. The fact that much can be learned, and many mistakes avoided, from the reporting of negative findings is persistently overlooked. Although perhaps reporting careful and sophisticated measurements involving intricate apparatus, these case reports, which usually discuss just a few subjects (and often only one), are inferentially worthless. Despite their appearance in professional journals, they are no more reliable than the sensational media stories already discussed, and certainly have no value as a basis for social policy.

Sometimes, after reading these isolated "promising reports" in either the media or in professional journals (or both), but usually after word-of-mouth endorsements among colleagues (one of the principal means by which physicians and researchers exchange information on innovations), someone may decide to check out the promising report on a series of cases—say, 25, or even 100. Some medical researchers seem to believe that the soundness of an inference is related to the number of observations from which it is derived, or perhaps the length of period of follow-up (see, for example, Vineberg, 1975; Sheldon et al., 1975). This paper will argue that such reasoning is seriously flawed because, while numbers are certainly important, other equally essential methodological criteria are overlooked, and such studies still constitute only promising reports.

Clinicians sometimes do attempt exploratory or pilot studies of the *effectiveness* of an innovation at this stage. Although well intentioned, these studies are usually also severely limited and can most appropriately be included in the category of uncontrolled observational reports. Chalmers discusses these studies and suggests that they may actually observe the conduct of properly designed and conducted evaluations:

> The so-called "pilot study" is a trap that may be the major factor leading to the lack of decent randomized controlled trials in the evaluation of new therapies. Unfortunately, when a physician decides he has an exciting new therapy, he usually feels he cannot start a controlled trial immediately because he is not sure of the dose and the patients to select; so he does a pilot study of consecutive patients. That prevents him from ever doing a randomized controlled trial for one of three reasons: He is so impressed with the efficacy of the drug in the uncontrolled trial that he cannot do a study for ethical reasons, and he publishes his "excellent results" in a preliminary paper. He concluded that a controlled trial should be done, but he does not do it because he is convinced that the drug works. It is often ten years before other clinical investigators, stimulated by a lack of success in less well patients, report equally uncontrolled negative series or finally do a controlled trial. A *second* possibility is that the originator of the therapy cannot do a controlled trial because the treatment seems so ineffective that he decides he cannot subject more people to it; yet it is entirely possible that it is the selection of patients who receive the treatment rather than the treatment itself that is at fault. This is especially true in the case of drastic "last resort" therapies. . . . At any rate, the therapy appears so unfavorable that a controlled trial would be unethical. The *third* possibility is that the therapy appears similar to other therapies, and the investigator has no incentive to spend his time doing a controlled trial to prove that a suggested therapy is no different from the standard. . . . *The only way to avoid this trap is to randomize the first patients.* (Chalmers, 1975a:755; emphasis added)

2. The Stage of Professional and Organizational Adoption

Up to this point support for the innovation appears somewhat disparate, coming from the manufacturers of the technology and/or from enthusiastic medical researchers. During this second stage more widespread and influential support is mobilized. Here we see movement from scattered support for the innovation to its *adoption* by powerful interest groups, involving professional associations, institutional structures, and other resources. The term "adoption" is employed to distinguish the scattered support evident during the first stage from the organized commitment of institutional resources during this second stage. It denotes a unique relationship with the innovation: the act of formally accepting and taking up some activity and using it as one's own, without the idea of its having been another's—to embrace or espouse it (Webster's Dictionary, 1976; Oxford English Dictionary, 1971). Such a special relationship must also be distinguished from "acceptance" of an innovation by the public, which denotes a more passive consent or approval of something, to regard it as proper, normal, or inevitable. Whereas professional *adoption* usually involves an investment (resources, time, reputation), public *acceptance,* as we shall see, suggests that people favorably receive or simply approve of something.

With regard to professionals and their associations, there are obviously many reasons for the adoption of innovations. Some physicians may be simply responding to peer pressure, known to be very strong in medicine (Coleman, Katz, and Menzel, 1966). Others may view it as an opportunity to deliver improved care, to be seen to be up-to-date, scientific, more professional (also strong motivations in medicine), or just helpful. Perhaps because of what Freidson (1971) terms their "clinical mentality," physicians may be precipitately eager to adopt innovations through their sincere desire to respond to the problems of disease and suffering that their patients may present. Warner (1977) has shown that rapid diffusion of new treatments occurred as a "desperate reaction" in the case of leukemia patients, when limited treatment alternatives were available.

Some commentators, who regard the professions as a conspiracy against the laity, consider personal financial gain as the motivation for physicians' adoption of innovations. Although this explanation is appealing in some circles, it is too simple an explanation of the phenomenon being discussed. Undoubtedly, some physicians, in common with workers in just about every occupation, may adopt an innovation because of a personal financial interest. This is just a fact of life and is certainly not unique to the occupation of doctoring (McKinlay, 1977b). But it is doubtful whether this is a primary motivation for the majority of physicians. In adopting innovations, physicians and their associations believe that they are being more effective, humane, scientific, or whatever, and *secondarily* derive financial benefit.

With regard to the adoption of innovations by medical organizations (hospitals, medical centers, health clinics), it appears that organizational and economic considerations may be more important than they are among physicians (Kaluzny, Veney, and Gentry, 1974). In adopting an innovation, administrators may, of course, be simply responding to intense pressure from their medical staff. Such a response, although consistent with the requests of physicians, may be motivated by a different set of reasons. For example, the adoption of certain innovations may be viewed as an attempt to enhance a hospital's reputation in the community, thereby improving its competitive position with respect to other hospitals. Additionally, adoption may be affected by the nature of a hospital's relation with other organizations and interests (insurance companies, banks, construction companies). One study reveals that expensive technologies diffuse more rapidly as the percentage of hospital resources derived from third parties increases (Cromwell et al., 1975; Kaluzny and Veney, 1977). According to Russell (1976:559) the paths of diffusion for hospitals have been quite similar for most of the recent major innovations: "In general, the facility in question first gained a foothold in large hospitals. Then, as large hospitals adopted it in increasing numbers, it began to spread down through the size distribution to smaller and smaller hospitals, with the smallest generally the last, and the slowest, to pick it up."

In a study of the diffusion of computed tomography (CT) scanners, Banta (1980) found that they followed the pattern of other expensive medical technologies in that the largest hospitals were also the first to adopt cobalt therapy, electroencephalographs, and intensive care units. The way in which hospitals at present adopt innovations not surprisingly results in some distributional inequalities. With respect to CT scanners, for example (Banta, 1980:261): "Only one of New York City's city hospitals, Bronx Municipal, has a scanner. Many large public hospitals whose main clientele are the the poor are without CT scanners; e.g., Bellevue and Kings County hospitals (New York), Charity Hospital (New Orleans), Cook County Hospital (Chicago), and Cleveland Memorial Hospital."

A hospital's affiliation with a medical school has been shown, in studies of intensive care units (Russell and Burke, 1975) and nuclear medicine facilities (Rappaport, 1978), to be related to early adoption of an innovation. Other studies (Cromwell et al., 1975; Banta, 1980) did not uncover this relationship.

Medical education gives the career of many innovations an early and influential boost and creates formidable impediments to the removal of those that eventually prove worthless or dangerous. All professionals are reluctant to alter practices that they have been taught. Innovations gain added legitimacy once they find their way into the medical curriculum and receive endorsement from influential educators in distinguished medical institutions. All students receive their first exposure to norms of practice from respected clinicians, who can recount first-hand experiences with a condition and its associated therapies. These experiences are essentially of the same quality as the promising reports (media stories and individual case histories) already discussed and should never be confused with reliable scientific evidence. Although they may suggest areas that are worthy of properly designed studies that may eventually yield such evidence, clinical experience or opinions can never be a substitute for scientific evidence, no matter how distinguished the observer or how numerous the observations. Unfortunately, this same clinical experience (frequently unsystematic observation) is the basis upon which most medical students learn. No wonder such a high proportion of what medical students are taught has a half-life of only a few years and comes to be viewed as worthless or actually harmful (e.g., radical mastectomy). The careers of many eventually discredited practices are temporarily prolonged through the support received from medical education, and by professional reluctance to relinquish what has been taught. With increasing specialization, students and practitioners may be trained to be dependent on certain practices or technologies; hence their continuing livelihood is to some extent contingent on the perpetuation of them. It is understandable, therefore, that some specialties are uncritically committed to particular interventions, and that they vigorously resist attempts to displace and sometimes even to evaluate them (surgical specialties are obvious examples).

It is essential that we be clear on the sources and quality of the information employed by physicians, hospitals, and medical educators as a basis for decision-making during this second stage in the career of an innovation. If this early information is defective, then subsequent action may be useless or harmful, and the resources devoted to it totally wasted. With regard to physicians, several studies have shown that a physician's adoption of a drug and his or her subsequent prescribing behavior is largely determined by drug industry sources (Silverman and Lee, 1974; Subcommittee on Health, 1974). One study on the adoption of a new drug found that detail men (the sales representatives of pharmaceutical companies) were the first source of information for about half the physicians, and drug-house mail periodicals for about a quarter. The final source of information, before adoption, was drug-house mail and periodicals for a third of the physicians, colleagues for a quarter, and professional journals for only a fifth (Miller, 1975; Stross and Harlan, 1979). Virtually all physicians use the *Physicians' Desk Reference* (PDR) for information on drugs; two-thirds use it four or more times a week (Subcommittee on Health, 1974). The PDR contains listings that are essentially the package inserts prepared and paid for by the manufacturers and subject to approval by the Food and Drug Administration (FDA). Although a minimal standard of accuracy in this information is ensured by FDA regulation, biases in reporting are to be expected from such interested sources.

An excellent paper by Waldron (1977:45) contrasts evaluations of Valium and Librium in two industry-sponsored sources (advertisements and the PDR) with what she considers to be two more independent sources (the *Medical Letter* and articles in the *New England Journal of Medicine*). She concludes that

the two industry-sponsored sources (the advertisements and the PDR) recommend these drugs for substantially more uses than the two independent sources (the *Medical Letter* and *The New England Journal of Medicine*). Aside from the obvious factor of motivation to sell, this reflects the difference between reliance on uncontrolled studies, in which apparent efficacy is inflated by placebo effects and spontaneous recovery, as compared to reliance on controlled studies. This discrepancy between drug industry sources and independent medical sources is greater in the earlier years when a higher proportion of the available studies were not properly controlled studies. An additional misleading aspect of advertising information for these products is the citation of 177 references in one ad of which 160 had nothing to do with the use recommended in the ad. . . . All four sources gave rather similar lists of adverse side effects, except in the earliest years when several important adverse effects were omitted in the advertisements and the PDR. . . . Industry sources

tended to evaluate these drugs more favorably when they were
newer. . . . Finally, the most striking time trend in these sources
of drug information is that before 1970, virtually all the information
available on Valium and Librium in *The New England Journal of
Medicine* was in the form of advertisements rather than articles.

Waldron's paper deserves careful attention by anyone interested in
the empirical basis (or lack of it) upon which innovations were adopted
by physicians, hospitals, and medical educators during this second
early stage in their career. Moreover, her analysis refers to the quality
of information available for the class of medical innovation (drugs)
for which there is the best quality control.

3. The Stage of Public Acceptance and State (Third-Party) Endorsement

Partly because of exposure to promising reports (Stage 1), but mainly
as a result of professional and organizational adoption (Stage 2), a
general approval (acceptance) of the innovation emerges among the
public. This approval broadens its base of support and creates a
constituency that can be appealed to in further advancing the career
of the innovation. Public acceptance takes the form of a generalized
belief that the innovation is a "good thing" and ought to be available.
It is usually less well formulated and organized than the boost received
from its adoption by professional and organizational interests. Having
once fostered acceptance and even a demand among the public, these
interests are in a position to satisfy it, while appealing to a demand
that they may have created as justification for their activities with
respect to the innovation.

In the typical career of an innovation being described, public acceptance is placed *after* the stage of professional and organizational
adoption, despite the frequent assertion by these interests that, in
adopting an innovation, they are simply responding to public demand.
Generally speaking, public demand or community enthusiasm for an
innovation must receive impetus and direction from professional interests that are already committed to the innovation. Demand does
not usually occur in a vacuum. At the same time, manufacturers,
professionals, and/or medical organizations may use public acceptance

or demand to legitimate their association with an innovation, and as a major reason for its expansion.

An innovation can be said to have "made it" when it eventually receives endorsement or support from the state and/or is underwritten by third parties. Two mutually supportive activities on the part of professional and organizational interests may induce the state and/or third-party insurance to underwrite certain innovations. The first activity, which can be termed the "indirect method," involves intensive lobbying with public officials, so-called expert testimony before legislative committees, campaign contributions to potentially supportive individuals and parties, and so forth. Certain important interests in the medical care field (American Medical Association, American Hospital Association, among others) have full-time lobbyists in Washington and strongly influence decision-making upon the allocation of state funds to medical research and practice. The second activity, or "direct method," involves obtaining support for the innovation among community groups or interests, which then pressure the state to support the particular innovation. The state's response to professional or organizational interests and public demand should not be viewed as a response to two separate constituencies, as they are sometimes depicted in the literature. Rather, they can be viewed as two methods—one direct and one indirect—by which the state is induced to underwrite a promising but yet-to-be-tested practice. There is nothing new in the suggestion that, generally speaking, the state and other third parties act *not* on the reasonable basis of reliable evidence, but on the basis of some combination of professional, organizational, and public pressure.

Again, it must be emphasized that despite the good intentions of well-motivated legislators and decision makers, the "authoritative" reports from state agencies, so-called expert testimony from authorities in the field, and the magnitude of the resources involved, *an innovation at this highly public third stage in its career usually remains without formal evaluation.* Usually, it still awaits a study that meets even minimally acceptable methodological criteria. The claims of manufacturers, the opinions of enthusiastic researchers, the well-intentioned adoption by experienced clinicians and educators, as well as public demand, are no substitute for a proper evaluation, and do not provide a rational, scientific basis for policy decisions. Once the state acts to support an

245

innovation and social policy is implemented, the career of an innovation can be viewed as having passed the point of no return.

The defective empirical foundation of the state's endorsement of an innovation is manifest in the research and development that the state subsequently funds. Having taken the step of endorsing an innovation (through, for example, reimbursement mechanisms and outright grants), the state, often through the funding of research and development activities regarding effectiveness, cost efficiency, and so forth, seeks to determine whether in fact it was the correct step to take. A careful review of the early careers of many different innovations reveals that, more often than not, the step was in quite the wrong direction and wasted resources, diverted professional and organizational resources to unproductive activities, and misled the public (Bunker, Barnes, and Mosteller, 1977).

Hemminki and her colleagues (Hemminki, 1980; Hemminki and Falkum, 1980) recently studied the number and quality of clinical trials in the applications submitted by the drug industry to licensing authorities in Finland, Norway, and Sweden. Many clinical trials were included but most of them were uncontrolled, otherwise deficient, or concerned only some of the indications applied for. Many of the reports cited had not been published and, since the submissions are secret, were not available to physicians or other researchers for evaluation. New drugs were sometimes registered for indications for which there were no good controlled trials. Thus, efficacy could not have been proved by the documentation included in the application. One suspects that a similar situation exists in most other countries.

4. The Stage of "Standard Procedure" and Observational Reports

There follows a period during which the innovation (having received professional and public support and legitimation through state endorsement and third-party coverage) achieves the privileged status of a "standard procedure." For a period of time it becomes generally accepted by interested parties as the most appropriate way of proceeding with a particular problem or situation. It is probably incorrect to refer here to the activity as an "innovation" (although we shall continue to do so in this paper), since at this stage it has graduated from being just another promising performance (something new with great potential) to the position of being an established and respected activity. Although there is a bias against reporting unsuccessful or untoward performances, they certainly occur but are usually dismissed as infrequent, the result of having poor material to work with, public misunderstanding, and so forth. So entrenched has the activity become that it takes rare courage for any individual or group even to question its effectiveness or desirability. To do so, as we shall see, is to invite retaliation from professional organizational interests, public indignation, and even in rare cases sanctions from the state.

Again, it should be recalled that, despite the resources and institutions already committed to the innovation at this midpoint in its career, it still remains without any formal evaluation. A clear example is provided by computer axial tomography (CT scanning), which was alluded to earlier. Banta (1980:263), after discussing the diffusion of this technology, suggests that:

> Despite more than five years of experience with CT scanning, its usefulness and ultimate place in medical care are largely unknown. The development and diffusion of CT scanners took place without formal and detailed proof of their safety and efficacy. The evidence existing today did not come from well-designed, prospective clinical trials, but from analyses of clinical experience. However, this evidence is restricted almost entirely to assessing diagnostic accuracy and usefulness, and gives little indication of the effects of CT scanning on therapy planning or on patient outcome. (See also Fineberg, Bauman, and Sosman, 1977.)

Virtually the same situation occurred with respect to electronic fetal monitoring (Banta and Thacker, 1979). Other examples are cited in companion papers in this issue.

The position of the innovation in any medical care system is further secured by the many comparative observational studies that are conducted as its career develops. These "studies" are not dissimilar to critics' reports in the theater, the not-always-independent opinions of supposedly knowledgeable individuals, who may have witnessed a performance, or even participated in its production. Several features of these studies should be highlighted: First, many are underwritten by the state as part of the effort already discussed to ascertain the effectiveness of an innovation *after* it has received general endorsement, and they usually take the form of retrospective studies, case reports, or follow-up investigations of an arbitrarily selected series of patients who have already been subjected to the innovation. Second, they are frequently initiated and conducted by the constituencies identified with the preceding stages (manufacturers, professional interests, and hospitals) who may have a vested interest in uncovering a beneficial outcome for the innovation. Thus, the objectivity of such observational studies could be seriously compromised. Third, these observational studies usually suffer crippling methodological limitations, such as inadequate sample size, restriction to a highly selective group of patients or problems, lack of an appropriate comparison group, use of subjective outcomes only (see Gore, Jones, and Rytter, 1977). Schneiderman (1975) provides examples (methyl GAG for myelogenous leukemia and 5-FU for certain forms of cancer) of how early uncontrolled results were actually misleading in evaluating potential cancer treatments. Another example is provided by clofibrate (Atromid-S), which was supposed to lower cholesterol in the blood and thereby prevent heart attacks, the leading cause of death in the United States. After thirteen years of widespread use and a proper evaluation (by the World Health Organization), it was found that users who took the drug regularly were 25 percent more likely to die of a broad range of disorders, including cancer, stroke, respiratory disease, and, ironically, heart attack, than those who got a placebo capsule! Fourth, although comparative observational studies sometimes provide useful information relating to the cost efficiency and social acceptability of an innovation, they seldom add much to knowledge concerning the *effectiveness* of the innovation in relation to the problem that it is designed to assist. Indeed, the term "evaluation" is becoming synonymous with studies of aspects of efficiency (Cochrane, 1972), and whether or not the recipients of an innovation (and sometimes even those who employ it) are "satisfied" (McKinlay and Dutton, 1974). Decisions concerning allocation of resources to or continuation of particular activities are increasingly influenced by whether such client or patient satisfaction is manifest.

In view of these and other limitations, it is difficult to determine from most observational reports whether the innovation is actually effective and whether some observed outcome may with certainty be attributed to it; for a review of the literature on observational studies see S.M. McKinlay (1975). For every one controlled trial that provides evidence against an innovation's effectiveness, there are sometimes literally hundreds of observational studies that produce support for it, at considerable public expense. This will be recalled at a later point when we consider the cost of properly controlled trials.

Chalmers (1975) reports that in 1970 there were 77 papers in professional journals reporting results on coronary artery surgery on over 5,000 patients. Only 2 of these studies were controlled and, unlike most of the remaining observational studies, both provided evidence against the effectiveness of this surgery. Elsewhere (Chalmers, Sebestyen, and Lee, 1970) he describes how 61 uncontrolled studies of emergency surgery for bleeding peptic ulcer resulted in enthusiastic support for the procedure, although the only 3 controlled trials available failed to demonstrate the superiority of this surgical intervention. Chalmers has also shown, in a review of clinical trials of anticancer agents, that only a very small percentage of trials are in any way controlled (Chalmers, Block, and Lee, 1971). In 1972 there were 152 studies reported in the English language medical literature of internal mammary artery ligation, but only 2 were properly controlled (made use of randomization), and both found the procedure to be of no value (Chalmers, 1972). One recent study critically reviewed 134 different articles published in English between 1965 and 1979 that compared ambulatory and inpatient care with regard to clinical outcome and economic cost. Only 4 of the 134 reports provided sufficient data to allow statistically valid conclusions (Berk and Chalmers, 1981). If it could be done, the costs of the hundreds of observational studies supporting the use of coronary care units (CCUs) (not to mention the costs of the units themselves) should be compared with, say, the costs of the Mather and/or Hill trials, which showed that most patients with myocardial infarction did as well at home as they did in the CCUs (Mather et al., 1971, 1976; Hill et al., 1978).

Coronary artery bypass surgery today (1981) is at about this fourth stage in its career. Having moved from the status of a promising report, through the stages of professional adoption and public acceptance, it now enjoys a favored position as a standard or conventional surgical means of handling heart disease for more than 100,000 patients annually (*New York Times,* 1980b). Medical workers and organizations are honestly committed to the procedure, believe it is an effective and ethical approach, and also derive considerable financial benefit from it. Public support for the procedure remains at a high level, and state and third-party arrangements underwrite most of its costs. To suggest that the procedure is ineffective, or even undesirable, is to court organized hostility and even ridicule. Despite the claims made for it, and the phenomenal investment of resources (estimated to be now around $2 billion a year in the United States), only one properly designed and conducted objective evaluation has been initiated and is still in progress (Murphy et al., 1977).

Mundth and Austen, after an exhaustive three-part review of around 150 different reports on surgical measures for coronary heart disease, were unable to turn up a single randomized controlled trial. At the time of writing they concluded that

> the duration of effectiveness of symptomatic relief, the effect of the functional status of the left ventricle and the effect on longevity have not yet been documented in toto. . . .
>
> *Controlled clinical trial is the ideal scientific solution for answering the questions raised concerning the effectiveness of coronary-artery surgical treatment.* . . . Whether randomized clinical trials comparing results of surgical versus medical therapy can be undertaken "ethically" has been a source of considerable debate. . . . However, when medical therapy has not been used or when it has been successful to a large extent in controlling symptoms, as in mild stable angina, *clinical trial with a prospective randomized study is ethically not only feasible but also advisable.* Similarly, meaningful data comparing the effect on longevity of surgical versus medical therapy can only be obtained with a randomized clinical trial. (Mundth and Austen, 1975:129; emphasis added)

Some features of this extensive report by two respected surgeons should be highlighted: first, the medical "evidence" for coronary artery bypass grafting (CABG) consisted entirely of observational reports (such as retrospective studies, case reports, clinical experience, follow-up studies); second, although not one randomized controlled trial (RCT) had been conducted among the more than 100 reports cited, the superiority of evidence derived from RCTs was recognized; third, proposals for prospective RCTs were alluded to with the hope that such studies could provide answers to the many questions that are still not completely resolved; fourth, it is reasonable to assume, on the basis of their commitment to the superiority of evidence derived from RCTs, that their practice would be influenced by the results (either positive or negative) of such studies.

Two years after Mundth and Austen's review, Murphy and his colleagues published preliminary results of the cooperative trial sponsored by the Veterans Administration (Murphy et al., 1977). This report confirmed what many people suspected, that CABG reduces the incidence and severity of angina but results in no difference in the survival of almost 600 patients with chronic stable angina (excluding those with obstructive disease of the left main coronary artery), randomized into medically and surgically treated groups, and followed for 21 to 36 months. The nature of the response to this and other trials will be discussed in detail in the following two stages (five and six) which are more directly concerned with RCTs. Braunwald (1977:663) in considering some of the criticisms of the Veterans Administration study suggests:

An even more insidious problem is that what might be considered an "industry" is being built around this operation; the creation of the facilities for open-heart operations in community hospitals in which no other cardiac procedures are performed and the enlargement of surgical facilities in teaching hospitals; the proliferation of catheterization and angiography suites as well as facilities for performing screening exercise electrocardiograms; and the expansion and development of training opportunities in clinical cardiology, cardiovascular surgery and cardiovascular radiology. *This rapidly growing enterprise is developing a momentum and constituency of its own, and as time passes, it will be progressively more difficult and costly to curtail it materially, if the results of carefully designed studies prove this step to be necessary.* (Emphasis added)

5. The Stage of the Randomized Controlled Trial (RCT)

Whether an innovation is worthwhile or not is an issue that, for many, appears to be satisfactorily settled by the sheer volume of observational reports. However, such reports never really place the issue of the *effectiveness* of an innovation beyond dispute. Byar and his colleagues (1976:79) have discussed the relative merits of different ways of assessing various medical treatments, and they conclude that "randomized clinical trials remain the most valuable method of evaluating the efficacy of therapies." Ten British and American statisticians have also reached the same conclusion (Peto et al., 1976, 1977). Although there are many understandable questions concerning RCTs, this author has yet to meet an informed researcher who doubts the inferential superiority of experimentally derived evidence (Guttentag, 1971; Riecken and Boruch, 1974). The ratio of observational reports to RCTs may be the order of 100 to 1 (as we have seen was the case with aortocoronary bypass for arteriosclerotic heart disease), but there are few who would not prefer experimental results, given a choice. The imbalance between the two types of studies results in large part from the difficulty of designing, and then implementing, an RCT in situations where an innovation is already standard procedure, and powerful interests and reputations are invested in its continuing success. It should be recalled at this fifth stage of a career that it is not really an innovation that is being considered for evaluation, but an activity that has become a norm in the field. In general, the more advanced the career of an innovation, the more difficult it is to undertake an RCT.

Anyone who has designed and implemented an RCT, or had one sabotaged, will be aware of the formidable obstacles that are placed in the path ahead and of the power of the interests that must be accommodated (Conner, 1977). Such obstacles tend to be glossed over in published reports. It is interesting to speculate on how many RCTs are initiated for every one that is successfully completed and eventually finds its way into print. The obstacles and objections to RCTs take many different forms (McKinlay, 1973). Some are legitimate and reflect genuine concern from various quarters. Others, probably the majority, are not legitimate objections and are designed to make proper evaluations virtually impossible, thereby protecting the innovation from potentially incriminating results. Ethical issues provide one excellent example. Some people, particularly clinicians, do have honest ethical and legal qualms concerning randomization (Kempthorne, 1977) and the withholding from a group of cases of some standard procedure that they consider worthwhile. Chalmers (1975a, 1975b) considers this issue and concludes that most ethical quandaries would be removed by randomizing the first patient before observations or reports could intervene and prejudice the physician or researcher.

Double standards exist over whether a study is considered ethical or not. On the one hand, it is ethical to subject all patients to an innovation, despite the absence of reliable evidence concerning its effectiveness, or its potential for harm. But, on the other hand, it is unethical to withhold the as yet unevaluated innovation from certain patients in order to ascertain its effectiveness and potential for harm. So-called ethical and legal objections are a major obstacle to the conduct of randomized controlled trials, although there are other problems such as their high cost, who should sponsor and conduct them, whether they are inappropriate to some interventions and situations, whether they can alter individual clinicians' behavior, and so forth.

Recognizing the legitimacy of certain objections, researchers often attempt to accommodate them in the design of an RCT—for example, by randomizing the first patient, by use of sequential techniques, permitting cases to be their own controls, etc. In making these accommodations and implementing a study in the real (sometimes hostile) world, certain methodological allowances must be made and certain categories of patients or conditions must perhaps be excluded. The researcher here has been forced by circumstances to depart from the ideal textbook design, and this obviously affects the generalizability and reliability of any inferences made. But without these methodological accommodations, the RCT would never have been permitted in the first place. These allowances, which are forced on researchers by practical considerations, are seized upon by critics to discredit the entire RCT. For example, some of the criticism of the eventual design of the first Mather trial of coronary care units versus home care for myocardial infarction came from the very interest groups whose initial objections determined what the original research design could be (Mather et al., 1971). It is analogous to someone saying they will not attend a party unless they can decide who is to be invited, and then complaining after the party that the company left much to be desired!

Sometimes the results of an RCT do show an innovation to be effective and these are immediately seized upon by its proponents and used to advance its career. More often, however, RCTs show innovations to be either ineffective or, at best, no more effective than existing and often much cheaper alternatives. Under these circumstances it is wasteful and perhaps unethical that proper evaluations of innovations should be postponed until the penultimate stages in their career. Imagine the potential for harm that could be avoided, and the resources saved, if innovations were routinely evaluated during earlier stages in their careers—certainly well before they become "standard procedure."

It is remarkable that the results of sometimes only one RCT so frequently create problems for the medical establishment and elicit defensive responses. Some of these reactions are discussed in the next section. Perhaps they are a measure of the flimsiness of the evidence employed up to this point by certain groups and organizations in support of, and as justification for, "standard procedure."

Up to this point we have distinguished several different types of "data" (but have employed the term very loosely). Stage 1 (promising reports) includes media stories that originate from manufacturing interests, and/or pilot studies on case histories that are essentially worthless but suggestive. A second type of data (clinical experience) was discussed in relation to Stage 2 (professional or organizational adoption). Again, such data do not constitute evidence of an innovation's effectiveness. While describing the elevation of innovations to "standard procedure" in Stage 4 we discussed the proliferation of a third kind of data—those derived from uncontrolled, comparative observational studies. Although these were considered more useful than either of the first two forms, they are still less reliable than a fourth form—the results from RCTs. One ought to be mindful of the different stages in the career of an innovation, and just how advanced that career usually is before data suitable for the formulation of social policies involving the allocation of public resources make their entrance.

6. The Stage of Professional Denunciation

We are concerned here with the defensive reactions that RCTs often elicit from the medical establishment when their findings appear to question what has become standard procedure. Although some of this reaction certainly constitutes legitimate criticism (concerning, for example, methodological, statistical, and ethical issues), much of it is simply a hostile response from a group self-interestedly protecting a domain of activity. Although often disguised in scientific and ethical jargon, such a response is not unique to medicine, but quite like the response of other groups and interests who perceive their livelihood and/or status threatened. It is understandable that a clinician would be defensive if a lifetime of "clinical experience" (one of the most valuable commodities in medicine) has been found to be simply wrong. Similarly, any researcher can be expected to vigorously defend the observational studies upon which his/her reputation has been built. I know few social scientists who would not be threatened by findings that run contrary to what they and their closest colleagues have espoused over many years. It should surprise no one that, in protecting their own interests and reputation, physicians respond like other human beings!

There are, of course, many ways of discrediting the results of an RCT that challenges some standard procedure. One favorite technique is to severely restrict the application of the results by depicting RCTs as impractical, ivory-tower activities, which seldom help in the handling of everyday problems in the real world. While perhaps conceding that disquieting findings may be applicable to experimental or research situations, clinicians may depict them as inapplicable to the everyday practice of medicine, or to what Lasagna (1974) refers to as "naturalistic" circumstances.

Professional denunciation often takes the form of letters to the editors of professional journals, particularly those that have the temerity to first publish the results of an RCT that question the effectiveness of some standard procedure. By mounting a write-in campaign, some interests can create the impression that there is more opposition than there actually is. At the same time, disquieting findings are often "put into context" by special editorials from "invited experts," who may attempt to reconcile the contradictory findings with their own clinical experience (Sanders, 1973). These experts may also be called upon to constitute a special committee, or working party, to evaluate the results of an RCT that pose enough of a challenge to standard procedure (Joint Working Party, 1975). Attempts are made to shore up an activity, the general standing of which is being threatened by an RCT, by appointing a panel of experts, or an "advisory group," which is expected to review any available evidence and make some recommendation (McKinlay, 1980). Such a committee was appointed in Great Britain after the publication of the first Mather (1971) trial. A federal advisory panel in the United States, headed by the chairman of the Division of Cardiovascular Diseases at the Mayo Clinic, recently considered the status of coronary artery by-pass surgery and enthusiastically endorsed it (National Institutes of Health, 1981). The claim that such special committees represent a genuine attempt to ascertain the proper place of certain innovations is strained if one analyzes the composition of these groups, and the interests they represent. Furthermore, it must be recalled that, to the extent that they review "data," these groups usually review (with the exception of the RCT) only the (methodologically defective) observational reports.

The issue of double standards is perhaps most evident during this sixth stage involving professional denunciation. The many defective observational studies conducted up to this point seldom receive adequate methodological and statistical scrutiny, whereas RCTs are subjected to the most stringent criticism, employing standards that are almost never invoked during the earlier stages. Questions are raised and motivations challenged that, again, are seldom raised during the earlier stages. There is absolutely *no* objection here to RCTs being subjected to the most gruelling methodological and statistical criticism. In an area such as medicine, with such a clearly documented potential for harm, there cannot be criticism enough. And if an RCT fails to meet even minimal standards of adequacy, it ought to be improved upon or disregarded. What is being questioned here is the near absence of any such criticism during the formative and strategically more important stages in an innovation's career. The nature of the scientific standards invoked, and the force with which they are applied, seem to vary depending on whether or not the results are supportive of what has become standard procedure.

Occasionally, the medical establishment seems simply to disregard the overwhelming evidence against some standard procedure. For example, in 1971, after many cases of vaginal adenosis and some carcinoma among young women whose mothers had received stilbesterol to prevent spontaneous abortion, the FDA issued a directive against the use of the drug for this purpose. Chalmers discusses this in a paper on "The Impact of Controlled Trials on the Practice of Medicine" and suggests:

> Obstetricians cannot be faulted for not anticipating such a long-term side-effect of the therapy. At the time of its use there was

no known toxicity, but was there any evidence of its efficacy? Between 1946 and 1955 thirteen evaluations of the efficacy of stilbesterol in preventing abortions in women with histories of habitual abortion and in diabetic women were carried out. Seven of the studies resulted in enthusiastic conclusions. None of these seven were controlled trials. Three had no controls, two employed historical controls, and in two studies the controls can be best called contrived, because the data were gathered after the results had originally been reported without any control patients. During this same period of time six studies revealed no evidence for efficacy of stilbesterol. All six of these had simultaneous control patients and three were double blind. In the 1950's randomization was not a commonly used procedure, and only one of the six was a randomized controlled trial.

These data should have been most impressive to practicing physicians. The evidence was overwhelming that stilbesterol had no effect in preventing spontaneous abortion in any group of patients, and six of seven textbooks of obstetrics came to this conclusion during the 1960's. Yet several studies of the marketing of stilbesterol in the late 1960's revealed that roughly 50,000 women received the drug during pregnancy per year, 15 years after six reasonably well-controlled studies showed it to be totally ineffective. The late appearing toxicity was irrelevant. (Chalmers, 1974:754)

It is reasonable then to argue that the success of an innovation has little to do with its intrinsic worth (whether it is measurably effective, as determined by controlled experimentation) but is dependent upon the power of the interests that sponsor and maintain it, despite the absence or inadequacy of empirical support. The power of such interests is also evident in their ability to impede the development of alternative practices (for which there may also be considerable observational support) that could conceivably threaten an activity in which there is already considerable investment.

7. The Stage of Erosion and Discreditation

One often reads reports of or, better still, witnesses an actual performance by some exciting new artist. For a while this artist is a major topic of conversation, receives rave reviews, much public recognition and support. Sometimes the artist is able, largely through good management and regulated exposure, to stay in the public eye for a period of time, and may eventually be more or less taken for granted. More often, however, he or she quietly disappears into obscurity, leaving the public wondering whatever happened to so-and-so. After such a promising beginning, what did the artist end up doing, and where is he or she now? Many promising careers are embarked upon, but few seem to survive and be established in the big time. The same phenomenon appears to be associated with the diffusion of medical innovations—whatever happened to that much heralded wonder drug, the machine that was supposed to revolutionize the practice of medicine, or the surgical procedure that offered new hope? Schneiderman (1975:68) urges us to "remember the number of drugs that have been Roman candles, making a bright and beautiful flash for a short time and then burning out."

After some period of time (often more than a decade), and ever so gradually, an erosion of support begins to set in. The enthusiastic claims made for the innovation during its earlier stages are modified somewhat; it is not as universally applicable as once thought; it is useful only for certain groups of the population, or particular types of or stages in an illness. Its career can sometimes be propped up for a while if it is combined with some other innovation or it may be relegated to the position of therapy of last resort—something to be employed after all other efforts are exhausted. Sometimes there is a scandal (e.g., thalidomide, dystilbesterol) and the innovation's career is abruptly terminated. And then, of course, people emerge who now claim to have had doubts about it all along! In these relatively rare situations the innovation may become so discredited that it is viewed as unethical to continue with it (e.g., radical mastectomy); it may eventually even be ridiculed. But scandal is not the only reason for a promising career's demise. More often it is simply eclipsed by some other rising star, and just drops out of public view. The innovation no longer enjoys public attention, little prestige is derived from association with it, cheaper alternatives become available, and so forth. Finally, it is relegated to that great dust heap called History. The slow demise of innovations is, indeed, consistent with the medical profession's resistance to change and preference for accepted procedures (McKinlay, 1973). Discreditation or discard usually occurs only when a *replacement* procedure becomes available.

From the above discussion it is evident that the typical career of most medical innovations is extraordinarily wasteful of scarce resources. To paraphrase Hegel, "What experience and the history of medical innovation teach is this—that the professions, hospitals, and the state never have learned anything from history, or acted on principles deduced from it." Innovation after innovation begins its slow, costly journey through the stages described only to end up—in the overwhelming majority of cases—either discarded or discredited. Is there no way of ensuring that more reliable information is available during earlier formative stages when the innovation is not yet firmly ensconced? Is there no way of temporarily curtailing the understandable, but so often premature, enthusiasm of the professions and medical organizations? Can the public and the state be encouraged to withhold their endorsement until some more reliable objective evaluation has been undertaken? How can some of the resources now consumed by wasteful observational reports be diverted into more reliable controlled experimentation? Is there some way of moving the evaluation of an innovation from the end of its career to some earlier beginning stage? Must we always remain uninformed by earlier experience and end up going through all these stages with every new innovation? Given our present knowledge of the disturbing ratio of careers embarked upon to those that are successful, is there no way of avoiding the endless repetition of our wasteful past (Fineberg and Hiatt, 1979)?

The particular innovations discussed illustrate a more general problem besetting most medical care systems: the repeated adoption of unevaluated innovations. Positron emission tomography, zeumatography, dynamic spatial reconstruction, and the numerous other costly innovations that are now lined up and seeking admission to the House of Medicine are of little intrinsic concern to this author. What is worrisome is the way in which just about all innovations, with active support of the state, slip into the medical care system of most countries without any proper evaluation either before or during most of their careers. The legal maxim that a person is presumed innocent until proven guilty appears also to apply to most medical innovations. They are assumed to be effective until they are shown *ad nauseum* to be ineffective. And on those occasions when something is shown to be ineffective, it is difficult to remove because of the pressure groups associated with, and even dependent upon, its survival. Unlike therapeutic nihilists, this author is certainly not opposed to any and all surgical, diagnostic, or pharmaceutical interventions (McKinlay, 1978). To be anti-innovation is obviously to be antiprogress. At the

same time, we must oppose premature state support for the introduction and proliferation of just about every promising innovation,
without any requirement that their effectiveness be properly demonstrated either before or at a very early stage in their careers.

A Strategy for the Future

Present patterns of social expenditure are clearly unrelated to any
widely accepted outcome measures, and many practices exist, or are
proposed, in the knowledge that they are either ineffective or questionable, or have never been evaluated on proper scientific grounds
(McKinlay, 1980). Such a situation was perhaps tolerable, although
not acceptable, during the 1960s, when there was considerable economic growth, and when the irrationality and waste described in the
first part of this paper did not require subtractions from existing
allocations. Most countries are now beset with structural payments
imbalances, uncontrollable inflation, deepening recession, ever-increasing unemployment, and negative or negligible economic growth
(McKinlay, 1980), which ought to preclude continuation of this
wasteful course (McKinlay, 1977a; O'Connor, 1973). In the United
States, for example, there are public movements to limit taxation,
cities increasingly cannot meet necessary expenses, and major industries are facing doubtful survival, despite heavy government support
(Tamaskovic-Devey and McKinlay, 1981).

Since many view the state as responsible for providing the greatest
possible benefit to the greatest number of people (utilitarianism), and
because the allocation of ever scarcer resources cannot continue as has
been described for the past, some clear criteria must be invoked to
inform social policy. Any policy based on ad hoc responses to defective
data and particular interest groups structurally precludes the state
from allocating resources in accordance with utilitarian principles.
Although the present irrational distribution of resources does occasionally help meet some social needs, there is no structural mechanism
for ensuring that it do so. It is therefore essential that some objective
(i.e., interest-free) criterion inform the allocation of at least public
resources to medical innovations. And the requirement that there be
proper *demonstrations of effectiveness* (preferably before their introduction

and diffusion) is such a criterion (Light, Mosteller, and Winokur, 1971; Gilbert, Light, and Mosteller, 1975). On the basis of this argument, the following premise should, therefore, inform all social policy:

Government Should Not Support through Public Funding for General Public Use Any Service, Procedure, or Technology, the Effectiveness of Which Has Not Been, or Cannot Be, Demonstrated.

This is not an unreasonable premise. The *public* ought to be confident that the services they receive and pay for are effective. *Workers* involved in the production and distribution of human services should wish to know that they are beneficially altering some condition or problem. The *state* ought to be concerned that public funds are not devoted to ineffective or questionably effective activities. Surely, it is irrational and nonutilitarian for the state, as at present, to estimate the possible costs and survey the social acceptability of some service without some previous demonstration of its effectiveness—i.e., its measurable contribution to some beneficial alteration in the natural course of some problem (Cochrane, 1972). This is indisputable.

It is no part of the present argument that ineffective services should necessarily be declared illegal or removed from the human service marketplace (McKinlay, 1978). People should be free to purchase just about any human service desired, no matter how ineffective. (If people want to undergo a coronary artery bypass graft—at a cost of around $20,000—then they should be free to do so). What is questioned here is whether, through public expenditures and/or third-party payments, the rest of society should be required to pay for such prodigal purchases.

There are a number of things that we need to consider urgently if we are to develop a human or social service system that can deal effectively with the problems that now plague our society:

—First, *we must determine, in some objective and independent fashion, the nature and magnitude of the human needs in our society.*

—Second, *all new services must be evaluated objectively (perferably and where appropriate by RCTs) before they are introduced.* There ought to be a moratorium on the widespread adoption and diffusion of any unevaluated innovations.

—Third, and in order to separate the grain from the chaff, *we should begin a systematic evaluation of the technologies that are already ensconced and widely accepted* but have never been properly evaluated.

—Fourth, if one subscribes to the view that society should be responsible for those who are generally recognized to be in need— that human services are an inalienable right—then *the state should be responsible for, and encourage the use of, only the services that have been shown to be effective*—that is, services that are able to beneficially alter the natural course of some recognized problem.

Now if *demonstrated effectiveness* can be generally accepted as the primary criterion for the allocation of resources (a necessary but *not* sufficient condition for the public funding of an intervention), then the methodology for the determination of effectiveness becomes a critical issue in social policy. It has been argued that one can determine the effectiveness of some program, or intervention, only through scientifically sound comparisons. For most people, RCTs represent the methodology of choice because there is no way, other than through experimentation (involving the objective—preferably random—assignment of cases to the intervention being evaluated, or to some appropriate alternative), that the matter of effectiveness can be placed beyond dispute. Consequently, *any social policy that seeks some distribution of public resources on the reasonable basis of effectiveness must also be concerned with the optimal methodology by which effectiveness can be demonstrated.*

Three principal criteria that may be employed to determine whether or not some proposed procedure, service, or technology (hereinafter referred to as an intervention) should be publicly funded, are presented *in order of logical importance.*

1. *Effectiveness. Whatever the intervention, it must first demonstrate some ability to beneficially alter the natural course of a clearly defined condition or set of conditions.*

- It is particularly important to demonstrate a benefit *over and above any possible placebo effect.*
- The demonstration of benefit must be as free as possible from important sources of *bias,* care being taken to minimize or adjust for, and document, any remaining biases.
- In general, the demonstration must involve some *comparison.* The proposed intervention must be demonstrably better than existing

procedures or services (if any) designed for the same purpose, and this improvement must be real, *not* a placebo effect.

- In determining any benefit of some proposed interventions, due account must be taken of any accompanying negative *side effects or added risks*. These must be incorporated in any outcome measure.
- The benefit should be applicable to as *wide a section of the population* subject to the condition as possible. This requires that the demonstration be carried out on as representative a group as is feasible.

2. Cost Efficiency. Where two or more proposed interventions of approximately equivalent effectiveness are available, that one should be preferred that involves the least cost.

- The *cost* of some proposed intervention must be *compared* with the cost of any existing procedures.
- The demonstrated effectiveness of the intervention, compared with standard or existing procedures, must be *related to the cost* of the intervention. In general, the costlier the intervention, the greater its demonstrated effectiveness must be *before* it can be considered an acceptable alternative.

3. Acceptability and Equity. A proposed intervention that is both effective and cost efficient is of no value unless it is socially acceptable and equally accessible to all the relevant subgroups of the society into which it is being introduced.

- A proposed intervention should be in a form that ensures its utilization by those groups whose needs it is designed to beneficially alter. If, for example, a condition is prevalent among the elderly and the proposed intervention requires a physical fitness usually associated with youth, then such an intervention is clearly inappropriate.
- When two or more interventions appear to be of equivalent effectiveness and cost efficiency, and are both of an appropriate form, some evidence of public preference may be incorporated in the decision-making process.

As stated, these three criteria (effectiveness, cost efficiency, and social acceptability and equality of access) are presented in order of logical importance. Each criterion is considered to be a necessary but not sufficient condition for the inclusion of the next criterion. For example, an intervention must demonstrate some effectiveness that is clearly attributable to the intervention, and *not* to a placebo, before any considerations of cost can be logically included in the decision procedure. At the same time, if effectiveness is demonstrated, it still may not be of sufficient dimension to justify possible increased cost of the proposed intervention.

In the context of the above formulation, the role of user preference or client satisfaction is clearly a minor one, and is important only if two or more interventions display equivalent effectiveness, cost efficiency, and appropriateness of form. One could argue that, given two equally effective interventions, one of which is more costly but preferable, the more costly should be chosen, as the less costly alternative will not be used (it is not preferred). However, it may be more efficient to render the less costly alternative more socially acceptable than to publicly fund the preferred, costlier intervention. One simply cannot evaluate the effectiveness (as defined in this paper) of an intervention by surveying the extent of consumer satisfaction. The public may be dissatisfied with services that are effective and of technically high quality, and satisfied with services that are ineffective and of poor technical quality.

Because *effectiveness* must be the key criterion in any consideration of a proposed innovation for public funding, the nature of the evidence for such effectiveness is of prime importance. The evidence submitted should be of such a form that: a) the worth of the evidence can itself be evaluated; and b) inferences and generalizations can be made from this evidence to the population to be exposed to the innovation. This evidence should consist, minimally, of carefully designed and executed studies, in clearly defined populations, using objective or reproducible outcome measures. Most studies should be of the form of experiments used to compare types of interventions, or surveys to estimate population characteristics.

With few exceptions, acceptable evidence of an intervention's effectiveness can be established only through comparative experiments (RCTs) that are as free as possible of sources of bias. Then and only then can there be confidence that the observed effect (if there is one) is *actually the result of the intervention.* Such experiments (trials) must minimally include the characteristics described by McKinlay (1981) (see also Chalmers et al., 1981; Nyberg, 1974; Wulff, 1977; Lionel and Hexelheimer, 1970).

Two caveats must be emphasized regarding any implementation of the decision procedure that is proposed above. First, there is *no* suggestion that the criteria of effectiveness, cost efficiency, social acceptability, and equality of access should be applied only to innovations newly proposed for public funding. Clearly, innovations already ensconced in our publicly funded human services system must be subjected to the same scrutiny. Moreover, it is likely that a large proportion of standard procedures or services would not meet even the minimally sufficient criteria and should, therefore, be excluded from further public funding if we are ever to receive value for money in human services.

Second, there is *no* suggestion that the criteria proposed should be applied only to particular innovations, or to those proposed by particular groups. Any intervention proposed for public support or funding (whether acupuncture, cardiothoracic surgery, chiropractic, income maintenance, psychiatry, social work, or transcendental meditation) should be subject to the same basic criteria. A situation must be avoided where, as at present, double standards exist regarding the criteria to be met, depending on the relative power of interested groups proposing or supporting some promising innovation.

References

Banta, H.D. 1980. The Diffusion of the Computed Tomography (CT) Scanner in the United States. *International Journal of Health Services* 10:251–269.

————, and Thacker, S.B. 1979. *Costs and Benefits of Electronic Fetal Monitoring: A Review of the Literature.* DHEW Publication No. (PHS) 79-3245.

Berk, A.A., and Chalmers, T.C. 1981. Cost and Efficiency of the Substitution of Ambulatory for Inpatient Care. *New England Journal of Medicine* 304:393–397.

Bloom, B.S., and Peterson, O. 1973. End Results, Costs and Productivity of Coronary-Care Units. *New England Journal of Medicine* 288:72–78.

Boston Globe, 1980. Doctor Cites Gains against Liver Cancers. October 7, 1980.

Braunwald, E. 1977. Coronary Artery Surgery at the Crossroads. *New England Journal of Medicine* 276:661–663.

Bunker, J.P., Barnes, B.A., and Mosteller, F., eds. 1977. *Costs, Risks and Benefits of Surgery*. New York: Oxford University Press.

Byar, D.P., et al. 1976. Randomized Clinical Trials. *New England Journal of Medicine* 295:74–80.

Chalmers, T.C. 1972. Randomization and Coronary Artery Surgery. *Annals of Thoracic Surgery* 14:323–327.

———. 1974. The Impact of Controlled Trials on the Practice of Medicine. *Mount Sinai Journal of Medicine* 41:753–759.

———. 1975a. Ethical Aspects of Clinical Trials. *American Journal of Ophthalmology* 79:753–758.

———. 1975b. Randomization of the First Patient. *Medical Clinics of North America* 59:1035–1038.

———, Block, J.B., and Lee, S. 1972. Controlled Studies in Clinical Cancer Research. *New England Journal of Medicine* 287:75–78.

———, Sebestyen, C.S., and Lee, S. 1970. Emergency Surgical Treatment of Bleeding Peptic Ulcer: An Analysis of the Published Data on 21,130 Patients. *Trans American Clinical Climatology Association* 82:188.

———, Smith, H., Blackburn, B., et al. 1981. A Method for Assessing the Quality of a Randomized Control Trial. *Controlled Clinical Trials*. In press.

Cochrane, A.L. 1972. *Effectiveness and Efficiency*. London: Nuffield Provincial Hospitals Trust.

———. 1979. 1931–1971: A Critical Review with Particular Reference to the Medical Profession. *Journal of the Royal College of Physicians of London* 14:2–12.

Coleman, J.S., Katz, E., and Menzel, H. 1966. *Medical Innovation: A Diffusion Study*. Indianapolis: Bobbs-Merrill.

Conner, R.F. 1977. Selecting a Control Group: An Analysis of the Randomization Process in Twelve Social Reform Programs. *Evaluation Quarterly* 1:195–243.

Cromwell, J., Ginsberg, P., Hamilton, D., and Summer, M. 1975. *Incentives and Decisions underlying Hospitals' Adoption of Major Capital Equipment*. Cambridge, Mass.: Abt Associates.

Fineberg, H.V., and Hiatt, H.H. 1979. Evaluation of Medical Practices: The Case for Technology Assessment. *New England Journal of Medicine* 301:1086–1091.

———, Bauman, R., and Sosman, M. 1977. Computerized Cranial

Tomography: Effect on Diagnostic and Therapeutic Plane. *Journal of the American Medical Association* 238:224–227.

Freidson, E. 1971. *Profession of Medicine.* New York: Dodd, Mead.

Gilbert, J.P., Light, R.J., and Mosteller, F. 1975. Pressing Social Innovations: An Empirical Base for Policy. In Bennett, C.A., and Lumsdaine, A., eds., *Evaluation and Experiment: Some Critical Issues in Assessing Social Programs,* 39–193. New York: Academic Press.

Gordon, G., and Fisher, G.L., 1975. *The Diffusion of Medical Technology.* Cambridge, Mass.: Ballinger.

Gore, S.M., Jones, I.G., and Rutter, E.C. 1977. Misuse of Statistical Methods: Critical Assessment of Articles in B.M.J. from January to March 1976. *British Medical Journal* 1:85–87.

Guttentag, M. 1971. Subjectivity and Its Use in Evaluation Research. *Evaluation* 1:60–65.

Hemminki, E. 1980. Study of Information Submitted by Drug Companies to Licensing Authorities. *British Medical Journal* 280:833–841.

———, and Falkum, E. 1980. Psychotropic Drug Registration in the Scandinavian Countries: The Role of Clinical Trials. *Social Science and Medicine* 14:547–559.

Hill, J.D., Hampton, J.R., and Mitchell, J.R.A. 1978. A Randomized Trial of Home-versus-Hospital Management for Patients with Suspected Myocardial Infarction. *Lancet* 1:837–841.

Joint Working Party of the Royal College of Physicians of London and the British Cardiac Society. 1975. *Journal of the Royal College of Physicians of London* 10:5.

Kaluzny, A.D., and Veney, J.E. 1973. Attributes of Health Services as Factors in Program Implementation. *Journal of Health and Social Behavior* 14:124–133.

———, Veney, J.E., and Gentry, J.T. 1974. Innovation in Health Services: A Comparative Study of Hospitals and Health Departments. *Milbank Memorial Fund Quarterly/Health and Society* 52 (Winter):51–82.

Kempthorne, O. 1977. Why Randomize? *Journal of Statistical Planning and Inference* 1:1–25.

Lasagna, L. 1974. A Plea for the "Naturalistic" Study of Medicine. *European Journal of Clinical Pharmacology* 7:153.

Light, R.J., Mosteller, F., and Winokur, H.S. 1971. Using Controlled Field Studies to Improve Public Policy. *Federal Statistics* 2:367–402.

Lionel, N.D.W., and Hexelheimer, A. 1970. Assessing Reports of Therapeutic Trials. *British Medical Journal* 3:637–640.

Mather, H.G., et al. 1971. Acute Myocardial Infarction: Home and Hospital Treatment. *British Medical Journal* 3:334–335.

––––––. 1976. Myocardial Infarction: A Comparison between Home and Hospital Care for Patients. *British Medical Journal* 1:925–929.

Mathur, V.S., et al. 1975. Surgical Treatment for Stable Angina Pectoris: Prospective Randomized Study. *New England Journal of Medicine* 292:709–713.

McKinlay, J.B. 1973. On the Professional Regulation of Change. In Halmos, P., ed., *Professionalization and Social Change,* 61–84. Sociological Review Monograph No. 20.

––––––. 1977a. On the Medical-Industrial Complex. *American Medical News* (April 11):26.

––––––. 1977b. The Business of Good Doctoring, or Doctoring as Good Business: Reflections on Freidson's View of the Medical Game. *International Journal of Health Services* 7:459–488.

––––––. 1978. The Limits of Human Services. *Social Policy* (Jan.–Feb.):29–36.

––––––. 1980. Evaluating Medical Technology in the Context of a Fiscal Crisis: The Case of New Zealand. *Milbank Memorial Fund Quarterly/Health and Society* 58(Spring):217–267.

––––––, and Dutton, D.B. 1974. Social-Psychological Factors Affecting Health Service Utilization. In Mushkin, S.J., ed., *Consumer Incentives for Health Care,* 251–303. New York: Prodist.

McKinlay, S.M. 1975. The Design and Analysis of the Observational Study: A Review. *Journal of the American Statistical Association* 70:351, 503–523.

––––––. 1981. Experimentation in Human Populations. *Milbank Memorial Fund Quarterly/Health and Society* 59 (Summer):308–323.

Miller, R.R. 1975. Prescribing Habits of Physicians. *Drug Intelligence and Clinical Pharmacology* 7:492–500, 557–564.

––––––. 1976. Prescribing Habits of Physicians. *Drug Intelligence and Clinical Pharmacology* 8:81–91.

Mundth, E.D., and Austen, W.G. 1975. Surgical Measures for Coronary Heart Disease. *New England Journal of Medicine* 293:13–19, 75–80, 124–130.

Murphy, M.L., et al. 1977. Treatment of Chronic Stable Angina. *New England Journal of Medicine* 297:12.

National Institutes of Health, 1981. Coronary-Artery Bypass Surgery: Scientific and Clinical Aspects. *New England Journal of Medicine* 304:680–684.

Newsweek. 1980. Scanning the Human Mind. September 29.

New York Times. 1980a. 3rd Dimension of Organs Seen on New X-Ray. October 12.

————. 1980b. Findings Are in Conflict on Value of Coronary Bypass Operations. November 18.

————. 1980c. U.S. Study Backs Bypass Surgery. December 6.

Nyberg, G. 1974. Assessment of Papers of Clinical Trials. *The Medical Journal of Australia:*381.

O'Conner, J. 1973. *The Fiscal Crisis of the State.* New York: St. Martin's Press.

Peto, R., et al. 1976. Design and Analysis of Randomized Clinical Trials Requiring Prolonged Observation of Each Patient. I. Introduction and Design. *British Journal of Cancer* 34:585–612.

————. 1977. Design and Analysis of Randomized Clinical Trials Requiring Prolonged Observation of Each Patient. II. Analysis and Examples. *British Journal of Cancer* 35:1–39.

Rappaport, J. 1978. Diffusion of Technological Innovation among Non-profit Firms: A Case Study of Radioisotopes in U.S. Hospitals. *Journal of Economic Business* 30:108–118.

Riecken, H.S., and Boruch, R.F., eds. 1974. *Social Experimentation: A Method for Planning and Evaluating Social Intervention.* New York: Seminar Press.

Russell, L.B. 1976. The Diffusion of New Hospital Technologies in the United States. *International Journal of Health Services* 6:557–580.

————. 1978. *Technology in Hospitals: Medical Advances and Their Diffusion.* Washington, D.C.: Brookings Institution.

————, and Burke, U.S. 1975. *Technological Diffusion in the Hospital Sector.* Washington, D.C.: National Planning Association.

Sanders, C.A. 1973. The Coronary-Care Unit: Necessity or Luxury? *New England Journal of Medicine* 288:101–102.

Schneiderman, M.A. 1975. How Do You Know You've Done Any Better? *Cancer* 35:64–69.

Sheldon, W.C., et al. 1975. Surgical Treatment of Coronary Artery Disease: Pure Graft Operations, with a Study of 741 Patients Followed 3–7 Years. *Progress in Cardiovascular Diseases* 18:237–253.

Silverman, M., and Lee, P.R. 1974. *Pills, Profits and Politics.* Los Angeles: University of California Press.

Sontag, S. 1978. *Illness as Metaphor.* New York: Farrar, Straus and Giroux.

Spodick, D.H. 1973. The Surgical Mystique and the Double Standard. *American Heart Journal* 85:579–583.

Stross, J.K., and Harlan, W.R. 1979. The Dissemination of New Medical Information. *Journal of the American Medical Association* 241:2622–2624.

Strupp, H.H., Hadley, S.W., and Gomes-Schwartz, B. 1977. *Psychotherapy for Better or Worse.* New York: Jason Aronson, Inc.

The Compact Edition of the Oxford English Dictionary. 1971. New York: Oxford University Press.

Tomaskovic-Devey, D., and McKinlay, J.B. 1981. Bailing Out the Banks: The United States and Private International Debt. *Social Policy* 11:8–17.

U.S. Senate. 1974. Subcommittee on Health, Committee on Labor and Public Welfare. *Examination of the Pharmaceutical Industry, 1973–74.* Washington, D.C.: Government Printing Office.

Vineberg, A. 1975. Evidence That Revascularization by Ventricular-Internal Mammary Artery Implants Increases Longevity: Twenty-four Year, Nine Month Follow-up. *Journal of Thoracic and Cardiovascular Surgery* 70:381–394.

Waldron, I. 1977. Increased Prescribing of Valium, Librium, and Other Drugs: An Example of the Influence of Economic and Social Factors on the Practice of Medicine. *International Journal of Health Services* 7:37–62.

Warner, K.E. 1977. Treatment Decision Making in Catastrophic Illness. *Medical Care* 15:19–33.

Webster's New Collegiate Dictionary. 1976. Springfield, Mass.: Merriam.

Wulff, H.R. 1977. Check List for Assessment of Controlled Therapeutic Trials. *Acta Neurologica Scandinavia,* Supplement, 60:79–80.

Acknowledgments: Much of the background reading for this paper was facilitated by a 1976 grant from the Milbank Memorial Fund. The paper has benefited from discussions with my colleagues Professors Mark Field, Sol Levine, S.M. Miller, and Dr. Sonja McKinlay.

Address correspondence to: Dr. John B. McKinlay, 59 Princeton Road, Chestnut Hill, MA 02167.

Advances in the Study of Diffusion of Innovation in Health Care Organizations

ANN LENNARSON GREER

Departments of Urban Affairs and Sociology,
and the Urban Research Center,
The University of Wisconsin—Milwaukee

Federal policy makers have been concerned with diffusion of innovation for some time. In the past, thought and policy were dominated by an assumption that innovation was good, progress to be welcomed. There continues to be an interest in encouraging diffusion of valuable innovations, those which promise to improve the quality of medical care or the way in which health institutions operate. However, in recent years, the desire to slow innovation has also been felt. Rapidly rising costs have focused attention on the need to contain the spread of costly, duplicative, and often medically questionable technologies. The 1960s concern of the Regional Medical Programs to diffuse technologies has been overtaken by a desire to restrain unnecessary adoption of innovation and to contain health system costs.

An understanding of the reasons for adoption of innovation is essential for those making policies intended to either speed up or slow down diffusion. As a guide to action, the literature is disappointing. It contains one well-developed theory concerned with the adoption of innovation by individuals, a cumbersome and inconclusive body of theory concerned with organization attributes as these influence organizational innovation, and a few first steps toward an understanding of the decision-making processes which characterize health institutions confronting opportunities to innovate.

Weaknesses in Available Theory

The great majority of studies investigating the diffusion of innova-

MMFQ / Health and Society / *Fall 1977*
© Milbank Memorial Fund 1977

tion fall within a common framework. "Classical" diffusion theory offers explanation of the adoption of innovations by single individuals who are first in a community to hear of and adopt innovations and who pass information along to others who also adopt. Numerous studies have analyzed (1) the role of individuals in information networks and (2) the character of information passed. There are severe limits to the applicability of classical theory to *organizational* adoption of innovation. It is impossible to assume an identity of interest among all participants within a complex organization such as a hospital, clinic, or public health department. Thus the assumption that single individuals adopt (and implement) innovations must be modified or discarded.

Researchers have evolved several strategies for circumventing this problem. One is to assume that *persons in positions of formal power* act on behalf of their organizations and may be therefore studied as individual adopters. A second is to assume that *organizations* behave as *individuals*. A third is to assume that *organizational wholes* adopt innovations and to relate organizational properties to the innovation process. A fourth is to assume that a group of organizational *decision makers* negotiate policies and determine the interests, resources, and strategies which they bring to the decision process. The first two strategies allow the use of concepts from classical theory. The latter two strategies constitute radical departures from classical tradition, and move toward organizational and political theory.

The utility of available diffusion theory is also limited by the dominating assumption that innovation is desirable. Scholars as well as policy makers are now questioning the validity of this assumption but research does not yet reflect this change in perspective. Because innovations have been considered to be valuable, *in general*, studies have focused on "innovativeness," defined as the number of innovations adopted by a person or organization. This focus has resulted in a theoretical blurring of innovation attributes. Classical theorists provided a list of innovation attributes which affect the speed of diffusion: relative advantage, complexity (understandability), triability, observability of consequences and compatibility with values. Little has been done however to consider these or other attributes as reasons for organizational adoption. Studies have tended to treat all innovations in the same way.

Available theory depends almost exclusively upon studies

which analyze the diffusion of procedures and programs among health organizations. When the adoption of hardware technologies is considered, the focus is usually on the introduction of computerized records or some other operational technology where hospital administrators are the decision makers. This leaves policy makers with the job of generalizing from these studies when faced with situations where physicians are the important decision makers.

Recent literature is characterized by another debilitating problem. Theory has not been emphasized. Studies of organizational innovation have tended to manipulate aggregate data, usually that collected by the American Hospital Association, in the apparent hope that patterns will emerge. The result seems to be general confusion. One comes away from a review of this literature aware of a large number of variables which show some promise as predictors. Yet patterns are elusive. The cry for improved and more consistent measurement techniques is common. But our willingness to retain or abandon a variable should rely not simply on confirmation but on relationships among variables in a meaningful body of theory.

In selecting articles for attention in this review I have given strong preference to articles with sound theoretical underpinnings and to exploratory studies which generate hypotheses. I believe that carefully conducted inquiries geared to generating or refining theoretically important variables show greater promise for advancing general theory than do artificially sophisticated research designs. Until coherent, empirically grounded theories of organizational innovation are available, large scale "tests" are premature and wasteful.

This review makes no pretense of comprehensiveness. Rather I have selected articles which are particularly useful in gaining an understanding of the diffusion of innovation in health organizations. I considered relevant for inclusion studies dealing with health institutions generally, the disparate nature of which is obvious.

In preparing this report, I reviewed the literature published since 1960. My focus was on adoption of health technologies (either physical or social) in organizational contexts. Innovation was defined, in most of the studies reviewed, as the adoption of a program or technology which is new to the adopting unit. I wanted to find studies having sufficient theoretical and methodological force to warrant confidence. Studies are somewhat arbitrarily classified into three research frameworks. The frameworks are themselves analytically distinguishable. Particular studies often contain components of more than one framework.

The three theoretical frameworks which provide the basis for organizing the studies derive from classical theory, organizational theory, and political theory. Several questions must be answered if we are to acquire an understanding of the diffusion process: (1) How do responsive individuals within an organization receive and adopt innovative ideas? Classical theory has much to say about this. (2) What aspects of organizations constrain or facilitate the adoption or implementation of innovations? Organization theory is helpful here. (3) What interests and values relevant to innovation are effectively represented in organizations? How are these expressed? What is the outcome? In answering these questions political analysis is necessary.

Theories of Diffusion

A. *The Classical Model: Information and Influence*

Ideas central to the classical diffusion theory were introduced in the 1930s when scholars studying the adoption by farmers of hybrid corn noted patterns of communication and influence. Elaborated since that time in a variety of studies, diffusion theory has been most fully developed in the work of Everett Rogers (Rogers, 1962; Rogers and Shoemaker, 1971). Rogers focused on the process through which a new idea is communicated by a person who is aware of it to another person who thereby becomes aware of and adopts the new idea. His formulation incorporated many ideas, two of which have been widely used in the study of organizational diffusion. These involve the classification of persons as local or cosmopolitan and the identification of opinion leaders.

Robert Merton first used the terms *"localites" and "cosmopolites"* (Merton, 1949). The former referred to persons whose ambitions and social satisfactions derive primarily from their participation in the local community, the latter to persons whose primary rewards and satisfactions derive from participation in one or more functional communities (such as a professional group or national corporation). The distinction was used successfully by Coleman et al. in their classic study of the adoption of new drugs by physicians (1966). Because they participate in and identify with national networks, "cosmopolites" are the first to get the word regarding available innovations and are first to adopt them. Cosmopolites tend to be younger, better educated, more technically competent, and more geographically mobile than localites.

The concept of the "*opinion leader*" came to diffusion theory through efforts of students of electoral voting to understand the effect of media on the decision of voters. The idea was introduced when studies failed to show a direct effect of media on voter decisions (Lazarsfeld et al., 1948). Rather, it appeared that some voters, "opinion leaders," are influenced by media sources and that these voters influence their associates. Opinion leaders are centrally located in their groups sociometrically, "belong" to the groups they influence (are thought to have the group's interest at heart), conform generally to group standards, are socially accessible to group members, and are considered technically competent.

These two ideas converge to the extent that both opinion leaders and cosmopolites rely on information which comes from outside the local group and are considered competent. Cosmopolites are potential opinion leaders. Used frequently to guide research, these ideas have encouraged examination of (1) the interpersonal networks through which information passes and influence is exerted; and to a lesser extent (2) the social characteristics, motivations, attitudes, competencies, and leadership skills of particular individuals.

Most research in the "classic" tradition occurred during a period of great faith in progress. Opinion leaders were uncritically considered to be promoters of innovation. Little thought was given to the possible role of leaders in slowing diffusion. However, neither the concept of the "opinion leader" nor the "cosmopolite" requires (or benefits from) a pro-innovation bias. As Tanon and Rogers (Gordon and Fisher, 1975: 51–77) note, opinion leaders may use their influence to speed up or slow down the diffusion process. Similarly, cosmopolites may, in perfect accord with the standards of their reference groups, distrust proposed innovation.

Individual Adopters Acting on Behalf of Organizations   The most interesting development in the application of these concepts is Becker's suggestion that opinion leaders are selective in their sponsorship of innovations (Becker, 1970). Becker studied the diffusion of innovations in ninety-five local health departments. He defined innovation as the introduction of new programs into local health departments and considered the local health officer to be the program adopter. His primary contribution was to divide innovations into categories of low and high adoption potential, defined as an innovation's probable ease or difficulty of diffusion. To assess ease of diffusion, Becker asked a panel of experts to rate innovations according to the extent to which they departed from existing values and institutions. Those innovations which departed least he characterized as "high adoption potential" (HAP) innovations. Those departing most he described as having "low adoption potential" (LAP). For study, measles immunization was selected as a HAP innovation, diabetes screening as a LAP innovation.

Becker found that different types of persons led the way in adopting the two types of innovations. Those earliest to adopt HAP innovations were young, liberal, cosmopolitan health officers who were frequently early adopters of innovations and who were considered innovative by their peers. Becker explains HAP adoption as follows: Early HAP adopters are persons who value and seek the professional prestige which their data shows is associated with a high rate of innovation. Persons so motivated seek out information sources which will provide them with early and scientifically sound information about new things in their field. Their "most valued sources of information" are those sources which provide early information, especially professional meetings outside the state and professional journals. Relying on the information available through these "cosmopolite" sources, leaders adopt a relatively large number of HAP innovations ahead of others in the local community.

These early adopters become known to local community colleagues as sources of practical information about innovations. Local colleagues seek them out for information concerning "costs, problems, political risks, likelihood of opposition from interest groups, efficacy of the innovation when initiated and so forth" (Becker, 1970: 269). Thus they are accorded a central place in the local innovation information network: they are innovation opinion leaders. Becker diagrams the adoption activities of HAP innovators as in Fig. 1.

The circumstances surrounding LAP adoption are more puzzling. While the usual leaders are holding back, unsure about the acceptability of risky programs, another type of officer may adopt, an officer who is older, less well educated, generally localite, not frequently innovative, and not viewed as innovative by peers.

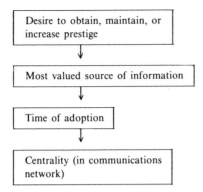

Fɪɢ. 1. Behavior of HAP Innovation Adopters.

Whereas HAP leaders are consistently innovative, LAP innovation pioneers are first to adopt only one or two programs. They do not acquire centrality as a result. Others do not usually follow their lead. If innovations they pioneer take hold, it is only after the usual group of HAP innovators have picked them up.

To explain the idiosyncratic nature of LAP innovation adoption, Becker suggests that localite pioneers may be innovating in response to desires of local constituencies. They may also feel more free to take professional chances since they have established places in their local communities. Becker's data did not allow him to explore LAP innovation further. However, his identification of a sub-category of positive innovation decisions suggests interesting questions. To be specific, consumer interests in health care may find entry into medical decision-making through localite opinion leaders. The idea that market considerations may encourage otherwise reluctant organizations to adopt consumer-desired innovations is common in the literature on business firm adoption (Schon, 1971; Utterback, 1974; Zaltman et al., 1973). This idea deserves further attention in the study of health care institutions.

The work of Kaluzny et al. (1974) includes an interesting finding relating to Becker's theory. Like Becker, Kaluzny et al. divide innovations into low and high risk categories. They examine the characteristics of twenty-three health departments and ninety-three hospitals which adopted innovative service programs. Like Becker, they find that classical concepts (in this case, cosmopolitan orientations of organization members and staff training) are strong predictors of new program adoption when the new programs do not diverge sharply from traditional activities. Also, like Becker, they find a different and confused pattern in the adoption of risky innovations.

The two studies are not comparable. Becker began with a specific theory. He sought to measure the variables relevant to it and control those extraneous. Kaluzny and his colleagues sought to measure the relative influence on adoption of a large number of variables suggested by a large number of theoretically dissimilar studies. Becker defines a specific risk: the risk of attempting influence where major departures from tradition are involved. Kaluzny et al. consider various types of risk: relative advantage (payoff), social approval, innovation complexity (ease of understanding), clarity of results, association with major activities, and persuasiveness. In spite of these many differences, these studies find a common pattern which warrants further study.

A similar dichotomy in explanatory power occurred in Bingham's study (1976) of the adoption of innovation in local government. Bingham found that two organizational variables (size of unit and availability of resources) were important predictors of the adoption of innovation by units of local government. Prediction was good, however, only for "process" innovations, innovations largely internal to the governmental unit and largely invisible to the public. None of the traditional organizational variables tested by Bingham explained "product" innovations. Bingham concluded that "these findings seem to suggest that 'invisible' innovations, those away from public scrutiny, may be much more predictable than those in the public eye." Bingham's conclusions are similar to Becker's in that they both suggest that when interest in an innovation is limited to professionals in the field it is quite predictable. Innovation patterns which are not predictable may be influenced by "random" (not understood) factors peculiar to the local community. Becker suggests that community forces may enter the professional agencies' decision-making process through localite officials. Bingham suggests simply that visible innovation draws the attention of interested parties in the community.

In a particularly interesting study of ninety-three public health departments, Mohr (1969) placed individuals motivated to innovate into organizational context. This study contains important elements of the organizational and political perspectives but most closely complements Becker's work. Indeed, Becker selected his sample of public health officers to overlap Mohr's and to make use of the latter's data.

Mohr emphasizes motivation to innovate, together with resources for innovation and obstacles to innovation. To assess motivation, Mohr examines the ideology and activism of public health officials. Ideology is defined by the health officer's opinion as to the proper scope of *public* health services as distinguished from privately supplied services. Activism is defined by the emphasis which the official places on activities directed to influencing groups in the community, acquiring additional support for the agency, relating the agency to community or professional groups, and identifying problems in the community. The public health officer who views the proper scope of public health activities as expanding into nontraditional programming and who is active in pursuing these goals is considered motivated to innovate.

Mohr speculates that motivation to innovate will be successful in direct ratio to the availability of resources in a given situation and in inverse ratio to obstacles to innovation. He begins with a person (a public health officer) who is motivated to introduce a new idea into an organization. The motivated innovator encounters obstacles to the successful introduction[1] of programmatic innovation. Obstacles may be cost (of materials, time, skills) or human factors (fears of organization members concerning their values, their job security, their self esteem). The innovator may have resources with which to overcome obstacles. These may include money, skills, authority, charisma, support of prestigious individuals, and self confidence. With these propositions Mohr specifies "why some of the many independent variables covered by previous studies were related to innovation; each indicated either a relative absence of obstacles or a relative presence of motivation or resources" (Mohr, 1969: 114).

Mohr suggests that lack of trained supervisory personnel is an organizational obstacle inhibiting innovation. Financial resources and the availability of trained supervisory personnel enhance successful innovation. Community size, the variable most strongly correlated with innovation, is important since large communities tend to have large public health departments. Because large public

---

[1] In Mohr's work successful introduction includes measures of the extent of implementation (personnel allocated to the innovations) as well as formal adoption.

health departments have greater resources, they are able to undertake a larger number of innovative programs.

It is very interesting; however, that Mohr finds that size, while it affects the total number of new programs a health department can offer, does not affect the *proportional* amount of innovation undertaken by a health department. Proportional innovation Mohr defines as the proportion of personnel resources allocated to nontraditional programs. Smaller departments devote comparable resources to innovation but soon reach a limit in the number of different programs possible. This is a result of (1) the limits on the divisibility of staff supervisory time, (2) the limits a small department faces in attracting and in justifying the hiring of specialized personnel which may be necessary for particular programs, (3) the limits on loose funds within the organization and the greater need, therefore, to obtain and respect the limits of categorical grants, (4) the more limited access of small departments to personnel and funds from state and federal sources.

In large departments there is greater likelihood of "slack resources," both funds and personnel available for allocation to new programs. The motivated health officer in a large department has the resources needed to overcome obstacles to adopting and implementing a large number of new programs. Why should the greater availability of slack resources lead to a large number of innovative programs rather than to a few done in more depth (as is the pattern in smaller organizations)? Mohr, following Cyert and March (1963), suggests that slack resources are used to pursue status-motivated innovation.[2] Relying primarily on Becker and on Mohr, it is possible to outline a sequence of behavior which results in the adoption of HAP innovations.

A health official motivated to adopt many innovations by a desire to obtain high professional status seeks out early sources of information (professional association meetings or journals, regional pioneers). The official selects innovations for adoption according to their adoption potential. He calculates the effect of anticipated obstacles and resources in determining adoption potential. Success in adoption results when resources are great enough to overcome

---

[2]As Becker's later study indicated, a health officer who adopts a large number of innovations is accorded prestige but a health officer who uses resources to intensively develop fewer programs is not.

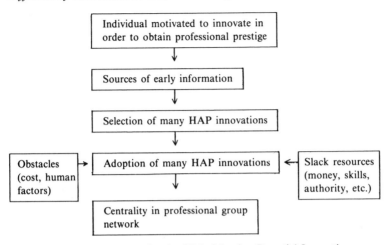

FIG. 2. Patterns of Adoption for High Adoption Potential Innovations.

obstacles. By virtue of being an early adopter, the innovator is sought out by colleagues for information and advice.

We seem then to have a theory which explains the diffusion of readily acceptable innovations among professionals, especially in organizations where slack resources are available. The theory falters as an explanation of professionally risky innovations or innovations falling outside the orbit of the professional group. The theory suggests that diffusion occurs primarily in response to the values held by professional groups and that these groups have during the past rewarded innovativeness. The applicability of the theory in the future would seem to depend upon continued belief of professionals that innovativeness is good. This may or may not imply a belief that innovations, on the whole, advance the field.

This theory offers useful knowledge to policy makers interested in slowing diffusion. Mechanisms which would make adoption more costly could offset advantages professionals acquire through innovation. The theory is less useful to those interested in encouraging the diffusion of disruptive, publicly visible, or otherwise risky innovations. Factors encouraging the adoption of these innovations remain largely unknown.

Organizations Treated as Individual Adopters Walker's study (1969) of diffusion of government innovations among American states is relevant to the understanding of diffusion in organizations since he suggests that organized groups behave like individuals. In studying adoption of innovation by state legislatures Walker asks: Why do pioneer legislatures adopt programs more readily than others? And, how do these new forms of service or regulation spread to other units? He looks at eighty-eight innovations and one hundred years of legislative history. He considers legislative adoption to constitute innovation.

Drawing directly on the information/influence body of theory, Walker speculates that innovators (legislatures viewed as "individuals" or composed of "individual innovators") fall into three leagues: national pioneers, regional pioneers, and followers. Innovation travels from national centers of legislative innovation *through* regional centers to parochial outposts. Like other potential adopters, legislators seek trustworthy sources from which to filter ideas and gain the information and reassurances necessary to adoption. The applicability of examples and information is evaluated by legislators in terms of the league to which they belong.[3] Regional opinion leaders identify with and emulate the front runners, yet provide examples which laggard states consider relevant to their own experience.

This characterization of regional "opinion-leader" states is confirmed in general by Walker's data. He does find exceptions which are not explained. In addition, he finds the regional model less applicable since 1930 than it was previously. He speculates that individuals in "parochial" states are increasingly involved in national networks (for example, professional associations and federal programs) as a result of increases in societal scale (that is, fewer people are "localities" by default, through lack of exposure to "cosmopolite" networks).

B. *Organizational Factors in Diffusion Theory*

Researchers who are concerned with adoption of innovation by organizations have found classical diffusion theory lacking and have turned to organizational theory for assistance in determining factors which influence organizational innovation. Available theory is de-

---

[3]Relevant to this point is Rowe and Boise's (1974) observation that diffusion of innovation is largely limited to functionally similar organizations: police, departments of public health, etc. Diffusion among disparate organizations may require different linkers.

rived principally from the work of management theorists interested in the behavior of corporations. Theories of organizational innovation have generally assumed known organization goals, particularly profit and hierarchy of command. Those who study organizations have tried to specify the consequences for the firm of a variety of structural and economic factors. Some of these factors tie into the classical interest in the flow of information. Others are quite independent.

Structural Factors   A number of variables describing organizational structure have been posed by investigators as important to organizational innovation. Studies of health organizations have drawn upon and adapted the formal organization theories of Simon (1957), Thompson (1967), Cyert and March (1963), March and Simon (1958), Perrow (1972) and others. In the process of applying and extending the theories of these men, a large number of variables have been studied. These include: organizational complexity, centralization of decision making, and formalization of rules and behavior as well as size and resource base.

The theoretical underpinning for these variables includes the following ideas: a diversity of tasks in an organization (*complexity*) requires employees with diverse backgrounds and perspectives. Organization members are stimulated by the diverse ideas which circulate within the organization as a result. Wide-ranging information becomes available to the organization through the multiple memberships of professionals in the organization. Difficulties encountered by managers in supervising diverse tasks leave individuals more freedom to innovate.

Centralization of decision making is thought to inhibit the adoption of innovation by reducing the flow of information among organization members and thereby the spread of new ideas. It is argued that members who do not hold high positions are not encouraged to contribute and may be discouraged from doing so by elite members. The latter are thought to protect the status quo since it is within the prevailing order they hold power. In a corollary fashion, organization members are likely to resist changes instituted from above because they have not had a hand in the formulation and distrust the consequences of the innovation for their security and comfort.

Formalization of rules and behavior is also thought to inhibit communication and therefore awareness of new ideas on the part of

organization members. Highly formalized rules limit the consideration of alternatives: organization members are less motivated to propose new methods and may be actually punished for deviation. In addition, value may be displaced from organization purposes to organization rules. The result is that change proposals elicit "resistance
to change" from members who have attached value to the rules.

There is supporting evidence for all of these interesting ideas.
There is also contradictory data. The lack of clear cut findings and
the consequent need for reassessment have highlighted the need to
compare definitions and measurements. A discussion of difficulties
encountered in applying the above theories follows.

Wilson (1966) argues that greater diversity in organizational
tasks encourages the proliferation of ideas but handicaps the actual
implementation of any one. Cooke (Zaltman et al., 1973) suggests
that the resolution of conflict between this apparent truth and the
findings of other scholars lies in the greater number of attempts
which occur in complex organizations. That is, the positive relationship between complexity and new ideas is greater than the negative
relationship between complexity and implementation. Even though
complex organizations adopt proportionately fewer of the projects
they consider, they have more adoptions overall as a result of
attempting so many.

Zaltman et al. (1973) suggest that decentralized decision structures inhibit rather than facilitate the adoption of innovation because those holding decentralized power may come to believe that
changes resulting from innovation will shrink *their* existing influence. Corwin (1969) argues that decentralized systems may provide
more opportunity for different groups and individuals to express
their differing points of view and thereby focus discontent which
might otherwise remain latent. Hage and Dewar's data (1973)
suggest that whatever positive effect decentralization may have is
counteracted by the inclusion of persons unable to agree. Mansfield
(1973) reports a *negative* correlation between the number of persons
required to approve an innovation and the speed with which an
industrial firm brings the innovation into use.

Zaltman et al. (1973) suggest that rule formalization *increases*
the ability of organization personnel to achieve implementation
by reducing role conflict and role ambiguity. Clearly specified
rules, he feels, (1) reduce uncertainty among personnel as to how the
innovation will affect their jobs and (2) minimize the likelihood that

new procedures will conflict with old ones. Farlee's account (1972) of the difficulties which developed around the use by hospital nurses of a new computerized record keeping system may support this proposition. The system was poorly adapted to actual routines and procedures. Cooperation was unrewarding because no person in authority took an interest in the nurses' compliance with it.

A number of scholars have now proposed a common resolution to the contradictions in the diffusion literature: there are stages to the innovation process not adequately differentiated and therefore not measured. At least four similar schemes have been proposed (Hage and Aiken, 1967; Rogers, 1962; Zaltman et al., 1973; French and Becker in Gordon and Fisher, 1975: 115–140). These schemes differentiate no fewer than three stages: (1) *ideas* enter the organization and are considered; (2) *adoption decisions* are made; (3) *implementation* occurs.

In the idea stage, information and creativity are very important. This stage requires flexibility, circulation of ideas, a variety of perspectives, and freedom from threat of excessive discipline. At the adoption stage, other factors become important: motivation, resources, and the ability to reach a consensus. In the final implementing stage, such factors as perceived legitimacy, disruptiveness, displacement, and trust become important. The various scholars who propose that diffusion researchers pay more attention to stages in the process do not feel available data can be sorted retroactively. Rather, it is necessary to collect data which will allow necessary differentiation to occur.

Stage theory explanations are not entirely satisfactory explanations of discrepant results, however. Most research has entered the process at roughly the same stage. That is, studies have tended to differentiate between organizations which have and have not formally introduced the innovations under study. Nor does stage theory address contradictions in reasoning which occur within stages, whether, for example, the inhibiting effects of organization groups protecting existing power arrangements are greater in centralized or decentralized organizations.

Two responses to the confusion seem in order. First, confusion will continue until scholars are more careful that their measurements refer to the same concepts. Downs and Mohr (1975) have provided a useful summary of the most common and most paralyzing conceptual and methodological difficulties. Second, characteristics of organizational structure may be less important than other variables or important only in conjunction with other variables (Mohr, 1969; Hage and Dewar, 1973; Bingham, 1976).

Economic Factors It may be argued that profit and non-profit organizations innovate for reasons of prestige when slack resources are available and immediate problems are met. Whether other knowledge of innovation gained through the study of profit-motivated industries is applicable to health care institutions is a topic worth examining. Scholars have generally shied away from suggesting that health care organizations are motivated by profit increase. Warner (1974: 443) suggests that in non-profit organizations prestige considerations may take the place of profit considerations.

Economic studies of industrial innovation have placed great emphasis on "relative advantage" as a reason for innovation. In general this has meant that an innovation promises profit advantage to the adopting unit: unit price is less than what would otherwise occur, a larger share of the market is captured, or a higher price is allowable. Anticipated advantage is tempered by the size of the investment required to bring it into use and the risk associated with possible failure. Fear of risk decreases as others in the field provide examples of successful adoption (Warner, 1974; Utterback, 1974), but increases to the extent that major technological improvements in the innovation itself are predicted. Major improvements which rapidly alter the innovation make delay in adoption advantageous (Utterback, 1974: 625). The speed of diffusion is positively related to the competitiveness of the industry or market. Warner quotes Nelson: "A firm may dawdle if the result is merely slower growth of profits, but it is likely to be activated when the result is a serious erosion of a previous profit or market share position. The pressures to adopt . . . innovations rapidly will be greater in reasonably competitive than in more sheltered industries" (Warner, 1974: 437).

Slack resources have frequently been identified as an important economic consideration in innovation. Slack resources are resources not required for ongoing operations or pressing problems. These "loose" resources may be allocated to innovation.

Slack resources also include uncommitted staff capabilities within the organization or available to it. Tilton (1971) suggests that one reason subsidiaries of large firms are capable of rapid imitation (diffusion) is that they have access to the specialists and professional personnel of the parent firm. According to Aiken and Hage, interorganizational cooperation has a similar outcome. When two or more organizations share resources, their combined resources make innovation more possible. "And here too, resource is understood to mean not only money, space, or equipment, but also staff which may be in short supply, depending upon the market and the qualifications needed" (Aiken and Hage, 1971: 78).

Because the objectives of profit-motivated industries and tax-supported agencies, such as public health departments, are different, few authors view economic models as relevant to public agency innovations. Several authors have attempted to apply economic theory to voluntary hospitals. Pauly and Redisch (1973) have argued that the voluntary hospital is a profit organization. They argue that physician staffs control and benefit financially (take the profits) from voluntary hospitals. The hospital is a "physicians' cooperative." In the absence of empirical data on the control structure of hospitals, the assumption that doctors act as a group and prevail in decisions seems unjustifiable. It may be argued, however, that economic models could apply to the radiology department and the clinical laboratory. The assumption that radiologists and pathologists are cohesive and important actors in the decision to adopt innovations in their departments is more easily justified than is the Pauly and Redisch assumption. However, even this assumption requires empirical confirmation.

Lee has suggested that hospital administrators seek to maximize not profits but "utility." In this model, where shareholders are absent, decisions are made to enhance the status and economic well-being of administrators. Lee notes that "the salary, prestige, security, power, and professional satisfaction of decision makers are dependent upon the prestige and status of the organizations with which the decision makers are associated" (Lee, 1971: 49). The status of the hospital is, in turn, a function of "the range of services available and the extent to which expensive and highly specialized equipment and personnel (including M.D.s) are available." The administrator is motivated to increase these hospital "inputs" to innovate, so long as he can cover costs incurred. Payment by third party payers which covers a hospital's expenditures without measuring improvements in outputs encourages adoption of equipment and service innovations.

Abt Associates (1975) picked up on Lee's model and provided supportive evidence for it. In a study of capital equipment purchases by Boston area hospitals, they found that equipment was not in full use, suggesting that it was purchased without respect to demand. Minimum effort went into estimating use and operating costs. Little or no attempt was made by hospitals to measure the effectiveness of a specific piece of equipment. Interviewees indicated that hospitals compete for physicians and patients and purchase new equipment to attract them.[4]

This single empirical study of the decision-making behavior of hospitals is highly suggestive. It would seem highly desirable for researchers to empirically determine the propriety of assumptions used in economic models and determine their applicability to health institutions. In general, one may observe that the usefulness of economic models will depend upon a better understanding of the decision-making structure of institutions and of the rewards and constraints surrounding innovation.

A Political Approach to Decision Making in Organizations

Relatively little scholarly attention has been paid to the political aspects of decision making in health organizations. What are the goals sought by different groups? What resources do they command? Who prevails? This omission is particularly glaring in the study of health institutions since the goals of these organizations are more various and more disputed than are those of business firms.

If decisions in health organizations are open to pressure from competing ideologies and interests, it becomes essential to determine the relevant actors in the decision process, including their objectives and the resources they can deploy to achieve desired ends. Political resources are resources which may be used to persuade or coerce others to cooperate in (apply their own resources to) the pursuit of goals desired by the leader. Although others may be included, Dahl's classic list includes: access to money and wealth; control over jobs; control over information and expertise; esteem or social standing; the rights pertaining to office; group solidarity; the right to vote; intelligence; education; time and energy (Dahl, 1961). This list can be adapted to particular needs.

[4]Several other authors concerned with hospital purchase of equipment assume that hospital purchase of innovative equipment is necessary to attract or retain physicians (Lee, 1971; Pauly and Redisch, 1973; Mills, 1972).

1. The Group Environment of the Health Care Institution Roos, with her associates (1974), seeks to understand hospital behavior in terms of the hospital's relationships with various interested parties which control resources the hospital needs. Each hospital is assumed to require: doctors, patients, patient support (third party payers), and capital funds for equipment and construction. The hospital must accommodate to the desires of those who control these essential resources. The relative emphasis which the hospital puts on quality, access, and efficiency is related to the emphasis that powerful groups place on these objectives. In examining this power, the authors look at hospital size and ownership structure (proprietary, government, or voluntary). Range of services offered (a measure of innovation) is examined as an aspect of quality. Measures are derived from archival data of the American Hospital Association.

Roos proposes that community doctors want a hospital which caters to the needs of their private practices (quality and access) and to their personal and professional freedom. Medical schools are interested in high quality medical training and research. (They are likely, therefore, to promote the acquisition of sophisticated equipment and techniques.) Government agencies are concerned with access to care (open admission, area-wide planning), with facilities, and with costs. Third party payers are also increasingly concerning themselves with cost. Philanthropic sources are attracted to projects which carry high prestige. It is interesting that these authors ascribe no concerns to patients since they ascribe no power to them. Patients are a necessary component of hospital activities but they are provided to the hospital by doctors and are paid for by third party payers. The latter two are considered to have power as a result of controlling the patient resource. Hospitals are analyzed by size and ownership for their relative dependence on each of the above. What resources do they need most and how many alternative sources are available to them?

The model these authors develop has a powerful logic. Using it and various measures of performance, they challenge common assumptions about how goals are determined in hospitals. They find, for example, that large government hospitals offer the largest number of sophisticated services. Roos suggests that "their heavy dependence on interns and residents for meeting staffing needs, and their extensive medical school affiliations, open up the larger state and governmental hospitals to strong medical school pressures for quality and service."

Krause (1971) has also proposed a scheme for relating political diversity to the adoption of innovation. He suggests that manufacturing corporations are particularly active in their efforts to promote the adoption of equipment and other products. Further, he speculates that the promotion of an innovation by a corporation is negatively related to the enthusiasm of health professionals. The less sponsorship elsewhere, the greater the efforts of the producing corporations to "sell" the innovation themselves. However, Krause argues that corporations normally act in coalition with other health interests. These include medical research physicians who want to undertake "frontier research" and others who want the prestige of advanced technology.

Krause argues that this latter category of fellow travelers was less likely in 1971 to include administrators of teaching hospitals than in the past. This group came under increasing pressure from community groups and from the federal government to provide community medicine. The activism of the poor and the anti-establishment physicians in the 1960s found reflection in hospital politics at the local level and in federal government priorities and budget allocations.

Krause suggests that non-teaching hospitals and community physicians are influenced by the corporations and the teaching hospitals, but lack necessary information on the effectiveness of innovations. Thus, he views non-university hospitals as the major victims of unscrupulous salesmen. According to Krause, they have paid for prestigious equipment which they have neither the patient volume to need nor the staff to maintain. From this perspective, the reluctance of local decision makers to adopt innovations may often represent sound judgment. Without additional information and possibly additional need or resources, local adopters may stand to serve other interests than their own.

This approach has not been well developed, yet its intellectual importance seems undeniable. The actual process by which adoption of innovation occurs in health units inevitably involves not only individuals with certain inclinations and organizations with certain properties but groups with certain interests. These interests will be among the obstacles and resources which will affect the success of those individuals who attempt to influence the behavior of a health organization. Their relative importance will be enhanced by organizational and environmental structure. Other candidates for study as political forces would include foundations, professional societies, banks, competing health units[5] and institutional donors such as the American Cancer Society.

2. Organizational Decision Making Roos (1974) also applied a political perspective to the decision-making process within the hospital. She studied an effort to consolidate the laboratories of four hospitals; two hospitals actually consolidated their laboratories. This split offered some of the advantages of an experimental design. Roos rejects the rational economical explanation for the merger since all four hospitals did not make the same "rational" choice. She also eliminated the theory that policies are made in consideration of the effect they are expected to have on physicians' incomes (Pauly and Redisch, 1973). Cost theory also failed to explain the different behavior of the four hospitals.

Roos analyzed the content of a large number of lengthy, in-depth interviews to determine the interests of various parties involved in the decision process. She identified events which caused the perspectives of participants to change, thereby providing a dynamic decision-making model. In general, she argues that innovation is a function of (1) political and technological events which affect hospitals; and (2) the performance satisfactions and dissatisfactions of groups within the hospitals. The latter is in part a function of the former which alters group perceptions of what is technically and politically possible. Roos proposes the following propositions to explain the laboratory consolidation in two hospitals and its rejection in two others.

Changes occur: (1) When there are changes in the goals of powerful groups. An example is the change which occurred in the position of administrators when they came to believe that the federal government would take action if they did not and therefore that they could maintain control only by anticipating government actions. (2) When the power of opposition groups is decreased. For example, the power of opposing board members decreased when the

---

[5]Kurt R. Student found, for example, that implementation of a new scheduling system in one hospital's admissions office was thwarted in part by the fear that doctors would send patients to another hospital (Griffith et al., 1976).

hospital confronted new needs to economize. The financial stress, to which consolidation seemed one answer, occurred as a result of the demands of community groups for increased care of indigents. (3) When the power of proponent groups increases. For example, the power of the younger physicians, the specialists, and those who favored closer cooperation with the medical school increased when the hospital's recruitment problems became severe. Another group (the pathologists) who favored consolidation gained power when they organized themselves into a self-controlling group. (4) When the old structure becomes obsolete for achieving goals. Medicare regulations reduced the ability of hospitals to subsidize money-losing departments through excess lab fees. Therefore, the incentive to have separate labs was reduced. (5) When performance gaps provide impetus to change. Satisfied groups are likely to oppose change rather than to be neutral since the known is familiar (and satisfactory) and the unknown may be bad (everyone can think of examples where experiments turned out badly). But dissatisfied groups seem to join coalitions for change. In this study, the unavailability of sophisticated laboratory services was felt most acutely by the medical school which felt the most advanced equipment was necessary for education and by the pathologists whose opportunities were limited by available equipment.

Roos concludes her study by noting that the rational model, in which the organization's best interests are assumed to govern, will not predict behavior. Organizational best interest (in this case economy) may be known to persons and even valued, but is apt to be of less concern than the more immediate interests of sub-units within the organization. Roos observes that laboratory cost reduction only became a high priority to groups within the hospital when they saw the possibility of controlling the savings involved and in applying them to immediate concerns. Consolidation was not achieved until issues of control were resolved.

Several other case studies reinforce the validity of both the organizational and political perspectives although emphases and conclusions vary. Farlee (1972) and Griffith et al. (1976) provide case studies of hospitals attempting to implement new procedures. In these accounts there is support for the idea that change induces insecurities on the part of individuals. It seems clear that in some cases diffusion rests on the ability of proponents to improve communication and clarify directives. Yet the case studies also show that within and among institutions, interests as well as motivation and resources do differ. Clearer communication or greater participation is not likely to alter these basic commitments.

Summary and Conclusions

This paper surveys the current research in diffusion of innovation as it applies to health organizations, and highlights suggestive studies. A reading of the literature reveals one well-developed theory. Classical theory has a good deal to say about individual responses to innovation, and about the circulation among professionals of information relevant to innovations. Recent studies suggest that professional norms which reward innovation, coupled with a desire of professionals to achieve professional esteem, result in predictable adoption by professionals of low risk innovations. Innovations which depart from professional norms or promise to be disruptive to community or professional relationships are more difficult to predict.

Organizational theory has produced a large number of variables which have been used in studies of innovation in health organizations. Among these the availability of slack resources, funds, and staff, has been a variable of considerable importance in predicting the adoption of innovation. Other factors are less clear. Conceptual and methodological problems have made an assessment of the role of structural factors difficult. Few empirical studies have examined the effect of economic factors in the diffusion of innovation in medical care organizations. Most of these organizations have been assumed to be free of profit-seeking behavior. Observers have questioned whether this is entirely so since some potential decision makers, such as pathologists, benefit economically. Others have suggested that hospitals (1) consume profits internally, and (2) spend resources to maximize prestige. Thus cost-related models of organization behavior are useful.

Political theory has contributed very little to innovation theory as yet. Since health organizations can quite justifiably be seen as pluralistic decision-making bodies, its increased use appears promising. Innovation in health care institutions may be studied from this perspective by (1) determining the goals and values of various parties interested in the introduction of an innovation; (2) identify-

ing the resources these parties command and the alliances they are
able to make; and (3) specifying the processes through which interested parties enter the decision-making process and negotiate a
conclusion.

Undesirable Diffusion

The application of classical diffusion theory is limited because of its
traditional assumption that innovation is beneficial. Scholars are
now questioning the validity of this assumption but research does
not yet reflect this changing perspective. Several activities are implied. The medical and social consequences of an innovation must
be assessed as must the cost effectiveness of adoption of innovations
by various types of health organizations. Then studies must establish the relationship of classical and organizational theory to *both*
useful and wasteful adoption. In addition, research should investigate the rejection and discontinuation of innovative technologies.

Attributes of Innovations

The value of an innovation and the desirability of its diffusion may
be seen as an aspect of a larger area of research neglect: the attributes of innovations as these affect diffusion. The assumption that
innovation characteristics influence the diffusion process was a
major tenet of classical theory. That the organization-focused study
and the innovation-focused study constitute valuable complements
is well demonstrated by two studies in a non-medical area of
diffusion. Walker (1969, 1973) and Gray (1973) used these alternative strategies in their investigations of legislative innovation in the
American states. Walker identified stable aspects of the environment (such as regionalism and the growing professionalism of the
public bureaucracy) which affected innovation patterns. Gray documented patterns in the spread of innovations which were specific to
characteristics of the innovations themselves.

  Scholars interested in medical innovations have demonstrated
an awareness of the need to reintegrate the innovation-focused
approach into the study of organizational diffusion. This reorienta-
tion has not, however, been reflected in empirical studies. Interest
has taken two forms. Four of the attributes identified by classical

theorists (advantage, understandability, triability, and observability) as well as some notions of structural and fiscal prerequisites to innovation use have been incorporated into a scheme proposed by Bernstein et al. (Gordon and Fisher, 1975: 79–114) for classifying medical innovations.

Others have suggested classifying innovations in terms of their likely reception by organized groups. This idea is related to the classical theorists' "compatibility with values" but goes beyond the embodiment of values by individual members to structural interrelationships. That receiving groups will resist innovations which threaten to alter prevailing behavior patterns and structures of control (and privilege) has been the assumption of the organizational and political theorists discussed in this paper. However, only Becker (1970) has made the "adoption potential" of an innovation *by medical organizations* a central component of research. Becker's scale involves indicators of relative benefit and communicability but also indicators of the extent to which behavioral change was implied by the innovation or reallocations of power were suggested. Schon (1971), Rowe and Boise (1974), and Roos (1974) have discussed the organizational meaning of innovation traits and provided social and political explanations for the resistance of organized groups to "beneficial" innovations.

Medical Technologies

In view of the federal government's interest in the optimal diffusion of medical technologies, it is distressing to note the almost total absence of studies which address such innovations. Available theory depends almost exclusively upon studies which analyze the diffusion of procedures and programs among health organizations.

While theory formulated to explain the diffusion of social organizational technologies is likely to be useful to the study of medical technologies, the direct extrapolation of findings cannot be justified. The difficulty may well lie in the insecurities of social scientists in dealing with medical technology. In view of the limited empirical study devoted to physicians in general, another explanation offers itself: real or imagined problems of access. Whatever the reason, the bias against the study of hard technologies and physician decision makers must be corrected if the limits of developing theory are to be determined and a broad-based theory constructed.

References

Abt Associates, Incorporated, 1975. *Incentives and Decisions Underlying Hospitals' Adoption and Utilization of Major Capital Equipment.* (HSM-110-73-513). Prepared for National Center for Health Services Research and Development, Health Resources Administration, Washington, D.C. (NTIS No. PB-251-631)

Aiken, M., and Hage, J. 1971. The Organic Organization and Innovation. *Sociology* 5:63–82.

Becker, M.H. 1970. Sociometric Location and Innovativeness: Reformulation and Extension of the Diffusion Model. *American Sociological Review* 35:267–282.

Bingham, R.D. 1976. *Innovation, Bureaucracy and Public Policy: A Study of Innovation Adoption by Local Government.* University of Wisconsin—Milwaukee, Urban Research Center Publication.

Coleman, J.S.; Katz, E.; and Menzel, H. 1966. *Medical Innovation: A Diffusion Study.* Indianapolis: Bobbs-Merrill.

Corwin, R. 1969. Patterns of Organizational Conflict. *Administrative Science Quarterly* 14:507–522.

Cyert, R.M., and March, J.G. 1963. *A Behavioral Theory of the Firm.* Englewood Cliffs: Prentice Hall.

Dahl, R. 1961. *Who Governs?* New Haven: Yale University Press.

Downs, G.W. Jr., and Mohr, L.B. 1975. Conceptual Issues in the Study of Innovation. Paper delivered at the Annual Meeting of the American Political Science Association, San Francisco.

Farlee, C. 1972. Failure of an Innovation: Computer-Generated Medication Schedules. *Hospital Administration* 16:43–51.

Gordon, G., and Fisher, G.L. (eds.). 1975. *The Diffusion of Medical Technology: Policy and Planning Perspectives.* Cambridge: Ballinger Publishing Co.

Gray, V. 1973. Innovation in the States: A Diffusion Study. *American Political Science Review* 67:1171–1185.

Griffith, J.R.; Hancock, W.M.; and Munson, F.C. 1976. *Cost Control in Hospitals,* School of Public Health, University of Michigan, Ann Arbor: Health Administration Press.

Hage, G., and Aiken, M. 1967. Program Change and Organizational Properties: A Comparative Analysis. *American Journal of Sociology* 72:503–519.

Hage, G., and Dewar, R. 1973. Elite Values Versus Organizational Structure in Predicting Innovation. *Administrative Science Quarterly* 18:279–290.

Kaluzny, A.D.; Gentry, J.T.; and Veney, J.E. 1974. Innovation of Health Services: A Comparative Study of Hospitals and Health Departments. *The Milbank Memorial Fund Quarterly: Health and Society* 52:51–82.

Krause, E.A. 1971. Health and the Politics of Technology. *Inquiry* 8:51–59.

Lazarsfeld, P.F.; Berelson, B.; and Gaudet, H. 1948. *The People's Choice.* New York Columbia University Press.

Lee, M.L. 1971. A Conspicuous Production Theory of Hospital Behavior. *Southern Economic Journal* 38:48–58.

Mansfield, E. 1973. Speed of Response of Firms in New Techniques. *Quarterly Journal of Economics* 77:290–311.

March, J., and Simon, H. 1958. *Organizations.* New York: Wiley.

Merton, R.K. 1949. *Social Theory and Social Structure.* New York: Free Press.

Mills, C.W. 1972. Technostructure and Medicine. *The Milbank Memorial Fund Quarterly: Health and Society* 50:143–158.

Mohr, L.B. 1969. Determinants of Innovation in Organizations. *American Political Science Review* 63:111–126.

Pauly, M., and Redisch, M. 1973. Not-for-Profit Hospital as a Physician's Cooperative. *American Economic Review* 63:87–99.

Perrow, C. 1972. *Complex Organizations: A Critical Essay.* Glenview, Illinois: Scott Foresman.

Rogers, E.M. 1962. *Diffusion of Innovations.* New York: The Free Press.

Rogers, E.M., with the assistance of F.F. Shoemaker. 1971. *Communication of Innovations: A Cross Cultural Approach.* New York: Free Press.

Roos, N.P.; Schermerhorn, J.R.; and Roos, L.L., Jr. 1974. Hospital Performance: Analyzing Power and Goals. *Journal of Health and Social Behavior* 15:78–92.

Rowe, L.A., and Boise, W.B. 1974. Organizational Innovation Current Research and Evolving Concepts. *Public Administration Review* 34(3):284–293.

Schon, D.A. 1971. *Beyond the Stable State.* New York: Random House.

Simon, H. 1957. *Administrative Behavior.* New York: Macmillan.

Thompson, J.D. 1967. *Organizations in Action.* New York: McGraw-Hill.

Tilton, J.E. 1971. *International Diffusion of Technology: The Case of Semi-Conductors.* Washington, D.C.: The Brookings Institution.

Utterback, J.M. 1974. Innovation in Industry and the Diffusion of Technology. *Science* 183:620–626.

Walker, J.L. 1969. The Diffusion of Innovations Among the American States. *American Political Science Review* 63:880–889.

———. 1973. Comment: Problems in Research on the Diffusion of Policy Innovations. *American Political Science Review* 67:1186–1191.

Warner, K.E. 1974. The Need for Some Innovative Concepts of Innovation: An Examination of Research on the Diffusion of Innovations. *Policy Sciences* 5:433–451.

Wilson, J.Q. 1966. Innovation in Organization: Notes Toward a Theory. In *Approaches to Organizational Design*, edited by J.D. Thompson. Pittsburgh: University of Pittsburgh Press, pp. 193–218.

Zaltman, G.; Duncan, R.; and Holbeck, J. 1973. *Innovations and Organizations*. New York: Wiley.

This paper was prepared for the Office of Planning, Evaluation and Legislation, Health Resources Administration, U.S. Department of Health, Education, and Welfare.

Thanks go to Daniel I. Zwick, Anabel Crane, and Arlene Zakhar for their critical comments.

Address reprint requests to: Ann Lennarson Greer, University of Wisconsin—Milwaukee, Urban Research Center, P.O. Box 413, Milwaukee, Wisconsin 53201

IV Two Policy Failures

The Impact of
Certificate-of Need Controls
on Hospital Investment

DAVID S. SALKEVER

THOMAS W. BICE

Certificate-of-Need (CON) controls over hospital investment have been enacted by a number of states in recent years and the National Health Planning and Resources Development Act of 1974 provides strong incentives for adoption of CON in additional states. In this study, we review the questions that have been raised about the effectiveness of CON controls and then we develop quantitative estimates of the impact of CON on investment. These estimates show that CON did not reduce the total dollar volume of investment but altered its composition, retarding expansion in bed supplies but increasing investment in new services and equipment. We suggest that this finding may be due to (1) the emphasis in CON laws and programs on controlling bed supplies and (2) a substitution of new services and equipment for additional beds in response to financial factors and organizational pressures for expansion. Finally, we caution against the conclusion that CON controls should be broadened and tightened, though our results might be so interpreted, because of the practical difficulties involved in reviewing and certifying large numbers of small investment projects.

Introduction

In the wake of rapid post-Medicare cost inflation, investment controls have emerged as important regulatory mechanisms for moderating the rise in health services expenditures. These controls take two forms: (1) legal prohibitions of unnecessary capital investment, and (2) financial controls, whereby a health care institution's eligibility to receive capital or operating funds relating to an investment project is dependent upon the approval of designated planning agencies. Presently, both types are widespread. Legal prohibitions are in effect through certificate-of-need (CON) laws in twenty-four states, and similar legislation has been proposed in seven other states (Lewin and Associates, Inc., 1974). Moreover, with the passage of P.L. 93-641, the National Health Planning and Resources Development Act of 1974, CON was slated for adoption by all participating states.

Several types of financial controls have been applied. Under

Section 1122 of the Social Security Act, reimbursements under Titles V, XVIII, and XIX for depreciation, interest, and other costs associated with an investment project in excess of $100,000 may be denied if the project is not approved by designated planning agencies. Under contracts from the U.S. Department of Health, Education, and Welfare, thirty-seven states now conduct Section 1122 reviews. Similar provisions ("conformance clauses") link Blue Cross reimbursement to project review by planning agencies or Blue Cross plans themselves in nineteen states. In all states, eligibility for capital investment subsidies through the Hill-Burton program requires planning agency approval, as does participation in construction finance programs in forty-two states.[1]

This spate of controls emerged only very recently and without the benefit of systematic research as to its likely consequences. The major federal initiatives, Section 1122 and P.L. 93-641, were promulgated within the past four years, and all but five of the existing CON laws were enacted since 1970 (Curran, 1974). The reasons behind this wave of enthusiasm for investment controls have yet to be studied in detail. It is distressing to observe, however, that decisions to adopt controls were taken despite the total absence of evidence as to their efficacy or secondary effects. Thus, a thorough review of relevant literature by O'Donoghue and Policy Center, Inc. (1974:67) led to the conclusion that

> ...there is no evidence supporting the effectiveness or efficiency of capital expenditures regulation. On the other hand, it is equally true that there is no evidence indicating that such regulation is ineffective or inefficient.

Of course, the fact that investment controls are already in place does not obviate the need for such evidence. Indeed, since changes in the extent or structure of these controls are possible, and perhaps even likely, systematic assessment of their effects may contribute crucial information for policy formulation.

The major objective of this paper is to provide such information on the quantitative impacts of investment controls. Specifically, we assess effects of CON controls on investment in hospital facilities. The limited nature of this objective should be noted, in that our focus is on only a subset (i.e., hospital in-

[1]Our description of investment controls is from Lewin and Associates, Inc. (1974: Chapter 3), which is current as of April 1, 1974.

vestment) of all potential impact measures[2] and on one particular form of control (i.e., CON). There are, however, several considerations which justify concentration on CON. First, it is the strictest form of control in that failure to win approval for projects usually means that institutions are prohibited from carrying out proposed investments. In consequence, CON is likely to yield measurable impacts. Financial controls, by contrast, impose only monetary sanctions which may be either insufficiently severe to alter hospitals' investment behavior or compensated for by other sources of revenue. Second, the CON approach will probably soon emerge as the predominant form of investment control. As Section 1523 of P.L. 93-641 provides an incentive for non-CON states to adopt CON legislation, other forms of investment control will become redundant and probably fall into desuetude. On this point, Lewin and Associates, Inc. (1974:158) observed that nine of the 14 states which did not participate in the Section 1122 program already had CON laws and that

> ...their lack of interest in the program was based on a belief that Section 1122 review would not add to their existing authority or that 1122 procedural requirements would conflict with state administrative practices.

Our concentration on hospital investment also seems warranted on several grounds. In addition to entailing substantial resource costs, hospital investment triggers increases in utilization and operating costs.[3] In consequence, limitations on investment effect savings in operating as well as capital costs. Furthermore, since control of hospital investment is the principal concern of CON programs, we assume that their effects will be most profound in the hospital sector. By the same token, failure to detect such impacts would be compelling evidence of their ineffectiveness.

We begin with a survey of arguments regarding presumed effects of CON regulation. With these as a background for interpreting our findings, we describe our methods and results.

[2]For discussions of a fuller range of impact measures that would be relevant for a more complete policy evaluation, see May(1974: 58-59)and Brown (1969).

[3]The literature documenting the positive effect of bed supply on hospital use, the so-called "Roemer Law," is extensive. A recent contribution is in Feldstein (1971a). For evidence of the positive impact of equipment and facilities on use and costs, see Davis (1969; 1974) and Berry (1974).

Following these are discussions of the results and conclusions pertaining to policy implications, and suggestions for future research.

Effects of CON:
Critical Views from the Literature

The putative purpose of CON legislation is to restrain costs of health care by limiting unnecessary expansion of health facilities and of services rendered in them. Much of the recent literature expresses skepticism about CON's ability to accomplish this; three principal arguments are advanced. First, some doubt the willingness of agencies administering CON programs to effectively control investment. Second, some question these agencies' ability to accomplish this aim. Finally, concern is expressed about the possible unanticipated effects of CON laws on providers' investment plans.

The thesis that CON agencies will be unwilling to vigorously control hospital investment extends the "capture hypothesis" from experience in other regulated industries. Noting that a regulatory body becomes a focal point for industry lobbying and a prize worthy of capture, critics chronicle the process whereby it comes to serve the welfare of the regulated industry instead of the public interest (Havighurst, 1973: 1178–1179; Hilton, 1972). The political economy of health planning, some note, is particularly conducive to such capture, for the planning agencies that conduct CON reviews in most states include among their board members representatives of hospitals. They are thereby accorded easy access to agency personnel and to influence over agency policy (Lave and Lave, 1974: 169). Furthermore, hospitals are often an important source of financial contributions required for agency survival and growth. Pluralism falters, as the countervailing power of consumers in the review process is diluted by their reliance upon providers and agency staff for technical expertise (Havighurst, 1973: 1183–1184). Consequently, critics allege that CON regulation is employed primarily to block entry by new providers (e.g., hospitals and other potential competitors such as HMOs and surgicenters) rather than to restrain expansion of existing hospitals.

This line of argument suggests that CON programs will effectively control only one type of hospital investment, namely, the building of new hospitals.⁴ Conceivably, it might even encourage expansion among existing hospitals by protecting them from competition for donor capital and patients. Were this so, the net effect on hospital investment would be only slightly restrictive at best.

Contrary to these expectations are two principal arguments that lead to the opposite conclusion. First, the existence of standards for review and requirements for public disclosure of rulings may militate against agencies' favoring existing providers at the expense of new entrants. Although such requirements permit considerable discretion in some states, and opportunities for obfuscation persist even when they are enforced, blatant discrimination against new entrants is presumably precluded. Second, existing providers may actually welcome CON control over their own investment opportunities. It may limit competition among hospitals (Posner, 1974) and enhance management's bargaining position vis-a-vis the medical staff.⁵ By holding that they have little power to prevent CON agency disapproval of investment plans to which they themselves accord low priorities, administrators gain the power necessary to forestall such plans. (Schelling, 1963). In sum, the presumption that CON agencies serve the interests of existing providers, even when true, does not necessarily imply ineffective control of hospital investment.

The principal doubts about CON agencies' ability to control investment stem from the limited nature of CON coverage and the scarcity of agency resources. Although most CON laws require certification for new construction and for significant increases in bed capacity, other potentially important types of investment are not controlled. Several states exempt all projects below a minimum capital expenditure, which ranges from $10,000 in New York to $350,000 in Kansas. In some states, expenditures for equipment or expansion of existing services that do not involve enlargement of physical plant are excluded from review. Thus, while there is considerable variability in the provisions of laws, a substantial portion of investment activity is beyond the reach of CON, and this is particularly true of investment not requiring new construction or bed

⁴It is also frequently argued that, in addition to blocking new entrants, CON agencies will impose stricter controls upon disfavored existing providers, particularly proprietary hospitals.

⁵Curran's (1974) observation that medical societies, unlike hospital associations, have not been strong advocates of CON is of interest in this context.

increases (Havighurst, 1973: 1165-1166).[6]

CON agencies' ability to review thoroughly all projects requiring certification is limited by financial and personnel constraints (Stuehler, 1973). Again, the analogy to regulation in other industries points to provider domination (Havighurst, 1973: 1178). Sparing little expense in defending its requests for approval, a large and politically strong institution may easily convince an understaffed and underfinanced CON agency not to incur costs required to develop a compelling refutation. Accordingly, the agency will adopt the path of least resistance, that is, approval. However, this course of events is only one possibility. Pauly (1974a:158-159) argues, for instance, that the path of least resistance for the agency is to disapprove plans for new hospitals and bed expansions. The consequences of erroneous approvals—empty beds—are highly visible, while those of erroneous disapprovals (e.g., longer waits for elective admissions) are less so.

These observations raise a general point, namely, that in the presence of severe resource constraints, CON agencies will be forced to make decisions about priorities and to adopt either implicit or explicit rules of thumb. Pauly's view implies a "when in doubt, disapprove" rule for investments in new beds, which is consistent with moratoria on such expansion declared recently by several areawide planning bodies. However, a more permissive rule of thumb seems more likely for new services and equipment, particularly those which constitute innovations in medical practice. Moratoria on such investments or disapprovals after cursory reviews open the CON agency to the charge of capriciously depriving the citizenry of the fruits of medical progress. As for priorities, our previous discussion of the provider domination thesis contains some suggestions as to how these may be set. Furthermore, it may be reasonable to hypothesize that more agency resources will be devoted to the review of proposals for new beds than to reviews of new service and equipment requests. Empirical support for this expectation is provided by Bicknell and Walsh's (1975:1057) observations on the Massachusetts experience with CON, which revealed that facility improvement proposals not involving new beds usually did not "attract the closer, technically more sophisticated scrutiny...normally reserved for bed-related applications."

[6]Summaries of CON coverage are in Curran (1974: 93-97), Havighurst (1973: 1145-1146), and Lewin and Associates, Inc. (1974: 173-185).

Several authors note that the mere existence of a CON law may influence hospital investment plans, although it is not clear whether the effect is to deter or encourage growth. Bicknell and Walsh (1975: 1059) hold that it reduces investment, arguing that

> ...a certificate-of-need program, merely by its existence, may discourage construction and capital expenditures by causing an anticipatory reaction on the part of providers.

Others, noting that CON is similar to franchising, hypothesize the opposite effect. According to Havighurst (1973:1171, n.104), for instance,

> [t]here would seem to be a danger that the certificate-of-need process may actually stimulate hospital construction by causing applicants to accelerate their plans in order to pre-empt others.

This reasoning is also applied to decisions about costly innovations in services and facilities (Roth, 1974). Being the first hospital in an area to install a $400,000 EMI brain scanner becomes expecially important if the chances of approval of second and third requests are nil.

From this brief review of literature, we have reason to doubt the presumption that CON controls will negatively impact upon hospital investment. Indeed, several arguments lead to the opposite expectation. Moreover, they suggest that the effect of CON will vary among different types of investment. Specifically, limitations on coverage and considerations of agency priorities and rules of thumb imply that the effect on investment in bed expansion and new construction is likely to be more negative than the effect on investment in new equipment and services. Of course, the extent to which these various hypotheses are consistent with actual experience is an empirical question, and it is to this question that we turn in the remainder of this paper.

Methods

Two principal strategies are available for quantifying effects of CON: (1) a descriptive approach and (2) an analytic approach. Using the former, the investigator would review CON applications over some period and enumerate amounts of capital expenditure avoided by disapproval or agency-mandated modifications. (Obviously, adjustments would be required when dealing with competing applications.) Although the descriptive approach has the virtue of simplicity, Bicknell and Walsh (1975), who applied it in their Massachusetts study, note that it fails to capture projects which might have been undertaken in the absence of CON but for which applications were never filed because a rejection was anticipated. Another defect is that this approach overlooks investment not covered by CON law, although it is possible that it is indirectly affected by CON control. Finally, the most serious deficiency of the descriptive approach is that it inevitably must lead to the conclusion that CON reduces investment.

In this study, we employ the second strategy, that is, the analytic approach. In this approach, the effects of CON are estimated by statistically controlling for factors other than CON which influence investment. The obvious weakness of this method is that it may lead to spurious causal interpretations about CON's effects when relevant non-CON factors are omitted from the analysis. (To minimize this possibility, we specify models to include most factors other research has shown to affect investment.) At least, however, the analytic approach does not prejudge the direction of CON effects.

Estimates of the investment impact of CON are derived from cross-section, multiple-regression analyses of investment by non-federal, short-term general and other special hospitals. The data employed in the analysis pertain to the 48 contiguous states and the District of Columbia (49 observations in all). Estimates of CON impacts were obtained for three different measures of investment: change in plant assets, change in bed supply, and change in assets per bed. The first of these represents the total dollar value of investment while the third may be viewed as a measure of increases in sophistication or capital-intensiveness of facilities. All three measures were defined over the 1968–1972 period. This period was chosen on the grounds (1) that it included some exposure to CON in a number of states and (2) that the confounding influences of Section 1122, federal price controls, and Blue Cross conformance clauses were less important than in later years.

Following the approach taken in other studies of investment (Ginsburg, 1970; Muller et al., 1975; Pauly, 1974b), we employ a regression model of the general form:

$$I = b_0 + b_1 D + b_2 A + b_3 X, \qquad [1]$$

where

I = hospital investment

D = factors influencing demand for hospital services

A = availability of investment funds

X = other factors influencing investment,

and the b_i's are regression coefficients. Estimates of CON impacts are obtained by two procedures. First, we estimate an expanded version of equation [1]:

$$I = b_0 + b_1 D + b_2 A + b_3 X + b_4 C,$$ [2]

where C is defined as the percentage of the four-year period from January 1, 1969, to December 31, 1972, during which CON controls were in effect.[7] In this equation, b_4 estimates the impact of CON. Our second approach estimates coefficients of equation [1] using data from non-CON states.[8] These estimates are then applied to data from CON states to obtain predicted values for the dependent variable, I. Differences between actual and predicted values of 1 for the 1968–1972 period for these states are interpreted as estimates of CON effects.

There is, of course, no perfect method for estimating CON impacts, and each of the two employed here has shortcomings. The former method assumes that the effect of CON is additive and proportional to the percentage of the four-year period in which controls were in force. We have no independent verification of these assumptions and it is at least possible that they may lead to erroneous conclusions. The latter method, while not requiring these particular assumptions, may still lead us astray if differences between actual and predicted investment in CON states are at-

[7]Dates of implementation used in determining the values of C were obtained from the descriptive study by Macro Systems, Inc. (1974), and were verified by telephone contacts with CON agency or planning-agency personnel in the individual states. Twenty states have non-zero values for C; only five (California, Connecticut, Maryland, New York, and Rhode Island) have values greater than 50.

[8]To obtain an adequate data base, some CON states with low values on C were included. For further detail, see the discussion of Table 4 in the next section.

tributable primarily to factors other than CON. This problem, however, is less important in the former method, which allows for differences between actual and predicted investment that are unrelated to CON. Since both methods are imperfect but complementary—in the sense that the major shortcoming of one is not shared by the other—we employ the prudent approach of applying both. The fact that both yielded similar results considerably strengthens our conclusions.[9]

Two specific forms of equations [1] and [2] are used in the regression analyses: (1) linear in percentage changes and (2) linear in logarithmic changes.[10] (Definitions of variables included in the regression equations are shown in Table 1; data sources are described in the Appendix.) The major advantage of these functional forms is that, while they are linear and additive, they incorporate the obvious restriction that the absolute impacts on investment of the CON variable (*C*) and of other "scale-free" independent variables, such as per capita income, should vary positively with the size of the state.

As the independent variables employed here are similar to those used in other studies, they require little comment. Demand variables, such as population size, income, and insurance, are included to capture the effects on investment of changes in demand for hospital services. The hypothesis that an increase in demand for services leads to an increase in desired capital stock, sometimes called the "accelerator hypothesis," predicts positive associations with investment. The occupancy rate may be viewed as a measure of demand pressure on available bed supply and, such, should be positively related to investment, particularly investment in new beds.[11] Net revenues, or the availability of internal investment funds, and Hill-Burton allocations, a measure of the availability of external investment funds, also impact positively upon investment

[9]Of course, several other methods of specifying CON impacts are possible. For example, quadratic (*C²*) or higher-order terms could be added to equation [2]. As time and resource constraints prevented our experimentation with other methods, we rely upon the consistency of findings reported below as evidence that other approaches would not have materially altered our qualitative conclusions.

[10]A third form with the logarithm of *I* as a linear function of absolute changes in the explanatory variables was also tested. Results are briefly discussed below in note 17.

[11]Ginsburg (1970: 104) suggests that the occupancy rate should be adjusted for size to account for larger hospitals' ability to function more comfortably at higher rates. Following his suggestion, we computed a size-adjusted occupancy rate from a size-

TABLE 1

Variables Included in the Analysis

	Percentage Change Equations		Logarithmic Change Equations	
	Form of Variable	*Name*	*Form of Variable*	*Name*
Dependent Variables				
Change in plant assets, 1968–1972	a	D2PA	c	D2LPA
Change in beds, 1968–1972	a	D2BD	c	D2LBD
Demand Variables				
Change in population				
1968–1972	a	D2POP	c	D2LPOP
1964–1968	a	D1POP	c	D1LPOP
Change in mean per capital income				
1968–1972	a	D2INC	c	D2LINC
1964–1968	a	D1INC	c	D1LINC
Occupancy rate in 1968	b	OCC	d	LOCC
Change in occupancy rate, 1964–1968	a	D1OCC	c	D1LOCC
Change in proportion of population with Blue Cross of Medicare hospital coverage				
1968–1972	a	D2BCM	c	D2LBCM
1964–1968	a	D1BCM	c	D1LCBM
Change in proportion of population with hospital insurance				
1968–1972	a	D2PH	c	D2LPH
1964–1968	a	D1PH	c	D1LPH
Change in number of physicians				
1968–1972	a	D2MD	c	D2LMD
1964–1968	a	D1MD	c	D1LMD
Change in number of specialists				
1968–1972	a	D2SP	c	D2LSP
1964–1968	a	D1SP	c	D1LSP
Availability of Funds Variables				
Ratio of total Hill-Burton allocations to 1968 plant assets				
1969–1972	b	R2HB	d	LR2HB
1965–1968	b	R1HB	d	LR1HB
1965–1972	b	RTHB	d	LRTHB
Ratio of total hospital net revenues to 1968 plant assets				
1968–1972	b	R2NR	d	LR2NR
1964–1968	b	R1NR	d	LR1NR
1964–1972	b	RTNR	d	LRTNR
Other Independent Variables				
Annual construction wages in 1970 (in thousands of dollars)	b	CW	d	LCW
Residents and interns per hospital bed, 1968	b	RI	d	LRI
Percentage of the 1968–1972 period with CON program in effect	b	C	d	C

a Percentage of change
b Level
c Change in logarithms
d Logarithm

311

by reducing the need for borrowing and other fund-raising efforts.[12] The number of residents and interns per bed is a compact, albeit crude, descriptor of average hospital type, included on the assumption that investment preferences vary among hospitals. Teaching hospitals, for example, may prefer expansion of scopes of services in response to increased demand over expansion of bed supply. Construction wages measure the cost of new capital, particularly new construction. Finally, independent variables relating to the 1964-1968 period are included to allow for lagged effects on investment.[13]

Results

The results of estimating investment regressions corresponding to equation [2] are shown in Tables 2 and 3. We begin our discussion of these results by considering the coefficients of *C,* which are of primary interest, since they represent the estimated effects of CON.

If CON programs have been effective in limiting total investment, this should be revealed by significantly negative coef-

occupancy regression and included this adjusted rate as an independent variable in several investment regressions. The results obtained were essentially similar in all respects to those obtained using the unadjusted occupancy rate.

[12]The view that availability of external grant funds should affect investment has recently been challenged by Pauly (1974b: 9). He argues that the *marginal* cost of investment funds, which is the critical financial variable in the determination of investment, is not affected by grant funds as long as any part of total investment is financed from borrowing. This argument depends, however; on the assumption that the per dollar cost of borrowing is constant, regardless of how much is borrowed. If this cost increases with the amounts borrowed, external grants would reduce the marginal cost for any given amount of investment, thereby increasing the amount invested.

[13]This simple method of accounting for lagged effects was employed by Pauly (1974b). We use it here because it avoids some practical and theoretical problems of other approaches. For example, proportional adjustment models (Feldstein, 1971a:866–868) imply that the initial impact of an explanatory variable is greater than its effect in subsequent years. In view of the long lags associated with certain types of hospital investment, this assumption is clearly inappropriate. Moreover, the usual method of estimating this sort of model by including lagged values of the dependent variable poses statistical problems which are not easily remedied when, as here, the number of observations is small. This difficulty also arises with more complicated lag models, such as polynomial distributed lags.

fieients for C in the total investment regressions (equations 2.1–2.3 and 3.1–3.3). In fact, these coefficients are all positive and all but one are insignificant. According to these estimates, CON programs clearly have not reduced total hospital investment.

However, the results for equations 2.4–2.9 and 3.4–3.9 indicate that CON programs have had a significant impact on the composition of investment. Specifically, the estimated coefficients of C in the bed-supply equations (2.4–2.6 and 3.4–3.6) are all negative and significant, indicating that CON restricted investment in new beds. By contrast, the corresponding coefficients in the assets per bed regressions (2.7–2.9 and 3.7–3.9) are all positive and significant. This suggests that CON programs have stimulated investment in modernization and in special equipment and facilities, thereby increasing assets per bed.[14] Moreover, the magnitudes of these estimated effects are relatively large. The coefficients in Table 2 imply that the effect of a CON program over the entire four-year period is to reduce the growth in beds by 5.4 to 9.0 percent and to increase assets per bed by 15.2 to 19.7 percent. Correspondingly, the coefficients in Table 3 imply a reduction in beds of about 3.5 percent and an increase in assets per bed of about 10 percent. A comparison with the mean increases in beds (9.3 percent) and assets per bed (37.7 percent) reveals that these estimated effects are indeed substantial.

Turning to the results for the demand variables, we observe that the coefficients for changes in population and insurance coverage are generally in the expected positive direction. The impact of insurance on assets per bed seems slightly stronger than its effect on bed supply. This agrees with Feldstein's (1971b: Chapter 4) thesis that growth of insurance increases hospital per diem costs by causing hospitals to upgrade "styles of care." However, changes in income had no appreciable effect on investment, and,

[14]Our coefficient estimates probably understate the positive effect of CON on these categories of investment because of the ways in which plant-asset data are recorded. Plant assets are generally defined at book value (i.e., the value at the time of construction or purchase) or a book value minus accumulated depreciation. Thus, increases in the costs of construction and facilities should lead to increased assets per bed with the addition of new bed capacity. However, if CON has reduced the growth of bed capacity, as our data suggest, this should also reduce the growth in assets per bed. Obviously, the positive effect of CON on other types of investment was strong enough to offset this reduction and to yield positive and significant coefficients for C in equations 2.7–2.9 and 3.7–3.9.

TABLE 2
Regression Coefficients for Percentage Change Equations
(*t*-statistics in parentheses)

Equation No.	2.1	2.2*	2.3	2.4	2.5*	2.6	2.7	2.8*	2.9
Dep. Var.	D2PA	D2PA	D2PA	D2BD	D2BD	D2BD	D2PAB	D2PAB	D2PAB
Constant	-0.197	-0.496	-0.392	0.076	0.294	-0.137	-0.263	-0.806	-0.150
C†	0.089	0.054	0.096	-0.090^c	-0.083^b	-0.054^b	0.197^b	0.152^b	0.157^b
	(0.75)	(0.48)	(1.04)	(3.12)	(2.44)	(2.19)	(1.82)	(1.52)	(1.91)
D2POP	1.960^a	1.404	1.362	0.367	-0.187	0.112	1.396	1.527	1.153
	(1.45)	(0.92)	(1.12)	(1.11)	(0.40)	(0.34)	(1.11)	(1.12)	(1.07)
D1POP	2.633^b	1.665	2.107^b	0.579^a	1.269^c	0.202	1.720	-0.039	1.717^a
	(1.77)	(1.13)	(1.80)	(1.60)	(2.84)	(0.57)	(1.26)	(0.03)	(1.47)
D2INC	0.374	-0.044	0.239	-0.043	0.073	-0.084	0.415	-0.121	0.341
	(0.80)	(0.09)	(0.58)	(0.42)	(0.47)	(0.76)	(1.07)	(0.27)	(0.94)
D1INC	-0.161	0.321	0.125	-0.267^b	-0.116	-0.085	0.213	0.420	0.225
	(0.36)	(0.67)	(0.32)	(2.42)	(0.80)	(0.83)	(0.51)	(0.98)	(0.66)
OCC††	-0.040		-0.014	0.038^b		0.059^c	-0.084^a		-0.090^a
	(0.57)		(0.23)	(2.24)		(3.60)	(1.32)		(1.66)
D1OCC		-0.258			0.078			-0.350	
		(0.43)			(0.43)			(0.65)	
D2PH	0.718^b		0.869^b	0.061		0.136^a	0.595^b		0.628^b
	(1.93)		(2.40)	(0.67)		(1.40)	(1.74)		(1.95)
D1PH	0.350		0.441^a	0.666		0.085	0.236		0.284
	(1.01)		(1.35)	(0.78)		(0.98)	(0.73)		(0.98)
D2BCM		-0.297			-0.196^b			-0.015	
		(0.90)			(1.96)			(0.05)	
D1BCM		0.207^a			0.058^a			0.115	
		(1.63)			(1.51)			(1.01)	
D2MD	-0.751			-0.478^b			-0.091		
	(0.75)			(1.96)			(0.10)		

	(1)	(2)	(3)	(4)	(5)	(6)	(7)	(8)	(9)
D1MD	-1.768[b] (1.88)		-1.854[b] (2.18)	0.462[b] (2.02)		0.262 (1.15)	-2.255[b] (2.61)		-2.077[c] (2.75)
D2SP		-0.147 (0.20)			-0.441[b] (2.00)			0.431 (0.66)	
D1SP		-0.721 (0.91)			0.359[a] (1.50)			-1.126[a] (1.59)	
R2HB	-0.935 (0.44)			-1.531[c] (2.92)			1.325 (0.67)		
R1HB	3.470[b] (1.75)			1.026[b] (2.12)	(0.95)		1.736		
RTHB		2.279[c] (3.37)	1.413[b] (2.36)		0.089 (0.44)	-0.218[a] (1.36)		2.023[c] (3.35)	1.608[c] (3.03)
R2NR	0.192 (0.78)			-0.033 (0.55)			0.218 (0.96)		
R1NR	0.002 (0.01)		0.182 (0.61)	0.005 (0.06)		0.077 (0.96)	-0.024 (0.08)		0.042 (0.16)
RTNR		0.065 (0.31)			-0.046 (0.72)			0.108 (0.57)	
CW	0.064[b] (2.10)	0.056[b] (1.76)	0.058[b] (1.97)	-0.021[c] (2.81)	-0.026[b] (2.53)	-0.023[c] (2.86)	0.086[c] (3.04)	0.086[c] (2.98)	0.083[c] (3.18)
R1		0.965[a] (1.46)			0.046 (0.23)			0.789[a] (1.34)	
R2	0.563	0.523	0.508	0.702	0.518	0.595	0.571	0.559	0.553

* Nevada excluded because of undefined values for independent variables.
† Coefficients shown are actual coefficients multiplied by 100.
†† Coefficients shown are actual coefficients multiplied by 10.
[a] Significant at the 0.1 level (one-tailed test)
[b] Significant at the 0.05 level (one-tailed test)
[c] Significant at the 0.005 level (one-tailed test)

TABLE 3

Regression Coefficients for Logarithmic Change Equations

(*t*-statistics in parentheses)

Equation No.	3.1**	3.2*	3.3	3.4**	3.5*	3.6	3.7**	3.8*	3.9
Dep. Var.	D2LPA	D2LPA	D2LPA	D2LBD	D2LBD	D2LBD	D2LPAB	D2LPAB	D2LPAB
Constant	-0.737	-0.736	-0.768	-0.121	0.743	-0.099	-0.858	-1.479	-0.669
C†	0.034 (0.82)	0.024 (0.56)	0.045[a] (1.48)	-0.034[b] (2.50)	-0.041[b] (2.69)	-0.018[b] (1.76)	0.068[b] (1.69)	0.065[a] (1.56)	0.063[b] (2.15)
D2LPOP	1.373[a] (1.43)	0.405 (0.42)	0.746 (0.84)	0.356 (1.12)	-0.216 (0.62)	0.237 (0.79)	1.017 (1.09)	0.621 (0.65)	0.509 (0.59)
D1LPOP	1.637[a] (1.59)	1.167 (1.07)	1.475[a] (1.62)	0.512[a] (1.50)	0.986[b] (2.52)	0.193 (0.63)	1.125 (1.22)	0.181 (0.17)	1.282[a] (1.46)
D2LINC	0.504[a] (1.37)	0.034 (0.08)	0.239 (0.67)	-0.066 (0.54)	-0.006 (0.04)	-0.124 (1.03)	0.570[a] (1.59)	0.040 (0.10)	0.362 (1.06)
D1LINC	-0.107 (0.27)	0.114 (0.26)	0.085 (0.27)	-0.294[b] (2.23)	-0.241[a] (1.51)	-0.088 (0.82)	0.187 (0.48)	0.355 (0.81)	0.173 (0.56)
LOCC	-0.122 (0.37)		-0.064 (0.20)	0.300[b] (2.70)		0.404[c] (3.81)	-0.422 (1.29)		-0.467[a] (1.54)
D1LOCC		0.038 (0.08)			0.057 (0.34)				
D2LPH	0.494[b] (1.85)		0.616[b] (2.37)	0.069 (0.78)		0.137[a] (1.56)	0.425[a] (1.63)		0.480[b] (1.92)
D1LPH	0.374[a] (1.50)		0.389[a] (1.59)	0.065 (0.78)		0.056 (0.68)	0.310 (1.27)		0.333[a] (1.41)
D2LBCM		-0.186 (0.68)			-0.179[b] (1.82)			-0.007 (0.03)	
D1LBCM		0.316[b] (2.31)			0.084[b] (1.71)			0.232[b] (1.73)	

316

D2LMD	-0.752 (1.04)			-0.447[a] (1.86)			-0.305 (0.43)		-1.484[b] (2.56)
D1LMD	-0.928[a] (1.32)		-1.317[b] (2.19)	0.407[a] (1.74)		0.167 (0.83)	-1.335[b] (1.95)		
D2LSP		0.006 (0.01)			-0.313[a] (1.46)			0.319 (0.54)	
D1LSP		-0.644 (1.01)			0.410[b] (1.80)			-1.053[a] (1.69)	
LR2HB	-0.063 (0.47)			-0.105[b] (2.35)			0.042 (0.32)		
LR1HB	0.211[a] (1.60)			0.073[a] (1.67)			0.138 (1.07)		
LRTHB		0.249[a] (3.37)	0.149[b] (2.31)		0.009 (0.33)	-0.032[a] (1.49)		0.240[c] (3.31)	0.181[c] (2.92)
LR2NR[††]	0.281 (1.08)			-0.030 (0.35)			0.311 (1.22)		
LR1NR[††]	-0.176 (0.70)		0.132 (0.63)	0.047 (0.56)		0.143[b] (2.02)	-0.222 (0.91)		-0.011 (0.06)
LRTNR[††]		-0.032 (0.08)			-0.071 (0.51)			0.039 (0.10)	
LCW	0.311[b] (1.91)	0.293[a] (1.62)	0.285[b] (1.78)	-0.168[c] (3.12)	-0.173[b] (2.67)	-0.161[c] (2.98)	0.479[c] (3.02)	0.467[b] (2.63)	0.446[c] (2.89)
LRI		0.480[b] (1.96)			0.084 (0.96)			0.396[a] (1.65)	
R^2	0.577	0.511	0.483	0.711	0.561	0.642	0.596	0.510	0.526

• Nevada, New York and Wyoming excluded because of undefined values for independent variables.
:• Massachusetts and New York excluded because of undefined values for independent variables.
† Coefficients shown are actual coefficients multiplied by 100.
†† Coefficients shown are actual coefficients multiplied by 10.
a Significant at the 0.1 level (one-tailed test)
b Significant at the 0.05 level (one-tailed test)
c Significant at the 0.005 level (one-tailed test)

contrary to our expectations, changes in physician supply affected investment negatively. Finally, while the occupancy rate has no measurable impact on total investment, it apparently alters the composition of investment by increasing bed expansion and reducing other types of investment. Ginsburg (1970: Chapter 6) reports an identical finding from his study of individual hospitals over the 1961–1965 period.

Among the other variables, construction wages was the most significant. Its negative impact on investment in beds implies that plans for new hospital construction are sensitive to cost factors. However, while an increase in construction wages reduces the physical quantity of new construction, it increases the unit cost. Our estimates show that the net effect of these influences on the total dollar value of investment (equations 2.1–2.3 and 3.1–3.3) is significantly positive. Also, the positive coefficients in the plant assets per bed equation reflect both the positive effect of construction wages on the unit cost of construction and perhaps a reallocation of investment funds from construction to equipment.

The coefficients for residents and interns per bed conform to expectations in that they are more strongly positive for plant assets per bed than for beds. The coefficients for the Hill-Burton variables display a similar pattern, which may reflect the program's recent emphasis upon modernization rather than expansion of bed capacity. Finally, we were unable to detect any appreciable effect of net revenues on investment.

Overall, our coefficient estimates conform to prior expectations, and the regressions explain substantial portions of the variances in the dependent variables. In addition, the coefficients of C are stable across regressions that vary in terms of functional form and the set of included explanatory variables. This attests to the validity of the estimates of CON's impacts in that they are not likely to be artifacts of having omitted other relevant independent variables.

To arrive at the second set of CON impact measures, we reestimated 12 of the regressions described above, deleting the independent variable C and exluding the five states where CON had been in effect throughout 1971 and 1972 (i.e., California, Connecticut, Maryland, New York, Rhode Island). The reestimated equations include: 2.2, 2.3, 2.5, 2.6, 2.8, 2.9, 3.2, 3.3, 3.5, 3.6, 3.8, and 3.9. We also reestimated equations 2.3, 2.6, and 2.9, deleting C and excluding the 11 states where CON had been in effect for five or more quarters during the 1969–1972 period. (These include the five states mentioned above, plus Minnesota, New Jersey, North Carolina, North Dakota, South Carolina, and Washington.) Coefficients from these 15 reestimated regressions were then used to predict changes in plant assets, beds, and plant assets per bed for the excluded states. Differences between predicted and actual values for these variables are shown in Table 4 for California, Connecticut, Maryland, New York, and Rhode Island.

The pattern of these deviations conforms precisely to the pattern of coefficients for C reported above. In almost all cases, actual increases in beds in these five CON states are less than predicted increases. Furthermore, increases in plant assets and in plant assets per bed are generally greater than predicted, but deviations for plant assets per bed are more consistently positive and larger relative to the standard errors of the predictions.[15]

A brief comparison of deviations among the five states may also be of interest, for CON programs in these states differ structurally. In California, for example, final authority for CON determinations rest de facto with area-wide CHP agencies. Maryland's state CHP agency renders final decisions, although area-wide agencies are important parts of the process. In Connecticut, New York, and Rhode Island, CHP agencies have only minor roles, and in New York the agency that issues certificates (the state health department) is also responsible for regulating hospital costs.

One might expect such differences to be related to the effectiveness of controls. Close interaction between CHP area-wide agencies and hospitals, we have noted, may facilitate provider domination and, in turn, less effective control where these agencies figure importantly in the review process. Conversely, where the major responsibility rests with a state agency concerned also with operating-cost implications of unnecessary investment (as in New

[15]Deviations between predicted and actual investment for the other six CON states in the regressions where they were excluded did not consistently follow this pattern. Only three of the six states had less growth in beds than predicted, but these three negative deviations were on average about twice as large as the three positive deviations. Four of the six deviations were also negative for growth in plant assets and in plant assets per bed. Here, however, average sizes of positive and negative deviations were essentially equal.

York), one might expect more stringent controls (Havighurst, 1973: 1180–1181).

Surprisingly, there is little correlation between the results shown in Table 4 and these structural characteristics. One of the two states where CHP(b) agencies are presumably most influential, California, was the least successful in controlling bed expansion while the other, Maryland, was most successful.[16] No state achieved visible success in controlling increases in plant assets and plant assets per bed.

We should be careful, however, not to overinterpret these findings, for comparisons among states based on a single set of deviations between actual and predicted values obviously lack reliability. They do suggest, however, that simple hypotheses about the relative effectiveness of CON programs based on comparisons of real or presumed structural characteristics may be misleading. The effectiveness of controls within a single state may depend greatly upon political forces, personalities involved, and special circumstances not readily visible from afar.

Discussion

In sum, our two methods of measuring CON's effects on hospital investment yield similar results. These results indicate that CON controls did not reduce the total dollar amount of investment during the 1966–1972 period, but significantly altered its composition by reducing growth in beds and increasing other types of investment. Employing several different regression models composed of different combinations of independent variables, we obtained stable results, which attest strongly to their probable validity.[17]

[16]Several difference between California and Maryland may account for this. In Maryland, a considerable portion of all hospitals are within the purview of the Baltimore metropolitan area CHP(b) agency, a relatively well-staffed and active body in which non-providers have played an important role. California's fragmentation of the state into twelve different CHP(b) regions may have encouraged leniency by allowing citizens in one area to pass on a share of the costs of additional investment to others throughout the state in the form of higher insurance premiums and taxes for Medicaid payments. These speculations are, of course, just that and, as such, invite more careful investigation.

[17]As mentioned above in note 10, a third regression model was also tested in which the dependent variables were expressed as logarithms of absolute changes (e.g., log [plant assets in 1972 minus plant assets in 1968]). Most independent variables were

TABLE 4

Deviations of Actual from Predicted Values
for Dependent Variables from Five CON States
(Standard errors for predictions in parentheses)

Dep. Var.	Equation No.**	California	Connecticut	Maryland	New York*	Rhode Island
D2PA	2.2	− 0.013 (0.189)	0.183 (0.173)	0.040 (0.210)	0.180 (0.224)	0.026 (0.183)
D2PA	2.3	0.068 (0.175)	0.296 (0.167)	0.066 (0.183)	0.065 (0.168)	− 0.005 (0.172)
D2PA	2.3†	0.031 (0.199)	0.293 (0.179)	0.042 (0.202)	0.080 (0.182)	− 0.005 (0.186)
D2LPA	3.2	0.025 (0.054)	0.094 (0.050)	0.039 (0.058)		− 0.049 (0.081)
D2LPA	3.3	0.040 (0.051)	0.112 (0.050)	0.020 (0.054)	0.037 (0.049)	− 0.008 (0.067)
D2BD	2.5	− 0.027 (0.058)	− 0.053 (0.053)	− 0.115 (0.064)	0.048 (0.068)	− 0.053 (0.056)
D2BD	2.6	0.040 (0.045)	− 0.033 (0.043)	− 0.099 (0.047)	− 0.034 (0.043)	− 0.077 (0.045)
D2BD	2.6†	0.055 (0.047)	− 0.027 (0.042)	− 0.104 (0.047)	− 0.018 (0.042)	− 0.078 (0.043)
D2LBD	3.5	− 0.012 (0.021)	− 0.021 (0.020)	− 0.042 (0.023)		− 0.004 (0.032)
D2LBD	3.6	0.011 (0.018)	− 0.016 (0.017)	− 0.033 (0.018)	− 0.016 (0.017)	− 0.010 (0.023)
D2PAB	2.8	0.020 (0.169)	0.237 (0.155)	0.182 (0.188)	0.099 (0.201)	0.093 (0.164)
D2PAB	2.9	0.014 (0.155)	0.318 (0.147)	0.187 (0.161)	0.103 (0.148)	0.092 (0.152)
D2PAB	2.9†	− 0.039 (0.173)	0.306 (0.156)	0.171 (0.176)	0.095 (0.153)	0.093 (0.152)
D2LPAB	3.8	0.037 (0.052)	0.114 (0.048)	0.081 (0.057)		− 0.045 (0.078)
D2LPAB	3.9	0.029 (0.049)	0.128 (0.047)	0.052 (0.051)	0.053 (0.047)	0.002 (0.064)

* Omitted values resulted from undefined values for independent variables.
**Equation number refers to the equation in Table 2 or 3 whose specification corresponds to that used in deriving predictions.
† Eleven CON states were excluded from the regression used to derive these predictions. In all other cases only the five states whose deviations are shown here were excluded.

321

Furthermore, our empirical findings are consistent with expectations derived from critical analyses of CON. That investment in beds was more effectively controlled than other investment in services and facilities accords with expected implications of provider domination, limitations in coverage of CON laws, and the likely response of CON agencies (in terms of setting priorities and rules of thumb) to the scarcity of resources. On the other hand, findings that total investment was not reduced and that the growth in assets per bed was actually stimulated by CON are somewhat surprising. These may be due to the franchising aspects of CON regulation, which, as we have noted, may encourage pre-emptive investment, or to the added protection from competitive pressures that these laws afford to existing providers. But there are at least two other explanations which should be considered.

First, one can reasonably postulate that strong pressures for capital expansion are operative within the management structure of many hospitals. The managerial preference for expansion of facilities and services appears to be characteristic of virtually all organizations (Perrow, 1970: 152–153; Starbuck, 1965), but it is probably strongest in non-profit institutions (such as most hospitals) where the significance of profit as a criterion of success is diminished. Furthermore, in the case of hospitals, these preferences are reinforced by the desires of staff physicians for the most up-to-date services, equipment, and patient accommodations. Since external market pressures for cost control are weak and expected profitability is of minor relevance in setting investment priorities, administrators and trustees are likely to be respossive to these desires. Indeed, failure to do so may impair the hospital's ability to compete for patients. These considerations imply that if one means of indulging the expansionist preferences of management and the medical staff is blocked by regulatory controls, alternative means that are not subject to regulation will be found. If CON prevents a hospital from adding the additional beds desired by the specialists

expressed as absolute changes instead of percentage changes or logarithmic changes. In this model, availability of funds variables were more significant predictors of investment, while population change was less so. However, findings with respect to C were identical to those reported in Tables 2 and 3. As a further check on the stability of the coefficients of C, we executed several regressions omitting one or more independent variables. Again, these coefficient remained quite stable. Finally, it is reassuring to observe that Hellinger (in press), using a somewhat different model in his multiple regression analysis of interstate variations in plant assets, has also found that CON has no significant effect on total investment.

on its staff, it can "compensate" these physicians (and thereby retain their custom) by installing facilities for cardiac catheterization, renal dialysis, and the like. Our findings suggest that this may in fact have occurred.

Second, there is the possibility that, for an individual hospital, investment in beds and other types of investment may be interrelated financially. The marginal cost of raising investment funds probably increases with total investment. In the credit market, as a hospital's indebtedness rises, its ability to obtain additional funds on favorable terms decreases. In the "philanthropy market," the yield of fund-raising efforts must certainly decline as more donors are solicited or the same ones are repeatedly solicited. Therefore, if a CON program successfully reduces amounts of funds spent on one type of investment (e.g., expansion of bed capacity), the cost of funds for other types (e.g., modernization and sophisticated equipment) is reduced, causing increases in these other types.

This argument is shown in Fig. 1, where *AB* and *AC* are the

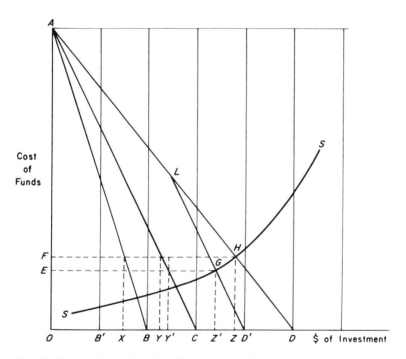

Fig. 1.   Demand for and Supply of Investment Funds.

323

hospital's demand curves for bed-investment and nonbed-investment funds, respectively, and SS is the funds supply curve. AD, the total demand for investment funds schedule, is the horizontal sum of AB and AC. In the absence of CON, equilibrium occurs at point H; the marginal interest cost is OF percent; total investment is OZ, of which OX is devoted to expanding bed supply; and XZ ($= OY$) is devoted to other investment. Suppose now that a CON program limits bed investment to OB'. The constrained total demand schedule is then ALD', and equilibrium is at point G, with a marginal interest cost of OE. While investment in beds is reduced to OB' other investment increases to $B'Z'$ ($= OY'$). The net effect on total investment remains negative, but it may be quite small. (This would occur if, for example, the segment of SS between G- and H is steeply sloped. When this segment is vertical, there is no decline in total investment.) Furthermore, the resultant decline in total investment may be further reduced or even eliminated by positive effects of pre-emptive investment and reduced competitive pressures.

As we have noted, our findings about the investment impacts of CON are both statistically robust and consistent with plausible expectations about the likely effects of CON regulation. However, in the absence of other studies offering corroboration and in view of the obvious policy implications of our findings, it is imperative that we attend to their possible limitations. One stems from our use of aggregated state data, which are not perfectly suited to our purposes. Planning and regulation ultimately occur in designated regions within states that are agglomerations of individual hospitals and localities which are probably quite heterogeneous. State aggregates, therefore, are averages across potentially quite diverse regions. Having relied upon published data, we have no independent means of assessing their reliability and validity, which is especially problematic regarding information on hospital plant assets and insurance coverage. Furthermore, we must note that our investment variables (changes in beds and changes in plant assets per bed) correspond imperfectly to the distinction between bed investment versus non-bed investment. A stronger test of our interpretations requires more precise measurement of non-bed investment in particular. Finally, non-random adoption of CON controls by states poses threats to the internal validity of our causal interpretations of CON's effects. States that adopted such legislation may differ systematically from others in terms of relevant dimensions not included in our analyses. If so, our causal reasoning would be spurious in some unknowable degree.

Because of these limitations, caution must be exercised in extrapolating our results to subsequent extensions of CON coverage. The self-selection of states into CON probably implies that our estimates will lead to upwardly biased effects when used to predict impacts in other states. Among those that subsequently adopt CON laws in response to P.L. 93-641, the restrictive impact on investment in beds will probably be less than reported here. Furthermore, as our results reflect only the effects of existing CON programs at a particular time, it would be incorrect to view them as necessary consequences of CON regardless of the nature of the review process and the circumstances in which it occurs. Indeed, the limited evidence presented here suggests that there is considerable variation in impact among existing programs. Finally, returning to our earlier caveat about the limited purpose of this analysis, we must note that CON is but one of several types of regulation currently in force or contemplated. Our findings cannot be used to predict the consequences of combining CON with other forms of investment, rate, and quality controls.

Policy Implications and Suggestions for Future Research

We have found that, while CON has controlled expansion in bed supply, it has stimulated other types of investment and, therefore, had little effect on total investment expenditures. One might be tempted to conclude that CON programs can be made more effective by tightening existing controls and extending them to cover all types of investment projects. The wisdom of this course of action is, however, by no means self-evident. Careful review of all certification requests, including the additional requests generated by extending the scope of CON, would require large additions to agency resources. Conceivably, the resources required for review might often exceed the costs of investment projects being reviewed. Such circumstances do not seem to constitute an optimal allocation of societal resources.

Other straightforward options are also undesirable in that they are either politically infeasible or at variance with CON's putative purpose, that is, to control cost inflation by deterring *unnecessary-* investment. For instance, CON agencies could adopt the general policy of denying certification for equipment and facilities except in cases where extreme and urgent need is demonstrable. Alternatively, substantial submission fees or even taxes on investment could be employed to discourage hospitals and other institutions from seeking certification. Although such measure have the superficial appeals of simplicity and economy, they are not particularly discriminating between needed and unneeded investments. Furthermore, they would most likely favor the large, wealthy institutions' interests even more than does the process currently in use.

The desirability of tightening or extending CON controls must also be considered within the total context of health-sector regulation. Realization of the impossibility of relying solely on CON to control health care costs (Bicknell and Walsh, 1975: 1060) leads to skepticism of arguments favoring such modifications of CON. Utilization controls and rate-setting policies which limit reimbursement for depreciation and operating costs relating to unneeded capital facilities may complement CON programs which focus almost exclusively on controlling bed supply.[18]

In concluding, we wish to stress our belief that the present study does not in itself provide an adequate basis for deriving specific programmatic policy options regarding CON. We have described several important limitations of our study which, we hope, can be eliminated in future research. In addition, there are other directions of complementary research that ought to be pursued if we are to attain a more complete understanding of direct and indirect effects of existing and proposed CON programs.

This paper is a part of a larger effort to assess CON's impacts on hospital operating costs and utilization and on investment in nursing homes, as well as on the types of investment reported here. Furthermore, using data from CHP(b) planning regions, we are examining effects of CON on bed supplies and the addition of specific facilities and services. Several other important questions invite investigation. For instance, study of CON's effects on the structure of the health care industry is warranted by the criticism that CON may block entry of new competitors, retard growth of

---

[18]In this regard, it is pertinent to recall that our results apply to a period (1968-1972) during which these other forms of control were relatively unimportant.

HMOs, and discourage investment in less costly alternatives to hospital care (e.g., surgicenters) (Havighurst, 1973). Longitudinal analyses of changes in CON's effects may also be revealing, for experience in other industries shows change in the behavior of regulators over time, in particular, a loss of reformist zeal and an increase in provider domination. With the recent adoption of other regulatory devices such as rate setting and PSRO, a detailed analysis of CON's interactions with them is especially relevant to current policy debate. Finally, as a means of verifying the reasoning behind our interpretations of findings reported here and for generating further insight, more descriptive studies like those reported by Bicknell and Walsh (1975) and Macro-Systems, Inc. (1974) are indicated. Having embraced CON as a cornerstone of nascent federal health policy, it is incumbent upon policy makers to evaluate carefully and extensively its effects. To do otherwise is inevitably to consign debate about CON to the realm of speculation, where undoubtedly the urge to regulate will prevail.

David S. Salkever, PH.D.
School of Hygiene and Public Health
The Johns Hopkins University
615 North Wolfe Street
Baltimore, Maryland 21205

Thomas W. Bice, PH.D.
Department of Sociology
Washington University
St. Louis, Missouri 63130

Support for this project is from the National Center for Health Services Research, U.S. Department of Health, Education, and Welfare, Contract Number HRA-106-74-57. The very competent research and computational assistance of William Harris, Margaret Solnick, and Barbara Vaeth is gratefully acknowledged.

Appendix

Data on beds, plant assets, net revenues, and occupancy rates in non-federal short-term hospitals were obtained from the *Guide Issues* of *Hospital, J.A.H.A.* Hospital insurance data were taken from the *Sourcebook of Health Insurance Data* (Health Insurance Association of America). Blue Cross hospital coverage figures were obtained from *Research and Statistics Notes* (Office of Research and Statistics, U.S. Social Security Administration) and from unpublished data provided by the Blue Cross Association. Medicare enrollment figures are published annually in *Medicare:*

Selected State Data (U.S. Social Security Administration). Construction wages were obtained from *County Business Patterns* (U.S. Dept. of Commerce) while per capita income and population figures were taken from *Sales Management: Annual Survey of Buying Power* (Sales Management, Inc.). Unpublished data on Hill-Burton allocations were provided by the U.S. Department of Health, Education, and Welfare. Finally, numbers of physicians, specialists, and residents and interns appear in *Distribution of Physicians* (American Medical Association). In certain instances, adjustments were made for missing data. These are described in a more extensive version of this appendix which is available upon request.

References

Berry, R.
1974   "Cost and efficiency in the production of hospital services." Milbank Memorial Fund Quarterly/Health and Society 52,3 (Summer): 291–313.

Bicknell, W.J., and D.C. Walsh
1975   "Certification-of-need: the Massachusetts experience." New England Journal of Medicine 292 (May 15): 1054–1061.

Brown, D.
1969   Evaluation of Health Planning. Health Administration Perspectives No. A8. Chicago: Center for Health Administration Studies, University of Chicago.

Curran, W.J.
1974   "A national survey and analysis of state certificate-of-need laws for health facilities." In Havighurst, C.C. (ed.), Regulating Health Facilities Construction. Washington: American Enterprise Institute for Policy Research.

Davis, K.
1969   A Theory of Economic Behavior in Non-Profit, Private Hospitals. Ph.D. thesis, Rice University.

1974   "The role of technology, demand and labor markets in the determination of hsopital cost." In Perlman, M. (ed.), The Economics of Health and Medical Care. New York: John Wiley and Sons.

Feldstein, M.S.
1971a   "Hospital cost inflation: a study in nonprofit price dynamics." American Economic Review 61,5(December): 853–872.

1971b   The Rising Cost of Hospital Care. Washington: Information Resources Press.

Ginsburg, P.B.
1970   Capital in Non-Profit Hospitals. Ph.D. thesis, Harvard University.

Havighurst, C.C.
1973   "Regulation of health facilities and services by certificate-of-need." Virginia Law Review 599(October):1143-1232.

Hellinger, F.
in   The Effect of Certificate of Need Legislation on Hospital Investment.
press   U.S. Social Security Administration.

Hilton, G.
1972   "The basic behavior of regulatory commissions." American Economic Review 62,2 (May): 47-54.

Lave, J.R., and L.B. Lave
1974   "The supply and allocation of medical resources: alternative control mechanisms." In Havighurst, C.C. (ed.), Regulating Health Facilities Construction. Washington: American Enterprise Institute for Policy Research.

Lewin and Associates, Inc.
1974   Nationwide Survey of State Health Regulations. Springfield, Virginia: National Technical Information Service (PB 236-660).

Macro Systems, Inc.
1974   The Certificate of Need Experience: An Early Assessment. Silver Spring, Maryland: Macro Systems, Inc.

May, J.
1974   "The planning and licensing agencies." In Havighurst, C.C. (ed.), Regulating Health Facilities Construction. Washington: American Enterprise Institute for Policy Research.

Muller, C., P. Worthington, and G. Allen
1975   "Capital expenditures and the availability of funds." International Journal of Health Services 5, 1(Winter): 143-157.

O'Donoghue, P., and Policy Center, Inc.
1974   Evidence About the Effects of Health Care Regulation. Denver: Spectrum Research, Inc.

Pauly, M.V.
1974a   "The behavior of nonprofit hospital monopolies: alternative models of the hospital." In Havighurst, C.C. (ed.), Regulating Health Facilities Construction. Washington: American Enterprise Institute for Policy Research.

1974b   "Hospital capital investment: the roles of demand, profits, and physicians." Journal of Human Resources 9 (Winter): 7–20.

Perrow, C.
1970   Organizational Analysis: A Sociological View. Belmont, California: Wadsworth.

Posner, R.A.
1974   "Certificates of need for health care facilities: a dissenting view." In Havighurst, C.C. (ed.), Regulating Health Facilities Construction. Washington: American Enterprise Institute for Policy Research.

Roth, E.
1974   "Certificate of need as a part of comprehensive health planning." Unpublished paper. The Johns Hopkins Medical Institutions.

Schelling, T.
1963   The Strategy of Conflict. New York: Oxford University Press.

Starbuck, W.
1965   "Organizational growth and development." In March, J.G. (ed.), Handbook of Organizations. Chicago: Rand McNally.

Stuehler, G.
1973   "Certification of need—a systems analysis of Maryland's experience and plans." American Journal of Public Health 63 (November): 966–972.

Milbank Memorial Fund Quarterly/*Health and Society, Vol. 56, No. 4, 1978*

The Annual Pap Test:
A Dubious Policy Success

ANNE-MARIE FOLTZ AND JENNIFER L. KELSEY

Graduate School of Public Administration, New York University; and Department of Epidemiology and Public Health, Yale School of Medicine

S CREENING FOR DISEASE among apparently healthy people has long been an important part of public health work. Certain types of screening have become national policy either through Congressional mandate or through informal diffusion. In recent years, the utility of screening tests has been increasingly debated by public health personnel (Fogarty International Center, 1976; Lave and Lave, 1977; Shapiro, 1977). Among the most common screening tests whose widespread use is being questioned is the Papanicolaou smear test, or "Pap" test, for cancer of the cervix (the neck of the uterus). During the past 30 years, this test has been promoted for annual use for all women over 20 years of age. So well established is the Pap test that in 1973 nearly 50% of the women over 17 years of age reported having had one during the previous year, and 75% reported having one at least once in their lives (U.S. Department of Health, Education and Welfare, 1975). Despite widespread use, and despite endorsement by the American Cancer Society and by the National Cancer Act Amendments of 1974, benefits of the Pap test remain unclear.

This paper is an examination of the rationale and development of policies for the use of the Pap test. As Shapiro (1975:83) pointed out:

> ... unfortunately, no provision was made years ago for a rigorous test of the efficacy of the Pap smear through randomized clinical trials and now because of its widespread acceptance as a diagnostic tool, it is no longer possible to do so.

Therefore, one has to pass judgment on the basis of available data, inconclusive though these data may be.

We will first review the scientific basis for establishing screening policies, and then assess the extent to which the Pap test meets these criteria for screening tests. We will then examine the question of why the annual Pap test has been adopted as national policy in the United States despite serious questions about its usefulness. In so doing, we will contrast the policies of the United States with those of the United Kingdom and Canada.

Criteria for Screening

When the National Conference on Preventive Aspects of Chronic Disease in 1951 (Commission on Chronic Illness, 1957) first established a definition for screening, it also set a precedent that public screening programs could be undertaken where the health benefits were directed to the individual rather than to society as a whole. This permitted the application of screening tests to diseases such as cancer, whereas previously they had been applied only to infectious diseases (Wilson, 1968; Hart, 1975; Rosen, 1975). Following this pattern, a few years later the Commission on Chronic Illness (1957) defined screening as:

> the presumptive identification of unrecognized disease or defect by the application of tests, examinations, or other procedures which can be applied rapidly to sort out apparently well persons who probably have a disease from those who probably do not. A screening test is not intended to be diagnostic. Persons with positive or suspicious findings must be referred to their physicians for diagnosis and necessary treatment.

Since 1968, the World Health Organization (Wilson and Jungner, 1968), McKeown (1968), Cochrane and Holland (1971),

Whitby (1974), Frankenburg and Camp (1975), and Cole and Morrison (1978) have summarized criteria that screening tests should fulfill before they are applied to populations. For purposes of discussion, we have combined these criteria into five groups, as listed below. Although failure of a screening test to fulfill any single criterion does not in itself completely negate the value of the screening test, most of the criteria should be met if a mass screening program is to be effective.[1]

1. *Importance of the Disease.* The disease should be an important health problem and have a high prevalence in the community.

2. *Characteristics of the Screening Test.* The test should be simple to administer, accurate, reliable, and acceptable to the population.

3. *State of Knowledge of the Natural History of the Disease.* The disease should have a recognizable latent or early presymptomatic stage, and its natural progression from latent to declared disease should be well understood.

4. *Efficacy of Treatment.* Diagnosis and treatment should be available for patients with recognized disease and should be acceptable to them. Consensus should exist on what is appropriate efficacious treatment.

5. *Justifiability of Screening Costs.* The costs of case-finding through screening must be politically and socially acceptable. This includes the cost of the test itself, the costs of diagnosis and treatment, and the personal and social costs associated with suggesting there is disease where none exists (false positive) and suggesting absence of disease where in fact it does exist (false negative).

---

[1]For example, phenylketonuria (PKU) is of low prevalence, but the test itself is accurate and simple, the natural history of the disease known, and the disease amenable to treatment, all of which help to justify the costs and make it an acceptable screening procedure. Nevertheless, of late, it too has come under criticism.

Screening for Cancer of the Cervix

1. *Is cervical cancer an important health problem with a high prevalence?*

Cancer of the cervix is not a major cause of death among women in Western countries. In the United States, as Fig. 1 shows, cancer of the cervix trails far behind heart disease and stroke as a cause of death, and it also trails behind several other major cancer sites in women. In 1976, 5525 deaths in the United States were attributed to cancer of the cervix, showing a steady decline from 7108 deaths in 1968 (U.S. Department of Health, Education, and Welfare, 1978b).

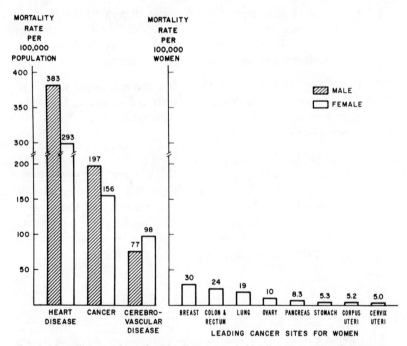

FIG. 1. Mortality rates from three leading causes and leading cancer sites for women in the United States, 1976. *Source:* U.S. Department of Health, Education, and Welfare. 1978b.

The average annual incidence rate for invasive cervical cancer from the Cancer Surveillance, Epidemiology and End Results (SEER) program (U.S. Department of Health, Education, and Welfare, 1978a) for the years 1973 through 1976 was 12.6 per 100,000. Applying this to the estimated number of women in the United States over this same time period (U.S. Department of Commerce, 1978) yields an estimate of the annual number of new cases of invasive cervical cancer of about 14,000.[2] From these mortality and incidence rates, it is evident that cancer of the cervix is a health problem of only moderate significance in the United States.

If a disease is of low prevalence in a community, screening brings in a low yield for a high effort. Moreover, the lower the prevalence, the less likely it is that a positive test will correctly identify a woman who really has cancer. This means that many women with positive test results but without disease will be referred unnecessarily for further diagnostic tests and treatment, with concomitant costs and worry.[3] The actual prevalence rates of cervical cancer, carcinoma in situ, and dysplasia are not known, since these rates can only be determined by surgery, which obviously cannot be undertaken on a sample of the general population. However, results of the Pap test indicate that cancer of the cervix is a disease of low prevalence in the general population. Stern and Neely (1963) found prevalence rates at initial screening of 5.4 per 1000 for dysplasia, 5.1 per 1000 for carcinoma in situ, 1.5 per 1000 for Stage 1 invasive carcinoma, and 1.0 per 1000 for Stage 2–4 carcinoma. The yield is even lower among those rescreened: among women with previously negative tests who had been screened from 1 to 7 years before, the respective rates were 2.4, 0.07, 0.09, and zero.

---

[2]It is realized that the SEER reporting areas are not completely representative of the United States, but they do provide a better cross section than any other source of incidence data.

[3]If the prevalence of a disease is 5 per 1000, the false-positive rate 5%, and the false-negative rate 20%, only about 8% (4 of 54) of those screened as positive will be true positives. If the false-positive rate is 20%, which is probably a more realistic figure, the false-negative rate still 20%, and the prevalence 2 per 1000, only about 0.8% (1.6 of 201.2) of those screened positive will be truly positive. In other words, 99.2% of those screened as positive will not be found to be truly positive by subsequent definitive testing. Thus, a costly burden is laid on the diagnostic facilities for an extremely low yield, while a psychological burden is placed on the women involved.

Among Connecticut women undergoing the Pap test between 1970 and 1974, the prevalence of invasive cancer ranged from 0.2 to 0.3 per 1000 women screened; for carcinoma in situ the prevalence rate ranged from 0.9 to 1.2 per 1000 women screened (American Cancer Society, Connecticut Division, 1976). Brindle, Wakefield, and Yule (1976) noted that almost 29% of the women screened in a program in northwestern England presented evidence of some gynecological disorder, and that among this 29%, about 2% had Pap test findings that required further investigation. Thus, although the yield among women with symptoms may not be low, among symptomless women in the general population the test is likely to yield few new cases for a large effort, especially if the women have had a negative test in previous years.

These differences in prevalence rates for cervical cancer result in part from variation in the types of women having Pap tests (Alvan R. Feinstein, 1978). These women come from at least four different groups represented in varying proportions in screening programs: 1) women not under current medical surveillance who would otherwise not have visited a gynecologist; 2) women under medical surveillance, visiting a doctor for some reason other than suspicious symptoms of cervical cancer, and who have the Pap test performed by that doctor during the course of that examination; 3) women for whom the Pap test is undertaken because they have signs or symptoms of cervical pathology; and 4) women previously found to be negative who are being reexamined. Each of these populations has particular prevalence rates, but very few studies take these different groups into account.

In addition, because the high frequency of hysterectomy has reduced the number at risk for cervical cancer, it is difficult to estimate accurately mortality, incidence, and prevalence rates for the disease. Nearly one-fifth of the women in the age range of 40–49, for instance, have had a hysterectomy (National Center for Health Statistics, 1966; Stern, Misczynski, Greenland et al., 1977).

2. Is the Pap test simple to administer, accurate, reliable, and acceptable to the population?

The Pap smear test consists of an analysis of Papanicolaou-stained cells taken from the uterine cervix (neck of the uterus) by scraping. The test may be taken in a doctor's office, clinic, or hospital. The procedure is quick, simple, and may cause some discomfort. Its safety has never been in question, and it seems to be readily accepted by women.

The primary purpose of the Pap test is to detect cancer or lesions that may be pre-cancerous. Traditionally, the results of the Pap smear are reported in five classes: I = normal; II = atypical; III = suspicious (dysplasia); IV = carcinoma in situ; and V = invasive carcinoma. Some laboratories use as many as seven classifications, however, and the names of the classes may vary. Classes III through V are considered "positive" by most physicians and require follow-up with the more definitive diagnostic procedure, ·the cervical biopsy.

The accuracy and reliability of the Pap test have not been established despite its use for over 30 years. The accuracy of the test has been stated to be between 95% and 100% (Dickinson, 1972c; American Cancer Society, 1975; Talebian, Shayan, Krumholz et al., 1977). This statement is misleading, however. With any condition of low prevalence, this statistic can hide a high rate of false negatives.[4]

Direct estimates of false-negative rates are not available, since this would require knowledge of the proportion of women known to have cervical dysplasia, carcinoma in situ, and invasive carcinoma who have negative Pap tests. Instead, false-negative rates have been estimated indirectly by comparing results from a first Pap test to findings in second and subsequent tests or by comparing first and second readings of the same smear. False-negative rates for a single smear estimated in these ways have varied considerably, but are for the most part about 20% (Yule, 1972) to 30% (Garrett, 1964).

A cervical scrape produces lower false-negative rates than vaginal aspiration (Shulman, Leyton, and Reed, 1974). Rates from cervical scrapes alone, from many different studies, range from 2.4%

---

[4]In this instance, the authors of these articles presumably use the term "accuracy" to mean the proportion correctly classified by the test out of all those screened. This is dependent not only on the false-positive and false-negative rates, but also on the prevalence of the disease. If very few people have the condition, most people will be correctly classified as negative. For instance, assume that 1000 persons are screened, of whom 5 are true positives; with a false-negative rate of 20% (1 of 5) and a false positive rate of 5% (50 of 995), the "accuracy" may be calculated to be 95% (949 of 1000). Even if the false-negative rate were 100% and the false-positive rate were 5%, 945 of 1000 persons would still be correctly classified. Thus, the statistics of 95% accuracy is misleading since it can hide a very high false-negative rate for a condition of low prevalence.

to 26% (Husain, 1976). Coppelson and Brown (1974), using various sources of data, estimated false-negative rates of 40% for dysplasia, 20% to 45% for carcinoma in situ, and 24% for invasive cancer. They concluded: "These studies show the false negative rate to be so high that it cannot be ignored in the design of strategies for cancer prevention."

This lack of repeatability in Pap tests has several causes. One is that the abnormal cells may be present in one sample and not in another. Sedlis, Walters, Balin et al. (1974) found that if two samples of cellular material were taken from a woman at the same time at least one-third of the time the abnormal cells seen in one sample would not be present in the second sample for carcinoma in situ, and at least half the time for mild or moderate dysplasia. Noting the reported false-negative rates of 25%, Sedlis et al. (1974: 296) stated: "Our results tend to support a view that in real practice, as opposed to highly selective studies, the prevalence of false negative results is probably much higher than generally believed." The authors concluded that taking two samples instead of one could increase by as much as 50% the chances of getting positive results. However, this would, of course, increase the false-positive rate as well.

A second reason for the lack of repeatability is that different cytologists reading the same slides report different results (Seybolt and Johnson, 1971; Lambourne and Lederer, 1973; Evans, Shelley, Cleary et al., 1974). Kern and Zivolich (1977) had two cytologists, four cytotechnologists, and four cytotechnology students examine 112 slides from 60 subjects. They found a high correlation among readers for dysplasia, but "significant disagreement" with 38% of the carcinomas in situ and 44% of the invasive carcinomas.

Data on false-positive rates are not available since one would need as a denominator a group of women known by a definitive method (surgery) to be free from cervical dysplasia, carcinoma in situ, or invasive carcinoma. To our knowledge, no estimates have been made of the false-positive rate either by direct means (such as assembling a group of women who have had hysterectomies for reasons unrelated to findings on the Pap test) or by indirect means. As noted earlier, even low false-positive rates in a disease of low prevalence result in high numbers of disease-free women being misidentified, thus creating high follow-up costs and unnecessary anxiety.

The problems of accurate assessment of the disease extend not only to the cervical screening but also to the diagnostic tool of biopsy. Inter-observer variation among pathologists has been frequently documented (Siegler, 1956; Kirkland, 1963; Cocker, Fox, and Langley, 1968; Lambourne and Lederer, 1973). For instance, in comparing histological diagnoses made by the pathologists submitting the specimens and by a panel of expert pathologists, Brudnell, Cox, and Taylor (1973) revealed disagreement in 32% of the 728 specimens examined. Moreover, the submitting pathologists were more likely to rank the specimens as being of greater severity (carcinoma in situ) while the panel of expert pathologists tended to rank them as dysplasia or other bland epithelial abnormalities. Brudnell et al. estimated a possible 150 unjustified hysterectomies out of their sample of 728 specimens. Hulme and Eisenberg (1968) found that pathologists were well aware of the variability, with one pathologist quoted as saying: "One man's CIS [carcinoma in situ] is another man's dysplasia."

Furthermore, there is also debate as to whether carcinoma in situ is really cancer or merely a frequent precursor. Dr. Lewis Robbins (1977) described some of the reasons for the confusion:

> The Pap smear isn't diagnosing cancer, it's diagnosing a precursor. Why do they call it cancer then? Because nobody would pay attention to it when they would call it a dysplasia . . . if you call it carcinoma-in-situ then they will examine it, do something with it.
>
> I remember a battle royal at Roswell Park in 1946. . . . The pathologist was saying that the Pap smear is no good. But [one physician in the group] said carcinoma-in-situ is not cancer but we have to call it cancer. The pathologist said we can't call it cancer if it doesn't metastasize or if it hasn't already metastasized. Well, they did.

If carcinoma in situ is a precursor of invasive cancer, then this would be demonstrated in the natural history. However, as Dunn (1977) pointed out in an interview:

> We are still arguing whether in situ is a pre-cancer or not. You know, pathologists got to the point they hated to say carcinoma in situ, because carcinoma has meant one thing to a surgeon—you take it out. The pathologist had a surgical specimen. He wasn't sure whether it was a cancer if it were an in-situ lesion.

In summary, the test is acceptable to most women and simple to administer, but its accuracy and reliability have been insufficiently documented. The available evidence is not encouraging.

3. Does cervical cancer have a recognizable latent or early presymptomatic state, and is its natural progression from latent to declared disease well understood?

It is assumed that dysplasia proceeds to carcinoma in situ, which in turn proceeds to invasive cancer. However, the frequency with which each of these progressions occurs is unknown. Moreover, diagnostic biopsies applied to the suspicious lesion may themselves alter the natural course of the disease.

Some suggestive data on the relationship between carcinoma in situ and invasive cancer have been derived from establishing correlations of socioeconomic status between groups with the two conditions (Wakefield, Yule, Smith et al., 1973). Other evidence for association of carcinoma in situ and invasive cancer was gathered by Cramer (1974)· the average age of women with carcinoma in situ is lower than that of women with invasive cancer; retrospective studies have revealed some overlooked cases of carcinoma in situ in invasive cancer; carcinoma in situ is often seen at the margins of frankly invasive lesions; and serial sectioning of carcinoma in situ specimens has revealed some stromal invasion on occasion.

The Canadian Task Force (1976), in summarizing all previous studies, concluded that the natural history of cervical cancer passed through three stages: dysplasia, carcinoma in situ, and invasive cancer, with the process taking perhaps 35 years. This is inferred from the evidence that the peak incidence of each of these stages occurs at progressively higher ages.

This indirect evidence is, however, insufficient. Some direct longitudinal studies have also been carried out. In Copenhagen, of 127 patients with diagnosed carcinoma in situ who were not treated, 33% had developed invasive cancer during a 9-year period (Peterson, 1956). Two other studies by Spriggs (1971) and Kinlen and Spriggs (1978) traced women in England with positive Pap tests (defined as invasive cancer or carcinoma in situ) who had refused biopsies. In the latter study, of 60 women so traced, one-third had negative tests an average of 5.2 years later, although all the women whose positive test regressed were under the age of 40 at the time of the first test. Kinlen and Spriggs concluded (1978:464):

> If these cases are representative, then one-third of the biopsies (usually cones) done in Britain because of positive cervical cytology are performed for lesions which are insignificant or would have disappeared if left alone.

These studies, because of their small samples and possibly self-selected populations are not totally reliable, and for ethical reasons, they are hard to replicate. Nevertheless, they indicate that regression can occur and that progression is not inevitable.

Nor does dysplasia always lead to carcinoma in situ. Stern and Neely (1963) found that dysplasia could appear rapidly and also regress, though it tended to appear again. In a study of women having shown dysplasia on a Pap test 1 to 7 years previously, 48% remained dysplastic, 40% regressed to normalcy, 11% progressed to carcinoma in situ, and 1% progressed to invasive cancer. Hall and Walton (1968) reported higher progression rates, 29% for those with severe dysplasia over a period of 1 to 14 years. Here again, it is likely that women with dysplasia are at a considerably higher risk for carcinoma in situ, but the progression is by no means certain.

Even if one assumes that the tumors do progress some of the time, the question still remains as to how quickly they grow. Great variation has been noted in the rate of growth of cervical tumors (Pederson, Høeg, and Kolstadt, 1971). A screening program offers the opportunity to identify slow-growing tumors with a long pre-invasive phase rather than fast-growing ones that quickly cause symptoms. With other forms of cancer, such as breast and lung, these fast-growing tumors unfortunately have been the ones associated with the worst prognosis (Charlson and Feinstein, 1974; Wells and Feinstein, 1977), and there is no reason to believe that this would not apply to cancer of the cervix as well. Unless tests are carried out every few months, these fast-growing tumors will be missed in screening programs.

In summary, women with cervical dysplasia are at higher risk for carcinoma in situ, and women with carcinoma in situ are at higher risk for invasive carcinoma. These progressions do not always occur, however, and certainly not at a constant rate. Much remains to be learned about the natural history of cervical cancer.

4. Are diagnosis and treatment available and acceptable to the public? Is treatment for cervical cancer effective?

Recommended treatment procedures have changed over time. By 1977, the usual procedure following a "positive" finding from a Pap test was a biopsy. In recent years, this biopsy has been recommended to be carried out using colposcopy (visualization and magnification of the cervix 15×). This is an office procedure and is more accurate than other types of biopsy. Other office procedures for excision of lesions include cryotherapy and electrocautery (Homesley, 1977). Before extensive use of colposcopy, and in the many areas where physicians trained in colposcopy are not available, the usual procedure has been to carry out a conization (removal of part of the cervix), which requires hospitalization. The extent to which colposcopy is available in the United States is not well known. Although most expert pathologists agree that it is not good practice to move directly from positive Pap tests to cone biopsies or to cryosurgery, or from punch biopsies to hysterectomies, the actual frequencies with which such procedures take place are unknown.

For cases of invasive carcinoma confirmed on biopsy, the usual procedure is total hysterectomy. Cases of carcinoma in situ may be treated by conization or cryosurgery if the woman is interested in future child bearing, but more likely by a total hysterectomy. In recent years, physicians in major medical centers have recommended not doing hysterectomies for cases of mild or moderate dysplasia but maintaining follow-up through colposcopic evaluation, biopsies, and further Pap tests. Since the patterns of diagnosis and treatment following positive Pap tests have not been surveyed in this country, it is difficult to know whether these recommendations represent actual practice or a sought-after ideal. Both biopsies and hysterectomies seem to have been well accepted by the medical profession and the public. For the most part, facilities have been available throughout the country.

The method of treatment of certain types of lesions has been debated. For example, Hulme and Eisenberg (1968) found that Connecticut hospitals varied in their treatment of micro-invasive carcinoma that is histologically on a spectrum between carcinoma in situ and invasive carcinoma. Two-fifths of the hospitals treated it as carcinoma in situ, an equal proportion treated it as invasive cancer, and the rest had no consistent policy. The issue in micro-invasive carcinoma (which goes by many different names), of whether to perform a radical or simple hysterectomy, is not easily resolved (Burghardt and Holzer, 1977; Benson and Norris, 1977).

Whether present treatment methods are effective has not been satisfactorily shown. The American Cancer Society, in its pamphlets to the public (1975), emphasized that, when pre-cancerous conditions and carcinoma in situ were detected sufficiently early, treatment was almost 100% successful. Several studies, however, have cited recurrences of carcinoma in situ or invasive cancer following treatment by either conization or hysterectomy (McIndoe and Green, 1969; Kolstad, 1970; Creasman and Rutledge, 1972). Kolstad and Klem (1976) estimated a 2% recurrence rate over a 10-year period following either hysterectomy or conization for carcinoma in situ. For most women, the disease recurred within 3 years, and the form of treatment seemed irrelevant.

The ultimate goal of mass screening for cervical cancer is to reduce mortality from this disease. Since adequate trials of the efficacy of the Pap test were not established when screening programs were first implemented, and since controlled randomized trials are now considered to be unethical, one has to conclude what one can from trends in mortality rates in areas where screening programs have been in effect, compared to areas without formal screening programs. This comparison is complicated by differences that may be due to other confounding variables such as socioeconomic status, by inadequacies in the reporting of mortality statistics (Feinstein, 1968), and by the knowledge that mortality rates for uterine cancer were decreasing before the Pap test was widely used.[5]

Analyses of trends in mortality rates for cervical cancer in areas where the Pap test is widely used have produced varying results, both when such areas are studied by themselves (Dickinson et al., 1972a and 1972b) or when such areas are compared to localities with lower Pap screening rates (Christopherson, Parker, Mendez et al., 1970; Ahluwalia and Doll, 1968; Kinlen and Doll, 1973; Cramer, 1974; Grünfeld, Horwitz, and Lysgaard-Hansen, 1975; MacGregor and Teper, 1978). However, it seems that in areas where the Pap test has been extensively used for a long enough period of time, there is a small but real decrease in mortality rates attributable to the Pap test. Even then, Pap screening programs have not been responsible for a substantial reduction in mortality.

Perhaps the most useful, although by no means conclusive, study was reported from Canada. Miller, Lindsay, and Hill (1976) studied mortality trends at the county and census division levels in

---

[5]Until 1949, mortality rates reported for uterine cancer combined the two parts of the uterus (the corpus and the cervix). Cervical, rather than corpus, cancer almost certainly accounted for most of the decrease in mortality rates before 1949.

Canadian provinces according to the intensity of screening activity; they also took into account census-derived indices of socioeconomic status that were known to be related to the incidence of cervical cancer. They found that, although much of the variation in mortality rates for cervical cancer from one area to another could be attributed to factors other than the intensity of screening, and although there was little evidence that screening brought about any decrease in mortality rates from 1950–52 to 1960–62, screening programs did contribute significantly to the overall reduction in mortality between 1960–62 and 1970–72.

None of these investigators took into account how much of the decrease in mortality from cervical cancer could be attributed to the increasing frequency of hysterectomies: this would, of course, mean that fewer uteri are at risk for developing cervical cancer. Estimates of the effect of hysterectomies on the decline of cervical cancer mortality rates vary from 10% (Lyon and Gardner, 1977) to 25% (Stern, Misczynski, Greenland et al., 1977).

Finally, none of the studies showing the effect of screening on cervical cancer mortality has been differentiated by recommended screening intervals for individual women. In Aberdeen, for example, women are recalled for screening every 5 years (MacGregor, 1976), while in British Columbia (Ahluwalia and Doll, 1968; Kinlen and Doll, 1973) and Louisville (Christopherson et al., 1970), the intervals are closer, but not specified. Yet all three programs report mortality rate decreases. Also, it is not always clear whether these screening programs include mostly women who are under medical surveillance anyway, or whether they attract high risk women who would otherwise not be screened.

5. Is the cost of case-finding through screening politically and socially acceptable?

A necessary condition for any effective program is that individual and social benefits from the screening procedures outweigh the costs such programs generate. Different ways of assessing costs and benefits have been tried with varying intensity and interest on both sides of the Atlantic and, at least in Britain and Canada, they have generated much debate. The issue is not so much whether the Pap test should be used, but who should be screened and with what frequency.

United Kingdom. In 1968, Knox in Britain had raised the issues of the cost of screening and suggested that the cost of preventing a clinical carcinoma would be £1000, about the same as the cost of treating it. In 1972, a *Lancet* editorial stated that large investments in screening at best would be likely to reduce mortality over a long period of time by only about 50%. (These latter findings were based on Knox's work.)

The next year, the *British Medical Journal* (1973) followed with an even stronger statement: "It is not a question of proving that screening has *no* value . . . but of deciding whether it has sufficient value to justify the risks and effort it entails" (italics in the original). This editorial prompted two defensive responses upholding the effectiveness of screening in reducing mortality: Christopherson (1974) cited studies in Louisville, Kentucky; and MacGregor (1974) cited data from Aberdeen, Scotland showing that the mortality rate in that area had been falling more rapidly than in the rest of the U.K.

Meanwhile, Brudnell, Cox, and Taylor (1973) had raised issues about unjustified hysterectomies because of improperly read histological specimens, and Richards (1974) had indirectly raised the issue of the personal costs of hysterectomy. Richards found that hysterectomy patients reported that an average of 11.9 months had elapsed before they felt completely convalesced, while a comparison group of women who underwent other forms of major surgery reported an average of 3 months. Certainly, this was an area in which little research had previously been done and demonstrated a concern not only for monetary costs but for personal costs as well.

The concern for costs and a conservative approach remained strong in Britain. Holland (1974) concluded that the *Lancet* series on screening "leaves the impression that total screening is hard to justify for any condition, save PKU." Randall (1974), in the same series, had stated that cervical cancer screening did satisfy most of the criteria for a selective screening program for high risk populations, but the wrong people were being screened.

These concerns were reflected in suggestions that doctors examining women under 35 years old be less zealous in taking repeat smears if there were no symptoms (Brindle, Wakefield, and Yule, 1976). The same year Knox (1976), using a more complex model than he had in 1968, concluded that a series of 10 screening tests for women between the ages of 35 and 80 years would be optimal and capable of preventing about 77% of all deaths from cervical cancer.

These calculations were made with the acknowledgment that much factual information, such as error rates and natural history of the disease, was still lacking and could noticeably alter conclusions. Nevertheless, in Britain, one could detect a clear trend toward less frequent use of screening because of its questionable effectiveness, its monetary costs, and its personal and social costs through high hysterectomy rates.

United States. In the United States, the debate on costs was unfolding differently, with the question of social costs or benefits receiving less attention. A program analysis by the Department of Health, Education, and Welfare as early as 1966 had suggested that one would save $1000 per case by treating carcinoma in situ early rather than invasive cancer when it appeared later (U.S. Department of Health, Education, and Welfare, 1966). Based on persons appearing for screening and treatment at the Mayo Clinic, Dickinson (1972c) found that money could not be saved by screening activity.

Another approach (Schneider and Twiggs, 1972) had been to estimate the annual costs of screening and not screening a theoretical population of 100,000 women. The authors concluded (1972: 857) that the only practical way to limit costs was to reduce the number of smears taken to one every 3 years in order to "relieve the overburdened health worker of the tyranny of the tedious 'Annual Pap and Pelvic'."

These last two estimates of costs and benefits were based on false-negative rates under 10%. In fact, the rates have been much higher. Estimating a 40% false negative rate, Coppelson and Brown (1974) concluded that the cost of delivering screening and follow-up services to 80% of the eligible women in America would amount to $1 billion, or 1% of the annual U.S. health expenditures.

In actual practice, monetary costs in the United States had been higher than one might expect, although most of these costs have not been formally reported. During 1974, 484,773 Connecticut women (American Cancer Society, Connecticut Division, 1976) had Pap tests at a cost of about $2.6 million for laboratory work alone.[6] This is about the same as the state expended annually for all its public maternal and child health services. The cost per case of cancer

---

[6]If we add to this the cost to the woman of $25 to visit the gynecologist, the total cost is $6 million.

detected, including invasive cancer, carcinoma in situ, and adenocarcinoma, was $3322, and this did not include the costs of the diagnostic biopsies.

The New England Journal of Medicine (1976) in an editorial raised the issue of whether the wrong women were being screened, since it was the middle-class low-risk women who were coming in for Pap tests, while the low-income high-risk women were not being seen in clinics. Six months later the same journal reported a round table discussion of the personal costs of the hysterectomies that usually follow a diagnosis of carcinoma in situ and sometimes even dysplasia. In this discussion, Cole (1976) noted that the discounted cost of providing women over 45 years with prophylactic hysterectomies to prevent future cancer would be about $9800 per year of life saved. The disadvantages would be the mortality rate of hysterectomies (estimated at 0.06% to 0.2%), and possible adverse metabolic and endocrine effects. Cole concluded that the benefits of hysterectomy for the purpose of cancer prophylaxis were insufficient to justify costs. Notman (1976) pointed out that a high rate of severe mental depression seemed to follow hysterectomies, and these effects were of sufficient importance that they should be taken into account and studied further.

Despite the comments on costs, despite the concern for excessive hysterectomies, and despite suggestions that screening should be carried out less frequently, many groups in the United States continued to support the annual Pap test. The recommendations of the Workshop on Uterine-Cervical Cancer in 1973 (Koss and Phillips, 1974) had called for cervical smears for all nonvirginal women (the designation by sexual activity rather than by age was a welcome recognition of at least one etiologic agent for the disease), and suggested that a cervical smear be done on all hospital in- and outpatients unless the patient had participated in a cytologic survey the previous year. The only concession on the question of cost came when the Workshop noted that "routine annual cytologic examinations cannot be justified economically in all patients." But having said that, the Workshop reneged: "This Panel cannot at this time make a firm recommendation about the frequency of cytologic examinations beyond the currently accepted annual interval." In essence, annual examinations were too costly but the panel refused to consider other options and continued, at least tacitly, to approve the annual exam.

As for social and personal costs, the Workshop recognized them in regard to dysplasia: "These lesions should be managed in the fashion most consistent with the well-being of the patient and, if appropriate, the preservation of her reproductive function." It is difficult to see how a physician would translate this general and ambiguous policy into practice.

One can get some inkling of the physician's expected response to this controversy from the *Journal of Family Practice*, an American journal devoted to disseminating information to family physicians. A 1975 review of the cervical screening literature (none more recent than 1969) pointed out that previous studies "suggest that cancer of the cervix is a slowly progressive disease requiring 5–10 years to progress from dysplasia to invasive carcinoma" (Frame and Carlson, 1975). The authors did not indicate that the progression did not always occur, nor that duration of the progression was not well established and probably the duration was longer than they indicated. One wonders how such statements influenced physicians in their decisions to perform or recommend total hysterectomies. However, the authors did diverge from the traditional annual Pap test philosophy by recommending the test be used only every other year.

The American Cancer Society had continued to stress the annual Pap test in its lay and professional publications. Moreover, it confused the public by implying that the Pap test was aimed at the detection of uterine cancer as a whole rather than just cervical cancer. The Pap test, as a rule, is designed to detect cancer only of the uterine cervix, the neck of the uterus. Moreover, uterine cancers other than those of the cervix at present have higher incidence and mortality rates. The following statements were made:

> If every woman had the test every year, most uterine cancer could be discovered in time for cure (American Cancer Society, 1968).

> A Pap test regularly, once each year, is the way to help protect yourself (American Cancer Society, 1973).

> The choice of a screening interval depends upon many complex factors, but is generally chosen to be one year (Nelson, Averette, and Richart, 1975).

> Each year, on some regular date, have a thorough health checkup . . . including a Pap test (American Cancer Society, 1976).

The American Cancer Society also noted that: "Total abdominal hysterectomy is, without question, the most commonly used form of definitive treatment" (Nelson et al., 1975). If analysts were raising questions about costs, frequency of screening, and excessive hysterectomies, they were not being heard in the public forum.

Canada. Canada, like the United States, had had a long running cervical cancer screening program. It had also supported epidemiological research. Unlike their counterparts in the United States, however, Canadian researchers had begun to question the value of all types of screening programs, perhaps in response to their universal provincial health insurance programs and high health costs (Sackett, 1975). Spitzer and Brown (1975) questioned whether a program of biannual health exams for all persons in the Province of Ontario would be worth the costs, considering how little was known about the benefits. He was more optimistic about the benefits of the Pap test.

However, the Pap test was already under scrutiny by a task force appointed by the Canadian government to produce a report on one of several programs and health care activities "whose effectiveness was in doubt" (Canadian Task Force, 1976: 981). Known as the "Walton Report" and published in June, 1976, it carefully reviewed the scientific evidence on the effectiveness of the Pap test, its availability, accuracy, and costs. It recommended for women at low risk Pap tests 1 year apart, then tests at 3-year intervals (if the earlier tests were negative) until the age of 35 years, and then Pap tests at 5-year intervals until the age of 60. High risk women, who were identified as those of low income, with early onset of sexual activity and multiple sexual partners, were recommended for annual screenings, but it was recognized that these women were the hardest to reach.[7]

Reactions to the Walton Report. The reaction to the report was swift in Canada and Great Britain, and lethargic in the United States. In Canada, the report had been published in the *Canadian Medical Association Journal* so that it received immediate and wide

---

[7]Whether users of oral contraceptives should be included among high risk women is subject to debate. At present, the evidence is unclear as to whether users of oral contraceptives are at high risk independently of other risk factors (World Health Organization, 1978).

coverage in the professional and the lay press. Although it acknowledged the scientific merits of the report, The Society of Obstetricians and Gynecologists was the group most unhappy with the reduction in frequency of screening (Schmidt, 1977: 972).

> The periodic examination is the mainstay of our present health care delivery system and . . . annual cytologic screening of the cervix is a reasonable safeguard against cancer.

Nevertheless, because of the vast publicity, Canadian women were informed of the need for less frequent Pap tests.

In Great Britain, reaction came in the form of editorials in both the *Lancet* (1976) and *British Medical Journal* (1976) within a few months of publication of the Report. Both journals summarized and commended the findings. Since annual Pap tests had never been a part of British policy, no changes were required, although the findings did help support those who had been concerned with the high costs of screening.

In the United States, the Walton Report was not so much disputed as ignored. An editorial in November in the *Journal of the American Medical Association* (Danilevicius, 1976) suggested that at least in the United States, based on the Louisville studies and some New York studies, the screening programs had potential for decreasing morbidity and mortality, and that "the natural history of carcinoma of the cervix . . . as well as the anatomic availability [*sic*] of the cervix for repeated examination are circumstances particularly suited to a screening program." Danilevicius concluded (1976:2099):

> Using consultations with gynecologists and availing themselves of the cytologic expertise of pathologists, the majority of primary care physicians could include all their female patients in successful, continuous cervical cancer screening and prevention programs.

It was as if the Walton Report had triggered a response of recommending increased rather than decreased screening activity.

At the end of September, 1976, the Cancer Control Division of the National Cancer Institute sponsored a conference on the "state of the art" of cervical cancer screening. The issue of costs was raised only in terms of reimbursement for Pap tests and follow-up by third party payers. Overall program costs were not addressed. The issue of frequency of screening was also raised. At the meeting, it seemed as if a consensus had emerged that annual screening should be continued. However, even though draft reports circulated informally, the conference had still not issued a final report by mid-1978, and it seemed unlikely that one would emerge. This indecisiveness may itself have been an indication of the impact of the Walton Report.

Since 1976, there has been a tendency among certain health professionals to move away from clear statements of recommended annual tests. With the annual health examination being questioned as well, Breslow and Somers (1977) suggested a lifetime health-monitoring program by which, for example, women 40 to 59 years of age would have a Pap test at 2- or 3-year intervals rather than annually. Even the American Cancer Society (1977: 17) rephrased its recommendations to suggest that: "Uterine cancer could be reduced dramatically as a cause of death if every woman had a Pap test with her regular health checkup . . . " Again, the term "uterine cancer" was used rather than cervical cancer, leading to confusion as to what the Pap test actually detects.

For the most part, however, Americans view the benefits of annual screening for all women as accepted dogma. The firm convictions of most health professionals are reflected in statements such as the following:

> Deaths from carcinoma of the cervix could be dramatically reduced if every adult woman had a Pap test annually. (Homesley, 1977)

These convictions have been communicated, as well, by the lay press:

> Young women should have an annual pelvic exam which includes a Pap smear. (*Glamour,* 1978)

> Getting rid of the concept that most people need a complete annual checkup would probably reduce our national health budget by several million dollars. (Let me add one caveat here. Most doctors still believe that women over 30 should have regular—probably annual—Pap smears, a test for cancer of the cervix, particularly if they are on the Pill.) (Nolen, 1978)

> Pelvic cancer cannot be seen or felt by a woman, therefore it is terribly important to have a Pap test at least once a year, starting at first menstruation or at least at first sexual activity. (Ask Beth, 1978)

In the United States, the political and social costs of screening are apparently acceptable. The annual program is not only accepted by women who pay the costs, but also by politicians in Congress who sponsor the program for those who cannot pay for it themselves. However, the costs in the United States have for the most part been hidden and ill defined. In contrast, Britain and Canada have found the political and social costs of an annual program unacceptable.

Persistence of Screening Policy

Why does annual screening persist as a policy in the United States if it is of dubious value?

What accounts for the differing points of view among British, Canadian, and American policy makers, and also among researchers themselves about their findings? One factor, already noted, is the state of the art, which is not as far advanced as those who work with the techniques or their results would like.

The second factor is the political environment for screening programs. To understand why the policy of an annual Pap test for all women over 20 years persists, we must examine the context for health policy-making in the United States. Screening enters the political context as soon as someone must pay for services not previously provided. For cytological screening in the United States, the individual woman pays for her visit and laboratory test, but laboratories, hospitals, screening programs, and cytologists in training have all been supported by public funds. Thus, public and private decisions are being made simultaneously. In Britain, and more recently, in Canada, virtually all funds for screening come out of the public purse one way or another. When funding for a screening program is mainly public, it is easier to assess competing priorities and determinations of need.

A program of dubious value such as the annual Pap test requires a fertile environment and an interested group of supporters in order to flourish. In the United States, the annual Pap test has had both. The fertile environment has been provided by American ideology, and the supporters have been a group most notably associated with the American Cancer Society. The contrasts between Britain and the United States help to illustrate how these factors have affected screening policy.

First, American ideology has always favored novelty and entrepreneurship. More than 150 years ago, de Toqueville (1955: 443) wrote that in America the idea of novelty is "indissolubly connected with the idea of amelioration." Americans often proceed with programs without assessing costs and benefits. Wilson (1963) noted that, whereas the British have emphasized the need for validating methods, Americans have tended to carry out screening before knowledge was great.

The number of new technologies implemented without appropriate clinical trials continues to grow in the United States and to be of some concern (Iglehart, 1977). Some, such as computerized tomography (CT scan), have been introduced regardless of the high costs of their use. Although Great Britain was the first country to pioneer these machines, they are not yet accepted there as standard equipment and, because of their costs, will probably not be for some time, if ever. In contrast, in the United States, hospitals and clinics throughout the country are vying with one another to purchase these expensive machines. Supporters say that new, important, and undreamed of uses have been discovered since the CT scanners were put into place. This may be a case where invention becomes the mother of necessity.

Other technologies may not only be costly, but potentially harmful as well. Coronary artery bypass surgery is so well established that about 60,000 operations are carried out yearly without the technique ever having been subjected to controlled trials to test its efficacy (Preston, 1977). The American rate of these operations is more than 10 times that of Great Britain or other western European countries.

American reactions to new technologies tend to be: Do what can be done, not do what needs to be done. The British tend to be conservative in their screening decisions: Do no harm. Americans think differently on social costs, as Hampshire (1976) noted:

> There is a notorious difference between Britain and the United States ... a deep difference, both of conscious feeling and unconscious strategy. The political argument between the parties in Britain typically circles around the question, How can we minimize the worst possible outcome being realized? In the United States the question is apt to be, How can we maximize the chances of the best possible outcome?

Second, the American political scene has traditionally been viewed by its analysts as an arena where competing interest groups with varying strengths, resources, and interests determine what policy is made (Truman, 1958). This viewpoint may be helpful in understanding the American commitment to mass screening. One distinguishing feature of the American health establishment is that it has been backed by a powerful lobby, the American Cancer Society (ACS), which has mobilized to promote cancer research, screening, and treatment. Its lobbying effort resulted in the establishment by federal law of the National Cancer Institute (NCI) in 1937. During the 1950s and 1960s, lobbying by the ACS and others was so successful that Congress during this period continuously raised appropriations of the National Institutes of Health (NIH), of which the NCI was a part, beyond the requests made by its own director (Strickland, 1972).

The ACS also played a key role in promoting the Pap test as the major and perhaps only cancer control device available (Breslow, 1977, I: 220). It sponsored the first interdisciplinary conference in 1948 and was (ibid., I: 225): "instrumental in providing the support necessary for establishing numerous cytology screening programs and cancer detection centers throughout the United States." In 1957, the ACS launched its "Uterine Cancer Year" which, with great publicity, was designed to promote the use of the Pap test for annual screening.

Meanwhile, the NCI had formed a cancer control branch which worked very closely with the ACS and supported screening projects at first to assess their feasibility and then, with the Louisville project, to attempt to demonstrate their impact on mortality (ibid., I: 225–232).

American Cancer Society activities culminated in the National Cancer Act of 1971. The "War against Cancer" was viewed with the same fervor as a moon shot or the development of the atomic bomb (Rettig, 1977), and the rhetoric was not always grounded in fact. The National Panel of Consultants on the Conquest of Cancer (1971: 42), a blue ribbon panel of scientific experts and distinguished laymen, reported to Congress:

> On a world-wide basis, cervix cancer is the most common form of cancer in women. Among all women in the United States, it is second only to cancer of the breast and, in low income groups, it is even more prevalent than breast cancer.

Figures elsewhere in the report as well as other sources, however, indicated that this statement was untrue. Yet, it has been widely cited. The Panel also maintained that studies had demonstrated incidence and mortality from cervical cancer could be greatly reduced if every woman were tested annually (ibid.: 42), even though the best data at the time could not confirm this.

When the National Cancer Act had been passed in 1971, a sub-interest group had wanted funds for the cancer control division that had supported Pap test screening programs and that had been phased out by NCI and NIH nearly 2 years earlier. This cancer control group had a staunch champion in Representative Paul Rogers (1972: 495), the Chairman of the House Subcommittee on Health and the Environment, who said about the cervical cancer control program: "This screening and testing was and is the most effective tool we have in fighting cancer." Partially in response to the efforts of a "working Group 8," which was formed to advise NCI on cancer control, in 1974 Congress amended the National Cancer Act to include (Section 409a): "programs to provide appropriate trials of programs of routine exfoliative cytology tests conducted for the diagnosis of uterine cancer."[8] Authorizations of $55 million for fiscal 1975 rose to $89 million by fiscal 1977.

The ultimate and worthy goal of the ACS is to eliminate cancer. Meanwhile, it must keep the disease highly visible in order to raise funds for its many campaigns. Thus, its policy to encourage mass screening programs also supports the organization's viability and visibility. Through the Society's efforts, screening for cervical cancer becomes national policy without any member of the public speaking for it and without the whole-hearted endorsement of epidemiologists. One should not be surprised that the ACS, with its $100 million budget, is concerned primarily with eliminating cancer, but the American public is hard pressed to counterbalance the ACS's powerful appeal with its own weaker public interests such as social, personal, and economic costs.

---

[8]Exfoliative cytology had to be specifically cited because the 1971 Act had been interpreted to mean that NCI's activities in cancer control were to be limited to new techniques. Hence, the Pap test, as an old technique, was excluded. The 1978 Cancer Act amendments, which removed this earlier ambiguity about new and old tests, therefore dropped the specific reference to exfoliative cytology or any other procedure (Rogers, 1978).

Given these political and ideological constraints, a change in policy seems unlikely even if new technological information were uncovered in the near future. The only change could come if health professionals, politicians, and the public itself were to think in terms of nationwide social and economic costs, and about competing priorities, and in terms of minimizing monetary and personal costs as well as maximizing benefits.

Conclusions

As currently constituted, screening programs for cancer of the cervix do not meet the criteria for mass screening annually of all sexually active women. In fact, both the Walton report and Knox's (1976) studies indicated the desirability of discouraging annual tests for women with several negative Pap tests and those who are at low risk for cervical cancer. Thus, the extensive advertising for annual tests should be stopped. The frequency with which women in different risk groups should be tested needs to be reconsidered, in light of the Canadian and British experience. Screening programs would also be more effective if studies were carried out concurrently to improve the readings of the tests and to minimize the number of unnecessary biopsies and hysterectomies.

In the United States the issue remains: Who should have a Pap test and how often? This is no longer just an issue between a woman and her doctor. Much of the use of the Pap test is now mandated by state and federal law. In many parts of the country, hospitals are required to carry out a Pap test on any woman admitted who has not had one during the previous 3 years. Federal regulations require federally-funded family planning clinics to take annual Pap tests on women requesting any type of birth control device, despite a very low yield of positive results.

Theoretically, one should not make policy without facts. Yet the present annual Pap test policy was made without reference even to those facts that were readily available. A new policy should now be instituted; enough information can be collected to make it feasible to do this within a year. Haste is appropriate, since no new policy is also policy—bad policy.

The most rapid and satisfactory mechanism for changing policy in this case would be a national task force charged with determining the appropriate standards and guidelines for using the Pap test for women of different ages and different risk groups. To operate effectively, such a body would have to be immune from many of the political pressures discussed earlier. This immunity would be best assured if the task force were located in a scientifically accepted and highly prestigious organization not already committed to the promotion of the Pap test program. The National Academy of Sciences comes to mind as one particularly appropriate organization. A second choice would be the National Institutes of Health. (Although the NIH have lodged within them the responsibility of cancer control programs, they have managed to maintain a fair degree of detachment at higher levels.)

The task force should be composed of experts in the fields of epidemiology, oncology, biostatistics, pathology, gynecology, economics, and policy analysis. If such understanding is not otherwise possessed within its specialist membership, the task force should include additional experienced persons sensitive to the special social and mental, as well as physical, problems women encounter in their roles as consumers of medical care. The task force should address itself both to immediate policy needs and to more long-term research requirements. Within 1 year of its formation, the task force should be able to use the basic findings of research undertaken to date to provide guidelines for physicians, clinics, and women as to the frequency with which the Pap test should be administered for different population risk groups during the next 4 or 5 years. The guidelines the task force will recommend after its year of deliberation are by no means clear-cut. As a *Lancet* editorial (1978: 1030) recently pointed out:

> Not enough is known for firm conclusions to be drawn about the best time for screening to begin and the best time for subsequent smears to be taken.

The editorial continued that a review was also needed of screening policy in the United Kingdom, particularly in the light of the fact that the British do not recommend screening women under 35 years of age even though women under this age appear to have an increasing incidence of cervical cancer.

Among the risk populations to be considered should be, first, all women with symptoms, then women of low income, women with early onset of sexual activity, and women with multiple sexual partners. Consideration should be given as to whether women taking oral contraceptives and women whose mothers took diethylstilbestrol (DES) during pregnancy should be included in high risk groups. The policy guidelines should be set in terms of overall epidemiological assessment of benefits and risks and costs to populations, not in terms of individual cases. Cost-effectiveness studies, such as those undertaken by Knox (1976), should be reviewed. If insufficient, others should be commissioned.

It is most important that the task force consider the Pap test in terms of its effectiveness in combatting cervical cancer, not in terms of its possible value as a means of luring women to gynecologists' offices once a year so that other examinations can be carried out. If reasons exist why all women should be seen annually by a gynecologist, or anyone else, then these reasons should be demonstrated independently through epidemiological evidence.

Meanwhile, the task force should have undertaken the equally important job of reviewing the status of research in the field of cervical cancer and should set in motion the research that would establish the following information: what is the reliability of the Pap test under normal as opposed to special research conditions? What are the true costs of a screening program, not only in terms of screening costs, but also in terms of diagnosis and follow-up treatment for all women in the United States? What diagnoses and treatments actually follow from positive Pap smears in the United States? This latter study will necessitate surveys of what constitutes a positive Pap smear in a sample of various rural and urban, university and non-university medical care centers in the United States, as well as surveys of what diagnostic and treatment modality usually follows from such a positive smear—whether it is colposcopy, punch biopsies without colposcopy, conization, or whatever. Data on the cost of each procedure should also be collected.

The treatment and risks resulting from these diagnostic procedures should also be reviewed. Currently, there is a notable lack of knowledge about what diagnostic and treatment modalities are used around the United States. Particular attention should be paid to the proportion of carcinomas in situ for which hysterectomies are recommended. It has been suggested that recently physicians have tended to recommend fewer hysterectomies for women still of childbearing age; however, there is little documentary evidence on this point. In view of the evidence that carcinoma in situ sometimes regresses, hysterectomy may not always be the treatment of choice, since a hysterectomy has its own mental and physical risks. Treatment by hysterectomy should be more carefully monitored in the future, particularly if it remains such a frequently performed operation in the United States.

It is possible, even likely, that after all these studies have been collected, the task force may want to revise its recommendations on the Pap test. Such a possibility should in no way discourage the group from using present knowledge to improve inadequate policies.

The task force is suggested as a particular solution for the case of the Pap test, a program that has been in force for 30 years without ever having been subjected to clinical trials. Ideally, new technologies should be regularly reviewed through regularly established services such as the National Center for Health Technologies in the Department of Health, Education, and Welfare, newly mandated by Congress in 1978. Until such review is a matter of routine procedure, ad hoc bodies, such as the task force recommended here, are the most adequate review mechanisms.

The successful diffusion of the annual Pap test is an excellent example of the ease with which a new technology or device can be rapidly disseminated to a population within a short period of time when given a great deal of publicity. Its widespread acceptance may, in part, have been dependent on the fact that it was directed to women who, as a group, seem to be more willing than men to undergo medical examinations. This misguided success may serve as a source of cheer for those who despair of ever getting any technologies diffused. It might better serve as ample warning that all medical devices and techniques need to be tested for safety and efficacy before they are diffused.

For nearly 20 years, American women have been bombarded with information issued by public service advertising that they should be screened annually for cancer of the cervix. One cannot be surprised that those American women who could afford it have gone dutifully to their gynecologists for annual tests. They have no interest in dying from cancer of the cervix, and the annual Pap test promises a cure, if cancer is caught early enough.

When the information is not correct, however, the federal government must reassess its policies and protect its citizens from inappropriate use of doubtful procedures. There is now ample evidence that it should not be national policy to screen all women for cervical cancer every year. The time for a policy change is long overdue.

References

Ahluwalia, H. S., and Doll, R. 1968. Mortality from Cancer of the Cervix Uteri in British Columbia and Other Parts of Canada. *British Journal of Preventive and Social Medicine* 22: 161–164.

American Cancer Society. 1968. *Cancer of the Uterus.* New York: American Cancer Society.

———. 1973. *Stay Healthy: Learn About Uterine Cancer.* New York: American Cancer Society.

———. 1975. *1976 Cancer Facts and Figures.* New York: American Cancer Society.

———. 1976. *Cancer Facts for Women.* New York: American Cancer Society.

———. 1977. *1978 Cancer Facts and Figures.* New York: American Cancer Society.

American Cancer Society, Connecticut Division. 1976. *Cytology Services in Connecticut, 1970–1974.* Woodbridge, Conn.: American Cancer Society.

Ask Beth. 1978. See Doctor. *New Haven Register* (April 28): 25.

Benson, W. L., and Norris, H. J. 1977. A Critical Review of the Frequency of Lymph Node Metastasis and Death from Microinvasive Carcinoma of the Cervix. *Obstetrics and Gynecology* 49 (May): 632–638.

Breslow, L. 1977. A History of Cancer Control in the U.S. with Emphasis on the Period 1946–1971. 4 vols. Los Angeles, Calif.: University of California at Los Angeles School of Public Health.

———, and Somers, A. R. 1977. The Lifetime Health-Monitoring Program. *The New England Journal of Medicine* 296: 601–608.

Brindle, G., Wakefield, J. and Yule, R. 1976. Cervical Smears: Are the Right Women Being Examined? *British Medical Journal* 1: 1196–1197.

British Medical Journal. 1973. Editorial. Uncertainties of Cervical Cytology. 4: 501–502.

———. 1976. Editorial. Commentary on Walton Report. 2: 659–660.

Brudnell, M., Cox, B. S. and Taylor, C. W. 1973. The Management of Dysplasia, Carcinoma in Situ and Microcarcinoma of the Cervix. *Journal of Obstetrics and Gynaecology of the British Commonwealth* 80(8): 673–679.

Burghardt, E., and Holzer, E. 1977. Diagnosis and Treatment of Microinvasive Carcinoma of the Cervix Uteri. *Obstetrics and Gynecology* 49 (6): 641–653.

Canadian Task Force. 1976. Cervical Cancer Screening. (Walton Report). *Canadian Medical Association Journal* 114 (June 5): 1003–1033.

Charlson, M. E., and Feinstein, A. R. 1974. Auxometric Dimensions: A New Method for Using Rate of Growth in Prognostic Staging of Breast Cancer. *Journal of the American Medical Association* 228: 180–185.

Christopherson, W. M. 1974. Letter. Mass Screening for Cervical Cancer. *British Medical Journal* 1: 453.

_____, Parker, J. E., Mendez, W. M. et al. 1970. Cervix Cancer Death Rates and Mass Cytologic Screening. *Cancer* 26 (4): 808–811.

_____, Lundin, F. E., Jr., Mendez, W. M. et al. 1976. Cervical Cancer Control: A Study of Morbidity and Mortality Trends Over a Twenty-One-Year Period. *Cancer* 38 (3): 1357–1366.

Cochrane, A. L., and Holland, W. W. 1971. Validation of Screening Procedures. *British Medical Bulletin* 27 (1): 3–8.

Cocker, J., Fox, H., and Langley, F. A. 1968. Consistency in the Histological Diagnosis of Epithelial Abnormalities of the Cervix Uteri. *Journal of Clinical Pathology,* 21: 67–70.

Cole, P. 1976. Elective Hysterectomy: Pro and Con. *The New England Journal of Medicine* 295 (5): 264–266.

_____, and Morrison, A. S. 1978. Basic Issues in Cancer Screening. Paper presented at the International Union Against Cancer Workshop on Screening. Toronto, Canada, April 24–27, 1978.

Commission on Chronic Illness. 1957. *Chronic Illness in the United States.* Vol. 1. Cambridge, Mass: Harvard University Press.

Coppelson, L. W., and Brown, B. 1974. Estimates of the Screening Error Rate From the Observed Detection Rates in Repeated Cervical Cytology. *American Journal of Obstetrics and Gynecology* 119: 953–958.

Cramer, D. W. 1974. The Role of Cervical Cytology in the Declining Morbidity and Mortality of Cervical Cancer. *Cancer* 34 (6): 2018–2027.

Creasman, W. T., and Rutledge, F. 1972. Carcinoma *in-situ* of the Cervix: An Analysis of 861 Patients. *Obstetrics and Gynecology* 39: 373–380.

Danilevicius, Z. 1976. The Walton Report. Editorial. *Journal of the American Medical Association* 236: 2098–2099.

de Toqueville, A. 1955. *Democracy in America.* Vol. 1. New York: Vintage Books.

Dickinson, L. M., Mussey, E., Soule, E. H., and Kurland, L. T. 1972a. Evaluation of the Effectiveness of Cytologic Screening for Cervical Cancer. I. Incidence and Mortality Trends in Relation to Screening. *Mayo Clinic Proceedings* 47 (8): 534–544.

———, Mussey, E., and Kurland, L. T. 1972b. Evaluation of the Effectiveness of Cytologic Screening for Cervical Cancer. II. Survival Parameters Before and After Inception of Screening. *Mayo Clinic Proceedings* 47 (8): 545–549.

———. 1972c. Evaluation of the Effectiveness of Cytologic Screening for Cervical Cancer. III. Cost-Benefit Analysis. *Mayo Clinic Proceedings* 47 (8): 550–555.

Dunn, J. 1977. Interview with Devra Breslow. In Breslow, L. *A History of Cancer Control in the U.S. with Emphasis on the Period 1946–1971.* Vol. 4, Appendix 6, p. 35. Los Angeles, Calif.: University of California at Los Angeles School of Public Health.

Evans, D. M. D., Shelley, G., Cleary, B. et al. 1974. Observer Variation and Quality Control of Cytodiagnosis. *Journal of Clinical Pathology* 27 (12): 945–950.

Feinstein, A. R. 1968. The Identification of Rates of Disease. *Annals of Internal Medicine* 69: 1037–1061.

Feinstein, A. R. 1978. Personal Communication. New Haven, Conn.: Yale School of Medicine.

Frame, P. S., and Carlson, S. J. 1975. A Critical Review of Periodic Health Screening Using Specific Screening Criteria. Part 3: Selected Diseases of the Genitourinary System. *Journal of Family Practice* 2: 189–194.

Frankenburg, W. K., and Camp, B. W., eds. 1975. *Pediatric Screening Tests.* Springfield, Ill.: Charles C Thomas.

Fogarty International Center (National Institutes of Health) and American College of Preventive Medicine. 1976. *Preventive Medicine USA: Theory, Practice and Application of Prevention in Personal Health Services.* New York: PRODIST.

Garrett, W. J. 1964. Symptomless Carcinoma of the Cervix. *Journal of Obstetrics and Gynaecology of the British Commonwealth* 71: 517–528.

Glamour. 1978. Beauty and Health Report. 76 (April): 168.

Grünfeld, K., Horwitz, O., and Lysgaard-Hansen, B. 1975. Evaluation of Mortality Data for Cervical Cancer with Special Reference to Mass Screening Programs, Denmark, 1961–1971. *American Journal of Epidemiology* 101 (4): 265–275.

Hall, J. E., and Walton, L. 1968. Dysplasia of the Cervix. *American Journal of Obstetrics and Gynecology* 100: 662–671.

Hampshire, S. 1976. Thinking About Social Costs. *The New York Times* (March 24): 39.

Hart, C. R., ed. 1975. *Screening in General Practice.* Edinburgh: Churchill Livingstone.

Holland, W. W. 1974. Taking Stock. *Lancet* 1: 1494–1497.

Homesley, H. D. 1977. Evaluation of the Abnormal Pap Smear. *American Family Physician* 16: 190–194.

Hulme, G. W., and Eisenberg, H. S. 1968. Carcinoma in-situ of the Cervix in Connecticut. *American Journal of Obstetrics and Gynecology* 102: 415–425.

Husain, O. A. N. 1976. Quality Control in Cytological Screening for Cervical Cancer. *Tumori* 62: 303–314.

Iglehart, J. 1977. The Cost and Regulation of Medical Technology: Future Policy Directions. *Milbank Memorial Fund Quarterly/Health and Society* 55 (Winter): 25–59.

Kern, W. H., and Zivolich, M. R. 1977. The Accuracy and Consistency of the Cytologic Classification of Squamous Lesions of the Uterine Cervix. *Acta Cytologica* 21 (4): 519–523.

Kinlen, L. J., and Doll, R. 1973. Trends in Mortality from Cancer of the Uterus in Canada and in England and Wales. *British Journal of Preventive and Social Medicine* 27: 146–149.

———, and Spriggs, A. I. 1978. Women with Positive Cervical Smears But Without Surgical Intervention. *Lancet* 2: 463–465.

Kirkland, J. A. 1963. Atypical Epithelial Changes in the Uterine Cervix. *Journal of Clinical Pathology,* 16: 150–154.

Knox, E. G. 1968. Cervical Cancer. In Nuffield Provincial Hospitals Trust, *Screening for Medical Care.* pp. 43–54. London: Oxford University Press.

———. 1976. Ages and Frequencies for Cervical Cancer Screening. *British Journal of Cancer* 34: 444–452.

Kolstad, P. 1970. Diagnosis and Management of Pre-cancerous Lesions of the Cervix Uteri. *International Journal of Gynaecology and Obstetrics* 8: 551–560.

———, and Klem, V. 1976. Long-term and Follow-up of 1121 Cases of Carcinoma in-situ. *Obstetrics and Gynecology* 48 (2): 125–129.

Koss, L. G., and Phillips, A. J. 1974. Summary and Recommendations of the Workshop on Uterine-Cervical Cancer. *Cancer* 33 (6, Suppl.): 1753–1754.

Lambourne, A., and Lederer, H. 1973. Effects of Observer Variations in Population Screening for Cervical Carcinoma. *Journal of Clinical Pathology* 26: 564–569.

Lancet. 1972. Editorial. The Value of Cervical Cytology. 2: 1236–1237.

———. 1976. Editorial. Walton Report on Cervical Screening. 1: 1337.

————. 1978. Editorial. Screening for Cervical Cancer in Young Women. 2: 1029–1030.

Lave, J. R., and Lave, L. B. 1977. Measuring the Effectiveness of Prevention. I. *Milbank Memorial Fund Quarterly/Health and Society* 55 (Spring): 273–289.

Lyon, J. L., and Gardner, J. W. 1977. The Rising Frequency of Hysterectomy: Its Effect on Uterine Cancer Rates. *American Journal of Epidemiology* 105 (5): 439–443.

MacGregor, J. E. 1974. Letter. Screening for Cervical Cancer. *British Medical Journal* 1 (Jan. 12): 77.

————. 1976. Evaluation of Mass Screening Programs for Cervical Cancer in NE Scotland. *Tumori* 62: 287–295.

————, and Teper, S. 1978. Mortality from Carcinoma of Cervix Uteri in Britain. *Lancet* 2 (Oct. 7): 774–776.

McKeown, T. 1968. Validation of Screening Procedures. In Nuffield Provincial Hospitals Trust, *Screening for Medical Care*. pp. 1–13. London: Oxford University Press.

McIndoe, A. A., and Green, G. H. 1969. Vaginal Carcinoma in situ following Hysterectomy. *Acta Cytologica* 13: 158–162.

Miller, A. B., Lindsay, J., and Hill, G. B. 1976. Mortality from Cancer of the Uterus in Canada and its Relationship to Screening for Cancer of the Cervix. *International Journal of Cancer* 17: 600–612.

National Panel of Consultants on the Conquest of Cancer. 1971. *Report prepared for the Committee on Labor and Public Welfare, U. S. Senate*. Document 92-9. Washington, D. C.: U. S. Government Printing Office.

Nelson, J. H. Jr., Averette, H. E., and Richart, R. 1975. *Dysplasia and Early Cervical Cancer*. New York: American Cancer Society.

The New England Journal of Medicine. 1976. Editorial. Papanicolaou Testing—Are We Screening the Wrong Women? 294 (Jan. 22): 223.

Nolen, W. A. 1978. Cutting Your Medical Costs in Half. *McCall's* 105 (August): 78, 172.

Notman, M. T. 1976. Elective Hysterectomy: Pro and Con. *The New England Journal of Medicine* 295 (5): 266–267.

Pedersen, E., Høeg, K., and Kolstad, P. 1971. Mass Screening for Cancer of the Uterine Cervix in Ostfold County, Norway: An Experiment. *Acta Obstetrica et Gynecologica Scandinavica* 11 (Suppl.): 1–18.

Peterson, O. 1956. Spontaneous Course of Cervical Precancerous Conditions. *American Journal of Obstetrics and Gynecology* 72: 1063–1071.

Preston, T. A. 1977. *Coronary Artery Surgery: A Critical Review.* New York: Raven Press.

Randall, K. J. 1974. Cancer Screening by Cytology. *Lancet* 2: 1303–1304.

Rettig, R. A. 1977. *Cancer Crusade: The Story of the National Cancer Act of 1971.* Princeton: Princeton University Press.

Richards, D. H. 1974. A Post-Hysterectomy Syndrome. *Lancet* 2: 983–985.

Robbins, L. 1977. Interview by Lester and Devra Breslow. In Breslow, L. *A History of Cancer Control in the U.S. with Emphasis on the Period 1946–1971.* Vol. 4, Appendix 6, p. 35, Los Angeles, Calif.: UCLA School of Public Health.

Rogers, P. G. 1972. The Need to Emphasize Preventive Medicine in Future U. S. Health Care Programs. *Preventive Medicine* 1 (Dec.): 493–498.

———. 1978. Personal communication. Washington, D.C.: U.S. House of Representatives.

Rosen, G. 1975. *Preventive Medicine.* New York: Science History Publications.

Sackett, D. L. 1975. Screening for Early Detection of Disease: To What Purpose. *Bulletin of the New York Academy of Medicine* 51: 39–52.

Schmidt, O. 1977. Cervical Cancer Screening Program: The SOGC's View. *Canadian Medical Association Journal* 116: 971–972, 975.

Schneider, J., and Twiggs, L. B. 1972. The Costs of Carcinoma of the Cervix. *Obstetrics and Gynecology* 40: 851–859.

Sedlis, A., Walters, A. T., Balin, H. et al. 1974. Evaluation of Two Simultaneously Obtained Cervical Cytological Smears. *Acta Cytologica* 18 (4): 291–296.

Seybolt, J. F., and Johnson, W. D. 1971. Cervical Cyto-diagnostic Problems — A Survey. *American Journal of Obstetrics and Gynecology* 109: 1089–1103.

Shapiro, S. 1975. Screening for Early Detection of Cancer and Heart Disease. *Bulletin of the New York Academy of Medicine* 51: 80–95.

———. 1977. Measuring the Effectiveness of Prevention II. *Milbank Memorial Fund Quarterly/Health and Society.* 55 (Spring): 291–313.

Shulman, J. J., Leyton, M., and Reed, H. 1974. The Papanicolaou Smear: An Insensitive Procedure. *American Journal of Obstetrics and Gynecology* 120: 446–451.

Siegler, E. F. 1956. Microdiagnosis of Carcinoma in-situ of the Uterine Cervix: A Comparative Study of Pathologists' Diagnoses. *Cancer* 9: 463–469.

Silverberg, E. 1975. *Gynecologic Cancer: Statistical and Epidemiological Information.* New York: American Cancer Society.

Spitzer, W. D., and Brown, B. P. 1975. Unanswered Questions About the Periodic Health Examination. *Annals of Internal Medicine* 83: 257–263.

Spriggs, A. I. 1971. Follow-up of Untreated Carcinoma in-situ of Cervix Uteri. *Lancet* 2: 599.

Stern, E., and Neely, P. M. 1963. Carcinoma and Dysplasia of the Cervix: A Comparison of Rates for New and Returning Population. *Acta Cytologica* 7: 357–361.

———, Misczynski, M., Greenland, S. et al. 1977. Pap Testing and Hysterectomy Prevalence: A Survey of Communities with High and Low Cervical Cancer Rates. *American Journal of Epidemiology* 106: 296–305.

Strickland, S. P. 1972. *Politics, Science, and Dread Disease.* Cambridge, Mass: Harvard University Press.

Talebian, F. Shayan, A. Krumholz, B. A. et al. Colposcopic Evaluation of Patients With Abnormal Cervical Cytology. *American Journal of Obstetrics and Gynecology* 49 (6): 670–674.

Timonen, S., Niemenen, V., and Kauraniemi, T. 1974. Cervical Screening. *Lancet* 1: 401.

Truman, D. B. 1958. *The Governmental Process.* New York: Alfred A. Knopf.

U.S. Department of Commerce. 1978. Bureau of the Census, *Current Population Reports.* Report P-25, No. 721 (April). Table 3. Washington, D. C.: U. S. Government Printing Office.

U.S. Department of Health, Education, and Welfare. 1975. Public Health Service, National Center for Health Statistics. *Characteristics of Females Ever Having a Pap Smear and Interval Since Last Pap Smear, United States, 1973.* Monthly Vital Statistics Report, Health Interview Survey, Provisional Data (HRA) 76-1120, Vol. 24, No. 7. (Suppl., October).

———. 1966a. Program Analysis: Disease Control Programs. Cancer. (Cited by Dickinson, L. M. 1972c. Evaluation of the Effectiveness of Cytologic Screening for Cervical Cancer. III. Cost Benefit Analysis. *Mayo Clinic Proceedings* 47 (8): 550–555.

———. 1966b. Public Health Service, National Center for Health Statistics. *Age at Menopause, United States, 1960–1962.* DHEW Publication 1000, Series 11, No. 19. Washington, D.C.: U.S. Government Printing Office.

———. 1978a. SEER Program (Surveillance, Epidemiology and End Results). *Cancer Incidence and Mortality in the United States,*

1973-1976. DHEW Publication No. (NIH) 78-1837. Washington, D.C.: U.S. Government Printing Office.

———. 1978b. *U.S. Vital Statistics: Mortality.* Unpublished Data: Trend C, Tables 292 and 292A, Death and Death Rates, United States, 1976. Washington, D.C.

Wakefield, J., Yule, R., Smith, A. et al. 1973. Relation of Abnormal Cytological Smears and Carcinoma of Cervix Uteri to Husband's Occupation. *British Medical Journal* 2: 142.

Wells, C. K., and Feinstein, A. R. 1977. Routine Radiographic Measurement and Prognostic Importance of Rate of Growth (Auxometry) in Patients With Lung Cancer (Abstract). *Clinical Research* 25: 266A.

Whitby, L. 1974. Definitions and Criteria. *Lancet* 2: 819-821.

Wilson, J. M. G. 1963. Multiple Screening, *Lancet* 2: 51-54.

———. 1968. The Worth of Detecting Occult Disease. In Sharp, C. L. E. H. and Keen, H., eds., *Presymptomatic and Early Diagnosis.* pp. 141-178. London: Pittman.

Wilson, J. M. G., and Jungner, G. 1968. *Principles and Practice of Screening for Disease.* Geneva: World Health Organization.

World Health Organization. 1978. *Steroid Contraception and the Risk of Neoplasia.* Report of a WHO Scientific Group. WHO Technical Report Series G19. Geneva. Switzerland: World Health Organization.

Yule, R. 1972. The Frequency of Cytologic Testing. (Abstract). *Acta Cytologica* 16: 389-390.

An earlier abbreviated version of this paper was presented at the 106th Annual Meeting of the American Public Health Association, Los Angeles, California, October 17, 1978.

Acknowledgments: We wish to thank Alvan R. Feinstein for review of an earlier draft of this paper, and *Milbank Memorial Fund Quarterly* referees for helpful comments.

Address correspondence to: Anne-Marie Foltz, M.P.H., Graduate School of Public Administration, New York University, 40 West 4th Street, New York, New York 10003.

V The Fiscal Crisis and Rationing by Science

Milbank Memorial Fund Quarterly/*Health and Society, Vol. 57, No. 2, 1979*

Special Report

Scarce Resources in Health Care

OFFICE OF HEALTH ECONOMICS (LONDON)

Over the past few years serious efforts have been made in Britain and elsewhere to achieve a more rational distribution of health care resources. It has often been assumed that an optimum supply of health care facilities could be achieved by the measurement of objective health care needs, and that, then, these resources could be fairly allocated to those requiring them. Unfortunately, well-intentioned as these attempts have been, the reality is that the problem is much more complex. This paper sets out some of these difficulties and offers some tentative solutions to the intractible problem of health care demands running constantly ahead of the supply of health care resources. It has no intention of arguing against the basic concept that National Health Service care should be rationally planned. However, it will call into question some of the notions which have arisen in the course of the discussion of this planning process.

Looking first, briefly, at the supply side of the equation, it is a fact that the availability of health care resources never has been and never will be determined by an objective measurement of need. The naive assumption that a National Health Service, or any other centrally planned health care system, could match needs and resources has proved to be a chimera. Instead, the resources which are made available for health care appear to be determined by a variety of complex socio-political systems which no one has yet been able to unravel. All that is known for certain is that an advanced form of Parkinson's law operates. It appears that to whatever extent health care facilities are expanded they will generally still all be used; and at the same time there will remain a steady pool of 'unmet' demands. For example, the number of hospital doctors in England and Wales rose by 130 per cent between 1949 and 1974 (OHE, 1977). Meantime, however, the 'waiting list' for hospital admissions has remained obstinately around the figure of 500,000 over the years. Very broadly, for every bed which the Health Service provides, there is another patient waiting to occupy it once the present incumbent has either been discharged or died.

The most plausible factor to explain the overall levels of provision of health care appears to be characterised by the maxim that 'the wealthier a country becomes, the higher is the proportion of that wealth which it devotes to health services.'[1] Figure 1, derived from an OECD study, shows an overall pattern in which the richer nations seem to devote more of their riches to health care.

---

1 The same is almost certainly true of education and social service as a whole. In this sense it can be argued that 'wealthier nations often tend to become more caring nations'.

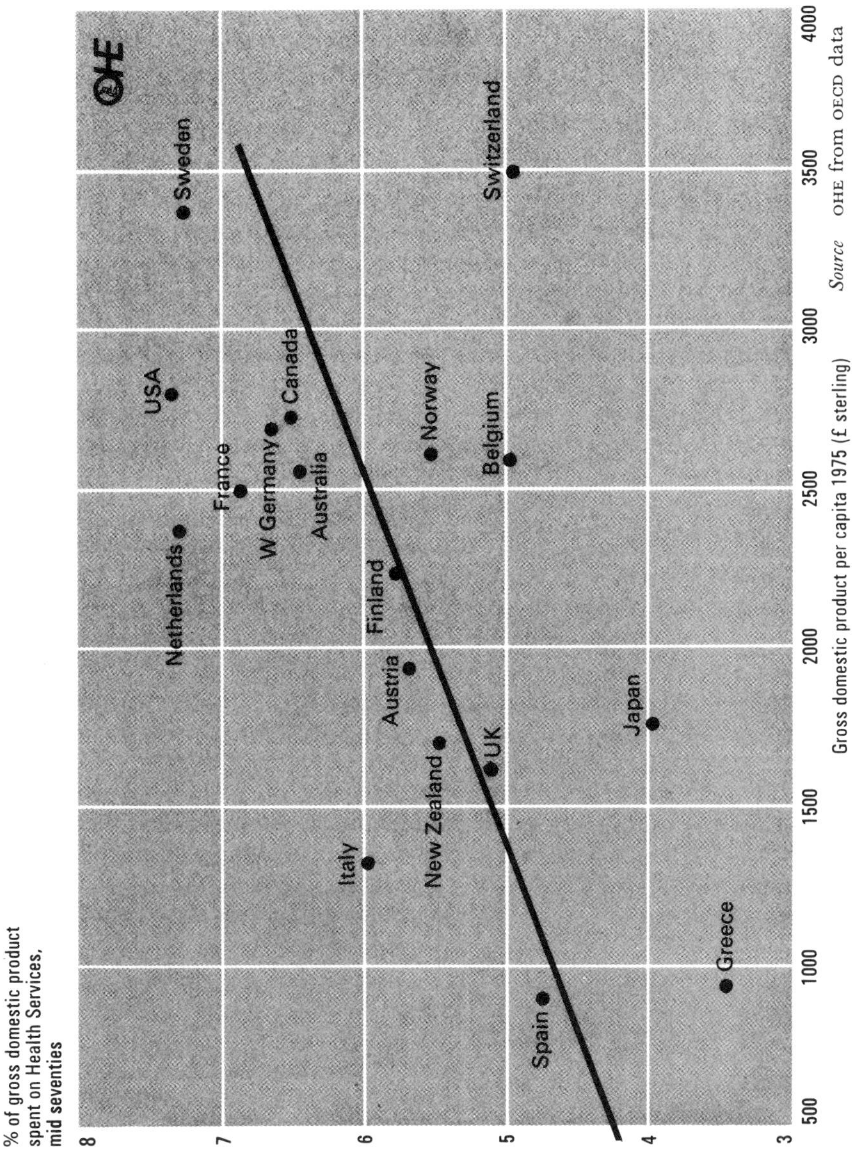

Figure 1 *Regression of 'health service expenditure as percentage of GDP' on 'Gross Domestic Product per capita' Organisation for Economic Co-operation and Development, Paris*

Note One possible explanation for this pattern of expenditure would be that the 'price index' for health care rises disproportionately in wealthier countries.

The Figure is based on somewhat shaky data, and there are discrepancies in the years used for expenditures for different countries. Nevertheless, it seems to lead to an inevitable conclusion that wealth rather than need still seems to be a prime determinant of the availability of health care. Traditionally that statement tended to apply to individual families; now in the late 1970s it appears to apply similarly on an international basis.

However, this paper is not primarily concerned with the availability of resources for health services. It is concerned instead with the use of these resources and how the problems of continuing shortages of health care arise and might be tackled. These are not local British problems. Difficulties in allocating scarce health care resources seem to occur world wide. Even the richest nations, devoting relatively much higher proportions of their greater wealth to medical care, face the same sort of problems of shortage as those which occur in Britain. Clearly additional manpower and money are not the answer.

Furthermore, the paper does not attempt to deal with the 'caring' side of medicine, with all its own problems and shortages. Clearly there is unlimited scope for improving the conditions of the mentally handicapped, the chronic sick and the elderly, for example. However, this paper, instead, is concentrating primarily on the difficulties which exist in the provision of 'curative' services, such as surgery, radio-therapy, physiotherapy and of course pharmacology. It is with shortages in these areas that the discussion will be concerned.

Originally in 1948, when the British National Health Service was initiated, there was a very real pool of untreated ill-health amongst the less wealthy which could readily be dealt with within the resources of available medical technology. This was illustrated by the sudden upsurge in the provision of dentures and spectacles which, because they had been relatively expensive, people previously had been unable to afford. But similarly, many patients could for the first time receive medical treatment free of charge for ailments for which they would previously have been unable to afford a doctor's consultation.

However, the pattern of demand and availability of care in the early years of the NHS was confused by a parallel (but unrelated) development. Coincident with this free availability of health care,

374

there came a number of notable medical advances. In many cases these originated from the newly emerging multinational pharmaceutical firms. The most striking of these new 'cures' was the treatment of tuberculosis (OHE, 1962). Within a very short period the long waiting lists for places in TB sanatoria disappeared, not because more beds were made available or because they were now 'free' but largely because chemotherapy had for the first time provided a readily successful treatment. In the same way, the infections such as pneumonia and scarlet fever could for the first time be effectively controlled by the antibiotics. As other examples, puerperal sepsis could be controlled and mastoid operations became obsolete. Indeed a whole range of similarly dramatic medical advances in the treatment of acute infections became available. Thus in the early years of the National Health Service there appeared to be relatively few 'shortages' of facilities because advances in chemotherapy made extra hospital resources available to treat more chronic sickness. In the early years it appeared that the dream of Beveridge and Bevan for a health service to cater for a steadily reducing need for treatment might be realised.

By the mid-1950s it was starting to be recognised that the control of infectious disease was to be an exception in the pattern of progress in medical care. By contrast, many other medical innovations such as advances in anaesthesia had the reverse effect. They increased the scope for expensive health care facilities rather than the reverse. Perhaps understandably, the architects of the NHS had overlooked this potential effect of technological progress on the capacity of medicine and surgery to deal with an ever-expanding range of technical medical problems. The reductions in demand for care which they had anticipated (and which had materialised, for example, in the case of tuberculosis) gave way instead to steady increase in the demands and apparent need for health care resources. This pattern of demand had never been foreseen in 1948. Had the state of medical art remained at the constant level which existed in 1948 – as doctors and politicians had expected it to do – there would have been little or no problem in 1978 in financing all of the very limited procedures to which doctors and surgeons would still be restricted.

Instead the reality is that pharmacological, biochemical, medical and surgical activities have all taken huge strides forward since the 1950s. Unlike the chemotherapy of tuberculosis these have often demanded increased resources. For example, brain surgery, transplant surgery, more precise biochemical diagnosis and a positive cornucopia of new medicaments for previously untreatable chronic illnesses have become available over the past thirty years. Medical and surgical practice has been transformed, and correspondingly the public have come to expect medical treatment in 1978 which bears little resemblance to their expectations in the 1940s.

It is important to make the point here, however, that it is not the public itself which has created the demand for new and more advanced therapy. People have never spontaneously demanded new medical technologies except in the most general sense of wanting 'a cure for cancer', 'a cure for the common cold' or relief in general terms from any symptoms which they might be suffering. They had few, if any, specific expectations.

Going back to the 1950s, it was not the sufferers from arthritis who were demanding the development of an artificial implantable hip. Hence, in this sense, there was no 'shortage' of hip transplant operations in the 1950s. The surgery did not exist in a satisfactory form and there was no specific public demand that it should be developed. It was medical scientists along with interested engineers who developed the artificial hip on their own initiative. Similarly, pharmacological treatment of acute anxiety or depression was not available to the public although these conditions were widespread and their existence was generally recognised. Hence there was no 'demand' for tranquillisers and anti-depressants. It was scientists in the pharmaceutical industry who developed the pharmacological innovations which could then be so widely prescribed.

Once again there was no public demand for an 'artificial kidney' in the 1950s. It was members of the professions who spontaneously developed the technology and who first offered it to patients whom it might benefit. Thus it is important to understand that medical innovation is not stimulated by public demand as such; it is stimulated by medical needs as seen by the innovators. The growth in available medical technology is stimulated by the technologists – academic and industrial scientists and the scientifically-minded doctors – themselves. It is the research workers – and not the public – who force forward the frontiers of medical science. It is the scientists who in a sense 'create' potential new 'needs' which can only be fulfilled if new resources are made available.

Nevertheless, once a new development has occurred, it tends to become 'news'. The media eventually focus on it and publicise it. But even at that stage the public and doctors may be relatively slow to awaken to the potentialities of new treatments which could prove lifesaving for themselves or their patients. The availability of renal dialysis, for example, was demonstrated in the United States in the early 1960s, but it was almost a decade later before there was a general demand for widespread dialysis facilities in Britain. And this was a particularly spectacular example of a lifesaving technological breakthrough. For less dramatic advances public and professional awareness may play very little part in the spread of the new technology. Although effective 'anti-depressant' medicines have been available since the late 1950s, the specific clinical state of depression may still sometimes be unrecognised either by patients or their doctors.

Thus in the earlier stages the demand for newer and safer treatments tends to be 'technology' or 'specialist' led rather than being called for in advance by the public or the professions at large. However, over a period of time the public and their doctors do come to expect that the new medical techniques (or new medicines) should be available for their benefit. It is at that stage that the problems of shortages in medical care reach the limelight.

All of this explains the unlimited potential demand for medical care which, since the mid-1950s, has been a constant feature of all health care systems. It is responsible for the 'shortages' and the 'queues' which arise in every health service where payments by the patient have ceased to act as a limiting factor on demand. One simple fact, however, should by now have become clear. The existence of shortages is inherent in any system of medical care which is more or less 'free at the point of access' and which nevertheless permits unlimited scientific innovation and progressive advance in the quality and scope of care which can be provided for its patients.

Controls on demand
Under the British National Health Service the primary responsibility for attempts to match this potentially unlimited demand against strictly limited resources falls on the shoulders of the family doctor. Every member of the public has the right to be on a family doctor's 'list' and the doctors are required under their terms of service to ensure that all necessary care is provided for the patients in their practice. Thus, except in an emergency, the family doctor is *intended* to be the only point of entry into the formal NHS system, and he can use whatever devices he likes both to limit the demands made on his own time and also to limit the demands made by his paitents on the specialist hospital services.

In doing this, he must implicitly define what he considers 'necessary' treatment under his terms of service.

Thus it is an unwritten and unwelcome responsibility put upon the British general practitioner that he has to try to make limited health care resources appear to meet all the justifiable 'needs' for medical care. He also has the even more difficult task of trying to satisfy all 'demands' for care – whether they represent legitimate needs or not. He has not been trained, and is often emotionally unsuited, to tell his patients that their demands for care are unreasonable. He may have an even more traumatic problem if he is faced with patients for whom he knows that effective treatment could be possible, if only sufficient resources were available.

However, although family doctors may have the initial responsibility in this respect, they do not usually face this latter problem alone. As in the case of renal failure, it is often the hospital consultant who ultimately makes the decision about whether specific lifesaving facilities can be made available for a particular patient.[2]

The general practitioner will also tend to learn by experience and by consultation with the hospital specialists what treatment is likely to be available in local hospitals for less dramatic operations, such as hernias or varicose veins. Here the family doctor can refer the patient to hospital, to spend perhaps months on a 'waiting list'. Alternatively, the family doctor can discourage the patient from seeking hospital treatment knowing that it is unlikely to be readily available. In many other cases, of course, the family doctor may genuinely consider that the patient's disorder is too trivial to justify referral to hospital. In all these variety of situations the family doctor and the hospital consultants together have to perform a precarious balancing act in trying to see that those most in need of treatment receive it, and that those in lesser need are still left satisfied with the limited care which they are receiving.

The concept of 'rationing'
Against this background, there has been much recent discussion of a concept which has come to be called the 'rationing' of health care. One of the most articulate arguments for the existence of 'rationing' under systems of health care came in a recent paper in the *Milbank Memorial Fund Quarterly* by the medical sociologist,

---

2 Specifically in the case of renal dialysis and transplant the hospital consultant may also be assisted in his decision by an advisory committee.

David Mechanic (1977). However, his is only one of many voices which have been speaking in terms of 'rationing' health care.[3] Because the usage of this term seems to be gaining ground without demur, it may be worthwhile pausing to examine the appropriateness of the word and of the concepts which lie behind its use.

In his Milbank paper, Mechanic re-emphasises the point that 'there is almost unlimited possibility for the continued escalation of medical demand and increased medical expenditure'. Based on this thesis Mechanic and others argue that there is (and must be) 'rationing' of resources. He goes on to explain that in his terminology 'techniques of rationing are in process of transition and most countries have yet to reach a reasonable end-point in this transitional process. The process is one of movement from *rationing by fee* through a stage of *implicit rationing* through resource allocation to a final stage of *explicit rationing*'.

However, 'rationing' is an odd word in this context and is not necessarily the right one to describe the process. In many ways, 'triage' used in its battle-field medical sense is more appropriate. This is the process of sorting those cases in most urgent need of attention, first, from those already too far injured to benefit from treatment and, second, from those whose minor injuries can conveniently wait until the immediate emergency has subsided. In a sense, this sorting process is similar to the principles of selection which every National Health Service doctor sometimes has to apply when trying to cope with the apparently inexhaustible demands from his many patients. He has to choose those who will most benefit from the limited resources at his disposal at that time. Another phrase which can appropriately be used instead of 'rationing' is 'priority selection', this specifically implies that not all in need of treatment will receive it.

By contrast, the word rationing was originally used to refer to the issue of rations to the armed services; it meant simply the daily portions issued to each man. It was only later, as far as the British public were concerned, that the use of the word 'rationing' had a connotation of shortage of supplies during wartime. In this situation, it came to mean the basic allowance of commodities to each person obtainable by purchase based on ration books of coupons.

Thus, rationing in the proper sense of the word did not arise from the growth of demand but from a need to control supply of

3   In particular M H Cooper recently published a book in Britain under the title *Rationing Health Care* (1977).

both kind and quantity. It is a control that is normally exercised on a large scale by central government through standardisation of products and production. If production and innovation can meet the market demand there is no need for rationing. It is only when a free market for some reason cannot be allowed by government that production and innovation come under control to produce rationing. Where demand exceeds supply and there are no controls, supply under private enterprise will move up to meet demand but there will be a price on the supply. Hence Mechanic correctly argues that traditionally price limited the choice of consumer of health services as it did in Britain in the 1930s and still does for many people in the United States in the late 1970s. This he calls *rationing by fee*. But this is not in reality rationing. In all Western industrial systems a corresponding system exists for all goods and services although its effect is masked because advancing technology makes alternatives available at lower prices. Thus the market for expensive new cars is limited – ie, 'rationed by fee' in Mechanic's health service sense – and most people must make do with cheaper alternatives. Indeed there are many who make do with obsolescent second-hand cars, lacking much of the latest technology, or else must go without a car altogether. However, it is now generally accepted that this sort of 'rationing by fee' or 'free market' is inappropriate in relation to medical care.

Mechanic next argues that the appearance of various forms of national health schemes produces *implicit rationing* because centrally-funded health care costs still prevent everyone having the best and most appropriate modern medical treatment. As has already been explained, medical technology has moved too rapidly ahead of what national budgets can afford out of their total financial commitments. The latest and best medical treatment may simply be too costly or else unavailable. 'The assumption is (he says) that physicians exercise agreed upon standards of care and that services are equitably provided in the light of the services'. This begs the question; it is a statement of his conclusion. The postulate of medical care (from which the argument *should* start) is that each doctor will do his best for each of his patients, in the light of his clinical knowledge and judgment, *with the resources available to him*. As long ago as 1959 the American Medical Association's House of Delegates had reached the conclusion that: 'The individual physician and the medical profession as a group must also be concerned with maintaining a proper balance between adequate medical care for the welfare patient and economical use of public funds . . . The individual physician, as the key person in the care of the welfare patient, must, there-fore, take into consideration not only the medical but the financial aspects of various acceptable modes of treatment.' (Roy, 1976).

Mechanic continues to expound this principle when he turns to *explicit rationing*. This 'is not only to set limits on total expenditure for care, but also to develop mechanisms to arrive at more rational decisions as to relative investments in different areas of care, varying types of facilities and man-power, new technological initiatives and the establishment of certain minimal uniform standards'. This concept of explicit rationing is further illumin-ated by Mechanic's note that 'the difficulty of imposing explicit rationing is more political than scientific'. Thus explicit rationing would be a political control system. It would begin with a budget-ary allocation of resources and proceed through a system of controls to set limits to facilities, manpower and its distribution, technical innovation and finally to the clinical judgement of doctors. 'Explicit rationing' does *not* mean that every individual is *guaranteed* equal access to appropriate medical care or equal shares. Treatment is still within the postulate that the doctor will do his best with the resources available to him but there are now such constraints on those resources as government decides; the end product is (as Mechanic says) bureaucratic medicine, governed by political decisions. Thus in a drift from what has been called 'rationing by fee'; through 'implicit rationing' to 'explicit rationing', the individual doctor would tend to pass from the phases of being a clinical 'entrepreneur' through being an 'expert' in apportioning scarce resources to the ultimate posi-tion of becoming a 'bureaucrat' or 'economiser', controlled in the resources available to his patients by a central authority. There is little doubt that this form of explicit rationing of health care would be unacceptable to many doctors and patients in a mixed economy such as Britain's. Many people would probably prefer to return to the principle of 'rationing by fee', for example through private health insurance.

'Rationing by science'
Before the concepts of implicit and explicit rationing had been so clearly enunciated by Mechanic and others, the epidemiologist Cochrane had already suggested that the problems of scarce resources could be alleviated in a process which he referred to as *rationing by science*. This was based on the observation that, when subjected to scientific evaluation, a substantial proportion of medical care appeared to be ineffective and hence unnecessary.

(Cochrane, 1971). Cochrane's argument was that if all this unnecessary treatment could be eliminated, the resources already available for medical care would probably be sufficient to meet all scientifically proven needs. This beguiling concept has much to commend it. However, difficulties arise both at the practical level and at a philosophical or sociological level.

First, in his book *Effectiveness and efficiency; random reflections on health services*, Cochrane concludes with a quotation from Agatha in Eliot's *The Family Reunion*:

> Not for the good that it will do
> But that nothing may be left undone
> On the margin of the impossible.

Cochrane implies, justifiably, that much of medical care has always been carried out on precisely this basis. It may be particularly true in life-and-death situations, but also no doubt often applies in attempts to alleviate less serious illnesses. There is often little or no scientific evidence that a particular treatment may benefit a particular patient, yet the doctor feels impelled to carry it out so that 'nothing may be left undone' even if there is only the remotest chance of success.

To a large extent this question of 'rationing by science' brings out into the open two essentially conflicting principles in medicine. On the one hand there are those medical scientists and epidemiologists who want specific proof of efficacy before a medical or surgical procedure is introduced; on the other there are the more sympathetic practicing physicians who have to deal personally with actual patients, who are both anxious and hopeful. Undoubtedly, practicing doctors should be more scientifically critical of the procedures which they request or undertake for patients under their care. But they have understandably always been reluctant to admit to their patients that medical science has nothing to offer.[4] In the last analysis they are still often going to suggest 'curative' treatments even if they know that on a statistical basis there may be little chance of success. In this situation, it is hard for the practicing doctor to face up to the fact that by ordering such an unpromising procedure he may – in the overall picture – be depriving other patients of treatments with strong chances in favour of success, such as renal dialysis and transplant or hip replacement. To use Mechanic's phrase, he is reluctant to

---

4 Doctors may often, of course, be able to offer symptomatic relief even if they cannot offer a 'cure'.

accept the existence of 'implicit rationing'. However, he would perhaps be even less happy to have to practice medicine under the principles of 'explicit rationing'.

Apart from this practical difficulty, a more philosophical argument has been advanced against the concept of 'rationing by science'. This is the sociological view that one of the most important theoretical effects of the British National Health Service has been to make *all* medical treatment freely available to the whole population. It can be argued that if the Health Service is viewed in this light, it is relatively unimportant whether the treatments provided are effective or not. On this basis it could be considered 'socially divisive' if the rich could buy ineffective medical care which was prohibited under the 'free' National Health Service. This appears as a totally irrational attitude from the point of view of medical scientists, who would argue in the reverse direction. In their view only *effective* medical care should be universally available, and it could be much more evenly distributed if 'free' ineffective procedures could be eliminated. Those with money should be left free to buy scientifically unproven care if that is the way they choose to spend it.

In any case, however, the important point for the physician is that whatever medical scientists and sociologists may feel on theoretical grounds, the practical problems described above still remain to be solved. Clearly, according to Mechanic's argument, 'rationing by science' would be no more than a particular aspect of 'explicit rationing'. The present discussion in many ways highlights the fact that medical practice, under any system of explicit rationing, could very easily degenerate into a system of medical bureaucracy, with the availability or non-availability of different procedures being determined by the authorities rather than by individual doctors.

What should by now have become clear is that the major problems of inequality in health care and the attempts to solve them arise from the expanding technological scope of medical care. Any meaningful attempt to share out equitably the available health care resources is bedevilled by the success of technological innovation. Technology is only desirable in a 'rationed' society when it increases the availability of existing scarce resources through improvements in productivity. By contrast, it has been pointed out that it makes a nonsense of any attempt to apportion equal shares when technology is continually creating new – and necessarily scarce – procedures. Thus inequality in health care has to be accepted if innovation is to be allowed to proceed. The ultimate results of bureaucratically apportioned – that is, 'explicitly rationed' – health care would inevitably be the virtual stagnation of medical innovation.

It is important, however, to make a distinction at this point in the discussion between 'high technology' innovation which involves substantial resources for every case treated as opposed to the alternative form of equally 'high technology' innovation which results in little more than marginal costs per case. The archetypes of these two alternatives are, of course, renal dialysis or transplants on the one hand, and the widespread use of a particular cheap antibiotic on the other. Both can be life saving and both have been costly to develop. However, surgery and elaborate medical procedures involve a repeated high cost for every patient treated, whereas most medicines can be prescribed at a relatively very much lower (ie, more or less 'marginal') cost per patient. In general the shortages which have been discussed so far refer only to the former type of innovation. Such 'shortages' have been almost unknown for medicines under the British National Health Service. It is only in a very few cases, particularly in hospitals, that some expensive new medicines (eg, for cancer) have probably been prescribed at less than optimum frequency primarily in an attempt to restrict pharmaceutical costs (Teeling-Smith, 1978).[5] However, for the normally-priced medicines used in general practice, their cost has very rarely been an over-riding consideration in a decision not to prescribe. Nor has there been any trace of shortages or restrictions in supply.

It is particularly ironic that general practitioners have, nevertheless, been made particularly aware of the cost of their prescribing through the activities of the Regional Medical Officers of the Department of Health and through their local medical committees. By contrast, very little effort has been made to force general practitioners to think in terms 'of the 'opportunity costs' of their decisions when they refer patients to hospital.[6] There is also evidence that general practitioners are generally aware of the cost of the medicines which they prescribe (OHE, 1975). Perhaps

---

5 A similar situation of course tends to arise with any very expensive new medicine: eg, cortisone when it was first introduced. It is only when mass production technology can bring down the price that it becomes readily prescribable.

6 An average NHS prescription in 1976 cost £1.56, whereas an average spell spent in an acute hospital cost £299.

they may even take costs into greater account when choosing a particular medicine than when they were recommending a much more expensive surgical procedure for example.

It is also important to distinguish between essentially 'research' costs as opposed to 'service' costs. This can be illustrated again in relation to the cost of chemotherapy in cancer. Here most forms of therapy are still in a relatively experimental stage, and their high price should, therefore, be regarded as a research rather than a service cost. This is obviously also true for much experimental surgery and other experimental medical techniques.

Yet another type of difficulty in distinguishing between initial costs of innovation and costs of individual treatments in 'service' can be illustrated by reference to advanced radiotherapy. Here the cost of the initial machine may be several hundreds of thousands of pounds. Once it has been purchased, however, the actual costs incurred in the treatment of each individual case will be marginal when compared to the original purchase price.[7] In this case the process of 'rationing', if that were to be the right word, would apply at two levels. First there is the decision whether or not to purchase the equipment. With limited capital funds the number which could be afforded is restricted. Second, once the equipment has been purchased, there is the decision as to which patients should be allocated time for treatment on it. Here in the first case a 'once-off' investment has been made which is different from the funds spent on pharmaceutical research and development, for example. Unlike the case of pharmaceutical research, a renewed heavy initial investment for radiotherapy must be repeated each time that a new machine is provided in order to make the facilities available for a new group of patients.

International factors

A further factor needs to be taken into account in a discussion of the contrast between very heavy 'sunk' research costs for a new medicine and the continuing high 'in-service' costs for other types of medical and surgical innovation. This is the international consideration. If a new medical innovation results in a new technique (such as surgery) this will in principle become freely available on a world-wide basis as soon as it has been reported in the medical

---

7 'Marginal' is here being used in its economic sense. The only costs for the actual treatment will be the materials used, staff time and an element of wear and tear on the machine.

literature. The country which initiates the procedure will gain little or no financial advantage over the others which start to use it once its benefits have been published. Conversely, each country which adopts the innovation must find the funds to implement it out of its own health care budget. They will gain freely from the knowledge embodied in the original medical or surgical research; but they are still left to find the substantial sums needed to implement this knowledge as a routine health care procedure. This is clearly the case, for example, with some transplant surgery.

By contrast, in the development of a new medicine the very high initial costs of research and development will be borne primarily by private industry in one or two countries. However, once the new medicine is marketed it will fairly rapidly become available world-wide. In this case, however, the innovation, as a chemical substance, will be patentable, and the initiator can be assured of commercial returns from his original research investment. Thus in general each individual dose will make a contribution (through profits or royalties) to the original innovator. But nonetheless the cost of the pharmaceutical treatment will approach the true marginal cost, especially for well-established medicines which have been on the market for several years. This is in contrast to the cost of surgery, where the full economic cost has to be borne on each occasion that the operation is performed.

There is a nice paradox here. In the case of general medical or surgical innovation the innovator gains little or nothing in direct economic terms. Yet those who benefit from the innovation will all pay the same high price as the innovator for the benefits of the procedure. On the other hand, a new pharmaceutical innovation will bring economic rewards to the firm which has developed it and to the economy of its country; but nevertheless those in other countries which use the innovation will pay only a marginal price. As the recovery of the orginal R and D costs can be on a world-wide basis, the contribution made by each individual treatment is relatively small. Thus the high technology 'transplant' type of innovation which brings little or nothing to its inventor is costly to all those who use it. The high technology development of a medicine on the other hand may bring handsome rewards to its originator, but is nevertheless still comparatively inexpensive in actual use. In the context of this paper, new medicines need rarely be restricted in their use on the grounds of cost. This is a marked contrast to the restrictions which have to be applied to the use of other types of high technology medical innovation, and which have been referred to as 'rationing'.

Against the background of this discussion, covering the nature of demand and technology in medical care, it is perhaps useful to return next to some first principles in medical care. In introducing the National Health Service, the Minister responsible, Aneurin Bevan stated that 'medical treatment and care . . . should be made available to rich and poor alike in accordance with medical need and by no other criterion' (Abel-Smith, 1978). However, it has already been explained that Bevan never envisaged the explosive growth in needs and demand which would flow from the technological revolution in medical care since the 1940s. He could never have foreseen a situation where almost unlimited resources could be devoted to medical practice, all of which can be justified if one accepts that doctors may freely pursue the practice of medicine at 'the margin of the impossible'.

Thus it is no longer feasible to provide medical care based on the 1940s concept of 'need'. However, this paper has also argued that any forms of bureaucratic control or 'rationing' have grave inherent dangers. Those responsible for the organisation of medical care have to face up to these growing problems. One way in which they might try to do so, would be by redefining the objectives of health. Rather than falling back on the traditional models of ill-health based on experience in the 1930s, new positive aims for health care could be stated as follows: a healthy childhood; a productive and satisfying adult life; and a comfortable old age. Increasingly, on this criterion, the test of medicine on a life span would be its success of the treatment in each of these periods of life to accomplish the aim set for the following period. It is now at least a questionable ethical medical service to mankind to treat at any stage for survival only. This refers, in particular, to some of the most expensive high technology medicine applied in the terminal stages of an illness. The objective of medical care should be to 'add life to years rather than years to life' (Lasagna, 1978).

However, this statement of objectives leaves many challenges unanswered. There might, for example, need to be a fundamental shift in public and professional attitudes to health, in which the individual would have to accept a very much greater degree of responsibility for his own well-being. This has recently been actively encouraged in Britain, particularly with the Health Education Council's campaign to 'Look After Yourself'. There would also need to be a greater acceptance of the inappropriateness of professional treatment when trivial symptoms are apparent. This leads to one of the most difficult areas of all, attempting to re-educate the public into believing that 'good health' is primarily their responsibility rather than that of the National Health Service. But there is also a need to educate people against expecting too much high technology medicine, especially if the outcome of the illness is unlikely to be affected.

Still seeking for solutions in these difficult areas, the example of triage in the armed forces has already been mentioned. However, analogy with military medicine cannot be pressed too far. Clearly, there is a danger, if one examines the military models, of reaching an extreme form of bureaucracy, or the worst sort of 'explicit rationing' to use Mechanic's phrase. However, in other respects, the objectives of military medical care are the same as those which should now be postulated for a National Health Service. The objective was to keep the army 'fighting fit'; that is to ensure that as high a proportion as possible were well enough to perform their daily duties.

This leads, of course, to the concept of preventive medicine, but in the present context it would need to have a much wider meaning than that usually attributed to it. It comes back to the objectives for health care set out above. Present behaviour and treatment should not only be concerned with current symptoms, but should more importantly be concerned with future prognosis at a later age. Nevertheless one has to face up to the fact that these statements of objectives – important as they are – seem to have very little bearing on the imbalance between needs and supplies which are continuously being aggravated by the advance of medical technology. 'Keep-fit' programmes and emphasis on preventive rather than curative programmes of medical care may have an important part to play, but it would be naive to assume that they provide any solution to the problems of shortages of health care with which this paper has been concerned. It is nevertheless an important step in the right direction that the World Health Organisation's meeting at Alma Ata in 1978 was so clearly oriented in favour of primary medical care in the broadest sense (WHO, 1978).

It is obvious that potentially unlimited demand for health care must be restrained, but this paper has argued that it cannot be 'rationed' in the usual sense of the word. This is partly because formal rationing would lead to further undesirable bureaucracy in medical care. It also implies equal medical needs for the population as a whole. More importantly it is undesirable because continued rapid technological innovation in medicine and surgery would make a nonsense of any bureaucratic attempt to ensure an equitable distribution of the most advanced forms of medical care. If health care were to be effectively 'rationed' it would be likely to stifle all further innovation in the more expensive branches of medicine such as transplant surgery. Instead of Britain being in the forefront of medical technology, it would become progressively more backward. From this it follows that some medical care under a National Health Service must always be unevenly available – if it is not simply to be unavailable altogether.

Perhaps most importantly of all the simple concept of 'rationing' health care ignores its intensely complex nature on both the 'supply' and 'demand' side of the economic equation. Figure 2 is an attempt to summarise the arguments in this paper and it offers the alternative 'OHE' and 'Mechanic' terminologies to try to explain the various interactions. Most of the discussion has ignored the 'caring' half of the equation at the top of the diagram, because this is perhaps even more complex than the 'curing' side. In the 'curing' half, the OHE box labelled 'priority selection (triage)' can, of course, be accused of begging all the questions which have been made explicit in Mechanic's terminology and discussions. There are, of course, elements in all Mechanic's arguments encapsulated in the 'priority selection' process. However, the burden of this paper has in many ways been that the process and interactions in the allocation of health care resources are indeed too complex to break apart and to describe in simple terms such as 'explicit rationing'. For all the reasons which have been described, health care resources are not, and cannot be, allocated on a rationing principle. A much more informal and flexible planning process is necessary, which inevitably leads to inequalities at least where the allocation of very high cost advanced technological procedures are concerned. There is also, of course, the need to channel an increasing proportion of the demand side of the equation into the box marked 'educated demand for medical attention'. Both the 'general demand for well-being' and 'high technology medicine' boxes undoubtedly contain substantial elements of 'unnecessary' – or at least unattainable – demand. Reducing these by better education would help to make the priority selection more effective by channelling a greater proportion of the resources into educated demands for medical attention.

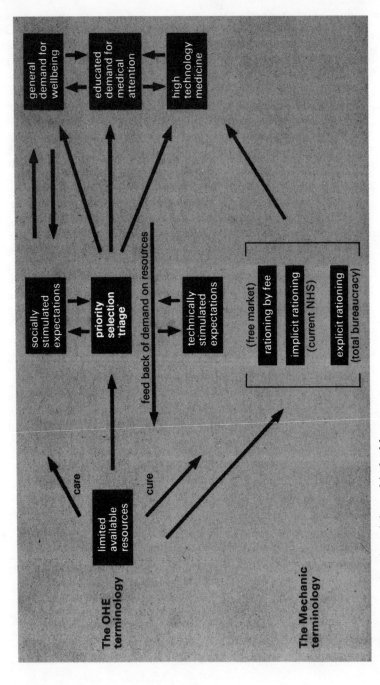

Figure 2 *Supply and demand in health care*

However, this paper has also drawn attention to the economic contrasts between expensive high technology medicine of different sorts. In some cases each treatment involves the use of substantial resources in manpower and capital facilities: these areas, such as transplant surgery, are the ones which have most conspicuously illustrated the shortages which are an inescapable feature of health care. In other cases, however, the economic costs are incurred primarily in the development stage. Pharmaceutical research and development is the most obvious illustration. For this latter type of investment, and the products resulting from it, there have been virtually no shortages. Instead there has been considerable acrimony over the 'marginal' price to be paid for the medicines which have resulted from the research investment.

Against the background of this discussion, it appears that much of the controversy over pharmaceutical prices in the past twenty years has been misguided. Throughout the world, the emphasis has tended to be on a cheap drug policy, attempting to restrict the multinational pharmaceutical innovators. Although these matters really lie outside the scope of this paper, it is clear from the discussion here that problems of health care shortages could be greatly alleviated if a larger proportion of illness could be treated with medicines rather than with very expensive medical technology. Insofar as the encouragement of pharmaceutical innovation can provide alternatives to surgery and other costly procedures, it should be vigorously encouraged.

In the early days of the Health Service, the chemotherapy of tuberculosis and other infections brought enormously cost-effective treatments to health care. There is recent evidence that such cost-effective treatments might now be repeated in other fields. An example here has been the recent development of a new medicine for the treatment of stomach ulcers. Previously these often needed complicated surgery, but now the taking of tablets may sometimes avoid the need for an operation. Studies in various countries are demonstrating the economic advantages of this shift from one type of health technology to another (Netherlands Economic Institute, 1977). Another current example is the use of medicines to dissolve gall-stones, which previously needed to be removed by surgery: again there are obvious economic advantages for the purely medical approach. The recent *Lancet* editorial suggesting chemotherapy for the treatment of brain abscess is only another of many examples (*Lancet*, 1978).

This, of course, goes back to the original precepts of Beveridge and Bevan in their design of the National Health Service. If disease really could be contained by the use of medicines and vaccines instead of having to be dealt with by very expensive technological procedures, it would help dramatically to reduce the apparently inevitable shortages. The demand for health care will never wither away, but perhaps its cost could be very much more effectively contained if pharmaceutical innovation were to be more actively encouraged.

The alternative is to continue indefinitely increasing the technological content of health care service procedures, and thus to exacerbate the current shortages. It has been argued that 'rationing' cannot solve the problem. It is, therefore, necessary to look to alternative technologies — and perhaps pharmacology in particular — to solve the present recurrent health care dilemma of excessive needs and demand perpetually outstripping available resources.

References

Abel-Smith B (1978). The National Health Service: The First Thirty Years. HMSO.

Cochrane A L (1971). Effectiveness and Efficiency: Random Reflections on the National Health Service. Nuffield Provincial Hospitals Trust, London.

Cooper M H (1977). *Rationing Health Care*. Croom Helm. London.

Lancet (1978). Chemotherapy of Brain Abscess. ii: 1081.

Lasagna L (1978). Contribution to the discussion at an OHE Symposium on 'Medicines for the Year 2000'.

Mechanic D (1977). The Growth of Medical Technology and Bureaucracy: Implications for Medical Care. Milbank Memorial Fund Quarterly, 55: 61.

Netherlands Economic Institute (1977). Present Cost of Peptic Ulceration to the Dutch Economy and Possible Impact of Cimetidine on this Cost. NEI, Rotterdam.

OHE (1962). Progress Against Tuberculosis. OHE, London.

OHE (1975). Sources of Information for Prescribing Doctors in Britain. OHE, London.

OHE (1977). Compendium of Health Statistics. OHE, London.

Roy W R (1976). Shattuck Lecture: An Agenda for Physicians and Legislators. *New England Journal of Medicine*, 295: 593.

Teeling-Smith G (1978). Cancer Chemotherapy: The Price to be Paid. *Journal of the Royal Society of Medicine*, 71: 633.

WHO (1978). Primary Health Care; a Joint Report by the Director-General of WHO and the Executive Director of UNICEF. Geneva.

 **Office of Health Economics**
162 Regent Street London WIR 6DD

The Office of Health Economics was founded in 1962 by the Association of the British Pharmaceutical Industry. Its terms of reference are:

To undertake research on the economic aspects of medical care.
To investigate other health and social problems.
To collect data from other countries.
To publish results, data and conclusions relevant to the above.

A more complete version of this paper appears as a monograph, No. 64, in a series on current health problems published by the Office of Health Economics, 162 Regent Street, London WIR 6DD. Copies are available at 35 p (£ 0.35).

Evaluating Medical Technology in the Context of a Fiscal Crisis: The Case of New Zealand

JOHN B. McKINLAY

Department of Sociology,
Boston University, and
Massachusetts General Hospital

N EW ZEALANDERS ARE TAUGHT, AND SOME EVEN believe, that theirs is "God's Own Country." Perhaps its geographical isolation and a generally favorable climate, combined with the equable disposition of its people, support this view. Ever so slowly, and painfully, New Zealanders are realizing that this is not now (if indeed it ever was) the case. Informed advice warns that the country is in dire economic circumstances. Some appreciation of these circumstances is essential if there is to be any understanding of the present state and future direction of the country's system of human services. Health care planners too often cannot, or will not, see that macroeconomic factors have just about everything to do with informed social policies concerning the public health. Indeed, they determine the very nature and range of policy options available for government. Such a truistic but necessary observation is the point of departure for the ensuing discussion.

This paper considers some problems and aspects of social policy concerning high technology as applied to medical care in New Zealand. The first section reviews several structural problems besetting the country's economy. These problems determine what is possible for future social policy, especially that concerning the proliferation of high technology. The second section describes the overall medical care system, highlighting three issues that are affected by, and them-

Milbank Memorial Fund Quarterly/*Health and Society*, Vol. 58, No. 2, 1980
© 1980 Milbank Memorial Fund and Massachusetts Institute of Technology
0160-1997-80-5802-0217-51/$01.00/0

selves compound, problems associated with high technology as applied to medicine. Unless social policy also addresses these seemingly separate, but closely related issues, no realistic social policy concerning high technology in medicine is possible. After this necessary background, the third section examines some aspects of medical technology, with specific examples, and offers suggestions for social policies in this area, in the context of New Zealand's overall economic situation.

The Serious Condition of the Economy

New Zealand is a small country covering an area of only 103,736 square miles and comprising three main islands—the North Island, the South Island, and the considerably smaller Stewart Island to the south—as well as a number of minor islands. The main islands are mountainous with rich coastal plains. The country is isolated from the rest of the world. Even Australia, of which it is sometimes thought to be an offshore island, is some 1200 miles away. In 1976, New Zealand had a population of 3,129,000; 2,700,000 (86 percent) of these were of European origin; 61,000 (2 percent) were Polynesian, and the remainder of other races (mainly Chinese and Indian).[1]

Recent *external* developments in international finance, over which New Zealand has little control, have exposed pre-existing structural weaknesses in the political economy, and heightened the country's economic vulnerability (United States Foreign Economic Policy Subcommittee, 1977; McKinlay, 1978a). Two such areas of vulnerability will be considered here as illustrations. First, the country's exports are commonly divided into two main categories: "primary" or agricultural

---

[1] Many of the statistics in this report derive from the New Zealand Planning Council's (1978) *Planning Perspectives: 1978–83.* My heavy reliance on this useful publication is hereby acknowledged. It was selected because 1) the Planning Council is probably the most authoritative source of economic information now available in New Zealand; 2) the material it uses is more or less up-to-date; and 3) as an appointed agency of the government, it tends to err on the side of caution and optimism. If, as the Planning Council suggests, the country is in dire economic straits, then it is indeed likely to be in such condition.

activities (mainly meat, wool, and dairy products), and "secondary" or industrial products (forest products and small-scale manufacturing exports). A disproportionate three-quarters of New Zealand's exports involve primary (traditional) products—a proportion that has changed negligibly over the last several decades—so that the economy is extremely vulnerable to overseas protectionism and world-wide price fluctuations. Nationwide alarm was expressed during 1978 when a television program simulated the economic decimation that would result from the introduction of a single disease that afflicts sheep.

A second example of New Zealand's vulnerability to external developments relates to oil: some 87 percent of requirements are imported. During the decade before 1973 (the year in which the OPEC cartel quadrupled oil prices), oil imports were equivalent in value to an average of about 5 to 6 percent of export receipts. By 1975, this figure had risen to about 21 percent. Government action to reduce volume brought the percentage down to 15.4 in 1977, but is unlikely to keep it there because of the heavy reliance of transport on liquid fuels (about 71.5 percent of total oil consumption) and oil price increases already scheduled by OPEC. Vulnerability through oil is a problem New Zealand shares with most other countries. When combined with vulnerabilities in other areas, however (e.g., remoteness, the high cost of overseas trade, a disproportionately heavy agricultural base, etc.), New Zealand appears precariously situated in the international financial area.

The recent precipitate decline in the terms of trade (the ratio of export prices to import prices), caused mainly by rising import prices, is further cause for concern. New Zealand's terms of trade, in contrast to the trend in previous postwar cycles of economic activity, improved little when other industrial countries moved out of the 1974–1975 recession, and has actually deteriorated further. In 1978 New Zealand had an unprecedentedly high deficit, over and above its already heavy borrowing, of $1446 million.* The range of actions that have been necessary to cope with (not solve) *external* developments (e.g., pricing policies, the dampening of demand, and taxation increases) have obviously had *internal* repercussions. For example, over the period

*Throughout this paper, figures in dollars refer to New Zealand dollars.

1973–1976, the growth of the volume of goods and services produced, the real gross domestic product (GDP), fell behind population growth. As the terms of trade deteriorated, New Zealand could purchase fewer imports for the value it earned through exports. After adjustment for the effect of both the deterioration in terms of trade (−12 percent) and the increase in population from 1973 to 1976 (5 percent), real income per capita fell by 14.4 percent over these four years. New Zealand's rate of inflation, although it usually follows the world rate, has recently lagged behind that of its trading partners, thereby further handicapping exporters and local industries, which must compete with cheaper overseas imports.

The resulting problem of unemployment is particularly hard on semiskilled and unskilled workers, new school leavers, the less-well-educated, and particular population groups such as Maoris and other Polynesians—those perhaps most in need of an opportunity to work. The number registered as unemployed continues to rise despite government provision of special work, the disincentive to register as unemployed because of the stigma of unemployment, and a net outflow during 1977 and 1978 of about 70,000 people.

This population loss is of particular concern, since many of these migrants are young skilled or professional workers, who leave New Zealand in search of more favorable employment opportunities. Nearly one-half of the emigrants between 1971 and 1978 were between ages 20 and 29; one-quarter were teachers, engineers, and other professional or technical workers, and nearly one-third were craftsmen or production workers, including machinists, electricians, and carpenters. The departure of workers in these categories, and in such large numbers, represents the loss of a resource for which the country will have even greater need in the future, if it is ever fully to recover from its present economic malaise.

Related demographic developments have tended to compound these difficulties. Of significance are the sharp decline in fertility rates, the immigration of Pacific Islanders (many of whom require considerable support through human services), and continuing internal migration from rural to urban areas, particularly of Maoris. The general fertility rate (the number of live births per 1,000 women aged between 15 and 44 years) has declined from a peak of 140.6 in 1961 to

83.2 in 1976. This decline, which is also occurring among the Maori population (who until recently experienced relatively high fertility rates) is of course being reflected in the changing age structure of the population. The elderly, as a proportion of the total population, continue to increase, and will require some expansion of the services concerned with their support in the community.

Attempts over the last several decades to broaden the country's economic base, through the expansion and diversification of manufacturing activities, have produced marked changes in the composition of exports and imports, and have altered traditional trading relations, but have not markedly lessened the country's economic vulnerability. New Zealand has few options in terms of natural resources, which consist primarily of some low-grade coal deposits and a little natural gas. To expand secondary industry, therefore, requires the importation of raw materials, which creates a new form of dependence on international trade. One authoritative report describes a new aspect of the country's economic vulnerability as follows:

> In colonial times, New Zealand's purpose was to supply agricultural commodities to Britain, and the nation's development was governed by fluctuations in world commodity prices. It is an ironic twist of fate that our efforts to insulate the economy through the development of manufacturing have in one sense widened the area of dependency and vulnerability, through dependence on imported raw materials and other inputs, to our industries. (New Zealand Planning Council, 1978)

Government maneuverability with respect to the public funding of services is restricted by the New Zealand taxation structure, which has been described by the Planning Council as "unattractive from a viewpoint of economic growth and also on the grounds of equity" (New Zealand Planning Council, 1978). Since it limits the range of options open to the state, particularly future public expenditure for human services, this tax structure and some of its consequences should be briefly described. New Zealand is distinctive in the proportion of total tax revenue raised in the form of personal and company income taxes. The proportion of total income taxes paid by private individuals in relation to that paid by companies has been growing: in 1959–1960 the ratio of personal to corporate income tax was 71:29, whereas in 1976–1977 it had risen to around 82:18. In 1966–1967, the average tax rate for a married person on an average wage was 11.8 percent: by 1977–1978, this rate had doubled to 23.2 percent. The tax rate on an additional dollar of income (the marginal tax rate) earned by a married person on the average wage in 1966–1967 was 22.5 percent: by 1977–1978 it was 45.5 percent. Although notoriously difficult to determine, the effective tax rate on company profits is authoritatively estimated to be as high as 78 percent. Some have suggested that the total income tax levied on the profits of many companies exceeds 100 percent of their real profits. Such high rates have a profound effect on, among other things, the incentive to work, save, and invest, and probably contribute to the current net outflow of New Zealanders to other countries. With regard to social equity, the current situation has been summarized as follows:

> While the tax structure is superficially very progressive (aimed to ensure that high-income earners pay not only absolutely but also proportionately more tax than low income earners) the actual situation is probably quite different, with a progressive tax structure applying to a wide band of wage and salary earners, but substantial scope for tax avoidance available to the highest income earners and little or no tax payable by those who have substantial wealth invested in a non-income generating form. (New Zealand Planning Council, 1978)

In summary, New Zealand can be described as a geographically isolated country of small numbers with an economy that is unusually vulnerable to setbacks on the international financial scene. It is now beset with serious structural payments imbalances (exacerbated by but not wholly attributable to the recent actions of the OPEC cartel), requires heavy overseas borrowing to sustain its present standard of living, is experiencing a deterioration in the terms of trade, and is being forced to cast around for new trading partnerships. The country is beset with labor disputes (which have not been discussed here), a precipitate rise in unemployment, a crippling tax structure, the ill-afforded loss of thousands of its younger, more skilled workers, along with other unfavorable demographic shifts. According to the New Zealand Planning Council (1978), the country, over the period 1978–1983, will be confronted with at least the following:

- A deficit between overseas receipts and payments.
- Negative economic growth and falling real income per head.
- Unemployment higher than at any time since the Depression.
- A continuing stream of New Zealanders leaving for other countries.
- Continuing high inflation.
- Tensions in industrial and social relationships.
- A slackening in the momentum of the drive for higher exports and for improved productivity in all sectors of the economy.

For those involved in health service research and planning in New Zealand, a difficulty is to persuade various interest groups (e.g., hospitals, the public, the professions) that these macroeconomic conditions will largely determine the future of the country's system of human services. The future of New Zealand's health system is often discussed as if the economic problems described do not exist, are only temporary, or can be rendered insignificant through "fine tuning." What is not now but must be recognized is that some appreciation of the country's economic condition is essential if social policy is to realistically confront and correct the structural problems besetting New Zealand medical care. Indeed, confrontation of these economic difficulties will determine whatever options are available for the future. Many of the problems associated with New Zealand's medical care system reflect, or are the consequences of, problems associated with the overall economy. In essence, whatever shape New Zealand's medical and health care system will assume in the future is dependent upon some recognition and solution of these problems in the overall economy. Visionaries do provide temporary relief from pressing realities, and sometimes foster useful alternative strategies. Eventually, however, one must return to the basic question for social policy (McKinlay, 1979a): What resources are likely to be available, and how can they be allocated so as to ensure value for money?

The Medical Care System

No real purpose would be served here by a detailed review of the history and organizational structure of New Zealand's medical care system, since the information is readily available elsewhere (New Zealand Government Printer, 1974, 1979). Instead, only the general contours of the system will be described before an exploration of three issues that bear upon the problem of high technology as applied to medical care, which is considered in the final section.

The Poor Return on Investment

What proportion of New Zealand's resources are consumed by medical care and what return does this investment yield? The pertinence of this social policy question is heightened by the preceding discussion of the country's economic plight. Figure 1 summarizes the changing distribution of central government expenditure since 1938. Over the last forty years, expenditure on human services (health and hospital boards and other social services and welfare benefits) has increased dramatically, from about one-third of all expenditure in 1938, to about one-half in 1978. For the fiscal year 1977–1978, $822 million was voted to health, a further $65 million to the Hospital Works Program (loan financed), $71 million to the Accident Compensation Commission, and $62 million to invalids and for sickness benefits and rehabilitation. In other words, in 1978 the total health-related expenditures by the public sector exceeded $1 billion, or 7 percent of the GNP.

Figure 2 gives some indication of the relative increase in both public and private expenditure on medical care over the period 1925–1978. Although government contributions have increased considerably over the entire period, the proportion of private contributions has changed little since the early 1940s. The way in which the government has allocated resources to three areas of health care since 1924 is depicted in Fig. 3. Hospital services have consumed the vast majority of the available resources, while public health activities have remained relatively constant. Community health care gained some ground at the

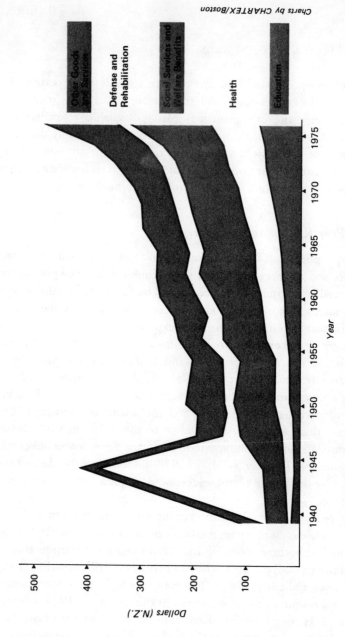

FIG. 1. Central government expenditures per capita at constant prices, 1939–1976. A wholesale price/gross domestic product index has been used as the deflator. Base year, 1965–1966.

402

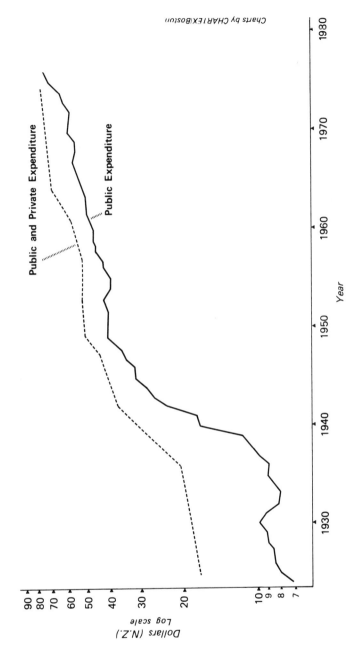

FIG. 2. Public (central government) and private expenditures on health per capita at constant prices, 1924–1978. The wage-rate index has been used as the deflator. Base year, 1965–1966. The estimates of private expenditure are tentative, particularly for the earlier years, and have been calculated on a conservative basis.

403

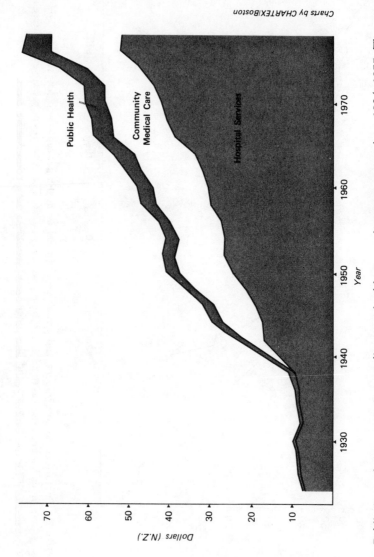

FIG. 3. Public (central government) expenditure on health per capita at constant prices, 1924–1977. The wage-rate index has been used as the deflator. Base year, 1965–1966.

Charts by CHARTEX/Boston

expense of hospital services during the 1940s, but has slowly lost ground over the intervening years.

Fostered in part by public debate over a 1974 White Paper (*A Health Service for New Zealand*), by knowledge of the changing nature of medical problems, and by the concern among some medical students, an interest in activities related to community health has emerged over the last few years (New Zealand Government Printer, 1974). At present, less than 3 percent of total government expenditure on health is devoted to such activities. Since there are now no extra funds for new programs (in large part because of the volume of existing commitments to hospitals and the potential opposition of a powerful hospital lobby), the government has responded by raising funds through the imposition of an added tax on alcohol and tobacco (known in New Zealand as the "beer and baccy" tax). Although some have heralded the new tax as an innovative approach to the funding of community health services, several factors make this view unacceptable. First, this new tax has not resulted in any change in the overall pattern of resource allocation to health care in the country. It simply provides some short-term funds that are added onto the much larger resources already flowing into traditional areas of medical care. It displaces nothing, and may even reinforce the traditional allocation format. Second, most of the funds generated through this added tax do not go to community health per se, but to hospital boards, either for administrative activities, or for previously unfunded hospital-based proposals that were resurrected and resubmitted. Third, it must be considered paradoxical and against sound principles of budgeting that community health activities should be funded, in large part, by a tax on the consumption of tobacco and alcohol. The implication here is that the more the public spends on alcohol and tobacco products, which are known to place people at risk to certain largely preventable illnesses, the more there will be available for community health activities, a large proportion of which are devoted to the alteration of these very same at risk behaviors!

Given the country's economic plight, it is timely to inquire as to what return such investment yields, in terms of, say, standard measures of the nation's overall health status. Figure 4 contrasts the decline in the standardized death rate with the proportion of the GNP

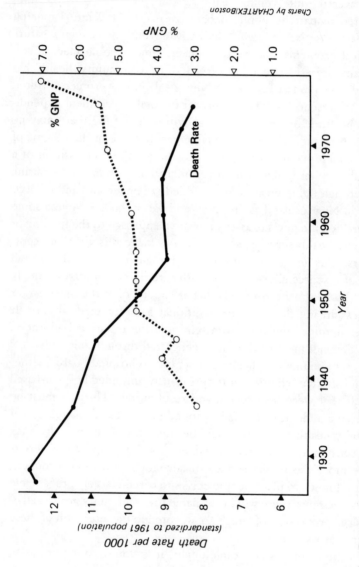

FIG. 4. Death rate per 1000 (standardized), contrasted with the proportion of the gross national product expended on health care, 1928–1975.

devoted to health care. Although the death rate declined dramatically between 1930 and 1955, it has leveled off over the last twenty years or so. But over this same period, the proportion of the GNP devoted to health care has more than doubled. The absurdity revealed by Fig. 4 is that the precipitate and still unrestrained increase in medical care expenditures began when almost all of the decline in New Zealand mortality this century had already occurred!

For non-Maoris since 1880, and for Maoris since 1950 (the earliest time for which reliable statistics are available), life expectancy at birth (the average number of years that members of a hypothetical group would live if they were subjected throughout their lives to the age-specific mortality rates observed at the time of their birth) has increased for both males and females, the increase being somewhat greater for non-Maoris. Nothing like the same improvement is evident in life expectancy at the other ages considered (20, 40, and 60 years). When life expectancy at different ages is considered, most of the gains during this century have resulted from the known decline in infant mortality, primarily from infectious diseases. And consistent with what has been shown by McKeown (1976) for England and Wales, and McKinlay and McKinlay (1979) for the United States, specific medical measures (either chemotherapeutic or prophylactic) appear to have contributed little to this reduction. Over the last twenty-five years or so, there has been little improvement in life expectancy at ages 20, 40, and 60 years, for either sex or ethnic group. Indeed, among Maoris, there may have been some decrease in life expectancy at age 60.

It may be that this discussion focuses on mortality and ignores the important areas of morbidity and disability where, it is claimed, medical care inputs may have had a detectable impact. In New Zealand, the *only* reliable information on the course of diseases over time, in large population groups, consists of mortality data. Other corroborative indications (e.g., prevalence data on morbidity, restricted activity days, bed days, days of limited activity, etc.), although sometimes available in other countries, are not generally available in New Zealand. New Zealand clearly has paralleled the mortality trends of most other similarly situated countries, and there is little reason to think that, overall, New Zealand has not done so with respect to other measures of output such as morbidity. If, as is likely, New Zealand has followed the pattern now evident in, say, the United States, then the expected life free of disability may not have increased with the small increase in life expectancy that appears to have occurred in some age categories (McKinlay and McKinlay, 1979). In other words, whatever slight gains in life expectancy have occurred at certain ages, they may have been merely gains in years of disability due, in large part, to chronic disease, and there may even have been some decrease in years free of disability. Certainly, from the mortality data that are available in New Zealand, it appears that the country is getting a poor return from its not inconsiderable investment in traditional medical care and, in the absence of corroborative morbidity data, there is no reason to qualify the contention that the present pattern of medical care inputs is yielding a poor return in terms of the nation's overall health status.

When limited resources are available, what is devoted to one area obviously subtracts from what is available for others. The vast sums devoted to the care (not cure) of such chronic conditions as heart disease, cancer, and stroke must subtract from what is available for areas with a potentially better return on investment, such as community health and primary health care. In the light of these data concerning the poor relation between medical care inputs and mortality outcomes (Cochrane, St. Leger and Moore, 1978; McKinlay, 1978b), it is reasonable to challenge the basis upon which resources are allocated to health care in New Zealand. The usual administrative response to such data is to maximize inputs to all aspects of the existing system in the hope that some beneficial outcome will occur somewhere. The economic vicissitudes already described have foreclosed the possibility of continuing this course for much longer.

General Structure

Like so many other countries, New Zealand has a hybrid system of medical care. Its origins can be traced to the English system, particularly the emergence of hospitals during the eighteenth century, and it was developed during the nineteenth century to accommodate the particular health needs of the population as it was distributed at that time. Since then the system has been disfigured by political pressures, public demands, professional self-interest and, more recently, massive and now habitual infusions of overseas technology. Medical care in New Zealand now rests, somewhat precariously, on foundations that have remained largely uninspected since they were first laid over a century ago. So ingrained is the commitment to the existing system, so powerful the interests behind it, and so institutionalized the response of simply adding more of the same, that it was only as recently as 1974, with the publication of a government White Paper (*A Health Service for New Zealand*), that a pattern of health care structurally different from the predominant hospital-based system was seriously contemplated. Until then, the provision of additions to, rather than replacements of, now outmoded hospital-based services had been the preferred response (New Zealand Government Printer, 1974).

Very briefly, the major components of New Zealand's medical care system are as follows:

1) *The minister of health* is a publicly elected member of the government (the majority party in Parliament) and a member of the prime minister's cabinet, who is responsible for all activities undertaken by the Department of Health, and usually covers issues and questions relating to health that may arise in Parliament. The prime minister alone decides who shall be minister of health, the decision being determined largely by political considerations (e.g., to balance perspectives in cabinet, ensure like-mindedness, political patronage, etc.). The minister may have some qualifications or experience in the area of health care, but usually does not. On occasion he/she may have had the advantage of serving an apprenticeship as "shadow spokesperson on health" before assuming a government's portfolio of health. Since there are general elections every three years, a minister is usually associated with the Department of Health only for this short period of time, before either the government is defeated, or he/she is promoted to more senior cabinet rank (e.g., education, industries and commerce, labor). This frequency of ministerial turnover presents difficulties for continuity of departmental policy. A minister may take up to a year to "find his feet" in a new portfolio. Since much of the third year in office is devoted to public posturing, with a view to a favorable result at the general election, little more than a year may be available for a minister to seriously implement new policies. The

minister must compete with other high-ranking cabinet members for his/her piece of the fiscal pie.

2) *The director-general of health (DG)* is a permanent civil servant and is responsible to the minister of health for the organization of the Department of Health, and for implementing any policy the government may have with respect to health care. The person occupying this position is statutorily required to be medically qualified but there is no requirement for the special training or experience that may equip him/her for such an important administrative post. A detailed account of the activities of the Department of Health is given in the annual report of the director-general of health, which the minister of health submits to Parliament.

3) *The deputy directors-general of health* are also permanent civil servants who are responsible to the DG for the organization and management of the particular division they head (e.g., clinical services, public health, hospitals, mental health, nursing, dental health, and administration). With the exception of the deputy director-general for administration, those at this rank are all medically qualified. Although they command considerable resources and manpower, they are not formally required to have special qualifications or experience in such fields as health planning, evaluation research, medical economics, social policy, or even management and administration.

4) *Hospital boards.* The country is divided into twenty-nine hospital districts. General and psychiatric hospitals in these districts are controlled by locally elected hospital boards. A hospital board of eight to fourteen members is elected every three years for each hospital district from the local population. It is the duty of every hospital board to provide, maintain, and staff such institutions, and such medical, nursing, and other services as the minister of health considers necessary. Until 1957, hospital board activities were funded jointly by the central government, contributions from the local authority, voluntary contributions and bequests, patients' fees, and social security payments. After 1957, local hospital boards were funded entirely by the central government, and their expenditures escalated. Despite several attempts to ensure that hospital boards work strictly within allocations approved by government, culminating in legislation in 1973 that rendered members of a hospital board personally liable for overexpendi-

ture, the regulations have proved difficult to enforce. The hospital board is the backbone of New Zealand's present medical care system. All activities, including nursing training, community health activities, and primary care radiate out from a hospital base. Hospital activities are not one part of a package of community health services; instead, they are the center around which all revolves. (Some even view community health nursing as a system in which hospital-based nurses drive out into the community to visit patients who are not able to go to the hospital.) The community health activities that have developed in recent years have been additions to, rather than independent replacements of, hospital-based activities. Those appointed to a senior post on the board (hospital board secretary, hospital superintendent, etc.) are not required to have special qualifications or experience in the area to which they are appointed. It is possible for a physician whose life has been spent in general practice to be appointed superintendent of a multimillion-dollar medical complex centered in a large hospital.

5) *Health districts.* In each of the eighteen health districts, which overlap hospital boards, there is a medical officer of health (MOH), who is always a medical practitioner and supposedly has special qualifications in public health. The MOH is involved with and is an advisor to all local authorities in the district. The approval of the MOH is usually required before action can be taken on health-related matters by a local authority, and sometimes the MOH is the first line of appeal against its decision. The MOH is required to keep the director-general of health and the board of health informed of deficiencies in the way the local authority carries out its responsibilities under the Health Act of 1956. Many people believe that changes in organizational structure and disease patterns have rendered the MOH a legacy of the past, which should be dispensed with.

The Public versus the "Private" System

There is much discussion in New Zealand of what are termed "private health services," and the nature of their relation to the public system. Since the arrangements to which the term refers can in no way be regarded as "private," this discussion is largely misplaced, and serves the interests of particular groups. Successive governments have supported the development of "private" hospitals on the ground that every private hospital bed is one less bed that the government has to pay for and maintain. But the general public, through the tax system, do in fact pay for and maintain "private" facilities. The position of these expanding private facilities has been secured through government-financed capital loans, various subsidy schemes, and periodic increases in hospital benefits. In other words, the growth of the so-called private system has continued virtually unchecked, and is heavily subsidized by the public sector, so much so that the term "private" is now a misnomer. Since 1938, all governments have accepted the compatibility of a dual system. Private health insurance has grown rapidly in the last several decades, especially since 1967, when premiums were made tax-deductible. Nowadays, about 10 percent of the population has some kind of medical care coverage through private health insurance.

The premise underlying the public system is that medical care should be free and readily available to all on the basis of need, rather than on the ability to pay. The growth of the private system is attributed to, or justified by, some purported deterioration in the public system that, it is claimed, jeopardizes the goal of readily available free care on the basis of need. For example, a so-called public desire for the alternative of private beds is often attributed to lengthy waiting lists for public beds, an issue that is of understandable public concern.

This matter of public hospital waiting lists illustrates a worrisome feature of New Zealand medical care: how the medical establishment, particularly "the profession," can contrive public demand and thereby manipulate the government into subsidizing a private system that is more favorable to its own interests. At least three important aspects of the medical system are conducive to such manipulation. 1) Medical services are provided in public hospitals largely by part-time or consultant physicians and surgeons, who frequently maintain parallel private practices. 2) Salaries or fees paid through the public hospital system tend to be low compared with fees charged privately. 3) The individual patient in a private hospital is responsible only for hospital expenses over and above a minimum allowance paid by the government (and even this excess may be paid through third-party insurance).

Given these conditions, it is easy for part-time physicians either to create a public hospital waiting list or to force patients into the private sector, at some extra cost to the patients, producing much higher income for themselves. Dr. A. may say to Mrs. B., upon agreeing that she should have her varicose veins stripped, that she must wait over a year if he is to perform the operation in a public hospital, or only a couple of days if in a "private" hospital—for which she must pay a little more. This does not represent a situation of "free choice," especially when patient *demand* has been translated into a *need* during a consultation. This situation is reinforced by the nature of the medical problems of the patients on public hospital waiting lists, which tend to be either nonurgent or elective surgical procedures. Only occasionally does a patient with a genuine emergency or urgent case experience difficulty gaining admission to a public hospital, an event seized upon by the media as newsworthy—an indication of its relative infrequency. In one particular hospital district, a relatively small waiting list increased rapidly after the opening of a private hospital, contradicting the original rationale for building this extra hospital. Some claim that the public hospital waiting list serves as an effective regulator of what may be unreasonable and insatiable public demand, a demand that is in large part contrived.

This phenomenon is further encouraged by a financial reimbursement system that favors hospital-based interventions over the less expensive, but just as effective, ambulatory procedures. By furthering a state of affairs in the public system that favors the alternative of private medical care, the medical establishment appears to have the government over a barrel. The interests that benefit from the existence of the private system also have a hand in the generation of problems in the public system that are a major justification for its (private system) existence. What is paradoxical is that government should so heavily finance the very process through which the "alternative" system is largely justified.

The issue of "private" versus public medical services in New Zealand remains problematic. While the government is being forced toward fewer beds because of economic considerations and, perhaps, evidence of the superiority of some ambulatory or outpatient procedures, private interests continue to expand even further, on the fairly safe assumption that the government will continue to pick up the costs. The position of one recent government was outlined as follows:

> The progressive improvement of State health services will restore true freedom of choice for patients. The Government believes that the true role of the private sector is to meet the medical needs of those citizens who freely and voluntarily elect to not use State provided health services and are prepared to meet the full cost of private services. Should they wish to meet this expense by private insurance, they should be free to do so. When it has been established that patients seeking private treatment do so from freedom of choice, and not in an effort to circumvent the difficulties of the public system, the real need for private health services will be more properly determined. (New Zealand Government Printer, 1974)

The Oversupply of Hospital Beds

An issue that continues to plague social policy in New Zealand is the way in which the government is locked into, and unable to significantly alter, patterns of resource allocation first established over a century ago. Although the problem is perennial in many different countries, and affects different areas of public expenditure, it is well illustrated in New Zealand with respect to the number and geographical distribution of hospital beds. During the nineteenth century, when New Zealand was a sparsely settled British colony, there was a short-lived gold rush on the west coast of the South Island. Although it is difficult to believe, the pattern of resource allocation established at that time (based on the distribution of population and the nature of the problems at that time) has persisted to the present day, despite the fact that the population distribution and the nature of the medical problems have changed remarkably over the ensuing century. Table 1 shows the remarkable increase in the number of hospital beds over the period 1874–1976.

Although the larger number of beds reflects the overall population increases, as expected, some marked regional anomalies remain. One reason is that hospital board expenditure remains subject to control by the minister of health who, in turn, is vulnerable to pressure from the medical establishment, public opinion, etc. To compound this, hospital board allocations for public hospital maintenance are based on

TABLE 1
The Increase in Public and Private Hospital Beds in New Zealand, 1874–1976

Year	Public Sector		Private Sector		Total	
	Number	Rate/1,000 Population	Number	Rate/1,000 Population	Number	Rate/1,000 Population
1874	1598	4.63			1598	4.63
1878	1974	4.31			1974	4.31
*1886	2822	4.55			2862	4.55
*1896	3708	4.99			3764	5.06
*1906	5296	5.66			5374	5.74
*1916	8612	7.49			8686	7.56
*1926	12548	8.91			12622	8.96
1936	15529	9.87	2596	1.65	18125	11.52
1946	18917	10.75	3254	1.85	22171	12.60
1956	22961	10.56	2822	1.30	25783	11.86
1966	25528	9.54	3644	1.36	29172	10.90
1976	27209	8.69	4982	1.59	32191	10.28

Sources: Provisional results of the 1976 census, New Zealand; and Department of Health, Wellington, New Zealand, 1978.
*The total includes some private beds, which were not consistently recorded for separate tabulation.

allocations made in the previous year, adjusted to take account of known increases in commitments, plus an allowance for normal growth. Funds are therefore allocated to local hospital boards, not primarily on the reasonable basis of population numbers, but rather on the established number of beds. The higher the number of beds per capita, the higher the allocation. This linear relation was investigated and produced a correlation of 0.65. Some of New Zealand's most populous areas, such as Auckland (800,000), North Canterbury (344,000), and Wellington (344,000), appear at the lower end of the scale in terms of both proportionate allocations and beds, whereas sparsely populated rural areas like Waipawa (13,000), the West Coast (34,000), and Taumaranui (12,000) appear toward the top end of the scale.

According to a recent report of the Organization of Economic and Cooperative Development, New Zealand currently spends proportionately more of its health dollar on hospital activities than any other country in the world. While there was an eight-fold increase in population over the period 1874–1976 (from 345,000 to over 3 million), there was more than a nineteen-fold increase in hospital beds (from 1,600 to over 32,000) in the same period.

Most countries do not support the high ratio of 10.2 beds per 1,000 population that now exists in New Zealand. The variation in the number of hospital beds available in different countries is in no way reflected in variations in either mortality or morbidity (Cochrane, St. Leger, and Moore, 1978; McKinlay, 1978b). In other words, a two-fold difference between countries in the proportion of resources devoted to hospital activities does not produce a two-fold difference in any of the standard output measures such as mortality or morbidity. The Department of Health recently issued some planning guidelines for hospital beds and services, which proposed that there be 8 beds per 1,000 population (Department of Health, 1977). This composite figure was arrived at after separate calculations of the ratio of beds that some feel are required in five different areas (pediatric, adult, geriatric, maternity, and psychiatric) per 1,000 age-specific population. Where these ratios originated, no one seems to know. They appear without any justification or reference. A ratio of 8 beds per 1,000 population is up to twice as high as the existing ratios in some other countries with a social and economic structure similar to that in New Zealand, and with almost identical mortality and morbidity outputs. The New Zealand Government (through the Department of Health) is now using these arbitrarily derived guidelines as a basis for social policy concerning the number and distribution of hospital beds.

Recognizing the absurdity of the level of bed provision recommended in these guidelines, let us consider how many beds are available at present. A comparison of the overall number of beds recommended (25,399) with the number actually available (31,836) revealed a surplus of some 6,437 beds. If we assume that the average hospital bed costs the state, say, $150 per day (whether or not it is occupied), then this surplus, over and above the high ratio proposed by the Department of Health, costs the New Zealand taxpayers in excess of $35 million each year, or around $12 for every man, woman, and child. And the state appears powerless to do anything about the oversupply of beds, even though it is forced to pay the bill. Wastage of such magnitude reveals how hollow the objection is that New Zealand simply does not have the resources to engage in proper health services research. Imagine the saving that would result for this small country if hospital bed numbers were brought down to the level most other similarly situated nations find adequate to their needs.[2]

A study of the relation between the number of hospital admissions per 1,000 population and the number of public hospital beds per 1,000 population revealed what Roemer (1961), among others, has already demonstrated for the United States: the higher the bed ratio, the higher the admission rate ($r = 0.45$).[3] In other words, the hospital

---

[2] Federal health planners in the United States have proposed the elimination of 100,000 unneeded hospital beds over the next seven years by reducing the ratio of general beds from its present 4.5 to 4.0 per 1000 population. Aside from the $80,000 capital investment in each of these unnecessary hospital beds, with an annual operating cost of $40,000 per bed, some $4,000 million ($40,000 × 100,000 beds) of America's resources are consumed each year by these superfluous beds (*New York Times,* September 29, 1977).

[3] Milton Roemer (1961) found that a sudden increase in the supply of hospital beds in one county in the eastern United States resulted in a prompt rise in the hospital admission rate and in the average length of stay for most patients. After years of "getting along" with a bed supply of 2.9 general beds

admission rate in New Zealand rises to fill the additional number of beds that are available in certain areas.

An even stronger linear relation (r = 0.74) exists between the number of public beds per 1,000 population and the average length of stay. In other words, where there is an excess of beds, not only does the rate of admission increase, but patients have a longer average stay. These factors combine to increase the probability of an individual's exposure to medical technology through hospitalization.

The hospital system is the conduit through which medical technology flows and becomes a permanent part of the health care system. Physicians abet this process by opening the spigot wider and wider. Some of this technology flows into socially useful areas and beneficially alters the course of some problems. Much of it, however, flows into areas that are either barren, or already "overtechnologized," and therefore are superfluous. Experience to date would suggest that the state, while protesting wastage and superfluity, is powerless to prevent them, and is forced to subsidize the whole process. This impotence in the face of the proliferation of high technology will continue until the state can effect some alteration in the hospital structure that now requires it, and without which so rapid an expansion could not occur. Controlling the hospital system is a necessary but not sufficient condition for controlling the proliferation of unevaluated high technology as applied to medicine.

The problem of the proliferation of unevaluated high technology (to be considered in the final section) cannot be separated from this problem of the oversupply of hospital beds. Some kind of vicious circle appears to operate. The medical establishment maintains that it must constantly expand hospital and related activities in order to accommodate new and ever more sophisticated technology. The

---

per 1000, the supply suddenly increased to 3.8 per 1000. At the old level, the hospital was not overcrowded, having an occupancy of 78 percent. With the increase in bed supply, however, there was an abrupt rise in the admission rate of the study hospital, and no compensatory decline in the admission rates of other nearby hospitals. At the same time, the average length of stay for 40 out of 53 patients increased. The utilization rate by Blue Cross members in the study hospital rose by 38 percent, in response to the 42 percent rise in the study hospital's bed capacity.

(mainly overseas) manufacturers of high technology maintain that new, bigger, more sophisticated technology is necessary in order that hospitals can be more cost efficient, achieve "economies of scale," and so forth. The activities of the constituent parts of the health system seem to be employed by each as a justification for the scale and direction of their own activities.

The Problem of Too Many Physicians

The structural problems besetting New Zealand health care cannot be compartmentalized or satisfactorily resolved through social policies initiated by New Zealand alone. They are related to other problems, and of a magnitude that now requires coordinated action by other governments as well. Nowhere is this more evident than in the oversupply of medical manpower, a situation New Zealand shares with most other countries. In the context of the economic difficulties now confronting the country, this problem must be considered of the highest priority for social policy. Because physician oversupply is so intertwined with other structural problems (e.g., the oversupply of hospital beds, the medical establishment's ability to steer the state, and the proliferation of high technology), action is necessary here if policy is ever to intervene effectively on these related problems, and vice versa. Moreover, since the oversupply of medical manpower is a problem shared with other countries, and because of the circulation of medical workers between different countries, social policy in this area must be coordinated with the programs of other countries, particularly such British Commonwealth partners as Australia, Canada, India, and Great Britain.

It is estimated that there were about 69,000 workers in the health sector of the New Zealand workforce in 1976: that is, 1 health worker for every 45 people in the total population, or 1 such worker for every 18 people in the workforce. By the turn of the century, when the population is projected to reach 3.7 million, these ratios are expected to decline to 36 and 14 respectively.[4]

Attention is focused on physicians because 1) they generate more

[4] These figures were prepared by the Management Services and Research Unit, Department of Health, Wellington, New Zealand, 1978.

costs for the state than any other category of worker; 2) reliable up-to-date figures are available on physicians from regular surveys by the Medical Council of New Zealand; 3) any increase in the number of physicians is integrally related to the proliferation of technology (the issue taken up in the final section); and 4) the problem of too many doctors is an area in which the state is now beginning to act. The abundance of physicians also illustrates how the common health problems of different countries now require social policies coordinated among countries. There is no uniquely New Zealand solution to the country's problem of oversupply of doctors. Any realistic solution now requires action by other countries as well. New Zealanders still talk about a "national health manpower policy," when the nature of the problem and all available data indicate that an international or multinational health manpower policy is required.

There are today just over 4,000 physicians in New Zealand, 1 for every 764 people. By the turn of the century (2001), the number is conservatively expected to double to 8,000, or 1 physician for every 465 people in the population (Salmond, 1978). The hospital board areas in North Island and South Island are sketched in Figs. 5a and 5b; Table 2 shows the population of each area, and the distribution of general practitioners (GPs) and hospital beds throughout the country. Some areas have a large number of doctors (fewer than 2,000 people per GP), and others seem to have relatively few (more than 4,000 people per GP). Clear concentrations of GPs exist in Northland, Tauranga, and Nelson, three well-known resort areas with very favorable climates. The large number of GPs in Otago, in the South Island, is probably an aberration attributable to the presence of what was until recently New Zealand's only medical school. It is noteworthy that a contiguous hospital board (South Otago) should be so undersupplied with doctors.

Why is any further expansion in the supply of physicians (possibly even the retention of existing numbers) bound to produce calamitous consequences for New Zealand's already fragile economy? Estimates vary widely, but it now costs about $80,000 to train a physician in New Zealand. The 1979 annual output of 243 medical graduates is expected to increase to 310 by 1981. As in most other countries, medical students are generally drawn from the highest social classes.

FIG. 5a. Hospital board regions and major population centers in North Island.

Although the costs of their training (currently about $19 million a year) are met through public funds, there is no requirement that physicians work for some period of time in the underdoctored areas already discussed, or that they remain in the country. Since the early sixties, the country has lost about one-third of its medical graduates by

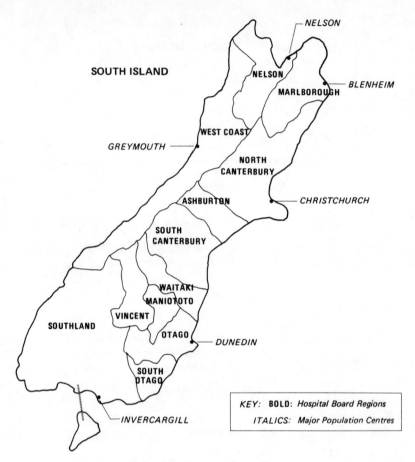

FIG. 5b. Hospital board regions and major population centers in South Island.

permanent emigration. In 1978, 171 emigrated overseas and 80 returned to the country, leaving a net loss of 91 New Zealand-trained physicians, over one-third of a year's total output! Over the last eight years, there has been a net outflow of 325 nationals, or the equivalent of three entire graduating classes.

Assuming that over the eight years 1970–1978 it cost an average of, say, $50,000 to train a physician, then the net outflow of 325 over this period represents an economic loss of around $17 million. At the present cost of around $80,000, the net outflow of 91 during 1978 represents a loss of over $7 million. For a country as small as New Zealand, with its economic problems and unique vulnerabilities, this represents a poor return on a very large investment. Even worse, these recent medical graduates contribute some of their best years to the economies of countries that are New Zealand's international competitors. In effect, New Zealand is underwriting some of the high costs of training physicians for its economic rivals—an international beneficence the country simply cannot afford.

Now it is true that, over the past eight years at least, this outflow of nationals has been offset by a net inflow of other nationals—971 since 1970, or an average of 121 a year (Salmond, 1978). Although many of these foreign graduates fill gaps in needed specialties, and undoubtedly contribute something to the overall health of the public, they sometimes exacerbate existing problems. Their training is sometimes inappropriate for the local scene; patients may have difficulty understanding foreign physicians. More important, foreign-trained physicians sometimes bring an inflated conception of what is possible, and demand the resources and technology to which they are accustomed (perhaps even dependent on) overseas. With only limited resources, there is sometimes difficulty fulfilling what must be considered, at least from the New Zealand viewpoint, grandiose expectations. One well-known specialist with overseas experience contends that six CAT scanners (one in each of the major cities) are essential if the country is to attract and hold appropriately qualified radiologists. Here the expansion of technology is being employed as an argument to attract highly trained medical graduates from abroad.

Over the last three years, the net overall gain in physicians has declined from 176 in 1976, to 88 in 1977, to a *net overall loss of 37 in 1978.*

The resources devoted to medical education and the losses incurred through emigration are undoubtedly a serious problem for so small a country. They are relatively minor, however, when compared with the costs physicians force the state to assume *after* their training. Upon graduation, each new physician can, without any real limit, authorize benefits, prescriptions, tests, procedures, and so forth that, under the present system, the state is obliged to finance. The annual cost incurred for the state by a GP has been estimated to be at least

TABLE 2

The Distribution of General Practitioners (Full-Time Equivalent) and Hospital Beds by Hospital Board Area in New Zealand

Hospital Board Areas	Area Population, 1976*		General Practitioners (Full-Time Equivalents)		Public and Private Hospital Beds, 1977	
	Number	Percent of Total Population	Number‡	Per 1,000 Population	Number§	Per 1,000 Population
North Island						
Northland	106,743	3.4	59.4	0.60	778	7.2
Auckland	796,506	25.5	360.7	.45	6990	8.8
Waikato	320,411	10.2	140.3	.44	3114	9.7
Thames	33,619	1.1	13.4	.40	282	8.4
Tauranga	66,387	2.1	36.9	.56	510	7.7
Bay of Plenty	44,467	1.4	11.8	.26	281	6.3
Waiapu	4,606	0.1	1.0	.22	44	9.6
Cook	41,136	1.3	18.3	.44	346	8.4
Hawkes Bay	121,508	3.9	41.6	.34	964	7.9
Waipawa	13,195	0.4	2.9	.22	210	16.0
Dannevirke	12,317	0.4	2.3	.19	149	12.1
Waiarapa	46,726	1.5	11.5	.25	376	8.0
Taumaranui	12,454	0.4	5.2	.42	139	11.2
Taranaki	99,312	3.2	41.9	.42	756	7.6
Wanganui	75,716	2.4	23.5	.31	599	7.9
Palmerston North	125,893	4.0	52.9	.42	1846	14.7
Wellington	344,338	11.0	137.3	.40	3526	10.2

South Island

	Population	%			Number	
Marlborough	31,649	1.0	13.4	.42	264	8.3
Nelson	64,352	2.0	39.8	.62	1214	18.9
West Coast	34,818	1.1	14.7	.42	760	21.8
North Canterbury	344,017	11.0	151.7	.44	4132	12.0
Ashburton	25,316	0.8	9.5	.38	317	12.5
South Canterbury	62,027	2.0	21.7	.35	511	8.2
Waitaki	22,576	0.7	7.2	.32	193	8.8
Otago	129,187	4.1	69.3	.54	2291	17.7
South Otago	17,159	0.6	3.9	.26	197	11.5
Vincent	9,483	0.3	3.2	.34	75	7.9
Maniototo	2,547	< 0.1	1.0	.39	33	13.0
Southland	116,568	3.7	35.9	0.31	939	8.0
Total	3,125,031	99.6†	1348.2	0.43	31,836	10.2

*Figures taken from the 1976 Population Census
†Total does not equal 100 percent, because of rounding.
‡These figures include the contribution of both "pure general practitioners" and general practitioners to the area of obstetrics and gynecology.
§Figures taken from data prepared by the Management Services Research Unit, Department of Health, Wellington, 1978.

$100,000, and the figure for some specialists has been put as high as $250,000. In a single year, a medical graduate commits the state to costs that exceed those already incurred during the six years of training. Given that a physician works for, say, forty years, a single medical graduate over a working lifetime commits the state to further costs far in excess of $4 million ($100,000 per year times forty years). Multiply this $4 million by the annual number of medical graduates (now 243) and the approximate potential annual commitment of the state is $1 billion—equivalent to 7 percent of the GNP, or the total annual amount the country at present spends on health! And this cost repeats itself every year. These rough figures are unadjusted for such factors as the effects of inflation and the immigration of foreign medical graduates, which would probably increase the amounts projected.

Early in 1979, the New Zealand Planning Council proposed that medical school intakes be gradually reduced by 25 percent. In implementing this proposal, the government, instead of taking the difficult but logical step of closing one of the country's four medical schools, has retained all of them and simply reduced the number of students in each, thereby actually increasing the cost of training a physician (because of the reduction in "throughput" per school). Although the action to reduce the number of medical graduates is a bold one and certainly not to be depreciated, it must be reinforced by action to dismantle part of the structure that exacerbates and reinforces the problem of the oversupply of physicians in the first place.

The Invasion of Unevaluated High Technology

Unless there is some collateral resolution of at least the issues discussed so far, the country will never resolve the problems concerning medical technology. For example, with the private sector absorbing the profitable, low-risk, low-technology, elective procedures, the public sector is left to support a disproportionate number of high-risk, high-technology procedures.

At the same time, unless the large number of public hospital beds is reduced to economically realistic levels and distributed more equitably, this major mechanism through which technology is introduced will ensure its survival. Since physicians' demands help stimulate the proliferation of high technology, some action is also required on the problem of the oversupply of physicians.

In other words, to move toward the resolution of problems associated with high technology, the state must move simultaneously on these problems that, at first sight at least, may appear unrelated. Moreover, effective social policies for each of these other areas requires collateral action on the problem of high technology. Piecemeal or compartmentalized social policies are unlikely to provide appropriate structural solutions to such structural problems (McKinlay, 1979b).

To properly understand the proliferation of unevaluated high technology anywhere in the world, it is necessary to trace it to its principal source: the world-wide invasion of the medical care sector by large-scale financial and industrial capital. Through the presence of such interests over the last several decades, the shape and content of medical care around the world are being dramatically transformed. Since the phenomenon is world-wide, no solution is likely to emerge from analyses and policies that are confined to particular national settings. To understand and act upon the proliferating high technology in New Zealand, the problem must be viewed in relation to developments abroad, especially in the United States (Waitzkin, 1979).

Elsewhere I have described how the medical care sector, at least in America, has been rendered a highly desirable arena for large-scale financial and industrial interests (McKinlay, 1977, 1978c). Although the features that make medical care so attractive are shared with other sectors of the economy, in the medical arena they cluster as a unique constellation that is conducive to reducing uncertainty in the market and to increasing the probability of high levels of profit. Some reasons are 1) the existence of a large and often captive market (all people are ill some of the time and some people are ill all of the time); 2) the primacy given by the public in the demand for medicine over other commodity consumption, and the apparent insatiability of this demand; 3) the facilitation of a control over the public; 4) the possibility of controlling a valued technology and thereby improving the competitive position; 5) the state acts as a guarantor of profit; and 6) through association with medicine, private interests may project an image of conspicuous benevolence. Some of these features have been associated with medicine for a long time, but others, particularly the partisan involvement of the state, have been fostered by those interests most likely to benefit from them.

Given these features (as well as internal pressures in other sectors of the economy), it is not surprising that large-scale financial and industrial capital has invaded and is now exploiting the medical care sector. Such multinationals as General Electric, IBM, Xerox, Kodak, Champion Sparkplugs, Firestone, among many others, have large medical enterprises within their corporate families. Aerospace companies are involved in everything from computerized medical information systems (Lockheed) to life-support systems (United Aircraft). Tobacco companies (Philip Morris manufactures surgical supplies), brewing concerns (Pabst Brewing makes drugs and pharmaceuticals), and transportation enterprises (Greyhound also manufactures drugs) are involved. In addition to these industrial institutions, many even larger financial institutions—commercial banks, life insurance companies, mutual and pension funds, diversified financial organizations and foundations—are increasing their association with medical care and experiencing phenomenal success. Many of these multinational concerns have assets in excess of the entire GNP of New Zealand, and many much larger countries. These institutions and their products have now become a permanent part of the medical care landscape around the world, even in so remote a country as New Zealand. Since there is usually some time lag before technology finds its way across the Pacific and into the New Zealand health system, the country is in a unique position to learn from both the successes and the failures of other countries. It may even be able to assume a leadership position through the provision of scientifically acceptable data to countries that, for reasons to be discussed, are now not able to obtain them.

Stages in the Introduction of Technology

During 1978, I was afforded a rare opportunity to identify the sequence of stages typically passed through when new technologies and interventions are introduced into New Zealand's medical care system. With its centralized organization and comparatively small size, the country may be uniquely suited to such a study. The following sequence was identified: First, the multinationals already described are constantly producing and aggressively marketing new technologies. An ever-increasing proportion of New Zealand's export earnings is diverted into imports of these products. Second, through the sales effort, the medical establishment (mainly physicians, independently and through the hospitals they run) is encouraged to demand the very latest and most sophisticated of this technology. For a physician to be unfamiliar with or lack access to this technology is considered deficient, unprofessional, and perhaps even culpably negligent! For a hospital to be without it means that its competitive position is somehow jeopardized. Only by "keeping up-to-date" (which implies ownership or control of the very latest technology) can physicians and hospitals hope to cope with emerging problems and public expectations. Third, additional local demand is fostered through powerful community groups. There is some justification for the joking suggestion that "Lions Clubs are the health planners of New Zealand"!

It is common for local community groups to raise funds for various technologies (CAT scanners, cardiothoracic surgery units, expensive ambulances) and then donate them to the public system. Although they are acting with the best of intentions, their activities exacerbate existing problems by continually implanting new technologies, thereby forcing the state to meet the operating expenses—a cost that is often far in excess of the purchase price that it has already declined to meet.

Up to this point, most of the activity in support of some new intervention or service involves self-interested groups and organizations that are generally outside the formal decision-making process. This, of course, is not to overlook the considerable behind-the-scenes or informal pressures they bring to bear. At this fourth stage, these local activities become joined with interests, processes, and individuals in the formal decision-making structure. Social movements often fail at this point through an inability to articulate their goals with interests in, and members of, the formal decision-making structure. Success during this fourth stage is therefore critically important if some new intervention or service is eventually to find its way into the state-supported medical care system. The public seems to have greater access to the formal decision-making structure in New Zealand than in, say, either the United States or Great Britain, perhaps because of such factors as relatively small population size and geographic isolation. The joining or engagement of informal outside interests with the formal structure can be achieved in several different ways. For example, community groups often put pressure on their member of Parliament (through letter-writing campaigns and local media efforts), who may respond by asking a formal question in Parliament. Such a question may extract a commitment to some undertaking from the government, which wishes to appear to be active or (especially in the case of an Opposition member's question) to remove the basis of some local complaint against the government. At this fourth stage, government, in various ways, accedes in the face of different political pressures and becomes committed to providing the intervention or service in question.

Eventually the state, through its various departments, purchases, underwrites, or subsidizes the new intervention or service. In the case of technology, the government pays the corporations that manufacture most of the technological hardware with export earnings. Manufacturers reinvest the profits and the whole cycle is repeated, albeit on an escalated scale. In a sense, the state fuels with one hand the fire that it is vainly trying to extinguish with the other.

The Matter of Effectiveness

Several features in this typical sequence must be of concern, but only one will be highlighted here: the absence of any prior demonstration of effectiveness. If the sales effort of the multinationals is vigorous enough, if the medical establishment deems it necessary, if enough of the public can be encouraged to demand it, sooner or later an intervention finds its way into the system, irrespective of its effectiveness or the resources diverted from other areas. The administrative rule of thumb in New Zealand (and most other countries) is that an intervention or service is presumed to be effective until it is shown to be ineffective. And even when research demonstrates repeatedly, and on commonly accepted methodological grounds, that it is ineffective, it is retained because of the power of the interests that become associated with, perhaps even dependent upon, its survival. A *Report of Family*

Statistics in New Zealand issued by the government's own Department of Statistics (1978) concluded that "it is probably true to say that hardly a single social welfare program operating in New Zealand today has had its effectiveness tested before, and after, implementation." Such a situation is by no means unique to New Zealand.

As one would expect in a country as small as New Zealand, there is a fairly tight-knit old-boy network among members of the medical profession. Until quite recently, there was only one medical school (Otago) and its graduates evidence considerable loyalty. It is not uncommon for all the major figures in the medical establishment (e.g., the director-general of health, some of the deputy director-generals, major members of the Medical Research Council, deans and professors of the medical schools) to have gone through medical school together. Someone once jokingly traced the origins of the New Zealand "medical mafia" to the class of 1954 (or thereabouts). On a number of occasions, when some proposal was being evaluated, particularistic allusions were made to someone's being "a good fellow when we were at Otago together." The failure of one foreign-trade medical school dean to establish a much needed primary care center in a relatively underprivileged area may be attributed not to the inherent worth of the proposal, but to his being "an outsider," and unfamiliar with "the New Zealand way of doing things."

The desire to do things "the New Zealand way," while certainly understandable, may be the country's most expensive national foible. The range of variability in illnesses and peoples is obviously not so great that New Zealand cannot, with safety, accept evidence from overseas. For what good reason can future social policy not be immediately informed by reputable overseas studies concerning the relative ineffectiveness of many standard medical practices? New Zealand certainly does not have the financial resources, or enough appropriately trained personnel, to replicate all of the expensive controlled trials that have already yielded definitive results. Nor are there always enough subjects to generate samples of sufficient size, from which reliable inferences may be drawn. This is not to suggest that New Zealand should not initiate clinical trials in strategic areas. Nor does a policy decision to routinely and systematically monitor overseas ran-

domized controlled trials (RCTs), with a view to their results inform-
ing social policy in New Zealand, necessitate undue delays while such
studies are completed. Enough reliable results are already available, in
many different areas, with which to immediately inform policy in New
Zealand (and elsewhere) on the rational allocation of scarce resources
to health care.

The Determination of Effectiveness

Some specific examples of decision-making in New Zealand will now
be considered by reviewing two topical technologies: cardiothoracic
surgery and computer axial tomography (CAT scanning). A couple of
years ago New Zealand was wrestling with the question of how many
cardiothoracic surgical units the country should have, and where they
ought to be located. In a country of New Zealand's size, with its
economic difficulties and scattered population, a decision on a single
technology may have repercussions for the entire system. When questions like this arise, and because "everyone knows everyone else," the
government sometimes, understandably, turns to overseas for advice
(as distinguished from evidence). A well-known and respected cardiothoracic surgeon was invited to New Zealand in order to review
the local scene and prepare a report with recommendations to the
government. The resulting report, although it apparently influenced
government policy concerning cardiothoracic surgery, for various reasons has never been released. Public and even parliamentary debate
on the number and location of units remains uninformed by this
report, even though the public paid for it. There are other concerns,
however. It was subsequently revealed that the particular overseas
consultant selected had a reputation for cardiothoracic surgery
empire-building. Moreover, the recommendations in the report derive from a perfunctory visit, supplemented by the crudest of vital
statistics. At the same time, it was widely known that the number of
operations performed annually at the several existing cardiothoracic
units was already below the minimum number considered by the
American Heart Association as necessary to maintain surgical competency in the area.

There may be some support here for the view that the advice of carefully selected overseas experts is used to legitimate a course of action that has already been decided upon by the local interest groups.

Another common response to public issues is to establish a committee to "investigate and report"—a practice that is by no means unique to New Zealand (Alford, 1975). This was the response when the government was first faced with pressure for the introduction of CAT scanners. The composition of the committee established by the Department of Health physicians to consider this issue was such that the future of this technology was more or less assured in New Zealand. The government eventually decided to allow one scanner to be introduced first, on the condition that it be properly evaluated before other machines were introduced. A special grant was provided for the purchase, installation, operation, and evaluation of the scanner. From discussions and correspondence, it became clear that the physicians most involved do not themselves have the necessary methodological or statistical expertise to undertake a scientifically acceptable evaluation, and there is no evidence of their consulting available epidemiologists and biostatisticians who presumably could provide such expertise. After discussions with knowledgeable physicians and in collaboration with an experienced statistician, a proposal outlining one possible approach to the evaluation of the CAT scanner was prepared. The proposal was rejected, not because of any technical considerations (which the physicians were ill-equipped to comment on anyway), but because of so-called ethical objections, which have never been clearly elucidated. What is particularly disturbing is that the Department of Health was unwilling, or unable, to enforce the condition upon which the scanner was introduced, even though it provided funds for this purpose. In essence, the interested parties have reneged on their commitment, and the Department of Health is powerless to force compliance. There are suggestions that, with a population of over 3 million, the country ought to have five or six scanners. On the basis of past experience, the composition of the committees to date, and the nature of the overseas advice received, it is reasonable to assume that the medical establishment will eventually be favored with them.

New Zealand may be uniquely situated in the world to undertake strategically important evaluations of some high technology, particularly because of the time lag between its establishment abroad and its introduction into New Zealand. This is well illustrated in the case of the CAT scanner. One common "ethical objection" to proper scientific evaluations (especially randomized controlled trials) concerns the withholding from individuals or groups of an already established intervention that, although without formal evaluation, is claimed to be effective. Now this "ethical objection" does not apply in quite the same way to newly proposed interventions that, at least at first, are in short supply. There is simply no way that all those perceived as "in need" can receive the purportedly effective new intervention in question. This situation of unavoidable scarcity in the beginning provides a unique opportunity for evaluation, without the usual ethical qualms. Some cases will not receive the intervention because there is not yet enough of it for everyone, not because it is deliberately withheld in the interest of evaluation research. Bradford-Hill has discussed this not unusual situation in relation to the introduction of streptomycin and the inactivated vaccine against poliomyelitis, both of which it would now be unethical to deliberately withhold for the purpose of an RCT. He argues that in such a situation

> it would have been unethical *not* to have seized the opportunity to design a strictly controlled trial which could speedily and effectively reveal the value of the treatment. [An evaluation] could proceed not only without qualms of conscience but with a sense of duty to do so. . . . Whenever a newly introduced drug or vaccine is scarce in its early days, then there presents an opportunity of which immediate advantage should, if possible, be taken. . . . With a serious disease in which the old offers very little hope of benefit, the new cannot be withheld. The chance of adequately and quickly assessing the value of the latter, if any, may never again occur. (Bradford-Hill, 1963)

New Zealand has long been dependent upon overseas experience, repeating the occasional successes and frequent failures of other systems. Its serious economic situation precludes the continuation of this wasteful course. New Zealand now finds itself in a unique position to evaluate certain technologies and provide information to other countries, which cannot themselves now undertake such evaluations. It is doubtful whether a properly designed and conducted RCT of, for example, CAT scanning, is now possible in either the United States or Britain. Since at present there is only one CAT scanner for New Zealand's population of over 3 million people, and that one is situated in the very north of the North Island, it is inevitable that some patients, deemed in need of this machine, will not be able to receive its purported benefits. This unique situation will almost certainly soon pass, as New Zealand follows the pattern of other countries in allowing this still unevaluated technology to become a permanent part of the medical care landscape. Such an opportunity to assess this technology adequately and quickly may never again occur, and ought to be quickly seized. Not to do so can be considered *unethical!*

Cardiothoracic surgery and CAT scanning are discussed to illustrate the magnitude of the resources that are, or could be, tied up in what is either a demonstrably ineffective activity or one whose effectiveness has yet to be established. They represent a very visible tip of the iceberg of ineffective or unevaluated procedures and services that exist in New Zealand. Many other examples could be cited: radical mastectomy seems to be unnecessary for many cancers of the breast (Bunker, Barnes, and Mosteller, 1977); coronary care units do not represent the optimal treatment setting for many myocardial infarctions (Mather et al., 1976; Hill, 1978; Hutter, 1973; Harpur et al., 1971); and injection compression sclerotherapy on an outpatient basis is better than inpatient surgery for varicose veins (Chant et al., 1972; Beresford et al., 1978; Adler, 1978). It appears that the benefits of electronic fetal monitoring during pregnancy do not always outweigh the risks (Banta and Thacker, 1979). When permitted to do so, nurses deliver medical care as effectively as physicians, by any outcome measure selected (Lewis et al., 1969; Spitzer et al., 1974; Chambers and West, 1978; Schlesinger et al., 1973; Burnip et al., 1976). Coronary artery by-pass grafting (probably the most expensive surgery undertaken today) has been shown by two RCTs to be questionably effective (Mathur et al., 1975; Murphy et al., 1977).

The specific cases considered here illustrate a more general problem besetting the medical care system (of New Zealand and many other countries): the repeated adoption of unevaluated overseas technology. Cardiothoracic surgery and CAT scanners, per se, are of little concern here. What is worrisome is the way in which procedures and services slip into the New Zealand medical care system, without any proper evaluation, either before or during their operation. Moreover, the state appears unable to stop paying the operating costs of the technologies it has already made a decision not to introduce. The legal maxim that a person is presumed innocent until proven guilty appears to apply also to technology associated with medicine. Any medically sponsored intervention is assumed to be effective until it is proven to be ineffective. And on those rare occasions when a procedure has been evaluated and shown to be ineffective, it is difficult to remove because of the pressure groups that become associated with and dependent upon its survival. I am certainly not opposed to cardiothoracic surgery, CAT scanning, or any other proposed technology. To be antitechnology is obviously to be antiprogress. What one should oppose is blind state support for the introduction and proliferation of all technologies, without any requirement that their effectiveness be properly demonstrated before or after introduction.

There are of course many human services that have been shown to be effective, on acceptable scientific grounds. For example, a broken leg, an acute asthmatic attack, or serious burns, should certainly receive effective medical treatment. But there is a vast range of services, procedures, and technologies—probably the majority—that, in New Zealand and elsewhere, have never been evaluated or shown to be effective on any grounds whatsoever, and may even be harmful. It is these questionably effective services that continue to tie up an ever-increasing proportion of New Zealand's ever-scarcer national resources, diverting funds from areas of more generalized effectiveness (e.g., community health and environmental management). The country cannot continue the naively conceived expansion of ineffective human services. Nor is it practical to begin the cavalier disposal of everything we have, a course recommended by visionaries such as Ivan Illich (1976). Both extremes are obviously absurd.

Effectiveness as a Basis for Social Policy

Since the state is viewed as responsible for providing the greatest possible benefit to the greatest number of people (utilitarianism), and because the allocation of resources cannot continue to be based on (contrived) public demand, professional claims, or blind Micawberism, some other criteria must be invoked to inform social policy. Any policy based on ad hoc responses to particular interests, structurally precludes the state from allocating resources in accordance with utilitarian principles. Although the distribution of resources on a particularistic basis may occasionally coincide with some social needs, there is no structural mechanism for ensuring this agreement. It is therefore essential that some objective (i.e., interest-free) criterion inform the allocation of whatever resources are available in the future. It has been argued elsewhere that the prior demonstration of effectiveness may be such a criterion (McKinlay, 1979a).

Is it reasonable for the state to support activities that are either known to be ineffective or have never been evaluated, or activities whose proponents will not allow them to be acceptably evaluated? Is it not reasonable to expect that health workers would want to be involved in an activity shown, through the very science that is supposed to shape their practices, to be effective? Surely a public, with uncontrived human needs, ought to be able to assume that the interventions they are subjected to, which they support through the taxation system, are known to be effective. Is there any good reason why the state should support, through public funding for general public use, any service or procedure whose effectiveness has not been or cannot first be demonstrated? If demonstrated effectiveness can be accepted by policy makers as the primary criterion for the allocation of resources (a necessary but not sufficient condition for the public funding of an intervention), then the methodology for the determination of effectiveness becomes a critical issue in social policy.

Some would argue for an observational study (for example, a social survey or retrospective analysis of case records to evaluate effectiveness) (McKinlay, 1976). Although such studies may be useful in determining parameters of need for and the social acceptability of some intervention, they can never put the logically more important matter of effectiveness beyond dispute. Such studies are confounded by major unknown biases of self-selection, and one can never be certain enough, at least for social policy purposes, that it was the intervention, and not something else, that produced the result observed. Such knowledge can only derive from at least one (preferably more) properly designed and conducted randomized control trial. Such experiments require that persons considered "in need" be randomly assigned to receive the new program (the treatment), or the old program, or no program at all (the control groups). This methodology can provide results that are more definitive than those obtained through other techniques, because at the outset of the program a comparison is established between two groups of clients who are similar in all ways except the important one: only the treatment programs are varied.

The strategy outlined could provide an appropriate structural solution to the structural problem of unevaluated techniques and procedures, which at present distort and threaten the future of the medical care system in New Zealand. Two additional points should be emphasized. First, there is no suggestion that the test of effectiveness, as a basis for resource allocation, should be applied only to interventions newly proposed for public funding. Clearly, interventions already ensconced must be subjected to the same scrutiny. Moreover, a large proportion of established procedures probably would not meet these criteria and should therefore be excluded from public funding if New Zealand is ever to receive value for money for its human services. No matter how long the intervention or practice has been in existence, if it does not meet the criterion of effectiveness, determined on acceptable methodological grounds, then it should receive no further support through public funding. Second, there is no suggestion here that the criterion of effectiveness should be applied only to particular interventions, or to interventions proposed by particular groups. Any intervention, whether acupuncture, cardiothoracic surgery, psychiatry, transcendental meditation, chiropractic, or whatever, should be subject to the same basic criterion. A situation must be avoided where, as at present, double standards exist regarding the criteria to be met, depending on the power of interested groups proposing or supporting some intervention.

A Prescription for the Future

This paper has considered some aspects of medical technology in relation to several structural problems besetting New Zealand's medical care system, within the broader context of the country's ever-worsening fiscal crisis. Some may consider the situation so extreme that structural reform is unlikely, and social policy a vacuous activity. I am under no illusion that this "warts and all" view of the present state of the New Zealand economy and medical care system will be at all popular. But it is generally consistent with the position of the government's own Planning Council, whose various reports have not been greeted with tumultuous applause. It is of course part of my strategy to present a realistic (some would say pessimistic) view of the existing crisis. However, social policies that will help bring about structural change are more likely to follow from a heightened consciousness of the crisis than from the present blind optimism. With this in mind, I have outlined a strategy that holds some promise for the future. Although this paper discusses a particular structural problem—the expansion of unevaluated high technology as applied to medicine—it illustrates a broader strategy and a methodology applicable to many other problems and areas of social policy. Obviously, many important details remain to be considered. They have been deliberately omitted from this paper in an attempt to draw attention to several major problems and principles of resource allocation relative to health care in New Zealand and elsewhere. If there can be no general consensus on these, or perhaps some other set of general principles, then no purpose will be served here by filling in specifics.

It may be claimed, by those who oppose *any* structural change, that New Zealand simply does not have sufficient resources, or enough appropriately trained personnel, to undertake the basic health services research and planning necessary for effective social policies concerning the public health. Such a claim is obviously specious when viewed in relation to the magnitude of resources that would be released in only one area *if* the government was prepared to enact its own optimistic hospital bed guidelines. There are many other areas where substantial savings could be effected. Furthermore, to postpone any change by claiming that there are just not enough appropriately trained professionals is to remain blind to, and further frustrate, the considerable talent available in New Zealand.

From an expatriate's view, New Zealand appears to have a sufficient number of appropriately qualified or experienced professionals, in enough of the relevant disciplines, strategically distributed in different arms of the health system and areas of the country, to take a first step toward structural change, perhaps along the lines of the 1974 White Paper (New Zealand Government Printer, 1974). New Zealand has professionals of international repute who, although sometimes overlooked in their own country, are second to none in their own fields of work. There are economists with interests in health in Otago, and in various centers in the North Island. The universities located at Auckland, Palmerston North, and Wellington have respected medical sociologists. There are a number of social epidemiologists of world stature in various locations. An innovative Corporate Planning Unit has been established in Wellington and is already providing a model for other hospital boards throughout the country. Excellent policy-relevant research and planning are already under way in the Department of Health's own Management Services and Research Unit. People with a broader vision of the problems and what is possible are located in Treasury, the Planning Council, the Department of Statistics, etc. A unique data base is available through the National Center for Health Statistics. Some primary care physicians, dissatisfied with traditional modes of practice, appear willing to experiment with alternative ways of organizing and delivering health care. Many nurses are chafing at their present wastefully constricting roles, and seek an input into community health that is more consistent with their training. Some medical students are responding to improved teaching in epidemiology and community health and seem prepared to look beyond the traditional specialties. Some persons in the Department of Health have an excellent grasp of economic realities and desire to do things in a better way. Although still generalized, there is some desire among the public for an improved health care system. In sum, enough people, appropriately trained and located, desire some movement.

An opportunity has now presented itself of which immediate advantage should, if possible, be taken. However, whether all these factors can bring about change depends, perhaps more than on anything else, on the caliber of the country's political leadership over the next few years, and the pressure that an informed public is able to bring to bear on that leadership. Very generally, there are two alternative paths along which the government may attempt to travel. One course (perhaps the easiest) is for the government to "kick for touch" and attempt to muddle through, by attempting to continue as before in the hope that enough people will be placated for the present government to be returned in three years. Should the minister of health decide (or be permitted by the Opposition) to simply "mind the store" over the next few years, then the structural problems already described will be further exacerbated. A second and more difficult course is for the government to begin an agenda of social reform based on some appreciation of the sorts of issues and principles outlined in this paper. Marc Lalonde (1977) chose this course while he was minister of health in Canada. Were it not for New Zealand's present fiscal crisis, the government would probably continue to play safe and choose the first alternative. But for reasons already discussed, this choice is no longer possible.

References

Adler, M.W. 1978. Randomized Trial of Early Discharge for Inguinal Hernia and Varicose Veins. *Journal of Epidemiology and Community Health* 32:136–142.

Alford, R.R. 1975. *Health Care Politics.* Chicago: University of Chicago Press.

Banta, H.D., and Thacker, S.B. 1979. Electronic Fetal Monitoring: Is It of Benefit? *Birth and Family Journal* 6:237–269.

Beresford, S.A.A., et al. 1978. Varicose Veins: A Comparison of Surgery and Injection/Compression Sclerotherapy (Five-Year Follow-up). *Lancet* 1:921–924.

Bradford-Hill, A. 1963. Medical Ethics and Controlled Trials. *British Medical Journal,* April 20:1043–1049.

Bunker, J.P., Barnes, B.A., and Mosteller, F., eds. 1977. *Costs, Risks and Benefits of Surgery.* New York: Oxford University Press.

Burnip, R., et al. 1976. Well-Child Care by Pediatric Nurse Practitioners in a Large Group Practice. *Journal of Diseases of Children* 130:51–59.

Chambers, L.W., and West, A.E. 1978. The St. John's Randomized Trials of the Family Practice Nurse: Health Outcomes of Patients. *International Journal of Epidemiology* 7:153–161.

Chant, A.D.B., et al. 1972. Varicose Veins: A Comparison of Surgery and Injection/Compression Sclerotherapy. *Lancet* 2:1188–1191.

Cochrane, A.L., St. Leger, A.S., and Moore, F. 1978. Health Service "Input" and Mortality "Output" in Developed Countries. *Journal of Epidemiology and Community Health* 32:200–205.

Department of Health. 1977. *Planning Guidelines for Hospital Beds and Services.* Wellington, New Zealand.

Department of Statistics. 1978. *Report of Family Statistics in New Zealand.* Wellington, New Zealand.

Harpur, J.E., et al. 1971. Controlled Trial of Early Mobilization from Hospital in Uncomplicated Myocardial Infarction. *Lancet* 2:1331–1334.

Hill, J.D. 1978. A Randomized Trial of Home-versus-Hospital Management for Patients with Suspected Myocardial Infarction. *Lancet* 1:837–841.

Hutter, A.M. 1973. Early Hospital Discharge after Myocardial Infarction. *New England Journal of Medicine* 288:1141–1144.

Illich, I. 1976. *Medical Nemesis: The Expropriation of Health.* New York: Pantheon.

Lalonde, M. 1974. *Nouvelle Perspective de la Santé de Canadiens.* Ottawa: Ministère Fédéral de la Santé et du Bien-être Social.

Lewis, C.E., et al. 1969. Activities, Events and Outcomes in Ambulatory Patient Care. *New England Journal of Medicine* 280:645–649.

Mather, H.A., et al. 1976. A Comparison between Home and Hospital Care for Patients. *British Medical Journal* 1:925–929.

Mathur, U.S., et al. 1975. Surgical Treatment for Stable Angina Pectoris. *New England Journal of Medicine* 292:709–713.

McKeown, T. 1976. *The Modern Rise of Population.* London: Edward Arnold.

McKinlay, J.B. 1977. The Business of Good Doctoring or Doctoring as Good Business: Reflections on Freidson's View of the Medical Game. *International Journal of Health Services* 7:459–488.

———. 1978a. A Confinement of Nonoptions: The Subordination of the Modern State through the International Debt Crisis. Unpublished paper, Department of Sociology, Boston University.

———. 1978b. A Note on Associations between Medical Care Input and Mortality Outcomes: Some International Comparisons. Unpublished paper, Department of Sociology, Boston University.

———. 1978c. On the Medical-Industrial Complex. *Monthly Review* 30:38–42.

———. 1979a. Epidemiological and Political Determinants of Social Politics Regarding the Public Health. *Social Science and Medicine* 13:541–558.

————. 1979b. The Decline of the House of Medicine. *Business and Society Review* No. 30 (Summer):55–61.

McKinlay, S.M. 1976. The Design and Analysis of the Observational Study: A Review. *Journal of the American Statistical Association* 70:503–523.

————, and McKinlay, J.B. 1979. Examining Trends in the Nation's Health. Paper presented to the American Public Health Association, New York, November 7.

Murphy, M.L., et al. 1977. Treatment of Chronic Stable Angina. *New England Journal of Medicine* 238:1259–1262.

New Zealand Government Printer. 1974. *A Health Service for New Zealand* (White Paper). Wellington, New Zealand.

————. 1979. *The Welfare State: Social Policies in the 1980s.* Wellington, New Zealand.

New Zealand Planning Council. 1978. *Planning Perspectives: 1978–83.* Wellington, New Zealand.

Roemer, M. 1961. Bed Supply and Hospital Utilization: An Experiment. *Hospitals (Journal of the American Hospital Association)* 35:36–42.

Salmond, G.C. 1978. *Medical Manpower Planning.* Wellington: Management Services and Research Unit, Department of Health, New Zealand Government.

Schlesinger, E.R., et al. 1973. A Controlled Test of the Use of Registered Nurses for Prenatal Care. *Health Services Reports* 88:400–410.

Spitzer, W.O., et al. 1974. The Burlington Randomized Trial of the Nurse Practitioner. *New England Journal of Medicine* 290:231–256.

United States Foreign Economic Policy Subcommittee. 1977. *International Debt, the Banks and U.S. Foreign Policy.* Committee on Foreign Relations, Washington, D.C.: U.S. Senate.

Waitzkin, H. 1979. A Marxian Interpretation of the Growth and Development of Coronary Care Technology. *American Journal of Public Health* 69:1260–1268.

Acknowledgments: Much of the background research for this report was undertaken while the author was a consultant to the Department of Health (New Zealand Government) and visiting professor of community health at the Wellington Clinical School of Medicine (Otago University). Particular thanks go to colleagues Dr. George Salmond, Department of Health, and Professor Ken Newell, Wellington Clinical School.

Index

Computerized tomography (CT) scanners (cont.)
Maryland state medical society's regulation of, 79
in New Zealand, 432–435
Conference on the Diffusion of Medical Technology, 198, 199, 210, 227
Conflict, in research, 220
CON laws. *See* Certificate-of-need laws
Coronary artery surgery. *See also* Chronic disease
and evaluation of medical innovation, 249–251
health care to, 427–428
and implementation without proper evaluation, 353
and technological proliferation, 427–428
Cosmopolitanism, 148–149, 152, 153, 154, 155, 160
"Cosmopolites," 274–275, 276
Cost containment. *See also* Hospital cost containment
through pharmaceutical innovation, 391–392
and quality of care, 166
Cost efficiency, 263
Costs, health care. *See also* Inflation, health care
and donation of technologies, 429
and failure to evaluate technology, 436
international factors in, 385–386
among medical innovations, 384
per physician in New Zealand, 426
for renal disease program, 92–93
for research vs. service, 385
and resource allocation, 118
and technical change, 113–114, 117–119
and technical operating expenses, 429
Costs, hospital
and adoption of medical technology, 175–176, 190
factors affecting, 180–182, 189–191, 194, 318, 322

Decentralization. *See* Centralization/Decentralization
Department of Health, Education, and Welfare (U.S.), 302
Diabetes. *See also* Chronic disease
and medical technology, 27–28, 30
research for, 30, 32
Diffusion of medical innovations. *See also* Innovation, program
erosion-and-discreditation stage of, 257–260

ethical considerations in, 252–254
and evaluation, 245–246, 247–250, 256–257, 259–265
momentum in, 251
pilot study in, 239
professional-denunciation stage of, 254–257
professional-and-organizational-adoption stage of, 239–244
"promising report" stage, 235–239
public-acceptance-and-state (third party) endorsement stage, 244–246
questions in, 274
randomized-controlled-trial (RCT) stage of, 251–254
role of advisory groups in, 255–256
role of clinical experience in, 242
role of comparative observational studies in, 247–248
role of drug industry in, 243
role of medical education in, 242
role of patient satisfaction in, 248, 264
stages in, 233–234
"standard procedure" and observational reports stage of, 246–251
suggested approach to, 261–265
Diffusion of medical technology. *See also* Technical change
and business interests, 427–428
and communication, 123
comparative observational studies on, 247–248
and CON laws, 84–85
criteria for, 201
and CT scanner, 75–77, 87
definitions of, 120, 201, 203n
factors in, 119, 121–124, 201–202
federal intervention in, 96–99
and health care inflation, 70–71
and hospital costs, 123
and inpatient revenues, 51
optimization of, 202–203
problem-solving process applied to, 204–210
and "profitability," 121
research and, 199–203, 213
and social values, 226–227
systems approach and, 203–204
and technological imperative, 47
and third-party reimbursement, 74
Diffusion theory. *See also* Adoption of medical innovations
and attributes of innovations, 294–295
centralization in, 283–284
classical, 272, 274–282
and community activism, 290

446

Government, federal. *See also* Regulation, federal
and CT scanners, 76–79
and evaluation of health practices, 112
examination of health technology by, 95–98, 100
and health policy of, 69–70, 79
and medical technology, 70
R & D role of, 46, 55–56
and regulation of health system, 79–82
and study of technology diffusion, 199
Government policy
and endorsement of medical innovation, 245–246, 354–355
and evaluation of medical innovation, 261, 262, 436–437

Health, and shifting attitudes, 387–388
Health care. *See also* Explicit health care rationing; Rationing, health care
cost of, 2, 71
impact of economics on, 394, 400
and mortality rates, 407
organizations, 1
rationing of, 2–14 (*see also* Rationing, health care)
Health care, in Britain
and innovation, 375–376, 377
unmet demand for, 372
Health care, hospital
effectiveness of, 416
unneeded beds for, 417n–418n
Health care, in New Zealand. *See also* Health care system, New Zealand; New Zealand
and death rate, 405–407
investment in, 405–408
distribution of physicians for, 423–424
effect on morbidity and disability of, 407–408
and emigration of physicians, 421–422, 425
expenditures on, 401–405
hospital costs for, 417
oversupply of hospital beds for, 414–419
oversupply of physicians for, 419–421, 423–426
proliferation of technology for, 418–419, 426–430
public vs. private expenditures on, 401, 403
Health care spending, and national wealth, 372–374
Health care system, New Zealand. *See*

also New Zealand
failure to test technologies in, 430–436
hospital board regions in, 421, 422
and hospital system, 418
old-boy network in, 431
and public, 429–430
public vs. "private" parts of, 401, 403, 414–414, 426
resources for improvement in, 439–440
role of directors-general of health in, 410
role of health districts in, 414
role of hospital boards in, 410–411
role of minister of health in, 409–410
structure of, 408–411
suggested approach to evaluation of innovations in, 437–438
Health insurance
and health care inflation, 59
and health technology, 48–49
and right to health care, 59 (*see also* National health insurance)
Health insurance, catastrophic, 91–94
further coverage suggested, 93
for renal disease, 92–94
Health Planning and Resources Development Act (1974), 301
as major regulatory law, 100
and medical technology, 80
Health technology. *See* Medical technology
Home health services, in innovation study, 136, 141
Hospital behavior. *See also* Visibility of hospital performance
and diffusion theory, 287–288, 289–290, 293
and outside groups, 203–204
Hospital care. *See* Health care, hospital
Hospital cost containment. *See also* Certificate-of-need (CON) laws; Costs, hospital; Efficiency, hospital
and area-wide cooperation, 51–52
via ceiling on capital expenditures, 56–58, 61
Congressional proposal of, 42
through CON laws, 111
definition of, 44–45
failure of, 106
government role in, 47–48
and health care inflation, 50
and health insurance, 59
through limit on total inpatient revenues, 50–56, 61–62
and medical education, 112

and Medical Service Plans (MSPs), 53
and medical technology, 43–45, 50–
  62, 106, 108–112
via prepaid group practices, 111
through rate-setting, 111
and R & D, 45–47, 53–55, 58
and reexamination of technology,
  111–112
and right to health care, 59–60
and shift of technology to private
  practices, 52–53, 57, 60–61
and standards for care, 60
Hospital Cost Containment Act, 42n
Hospital cost inflation. *See also* Inflation, health care
factors in, 110
and hospital rating systems, 123–124
impact of technology on, 105
and reimbursement system, 111
technical change as cause in, 116–118
Hypertension, 27, 30

Implicit health care rationing, 3, 5–7,
  379, 380. *See also* Explicit health care
  rationing
and doctor-patient relationship, 13
by prepaid group practices, 14
as resource allocation, 380–381
Industry lobbying, 304
Inflation, health care. *See also* Costs,
  health care; Hospital cost inflation
extent of, 2
and health insurance, 48–49
and health technology, 44, 47–49, 70–
  74, 165
and hospital cost containment, 50
and medical device amendments, 90–
  91
in Medicare, 99
and national health insurance, 4–5
and right to health care, 59
role of research policy in, 94
and technological imperative, 99
and third-party payments, 4
Innovation, definition of, 201, 273
Innovation, program. *See also* Diffusion
  of medical innovation; Medical
  innovation
and administrator's values, 148–149,
  152, 153, 154, 155
and attributes of activities, 138–140,
  142, 161
centralization and 146–147, 152, 153,
  154, 155
cosmopolitanism and, 148–149, 152,
  153, 154, 155, 160

diffusion of, 233–235
factors in, 144–149
and formalization, 146–147, 152, 153,
  154, 155, 160, 161
in health departments, 136, 139–144,
  152–153, 156–160
in high-risk services, 142–143, 144,
  151, 153, 155, 157–159, 160
in hospitals, 136, 139–144, 154–160
in low-risk services, 142–144, 151,
  152, 154, 156–157, 160
measure of, 137–144
methodology of study on, 134–149
organizational performance and, 147–
  148, 152, 153, 154, 155, 160
organizational size and, 145–146,
  149–156, 159
problem areas in, 133–134
professional training and, 148, 152,
  153, 154, 155, 160
slack resources and, 145–146, 152,
  153, 154, 155
Innovation, research
conditions for, 219, 221–222
and research administration, 222–223,
  224, 225
Interdisciplinary approach, in social research, 213

*Journal of the American Medical Associa-
  tion,* 350
Journal of Family Practice, 348

Kennedy, Edward M., Sen., 95, 98, 100
Kidney, artificial, 376

Lancet, 345, 350, 357
Librium, 243–244
"Localites," in diffusion theory, 274–
  275, 276–277

Manufacturers, and diffusion theory,
  290–291
Mechanic, David, 379–381, 389–390
Medical Audit Procedures (M.A.P.)
  program, 192–193
Medical care. *See* Health care; Primary
  medical care
Medical device amendments (1974,
  1976), 87, 88–91
aim of, 90
and conflicting criticisms toward technical change, 114–115
definition of device under, 88–89
impact on health care costs of, 90–91
and medical technology, 80
as major regulatory laws, 100

Problem-solving process. *See also* Research administration; Social research
administration of, 216
determination-of-relations-among-variables stage, 205–206, 224
establishment-of-causality stage of, 205, 206–207, 225
evaluation stage in, 205, 209, 225
manipulation-of-causal-variables stage, 205, 207, 225
problem-delineation stage, 204–205, 224
and research administration, 223
six stages in, 204–210, 224, 225
variable-identification stage, 205, 224
Professional Standards Review Organizations (PSROs)
and medical technology use, 83, 84
and physician attitudes, 82
Professional training, and innovation, 148–149, 152, 153, 154, 155, 160
Program innovation. *See* Innovation, program
"Promising reports" stage, in diffusion process, 235–239
Public demand, and medical innovation, 244–245, 376–377
Public interest, as goal of CON laws, 304, 307

Quality of care, 201
Quality of hospital care, 166. *See also* Adoption, health technology

Radiotherapy, and research vs. service costs, 385
Randomized clinical trials, of Pap test, 332
Randomized controlled trials (RCTs)
discrediting of, 255
ethical issues in, 252–254
for evaluation, 437–438
and medical innovations, 234, 252–254
as methodology of choice, 262, 264–265
obstacles to, 252–253
Rate setting, 111
Rationing, health care
conditions for, 379–380
and doctor-patient relationship, 12–14, 381
explicit, 3, 7–9, 379, 381
by fee, 3–4, 379, 380
implicit, 3, 5–7, 379, 380
need for, 379

objections to, 389
and physician attitudes, 382–383
and primary medical care, 9, 11–12
rationale for, 2–3
as response to unmet demand, 378–379
by science, 381–383
social divisiveness as objection to, 383
two levels of, 385
RCTs. *See* Randomized controlled trials
Regulation, federal, 79–82. *See also* government, federal
and CON laws, 84–87
of medical devices, 87–91
of medical technology, 100
reasons for, 80–81
in renal disease programs, 92–94
Rehabilitation services, 136, 141
"Relative advantage," 286
Research, biomedical. *See also* Research administration; Problem-solving process; Social research
negative findings in, 238
questioning of, 200
Research administration
contingency model for, 223–226
findings on, 220, 221–223
guidelines for, 218–219
and innovation, 222–223, 224, 225
and problem-solving approach, 223
and productivity, 222–223
and social values, 226–227
study on, 220–221
Research and development (R & D). *See also* Technical change
capital expenditures ceiling on, 58
as cost factor, 386, 391
inpatient revenue limit on, 53–55
and federal government, 46, 55–56
and health care inflation, 46
and medical technology, 45–46
need for information on, 115–116, 124
and private industry, 46
Research policy
government assessment of, 95–98, 100
and health care costs, 94–95
on program innovation, 161
Research priorities
and administrative organization, 37
and chronic diseases, 29–30, 37
Resource allocation. *See also* Rationing
explicit rationing in, 381
and health care costs, 118
implicit rationing, in 380–381
and medical innovation, 383–384

and medical technology, 108–110
military medicine model for, 388
and shift in attitudes toward health,
387–388
and perceived quality of service, 109–
110
and pharmaceutical innovation, 391–
392
and preventive medicine, 388
through rationing by science, 381–383
scheme for, 389–390
through triage, 379
Resource allocation, in Britain
by family doctors, 377–378
way of determining, 372
Resource allocation, in New Zealand
outmoded patterns of, 414
problems in, 408
Revenue limitations, total inpatient,
50–56

Scarcity, health care. See Resource
allocation
Schizophrenia
and medical technology, 27, 30
research for, 30, 32
Sciences
developmental stages of, 211–213
and social research, 211, 219
Screening. See also Pap test screening
chronic disease, 136, 141
criteria for, 333
definition of, 332
Senile brain disease (SBD)
impact of medical technology on, 23–
25
prevalence of, 23–24
research suggested for, 30, 31–32
Slack resources
in diffusion theory, 280, 286–287
and innovation, 145–146, 152, 153,
154, 155
Social research. See also Diffusion
theory; Problem-solving process; Research administration
basic-vs.-applied, 216–217
conflict in, 220
developmental level of, 210–213
in diffusion theory, 204
findings on research administration,
217–220, 221–223
funding patterns in, 215
innovation in, 219, 221–222
institutional settings for, 214–215
interdisciplinary approach in, 213–
214

on medical technology diffusion, 198–
200
normal science and, 211, 219
paradigm in, 211
and personality attributes, 220; 224,
225
and phenylketonuria (PKU) program,
208–209
predictability in, 217, 220
problem-solving process in, 204–210,
224–225
proposed approach for, 198
scientific method in, 227–228
study on research administration,
220–221
and Tavistock studies of British coal
mines, 207–208
urgency in, 217
Social sciences. See Social research
Social Security Act amendments (1972)
and health technology, 80, 81–82
as major regulatory law, 100
Social work, in innovation study, 136,
141
Specialization
and health care rationing, 9
and medical technology, 35, 47
Spina bifida, and medical technology,
28, 30
Standards for care
and explicit rationing, 7
and hospital cost containment, 60
and implicit rationing, 6
and system of payment, 13
Stilbesterol, 256–257
Sulfonamides, 19–20

Tavistock studies of British coal mines,
207–208
Technical change. See also Adoption of
medical technology; Diffusion of
medical technology; Medical
techology
criticisms toward, 113, 115
and economic environment, 113
and health care inflation, 113, 114
need for assistance for, 113–114
need for information on, 115–116,
124
phases in, 113
quality vs. cost, 112–113
surgical cost-benefit analysis of, 118–
119
Technological imperative
and cost escalation, 4
and explicit rationing, 14
of physicians, 47
and use of resources, 109–110

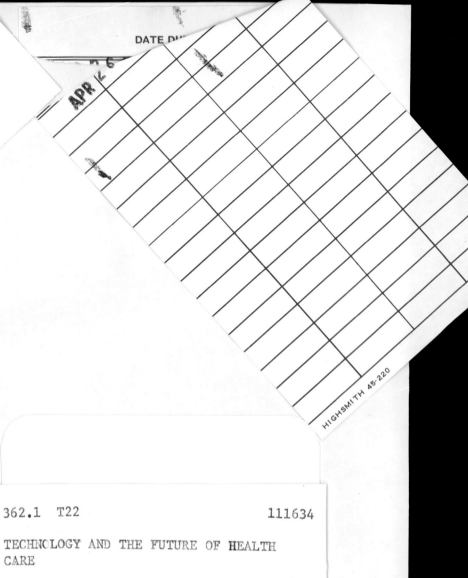